THE ATLAS OF STATES

For Anne

THE ATLAS OF STATES

Global Change 1900–2000

A.J. Christopher

Department of Geography, University of Port Elizabeth, South Africa

JOHN WILEY & SONS, LTD

Chichester • Weinheim • New York • Brisbane • Singapore • Toronto

Other Wiley Editorial Offices

John Wiley & Sons, Inc., 605 Third Avenue,
New York, NY 10158-0012, USA

VCH Verlagsgesellschaft mbH, Pappelallee 3,
D-69469 Weinheim, Germany

Jacaranda Wiley Ltd, 33 Park Road, Milton,
Queensland 4064, Australia

John Wiley & Sons (Asia) Pte Ltd, 2 Clementi Loop #02-01,
Jin Xing Distripark, Singapore 129809

John Wiley & Sons (Canada) Ltd, 22 Worcester Road,
Rexdale, Ontario M9W 1L1, Canada

Library of Congress Cataloging-inPublication Data

Christopher, A.J.
        The atlas of states: global change 1900–2000 / A.J. Christopher.
            p.   cm.
        Includes bibliographic references and index.
        ISBN 0-471-98613-5 (alk. paper)
        1. Atlases. 2. Boundaries—History—20th century—Maps.
    I. Title
    G1046 .F2C5 1999 <G&M>
    921—DC21   99-19391
                                                         CIP
                                                        MAPS

British Library Cataloguing in Publication Data

A catalogue record for this book is available from the British Library

ISBN 0 471 98613 5

Typeset in 10/12 pt Times by Hilite Design & Reprographics Limited
Printed in Great Britain by L&S Printing, Worthing, West Sussex
Bound by Bookcraft Ltd, Midsomer Norton, Somerset
This book is printed on acid-free paper responsibly manufactured from sustainable forestation,
for which at least two trees are planted for each one used

Contents

List of maps

Preface

The changing political pattern of the world has excited emotional and analytical debate throughout the ages, more particularly since maps came into more frequent use in the seventeenth and eighteenth centuries. The rise and fall of empires and states and their ever changing political boundaries have been recorded and charted in great detail, while numerous speculative, imperialistic and idealistic plans have been drawn for future configurations of the world. Popular curiosity with the map of the world and the recording of its partition among the various political entities has nowhere been so intense as at the beginning of the new millennium, when it is allied to a heightened anticipation of significant changes in the world order. As such, maps have exercised and continue to exercise a powerful influence over the minds of numerous politicians, academics and members of the general public. This may be attested to by the omni-present political maps displayed everywhere from school classrooms and company boardrooms to television screens and the Internet. Particular notice might be given to the use of the state outline whether on the national flag of Cyprus or in the manner in which President Yasser Arafat draped his keffiyeh over his right shoulder to represent the map of pre-partition Palestine. Despite predictions of globalisation, and the dawn of the information age encompassing the world, Geography, in the sense of the distinctive character of place and space, is very much alive and well at the beginning of the new millennium.

The many stages in the constantly changing political pattern of the world have been recorded in the maps produced by contemporary cartographers and subsequently reinterpreted by the compilers of historical atlases. In the process apparently immutable patterns, perceived, at the time, as being as permanent in outline as those of the continents, have dissolved in a hundred years of remarkable transformation. It is this fascination with the political map of the world and its frequent changes in the twentieth century, together with speculation over the likelihood of change in the new millennium, which form the basis of this study.

The author's interest in the subject goes back to childhood and began with the study of maps and atlases, particularly those which enabled comparisons to be made between the different editions available to him, covering a span of more than fifty years. Later at school he was introduced to the territorial and political intricacies of the Eastern Question and the emergence of the modern Balkan and Middle Eastern states in the nineteenth and twentieth centuries. To this basis was added an interest in philately, which with geography, stimulated an appreciation of the globe as a whole and the countries which currently existed and which had existed in the recent past. Towards the end of his school career Political Geography was included in the curriculum, and fortunately the opportunity to study this sub-discipline was continued at university.

The era covered by the author's formal education was one of rapid and far-reaching political transformation, beginning towards the end of the Second World War and ending twenty years later. The spirit of the age was perceptively encapsulated by the then British Prime Minister, Harold Macmillan, in his didactic, but epoch making, address to the South African parliament in Cape Town in February 1960, at the conclusion of an African tour. It is worth quoting at some length to summon up the feeling and context of the age:

Ever since the break-up of the Roman Empire one of the constant facts of political life in Europe has been the emergence of independent nations. They have come into existence over the centuries in different forms, with different kinds of Government, but all have been inspired by a deep, keen feeling of nationalism, which has grown as the nations have grown. In the twentieth century, and especially since the end of the war, the processes which gave birth to the nation states of Europe have been repeated all over the world. We have seen the awakening of national consciousness in peoples who have for centuries lived in dependence upon some other power. Fifteen years ago this movement spread through Asia. Many countries there of different races and civilisations pressed their claim to an independent national life. Today the same thing is happening in Africa, and the most striking of all the impressions I have formed since I left London a month ago is of the strength of this African national consciousness. In different places it takes different forms, but it is happening everywhere. The wind of change is blowing through this continent, and, whether we like it or not, this growth of national consciousness is a political fact. We must all accept it as a fact, and our national policies must take account of it.

(Macmillan, 1972: 156).

The relationship between political power and geography remained a matter of ongoing personal interest in the ensuing years as the pace of global change apparently slackened in the 1970s and then in the 1990s accelerated once more. The close connection between politics and geography was emphasised by the series of research projects undertaken thus far in the author's academic career, notably those investigating land issues and apartheid in southern Africa, the colonial impact in Africa and the worldwide imprint of British colonialism. Recently John Wiley and Sons, through the intervention and encouragement of two enterprising publishers, Tristan Palmer and Louise Portsmouth, provided the impetus which enabled the gathering together of thoughts on the subject and the compilation of the present volume.

It is necessary to warn the reader to exercise a degree of caution in the interpretation of the Atlas. Maps, despite their authoritative appearance, are not neutral documents. The complex links between cartography and culture and civilisation have been clearly demonstrated by Norman Thrower (1972). The Atlas is thus embedded within the cultural milieu of the late twentieth century academic world. It must further be noted that the propaganda value, of even the most objectively constructed maps, to support particular political programmes has long been recognised. The geopolitical maps produced in Germany and its neighbours in the period between the two world wars present a particularly well known case. Mark Monmonier (1991) has further demonstrated that maps are frequently constructed to convey a misleading impression. Inevitably any atlas, through the compiler's selection of map projections, subject matter, colour schemes, etc., can subtly influence the message portrayed. The material presented in the present work has inevitably had to rely upon a personal selection of themes. Because of the frequency of significant changes, attention has tended to be directed towards Europe, and so there is apparently a neglect of the Americas. This reflects the, no doubt welcome, stability in the state system of the Americas and the far more tumultuous and destructive history of Europe in the last one hundred years.

The Atlas endeavours to show the transformation of the pattern of independent sovereign states of the world in the course of the twentieth century. It accordingly records the emergence of new states and the demise of others, and ventures to offer some pointers to the future in possible new entities and possible failures in the light of the experience of the twentieth century. Consequently a substantial number of maps of sub-sovereign state level units whether 'states', provinces, counties, kingdoms or colonies have

been included, as it is they which frequently have been the territorial precursors of later sovereign states. Sub-state governmental units have played a significant role in the evolution of the world political map and provide the best key to the potential additions to 'the community of nations' in the future. The emphasis in the Atlas is thus on change, as a countermeasure to the apparent permanence of the printed map and the essential conservatism of human beings in general and political leaders in particular, who tend to resist change.

The work is arranged with an introduction presenting a general theoretical background to the nature and characteristics of the state and the mythology and practice behind it. Allied to the physical nature of the state as a defined piece of mappable land is the concept of the nation, which has dominated the political rhetoric of the twentieth century and seems set fair to do so for the foreseeable future. The theoretical section is complemented by a brief historical background indicating the evolution of the world system in the nineteenth century. There follows the main body of the Atlas, arranged in ten chapters. This begins with an extended examination of the state pattern of the world in 1900 as the base date for the discussion and concludes with an assessment of the world pattern in the year 2000. In between are a set of chapters dealing with eras of change. Some eras are relatively short and are associated with dramatic regional transformations, including the two world wars and their immediate aftermaths and most recently the post-Cold War era. Other eras are of longer duration, with the range of changes more restricted and globally focused. A certain degree of overlap is necessary in order to complete the picture. Thus later developments are dealt with in some chapters to avoid repetition. For example, Argentina and Colombia appear as foundation states in Chapter 2, but events up to the 1990s have been included as they maintained a remarkable degree of stability throughout the century. The volume concludes with a chapter of reflections, examining some of the major themes of the century and offering pointers to the future. Throughout, each section is illustrated with a map indicating the states involved.

In a project of this scale there are many people to whom a profound debt of gratitude is owed. The library staff and Research Committee of the University of Port Elizabeth deserve special mention for their support while this research was being undertaken. In addition, the author wishes to record his appreciation of assistance rendered by the staffs of the Berkeley Library and the Department of Geography at Trinity College Dublin while on sabbatical leave and subsequently during a further visit to complete the manuscript. Over many years the author has made use of the extensive resources of the British Library and the Royal Geographical Society in London, and wishes to thank their staffs for their dedication to the promotion of international scholarship.

There are also two particular personal debts which I readily acknowledge. The first is to Wilma Grundlingh, to whose cartographic skills the visual impact and enjoyment of the volume is due. Wilma undertook the task with enthusiasm and professionalism, which lightened the author's load considerably. Finally, I wish to acknowledge the continuous and loving support offered by my wife, Anne, who has lived with the Atlas project for a number of years and has helped to make the whole exercise so enjoyable and worthwhile.

Port Elizabeth
September 1998

A Note on Sources

The maps have been compiled using information from a number of sources, notably the various editions of the *Times Atlas* published since 1900, Engel (1962) *Grosser Historischer Weltatlas*, Darby and Fullard (1970) *New Cambridge Modern History Atlas*, and Putzger (1997) *Historischer Weltatlas*. In addition, specific material was modified and included from: Clericy (1910) (Fig. 2.6); India (1914) (Fig 2.10); Great Britain (1903) (Fig 2.19); Marriott (1917) (Fig 3.2); Fischer (1967) (Fig. 4.1); Bowman (1928) (Fig. 5.6); Toschi (1931) (Fig. 6.1); Schofield (1996) (Fig. 8.9); Ajayi and Crowder (1985) (Fig. 9.5); Cyprus (1976) (Fig. 9.14); United States (1992) (Fig. 10.4); Allen and Turner (1988) (Fig. 12.11).

CHAPTER 1

Introduction

The political map of the world underwent dramatic changes in the course of the twentieth century and looks set to undergo equally spectacular developments in the new millennium. Yet the human propensity for selective amnesia and psychological adjustment to change are such that the present situation nearly always appears to be taken for granted as a scene of constancy, and other configurations of the map regarded as belonging to the distant past. The political maps of the world presented in atlases, displayed in classrooms, broadcast on television screens, even those reproduced in advertisements and corporate logos, often appear as immutable to the observer as the outlines of the continents themselves. Such perceptions are misleading. Even a most cursory reading of history immediately indicates how ephemeral the present political map is and how many revolutions in the distribution of states and territories there have been in the course of the past millennium (Blouet, 1996; Darby and Fullard, 1970; Engel, 1962; Putzger, 1997). It is through an appreciation of the scale and character of past changes and indeed the inevitability and desirability of change that it will be possible to face the recurring challenge of redrawing the state pattern in the new millennium.

A substantial body of literature on the global pattern of states has been built up since the publication of the first political geography text by Friedrich Ratzel in 1897. Attention has generally centred upon the individual political unit and the wider patterns of political power as impacting most powerfully upon an individual's life (Johnston, 1982). Isaiah Bowman (1928) in *The New World* surveyed the post-First World War settlement, while emphasising the continued vitality of the world system. Gordon East and Arthur Moodie (1956) did the same for the post-Second World War era. However, the very speed with which events rendered old theories and old maps obsolete resulted in continued texts seeking to explain the map of the world, including Alexander (1957), Dikshit (1997), Glassner (1996), Muir (1975), Pounds (1963), Short (1993) and Taylor (1993a, 1993b) to name but a few. The dynamic nature of the state system attracted more speculative attempts to interpret and direct policies (Mackinder, 1919; Parker, 1985).

The twentieth century was distinguished by a high degree of global integration. The single world system had in large measure been achieved by 1900. Thereafter events in one part of the world influenced those in other parts on a scale never before witnessed (Wallerstein, 1974). The essentially Eurocentric system which had dominated an increasing sector of world politics until 1918 gave way to a new era of global politics. Indeed during the First World War the era characterised by A.J.P. Taylor (1954) as 'the struggle for mastery in Europe' was superseded by one characterised by Eric Hobsbawm (1995) as 'the age of extremes'. It is regrettable to have to comment that war and violent revolution characterised much of the political debate in the twentieth century (Kliot and Waterman, 1991; Pepper and Jenkins, 1985). The most costly of these wars, the First and Second World Wars (1914–1918 and 1939–1945) and the Cold War (1947–1991) were fought on a global scale and directly affected the majority of the states of the world. This had not been true of earlier 'world wars', the Seven Years War (1756–1763) and the Revolutionary and Napoleonic Wars (1792–1815), which had hardly impinged upon the interiors of Africa and Asia or the Chinese and Japanese realms (Pocock, 1998).

Changes in the world state system were prompted by numerous decisions taken by individuals and collective groups responding to the opportunities offered by the complex interaction of political, economic and social developments. The colonial empires attained their apogee in the early twentieth century as the political penetration of the European powers reached its limit and the economic integration of the world was largely accomplished. In territorial terms the political expression of imperialism was the colonial dependency. Also originating from the European hearth was the concept of the nation and its related ideology, nationalism. The spatial political expression of nationalism was the nation-state. Added to these concepts were the populist ideologies of democracy, socialism, communism and fascism, which were manipulated to exert a powerful control over diverse populations during the century. The resultant conflict between seemingly incompatible political systems resulted in a marked instability in the states which formed the world system. The evolution of the inter-state system was set against the background of rapidly increasing population numbers and more conspicuous disparities in the distribution of wealth on a global scale.

Although the magnitude of change was remarkable, with critical periods of state birth and death, there were also forces of inertia, which enabled a significant number of states to remain as constant features upon the world map. In a few cases they were so stable that they retained exactly the same external boundaries over the century. Although such cases were rare, the majority of world statesmen resisted change and sought stability and the retention of the status quo. This is understandable amongst the politicians directly concerned with the promotion of peace and the military leaders concerned with the preservation of a state's territorial integrity. In addition, the leaders of the international organisations throughout the century tended towards the same conservatism and adherence to the status quo. It may therefore be asked, why were the states of the world so unstable and what changes may be expected in the future? This Atlas seeks to provide a few pointers to the answers to these questions.

Some understanding of the nature of the state is required as to the spatial and territorial entity into which the world is divided in political terms. Although it is the sovereign independent state which usually appears in the literature, non-independent colonial, federal or dependent states have been significant factors in the evolution of the world pattern. It was usually from this pool of non-independent states that the majority of the new states of the world were created, and from which many of the potential states of the future may emerge, as they possess many of the attributes of sovereign states. However, an analysis of their characteristics opens up other issues, which have been dealt with elsewhere (Krishan, 1988).

The other significant concept introduced into any discussion of the state is that of the nation, as it corresponded with the population of the state. This concept is open to two very different interpretations. At a legal level of analysis the definition of a nation may imply no more than formal residence within the territorial limits of a state. However, emotionally the nation may be a very different community of people, with shared social and cultural traits. Exact coincidence between the legal and emotional nations is rare. When the gap between the two becomes too wide then the state involved becomes severely strained and radical change may be the outcome. The twentieth century has been particularly afflicted with national conflict arising from the interaction of often irreconcilable nationalisms.

The combination of the concepts of the state and the nation into the 'nation-state' has generated one of the most powerful political concepts of the twentieth century. The logical outcome, the facile idea of 'one nation, one state', permeated the politics of the twentieth century with often disastrous results, leading ultimately to genocide and ethnic cleansing. On the other hand, there has been a confusion of the concepts of state and nation, so that the terms are used interchangeably. As an example, weather forecasts predicting fine weather or rain 'across the nation' indicate an acceptance of the terminology, through the use of a 'people oriented' image, in marked contrast to the 'nation' conceived in the pursuit of a genocide.

As a counter to the excesses committed in the name of nationalism, the concept of multi-nationalism has been promoted both in socialist and in liberal democratic terms. The concept has earlier precursors in imperialism, where diverse multi-ethnic and multi-cultural populations were tolerated, and indeed even encouraged, although political power was usually restricted to the acculturated citizenry or elite. The same tolerance is discernible in the development of the internationalism of the twentieth century which similarly has sought to minimise the force of nationalism. The Soviet multi-national experiment ultimately failed, with the revival of the national separatisms, which accompanied the democratisation process. The outcome of the present experiment in European integration remains to be tested, based as it is upon legal definition and the shared Christian heritage. However, it would be true to state that nationalism, or rather the political exploitation of nationalism, has been the driving force behind many of the conflicts that bedevilled the twentieth century.

The State

At an initial basic level of analysis the concept of the state is relatively straightforward. The state is recognised by its four main attributes, namely: a territory, a resident population, an organisation and a measure of power. However, a closer examination of each of these attributes raises more questions than it answers. In certain respects this is because in the final analysis a state requires a distinctive raison d'etre, or reason for existence, which is remarkably difficult to define.

Territory

The territorial nature of the state is the distinguishing element when discussion of societies and nations are involved. It is the spatial unit which appears upon the political map of the world and is designated the state. Indeed a wide literature on the state and the problems of drawing boundaries for individual states has developed (Glassner, 1996; Prescott, 1987). An examination of the territorial nature of the state indicates that there is no standard or norm by which to measure the territory of the state. States have been formed which may measure no more than a few hectares, while others have embraced over a quarter of the earth's surface.

Small states suffer from a lack of resources and often of manpower, while large states benefit from an abundance of both. Yet there has been no universal trend towards the creation of a single world state, to parallel the emergence of a single world economy since the fifteenth century. The issue of containing diversity and the logistical problems of keeping large entities together are apparent as expansionist states develop to a stage of 'imperial over-reach' (Kennedy, 1988). At this stage decline begins and disintegration has generally become inevitable. On the other hand, small states are vulnerable to incorporation by stronger neighbours, while large countries have, until the advent of the intercontinental ballistic missile in the 1950s, been able to benefit from defence in depth.

Although the ideal state, based upon the military requirements of defensibility, has been considered to be a single contiguous piece of territory, many have detached exclaves and islands (Catudal, 1979). Some have extreme elongated shapes presenting problems of communication, while others have to rely upon their neighbours to facilitate communication between different parts of the national territory. The boundaries of some are clearly defined either as physical features or mutually accepted historic lines, while others have been subject to great instability, without invalidating the existence of the state. Indeed there appears to be no spatial limitation upon the form of a state.

Population

A resident population is also a basic attribute, as states are essentially the products of societies. Again the size of population necessary to sustain a state cannot be determined. A sovereign state with under one thousand inhabitants does appear on the world map, but it is sustained by the contribution of the populations of other states. A few thousand people are necessary to maintain a viable society and therefore provide for the biological perpetuation of the group. Once more, large numbers provide the labour to generate wealth and the military power for expansion, but large size usually results in the emergence of sectional interests, which may undermine the viability of the state. This aspect is more fully examined in the discussion of the concept of the nation. Sustained population growth in the twentieth century has resulted in the emergence of two states with over one billion inhabitants apiece, which despite their internal problems appear capable of long-term sustainability. So far there does not appear to be an upper limit to growth. It is this requirement of a permanent population which excludes Antarctica from discussion in this volume. Since December 1959 the continent has been subject to exploitation and management by international agreement (Chaturvedi, 1996).

Organisation

States are essentially organisations, whereby the two elements of territory and population are brought together and the relationship codified (Medved, 1997). The level of organisation has changed markedly through time and has differed from place to place. However, in the twentieth century a high degree of standardisation has been apparent as concepts of the state developed in Europe have been adopted by or imposed upon other parts of the world. The basic organisational model was most clearly set out in the pre-monetised feudal system, where at each level of society land was received in return for rendering services. The sovereign, as the owner of all land, distributed it to his tenants-in-chief (nobles) in return for their military support and payment of taxes (in kind or later bullion). At the lowest level, the lord of the manor distributed the land to the peasantry, in return for rent in agricultural products and labour dues. Variants of this hierarchical arrangement were present in large parts of the world until recently and its basic elements have been subsumed into other more egalitarian societies where land remains an essential part of power relations.

Parallel with feudalism came the thread of organised religion in the service of the state. All religions have sought to influence the actions of society and its individual members. However, the inspiration of the divine has enabled rulers to harness the power of the innate fear of death to their own purposes. Rulers were often endowed with divine properties, and acted as God's vice-regents on earth. Thus whether it was the concept of divine right as practised in Christian states or the respect claimed by the Japanese Emperor before 1945, the state was imbued with religious connotations. Therefore to defy the ruler or the state was to incur God's wrath. For the offender, condemnation to death in this world, could also incur consignment to the everlasting fires of hell in the next. The organised religions thus often acted as extensions of the state, and indeed the local priest was often the only 'official' in small communities, offering a range of services beyond the strictly religious.

However, governmental organisations have become more complex and all pervasive in the twentieth century, as the state apparatus expanded from an essentially military organisation designed to defend the state territory and extract tribute and taxation, to one designed to facilitate economic activity, and ultimately to provide social services (Clark and Dear, 1984). Internal coercion, through the legal system, and external defence, through the army and navy, consumed much of the budget in states throughout the world. The sovereign, and the presidential successor, thus took on a highly militarist character. State success was measured in military might and the ability to defend and expand the national territory. Subsequently states became responsible for the provision of basic services which facilitated economic development, notably the police, schools, postal systems, and often the railway and airways systems. As a result, until the late twentieth century the proportion of the population working directly for the state increased rapidly to supervise and control the population. Social spending has increased dramatically as levels of national wealth have increased in the twentieth century. Social welfare, the care of the population 'from the cradle to the grave', became a significant aspect of the Socialist state. Ultimately in the Communist states, all economic activities were nationalised and run by the state. The state attempted to organise every aspect of its citizens' lives. Since the 1980s the universal trend has been towards the scaling down of state organisations.

The internal organisation of many states created in the twentieth century has been remarkably weak. The 'quasi-states' of Africa are a point in hand (Jackson, 1990). However, even when the administrative machinery of the central government collapses completely and there is no recognisable government, the state as a geographical entity on the map survives (Zartman, 1995). Whereas prior to the Second World War, collapse would almost certainly have involved incorporation into a more powerful neighbour, after 1945, the international community was willing to support states without governments and assist in the reconstruction of viable administrations.

Power

Power can be measured as that needed to maintain internal order, and that required to retain external independence. As alluded to in the previous section, much of the state organisation has been and still is devoted to these twin purposes.

Measures of internal coercion increased as the government apparatus and bureaucracy became more sophisticated. The ultimate measures of control through terror were devised by the Soviet Union and National Socialist Germany with their secret police and death camps. The police state, with its rigid control of people's activities, became more effective in the twentieth century as modern technology was harnessed to the purposes of the state governors. The all-pervading system of state-controlled terror evolved by V.I. Lenin and Joseph Stalin after the Russian Revolution in November 1917 was the model for others seeking to control the evolution of society and eliminate any opposition, however insignificant (Carrere d'Encausse, 1981). The massive surveillance exercises undertaken by states such as the German Democratic Republic became an end in itself, availing the government comparatively little return for the resources expended. In South Africa the white minority National Party government retained control and imposed apartheid on the black majority through the exercise of extensive repression by the army, police and secret services. As Colonel Eugene de Kock, one of the senior policemen of the repressive system stated: 'No member of the former government ... could go to bed at night thinking they were in charge of the country because they were kept in their position by the South African Police, the Defence Force and the intelligence structures' (*Eastern Province Herald*, 2 October 1997).

External power has usually been measured in terms of military power. Conflict was thus virtually inevitable, until the devastation caused by wars in the twentieth century reduced their scale, if not their death rate. Indeed, in some states, war was regarded as the chief objective of the government and considered necessary for the 'good of the nation'. The various fascist ideologies linked war to the development of the nation. The military therefore has often played a pivotal role in the development of the state through the inculcation of national ideals. On the other hand, the defeat of the army could mean the annihilation of the state. Thus during the colonial period small states were incorporated as a result of defeats in campaigns fought by colonial armies dedicated expressly towards the extension of the empires.

Calculating state power was usually done in military terms. In the early twentieth century, the numbers of soldiers and armaments were counted and compared as a measure of power. The naval arms race was calculated in terms of ships of various classes, as new weaponry, for example the 'dreadnought' class warship, had the potential to change the balance of power before the First World War. Thus countries with large standing armies, such as Russia, appeared formidable on paper, even if its organisation was weak. On the other hand, the United States was usually left out of military calculations before the 1940s because it lacked a significant standing army. The ability of Afghanistan to defend and preserve its independence by military means against its British neighbours before 1947 and its Russian neighbours thereafter suggests that basic numerical power equations may not always work (O'Ballance, 1993).

States were not continuously at war, although preparation for war often dominated periods of 'peace'. The development of diplomacy, alliances and international organisations reduced the level of armed conflict and in effect projected national power through other means. Skilful diplomacy enabled states to achieve their objects through a combination of the threat of force, bribery and mutual self-interest. States such as the Ottoman Empire in the nineteenth century had been able to stave off partition as a result of careful diplomatic manoeuvring in order to exploit the rivalries of its enemies. Smaller and weaker states had to achieve their objectives through diplomatic means. Concepts of collective security and the support of the international community have been common in the post-1918 era in the survival of states lacking traditional military power.

Economic power has been more difficult to measure, just as economic warfare has been more difficult to wage. Figures for the production of key products, such as coal and steel early in the twentieth century, or microchips and computer systems at the beginning of the new millennium, have been used, as have figures for gross domestic product, to assess relative national power. Again, a comparison at face value of the apparent overwhelming economic strength of the United States and the almost total poverty of some other countries hides the many nuances of the state system.

The ability of the state to secure and retain the recognition of its separate sovereign status is the ultimate test of external power. The recognition of independence separates the sovereign state from a dependency or any other form of local state. Some local states, such as California (United States), Tatarstan (Russia) and Catalonia (Spain), exercise considerable powers, control substantial budgets, which are larger than most independent states, and even maintain governmental offices in foreign countries, but they are not independent. They do, however, present a significant form of political unit which has many of the attributes of sovereign states (Paddison, 1983). In most cases they are component units of a federation, where relations between the central government and the states are constitutionally regulated and guaranteed. Indeed in a number of federations the federal states claim sovereignty (Dikshit, 1976).

Raison d'etre

States also possess some means of defining themselves, their raison d'etre or state idea, in order to distinguish themselves from other states (Hartshorne, 1950). One of the most significant in the early part of the twentieth century was still the monarchical justification, although this had largely disappeared a hundred years later. The state was linked to the person of the monarch, through a mystical divine intervention, 'the Grace of God' or 'the Mandate of Heaven'. The monarchical principle of encompassing the state loyalties of the population is highly significant as providing markers in a country's history. The reigns of succeeding kings and queens are given significance and much national history is written as an account of the monarch's reign. Periods of relative greatness, including the Victorian age in Great Britain, the Napoleonic age in France, or that of Suleiman the Magnificent in Turkey, parallel those named after the dynasties, the Han or Ming of China or the Moghul of India. Personal and group identification of subjects with the monarch provided the state's binding mechanism. The endowment of the monarch with religious connotations provided for the effective cementing of society. Thus the Russian imperial anthem made no reference to the state, only to God and the Czar:

God bless the noble Czar! Grant him Thy Grace:
In war, in peace, O hide not Thou Thy face!
Blessings his reign attend, Foes be scatter'd far.
May God bless the Czar! God save the Czar!

(Fagge, 1914: 4)

However, the most frequently expressed raison d'etre is that of the state as the expression of the nation. Thus the state exists to serve and represent the nation. In ideal terms therefore the French Republic embodies the loyalties of the French nation and the government is responsive to the aspirations of the nation. This presupposes the existence of more than a legally defined nation, but an emotional nation created by the state or inherited from a sense of common origins, and sharing a common purpose, as exemplified by the French national anthem:

Ye sons of France, awake to glory,
Hark, hark what myriads bid you rise;
Your children, wives and grand-sires hoary
Behold their tears and hear their cries
Shall hateful tyrants mischief breeding.
With hireling host a ruffian band pollute and desolate the land
While Peace and Happiness lie bleeding?
To arms! To arms, ye brave. Th' avenging sword unsheathe!
March on! March on! All hearts resolved,
To Liberty or Death!

(Fagge, 1914: 2)

The nation

If a territorially based state is relatively easy to identify, the concept of the nation is more difficult to establish (Seton-Watson, 1977; A.D. Smith, 1991). Indeed Benedict Anderson's (1983) concept of 'imagined communities' conveys the nebulous nature of any quest to define the nation. Two basic approaches to its identification are discernible, namely the primordial and the legalistic. The primordial nation takes as its origin such concepts as the common ancestor and the common group, sharing a common history, usually on a common territory (Smith, 1986). The group is linked by a common language and usually a common religion or set of beliefs and ways of cooperating. The key to such a group is its psychological strength in perpetuating itself and passing on the common myths and beliefs to succeeding generations. The group is able to envelop the individual in a sense of common purpose, shared identity and collective power. Ultimately the group may call upon the individual to sacrifice his or her life for the good of the nation in war or other service. Such an act is taken to bind the nation more closely together in order to bear witness to the sacrifice as part of the shared experience (Ehrenreich, 1997). In this manner nationalism became 'the religious force of modern times', inspiring spiritual feelings and impulses (Rudolph and Good, 1992: 5). The power of such a mythology is reinforced by education systems inculcating national awareness, as exemplified by a popular British school hymn by Cecil Spring-Rice:

I vow to thee, my country, all earthly things above,
Entire and whole and perfect, the service of my love;
The love that asks no question, the love that stands the test,
That lays upon the altar the dearest and the best;
The love that never falters, the love that pays the price,
The love that makes undaunted the final sacrifice.

(Headmasters' Conference, 1949: 294)

The appeal to the primordial group has been extremely powerful in the era of nationalism. The terminology used in the declaration of Irish Independence in April 1916 makes this link between the living and the dead, and their claim to the future as part of a common experience:

The Provisional Government of the Irish Republic
To the People of Ireland.
IRISHMEN AND IRISHWOMEN: In the name of God and of the dead generations from which she receives her old traditions of nationhood, Ireland, through us, summons her children to her flag and strikes for her freedom.
Having organised and trained her manhood through her secret revolutionary organisation, the Irish Republican Brotherhood, and through her open military organisations, the Irish Volunteers and the Irish Citizen Army, having patiently perfected her discipline, having waited for the right moment to reveal itself, she now seizes that moment, and supported by her exiled children in America and by gallant Allies in Europe, but relying in the first on her own strength, she strikes in full confidence of victory.
We declare the right of the people of Ireland to the ownership of Ireland, and the unfettered control of Irish destinies, to be sovereign and indefeasible. The long usurpation of that right by a foreign people and Government has not extinguished the right, nor can it ever be extinguished except by the destruction of the Irish people. In every generation the Irish people have asserted their right to national freedom and sovereignty; six times during the last 300 years they have asserted it in arms. Standing on that fundamental right and again asserting it in arms in the face of the world, we hereby proclaim the Irish Republic as a Sovereign Independent State, and we pledge our lives and the lives of our comrades-in-arms to the cause of freedom, of its welfare, and its exaltation among the nations.
The Irish Republic is entitled to, and hereby claims, the allegiance of every Irishman and Irishwoman. The Republic guarantees religious and civil liberty, equal rights and equal opportunities to all its citizens, and declares its resolve to pursue the happiness and prosperity of the whole nation and of

all its parts, cherishing all the children of the nation equally, and oblivious of the differences carefully fostered by an alien government, which have divided a minority from the majority in the past.

(Younger, 1970: 34–36)

A powerful reinforcement of this concept is the belief in divine intervention in history in support of a particular, 'chosen', people. The idea of a Covenant or agreement with God has been particularly powerful (Akenson, 1992). The compact has often been linked to a particular piece of land granted by the deity in return for obedience to His laws. The Covenant thus provides a remarkable degree of both personal identity and social integration and common purpose. The archetype of such a bargain in the Western tradition has been the Old Covenant linking the descendants of Abraham, through obedience to God, to the land of Palestine. In the Biblical Book of Genesis (17: 7–8) Abram, henceforth to be called Abraham, is promised by God: 'And I will establish my covenant between me and thee and thy seed after thee in their generations for an everlasting covenant, to be a God unto thee, and to thy seed after thee. And I will give unto thee and thy seed after thee, the land wherein thou art a stranger, all the land of Canaan, for an everlasting possession; and I will be their God'. The land itself is further defined (Genesis 15: 18): 'The Lord made a covenant with Abram saying, unto thy seed have I given this land, from the river of Egypt unto the great river Euphrates'. The sense of identity associated with a particular piece of land gave focus to Judaism even in exile (Davies, 1982). This appears to be a feature associated with 'diaspora nations', displaced from their historic homelands (Chaliand and Rageau, 1995).

The Biblical Covenant provided the example, and indeed much of the imagery, for other Covenants, notably that by the Afrikaners in South Africa before the Battle of Blood River in 1838 and the Ulstermen in 1912 before the imposition of Home Rule on Ireland. All three of these Covenants have had most significant impacts upon the history of the twentieth century as they were place specific, in linking a particular people to a particular piece of land in spiritual terms. Significantly, the Covenant has often been accompanied by the idea of the biological purity of the 'holy people' and the exclusion of others from their midst.

Language

The most powerful binding factor in the creation and maintenance of a nation has been a common language (Williams, 1994). Indeed this virtual prerequisite was recognised by both ethnographers and politicians and a vast literature has been developed identifying linguistic groups. It has widely been assumed that a common language has been essential for the development of any common identity. It is through language that individuals are acculturated in their formative years. The concept of a mother tongue, learnt from one's mother, as the basic means of childhood education has been of considerable significance. This is not to detract from the importance for some people of being conversant in several languages, and using them for different purposes and different audiences. The linguistic education of the Emperor Franz Joseph of Austria-Hungary is a case in point. In addition to familial German and ecclesiastical Latin, he learnt French as the international language of diplomacy and aristocratic society, together with Hungarian, Czech, Polish and Italian as the languages of his subjects (Bled, 1994). However, the strictly utilitarian aspect of a language easily becomes embroiled in the political discourse of nationality.

Many of the identifiable linguistic groups are small with, at times, under a thousand speakers (Moseley and Asher, 1994). Papua New Guinea and adjacent Indonesian Irian Jaya constitute a region of significant linguistic complexity, reflecting the physical isolation of many communities and their relatively recent contact with outside peoples. As late as 1998 small groups of people with no previous contact with outside groups were still being identified in the Amazon Basin.

Language is also written and has increasingly constituted an essential means of linkage. Letters, documents, books, journals, newspapers and computers have become significant means of disseminating information. Written languages differ from spoken in their greater degree of standardisation. Mutually unintelligible accents and dialects are rendered compatible in a standard written form. Writing thus enabled a wider degree of communication than the spoken word. The most apparent case is Chinese, for which the written language was standardised in classical times, about 200 BC, by the Mandarins, the imperial scholars and officials. Thereafter it was maintained and enhanced through the production of a classic literature and the invention of printing (Forrest, 1973; Norman, 1988). In written form the idiographic script was suited to the transfer of messages between people who spoke a wide variety of tongues. In spoken form the Imperial court provided the standard form, adopted by all who had dealings with it. It was only in 1917, after the revolution, that the development of a standard spoken form was adopted as official policy.

However, the complexity of the written form was a hindrance to its diffusion following the introduction of compulsory mass education after 1949. This was compounded by the development of radio and television, which seriously challenged the apparent linguistic unity of the country. The proposed conversion to the simpler Latin script, following the national adoption of the Mandarin form of spoken Chinese, represents yet a potential further stage in the language's evolution. In this way linguistic unity may not be as apparent as the recognition of a national language may suggest. The position of Thai as the national language of Thailand, and of the royal court, occupies an analogous position, disguising spoken linguistic diversity with written uniformity (Smalley, 1994). The 80 languages in the country are subsumed through the religion, national hierarchies and education in creating a national identity.

The assumption that it is language which defines membership of the nation has been pervasive in Europe since the French Revolution and the development of the philosophy of nation building. Hence the various languages spoken in Europe and in certain other parts of the world have been identified as indicators of national identity. Much academic and political attention was directed towards the identification and classification of languages and their development. From there it was but a short step towards the promotion of linguistic nationalism. Small differences were identified and cases made either for their recognition as separate entities or for their merging with near neighbours. Such decisions lay largely within the domain of the state.

Influence of the state

The second most important means of defining the nation has been the state itself. Thus birth in a particular place usually confers membership of the state within the boundaries of which the birthplace is situated. In the monarchical state the allegiance of the subject to the territorial sovereign was the principle of the relationship. The sovereign could have many guises, as for example the various local titles of the Emperor of Austria before 1918, and hence subjects might be highly diverse in character, with few pressures exerted towards uniformity. Furthermore, change could occur through descent, even cession as a part of a territorial dowry for the sovereign's daughter. Arranged marriages for heiresses were significant elements in the evolution of the state pattern in the pre-modern era. Modern Spain owes much of its present spatial form to the marriage in 1469 of Isabella of Castile and Ferdinand V of Aragon, both to become sovereigns of their respective kingdoms in their own right. The subsequent conversion of the two kingdoms into the Spanish nation-state was a long and bitterly contested political process.

The state has played a significant role in determining the character of the nation. Within the modern nation-state the pressures towards uniformity have been most intense. The state through its communication system, legal system, and later education system has exerted considerable pressures upon people to conform to the national ideal in terms of language, culture and political allegiance. Beginning in the nineteenth century in Europe and spreading elsewhere, government bureaucracy expanded dramatically as the central government regulated ever greater sectors of their subjects' lives. At school, compulsory education involved the inculcation of basic reading and writing in the standard state language. Individual dealings with bureaucracy involved paperwork, again in the official state language, together with contact with officials often drawn from other parts of the country, who spoke nothing else but the state language. Compulsory military service in a number of countries contributed to a greater degree of uniformity between young men from different parts of the country, as well as a military education system instilling politically correct views promoting national ideals. The state also had the ultimate control over documentation, and personal papers, which could determine not only the nationality of the subject, but wider aspects of his or her life from residence permits to food rationing books. Naturalisation and the issue of a passport to travel were strictly within the competence of the sovereign state.

In some cases uniformity was accepted, even embraced wholeheartedly, by minority group members as a means of gaining access to the social, economic and political advantages that integration into the dominant group could secure. In certain respects this was accomplished with the maintenance of inherited forms of speech, even completely different languages. However, major shifts in language usage did take place, as the use of English came to predominate in Ireland, French over Breton in Brittany, and Spanish over Basque in Navarre. In other cases reaction to the imposition of another language gave rise to the establishment of cultural and linguistic societies, which sought to capture and revive the 'pure' speech patterns of the old and the peasantry, relatively unaffected by the pressures of education in a foreign tongue. The initial aim of such societies was to promote the national heritage. Often a separate statehood was not contemplated by such cultural movements until the collapse of the centralising state.

On occasion home language and national identification became detached. The plight of the German-speaking population of Alsace under French rule until 1871 is a case in point (Ellis, 1976). Prior to the Franco-German War of 1870–1871, the German speakers of the province had been subjected to an intensive acculturation programme by successive French governments, which regarded the population to be potentially pro-German. It has been suggested that the imposition of German rule in 1871 was the defining moment when the majority of the population appreciated that they had been sufficiently acculturated into the French state, as to be ill-fitting in the new German nation-state. In this case language did not necessarily define the nation.

In defining the national language the state rulers may have several choices. In many states the choice is obvious and the resources of the state are placed behind the promotion of the state language. The Académie Française guards the purity of the French language as its use is officially regulated and promoted. It is based on the language of the former royal court and the Isle de France around Paris, which once codified was imposed upon the remainder of the country. The imposition of the politically dominant group's language upon the remainder of the country remains the almost universal norm. This may vary from the imposition of Arabic on the southern Sudan, to Malay in North Borneo and Sarawak. A few countries may promote regional languages, usually associated with autonomous regions, such as Chechen or Yakut in Russia. Others may have more than one official language, such as Switzerland, Belgium and Canada, to accommodate the various communities, but the implementation of such policies is usually highly contentious and tends to dominate political debate.

The idea that there should be a distinctive national language for the state has engendered the revival of languages which declined during periods of alien rule. Thus in Ireland the government after 1922 promoted Irish as the official language. On the other hand, one language may be taken and elevated to the national language to emphasise distinctiveness from their neighbours or previous rulers. The development of Swahili in Tanzania or Hindi in India are examples. However, the need to promote interaction between members of the nation may result in the retention of colonial languages as a less contentious policy than imposing one of the many local languages on the remainder of the population. Thus most countries in Africa, South of the Sahara, have retained either English, French or Portuguese as their official languages in the post-independence era to act as linguae francae and for

governmental record, but significantly, not as replacements for home languages, or use generally in daily communication with members of other indigenous linguistic communities (Laitin, 1992).

The outcome of the majority of national language policies has been the imposition of a language upon non-mother tongue speakers. Ultimately the eradication of the minority languages is often the officially desired aim, whether in a colonial empire or the nation-state. Indeed language policies can be extremely oppressive and restrictive for those not speaking and communicating in the state language. Conversely the promotion of regional languages can be disruptive to national cohesion in opening areas of linguistic misunderstanding, even non-comprehension between members of the nation.

Change

Nations are not static entities. They evolve as their membership changes through the generations. Thus nations have to define themselves in each age, with reference to inherited tradition and the need to adapt to new circumstances. The interpretation and invention of tradition assumed a significant role in the development of the nation as economic and societal changes transformed national politics (Hobsbawm and Ranger, 1983). Attention has been directed towards modernisation and change in Western societies in the nineteenth century and globally thereafter, which, in France, transformed 'peasants into Frenchmen' (Weber, 1976). Similar transformations have been identified in other centralised states when confronted with the challenges of modernisation (Knippenberg, 1997). Such inventions were not confined to Western societies. The creation of a national mythology in Japan after the Meiji restoration of 1868 was an essential part of the modernisation of the state. The state myth of the lineal descent of the Emperors from Amaterasu Omikami, the legendary Sun Goddess, established the permanence of the dynasty and a chronology which could be traced back to the foundation of the Empire in 660 BC (Large, 1992). Similar processes are in progress elsewhere as urbanisation and national acculturation coincide (Roberts, 1995).

Parallel with this was the evolution of colonial societies, both indigenous and settler, into nations. Europeans emigrated to other continents in substantial numbers from the sixteenth century onwards. The permanent colonists, after a couple of generations, tended to view their home as being located in the colony, not the country whence their ancestors had come. Governments attempted to maintain some degree of conformity with the homeland, but the different social and physical environments, notably the greater opportunities for less restricted economic and political advancement in the colonies, led to conflicts. The creation of a local identity did not necessarily mean the creation of a new nation. However, differences of outlook led to political separation, beginning with the United States in 1776. The later British dominions broke the links with the homeland through constitutional evolution in the mutual recognition of the differences. Defining moments such as the Australian and New Zealand participation in the disastrous Gallipoli expedition in 1915 significantly contributed to the feeling of separation from Great Britain.

Not all settler communities were able to establish self-sustaining communities. Africa proved to be particularly uninviting. The Dutch settlers in South Africa evolved into the Afrikaner nation, to be joined by English-speaking and other European immigrants to produce the short-lived 'White South African' nation. The White settlers in Rhodesia created and sustained an independent state and nation for 15 years, only to fail in confrontation with the African majority, which defined the nation in very different terms. In colonial Algeria the emergence of a European Algerian nation was discouraged by the French government upon which the settlers ultimately relied for survival (Ageron, 1979). Two colonial societies, the Dutch of South Africa and the French in Canada, became isolated from their metropolitan societies and evolved in cultural opposition to the dominant British regime (Harris, 1977). Each society evolved into a new nation, which experienced considerable ambivalence in its relationship to other South Africans and Canadians.

The colonial period also created a large number of colonial states which at independence were faced with the task of nation building. It is significant that few sought to define the nation in linguistic or cultural terms but pursued the state-dominated approach to nation building. In some cases the problems were too great and the states collapsed, while in others the state apparatus was directed towards the aggrandisement and enrichment of a small clique of politicians and army officers. However, the creation of nations out of the diversity was pursued with greater success in other cases. Thus Nigeria with its history of conflict and military government has created a recognisable nation in large measure through the policy of reconciliation pursued after the civil war (1967–1970). However, the imposition of the Western concept of the nation-state upon the continent of Africa was justifiably described as 'the Black Man's Burden' (Davidson, 1992). Correcting the abuses of the past and achieving viable alternatives has been problematical (Darkoh, 1996). Differing ideas of

community and clientship in constructing the nation in a manner more in line with African traditional societies were adopted in some states in the 1980s and 1990s with a view to embracing the cultural and ethnic diversity of the continent, within the inherited colonial state framework (Bayart, 1993; Mamdani, 1996).

Just as nations are created, so they may die and be subsumed within another entity or become no more than a regionalism. Assimilation to this extent has proved possible whether by Manchus in China or by Galicians in Spain. The loss of political independence has been a significant cause of national re-evaluation. The loss of Scottish independence in 1707 led to the formulation of the concept of a British nation, of which the Scots were the 'North British'. This submerged identity appears to have been adequate in a period of economic growth and the era of Empire. However, it may not survive nationalist revival. Similarly Joseph Stalin commented in 1920 upon the nationalities of the former Russian Empire that: 'either these nations had no independent existence of their own, or they lost it a long time ago' (Dziewanowski, 1977: 82). In this he was following Karl Marx, who consigned 'history-less' peoples to assimilation (Velychenko, 1993: 19). In most cases the loss was temporary, even imaginary. Soviet policies were ultimately to lead to their revival, under the false premise that economic class transcended and could supersede nationality as the basis of personal identity.

In many colonial enterprises many incipient nations were eliminated either through direct extermination or the destruction of the group's culture and economic base. The European colonisation of the Americas was particularly destructive in this respect (Josephy, 1994). It does, however, raise one of the significant issues of recent history, namely the pursuit of genocide as a means of eliminating a minority and imposing uniformity upon the nation. Furthermore, as Gerard Prunier (1997: 237–238), the chronicler of the Rwandan genocide of 1994, has warned: 'genocides are a modern phenomenon – they require organisation and they are likely to become more frequent'.

Multi-nationalism

Prior to the rise of modern nationalism in the nineteenth century, cultural differentiation was a general state of affairs. Imperial powers included diverse nations and groups within their boundaries and sought to include them within the polity. In other cases they were invited to settle as a means of promoting the development of the Empire. Thus St Stephen, the first king of Hungary (1001–1038), advised his successor that:

The utility of foreigners and guests is so great that they can be given a place of sixth importance among the royal ornaments. The Roman Empire, too, became powerful and its rulers glorious and august by the fact that from everywhere the wise and noble men were flocking into that country. For, as the guests come from various regions and provinces, they bring with them various languages and customs, various knowledge and arms. All these adorn the royal court, heighten its splendor, and terrify the haughtiness of foreign powers. For a country unified in language and in customs is fragile and weak. Therefore I order thee, my son, to receive them with good will and to nourish them honestly in order that they abide with thee more joyfully than elsewhere.

(Jaszi, 1929: 39)

The same pride in the cosmopolitan character of the population is echoed nearly 900 years later by the Census Commissioner in Calcutta, the then capital of the British Indian Empire, in 1911 who rejoiced that:

It is no exaggeration of language to describe the population of Calcutta and suburbs as an agglomeration of races, for no less than 397 separate nationalities, races and castes are returned. Nearly all the races and nationalities of the civilized world are represented, and the castes are drawn from all over India.

(India, 1913: 41)

However, it might be argued that the Western taxonomic desire to classify societies and define small variations led to the creation of distinct communities where none existed beforehand (Barrier, 1981). This ultimately led to the deliberate falsification of the census results in order to promote political parties which were based on ethnic support (Ahonsi, 1988).

Just as the economic development of Hungary in the eleventh century involved the settlement of people with skills in remote parts of the kingdom, so in the twentieth century the development of the Indian Empire involved significant mass migrations to the hubs of economic activity. Indeed the histories of the colonial empires recorded substantial migrations of people ranging from administrators and soldiers on short-term service to permanent migrants, whether free or forced, who provided the labour for new economic or social developments. The two largest migrations were associated with the migration of Europeans to other continents and the subsequent establishment of European based societies elsewhere on the globe, and the forced migration of African slaves and Asian indentured labourers to plantations and other enterprises in lands controlled by the colonial powers. The result was in certain respects an added complexity to the world ethnic pattern and at one extreme the creation of multi-ethnic populations, but at the other extreme the replacement of an indigenous society by a new immigrant society, in the image of Europe or a form of Africa or Asia transplanted to another continent. The multi-ethnic populations possessed their own dynamics, which resulted in conflict after independence, and on occasion expulsion back to their respective ethnic homelands (Horowitz, 1985).

The post-colonial, multi-ethnic states, notably the United States, Canada, Australia and New Zealand, have pursued policies of multi-culturalism since the 1970s. These have attempted to accommodate all the diverse populations present within the states, without the coercion previously applied to conform to the accepted norm. This has resulted in the jettisoning of much of the inherited colonial and post-colonial cultural baggage of European origin. In this respect the legal definition of the nation thus became the sole means of definition as the concepts of a shared language and a common culture were rejected as too narrow to encompass the diversity of the new national identity. Equally intriguing has been the symbolic concept of 'the rainbow people' as propounded by Archbishop Desmond Tutu in South Africa (Maimela, 1996: 90). Following the abandonment of apartheid and racial segregation, the diverse ethnic and linguistic groups were considered to be bound together by a common historical experience, a clear case of the state boundaries defining the nation.

Nation and State

There are few states where either the primordial or the legally defined nation fits the state territory exactly. The closest fits are those which have experienced a considerable degree of isolation. Iceland, which has received few immigrants since the initial period of settlement in medieval times, is close to the theoretical ideal. Some of the Pacific islands are in a similar position. Several centuries of self-imposed political isolation in Korea and Japan resulted in the creation of relatively homogeneous societies, although in the latter case the continued colonisation of the northern and southern islands incorporated people of non-Japanese stock and cultures, notably the Ainu of Hokkaido, into the Empire, who were then subject to acculturation (Siddle, 1996).

At the other end of the scale are the Gypsies (Romani), who have never controlled their own state and uniquely have no group attachment to a particular ancestral homeland (Fonseca, 1996). In this they differ from other exiled and scattered stateless nations which have ancestral lands to which they may wish to return and even establish their own nation-states. The creation of the state of Israel by the Zionist movement is one of the most powerful examples of a people situated in a diaspora regaining their historic territory. The Gypsy Holocaust, which paralleled that of the Jews in the Second World War, produced no parallel demand for the security of a separate state.

The complexity of the majority of nations is such that the problem of holding them together has been one of the major goals of state policy. In some cases internal strains are slight, in others it was ultimately impossible to achieve any long-term feeling of commonality. Furthermore, secure nations may become insecure at other times, particularly during periods of rapid change when the state's raison d'etre is subject to question, notably in periods of relative decline.

In any discussion of the world map in the last two centuries, concepts developed in Europe have dominated intellectual thought in the same manner that European or Western force of arms dominated the world politically. The European-based concept of the nation-state, whether symbolised by a monarchy or a republic, has been the dominant factor in state formation and preservation in the twentieth century. Similarly European-derived ideologies of socialism and communism were offered as counters to the excesses of nationalism in the international arena after 1917, but collapsed in the early 1990s. Universalism and the uniformity of liberal democracy, however, did not emerge thereafter, as basic cultural or 'civilisational' values exerted their dominance (Huntington, 1996). Re-integrating the concept of civilisational distinctiveness into that of the Western derived nation-state, as non-Western societies recover from a long period of subjugation to Western ideas, will result in further instability in the state system.

It is proposed to examine briefly the world in 1800 and the changes wrought in the nineteenth century, most particularly in the European heartland of the world system, as a backdrop to a more detailed examination of the world map of the twentieth century, which forms the main contents of this atlas. The rapid changes in Europe between 1810 and 1815 are particularly notable, as is the relative stability thereafter until 1900. Broad governmental changes in the twentieth century, together with an appreciation of civilisations upon which the state system depends, complete the introduction.

1.1   THE WORLD IN 1800

In 1800 the states of the European world system dominated only sections of the world. Although the states comprising the European world system were in a phase of aggressive expansion, they had yet to incorporate large sections of Africa and Asia (Wallerstein, 1989). The Chinese Empire remained the most significant economic and political rival to Europe as constituting a separate world system. The Empire remained isolationist in attitude and self-sufficient in its economy as the outcome of the unsuccessful British mission to China under Lord Macartney in 1793 demonstrated. The Emperor Ch'ien-lung saw no point in establishing a permanent embassy and stated that 'We possess all things. I set no value on objects strange and ingenious, and have no use for your country's manufactures' (Hsu, 1983: 161).

Other countries such as the Ottoman Empire, Korea, Japan, Persia, Morocco, Ethiopia, the Central Asian khanates and the West African emirates were linked to the emerging world system to only limited degrees, and were able to maintain and enforce isolation where deemed necessary. Virtually the whole of the interior of Africa and other extensive tracts of the world had not been mapped and its state system remained relatively untouched by European economic or political penetration. Indeed exploration was to be one of the major themes in European history in the nineteenth century, a project intimately linked to the integration of the world economy (Cameron, 1980).

In South and Central America the Spanish and Portuguese Empires continued to dominate the map. Effective administrative control of the Amazon Basin or Patagonia was minimal and indigenous societies within those regions survived independently, even if no longer recognised on the political map. Similarly the still extensive British North American possessions were in practice limited to small colonies of settlement on the United States border and isolated posts elsewhere. The United States of America extending between the Mississippi River and the Atlantic Ocean represented a new post-colonial state, and was engaged in the creation of its own empire in the interior of the continent (Meinig, 1986). Its political significance lay in the future as the first of the overseas European communities to establish an independent state, free of imperial control.

The British and the Russians were actively engaged in the expansion of their empires in Asia. The former fought a series of successful and decisive campaigns in southern and northern India between 1792 and 1803. In the latter year Delhi was occupied and the Moghul Emperor was reduced to the status of a dependant of the Honourable East India Company. The Russians were engaged in the conquest of the Caucasus region. In 1801 the accession of Georgia to the Russian Empire was a significant

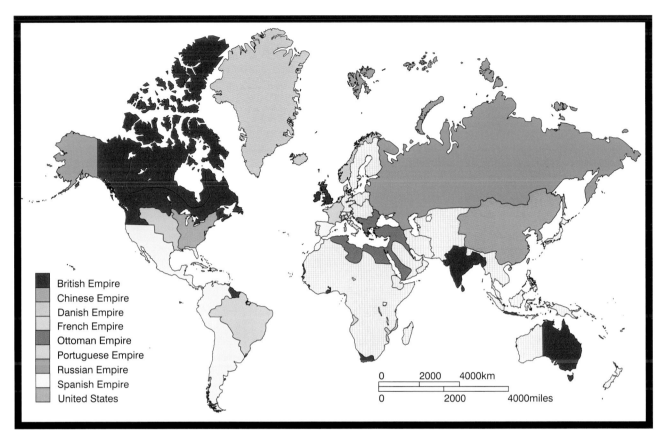

Map 1.1 The world in 1800

development in moving south of the mountain chain. In North America the Russians established trading posts in Alaska in the late eighteenth century and by 1812 a chain extended to California, contending with Spanish posts in California and British posts in the Oregon Territory. The United States' interest, symbolised by the Lewis and Clark expedition of 1804–1806, completed the complex imperial overlap in the region. Yet over these vast territories, imperial control was nominal and indigenous societies continued to operate as independent entities without reference to their nominal sovereigns.

The balance of power between the colonial empires outside Europe was undergoing rapid change. Great Britain had successfully conquered a number of the smaller colonies of France and its allies and was the dominant world sea power. The most significant seizures were the Cape of Good Hope, Ceylon and Guiana seized from the Dutch, Trinidad from the Spanish and the 'temporary' occupation of Malta and the remaining French West Indian islands. In addition, Great Britain was in the process of displacing the Dutch from their East Indian colonies.

1.2 EUROPE IN 1800

It is proposed to present the pattern of the state system of Europe not only for 1800, but also for 1812 and 1815, in order to illustrate the instability at the core of the dominant world system. In 1800 Europe and its overseas dependencies were convulsed by a series of wars which began with the deposition (1792) and execution (1793) of King Louis XVI of France and were only to end with the French defeat at the Battle of Waterloo in 1815. The period following the French revolution had been marked by large-scale conflict as the French Republic assumed military ascendancy on the continent of Europe. The enlargement of France to incorporate the lands within its 'natural frontiers' of the Rhine, the Alps and the Pyrenees had been completed. In addition, a series of satellite republics in the Netherlands (Batavian Republic), Italy (Cisalpine, Ligurian, Roman and Parthenopic Republics) and Switzerland (Helvetic Republic) marked a new era in European politics, as nationalism became the driving force of the revolution.

National liberation and the concomitant formation of nation-states was the message taken by French forces across the continent in an attempt to overthrow the pre-existing monarchical systems.

In the process the elimination of a large number of minor states resulted in the removal of many of the features of the medieval map of the continent. A host of small German states had been ruthlessly incorporated into their larger or more successful neighbours. Those eliminated included the numerous independent bishoprics and free cities, which had been able to achieve formal statehood as a result of the weakness of their nominal sovereign, the Holy Roman Emperor under the Treaty of Westphalia in 1648. In their place several medium-sized German states had emerged which contended for regional supremacy. Brandenburg-Prussia, with its independent base in East Prussia, which lay

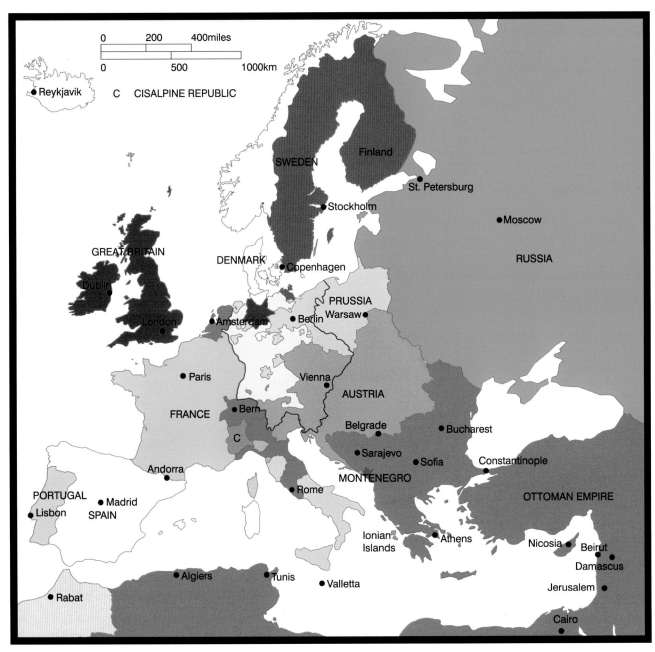

Map 1.2   Europe in 1800

outside the Holy Roman Empire, had expanded to become one of the major powers of the continent.

The map of eastern Europe had also been redrawn as a result of the three partitions of Poland, which had completely removed the kingdom from the map of the continent in 1795. Other venerable states to disappear included the Italian republics of Genoa and Venice in 1797 and the Sovereign Military Order of Malta in 1798, all as a result of the French intervention in the region. Similarly the replacement of the States of the Church by the Roman Republic marked a highly symbolic break with the past.

1.3   EUROPE IN 1812

The French-dominated European system was to be further developed in the ensuing twelve years as the Republic was transformed into an Empire under Napoleon Bonaparte in 1804. The satellite republics were either incorporated directly into France or became kingdoms under Napoleon's siblings. In the cases of Italy, Switzerland and the Confederation of the Rhine, Napoleon retained direct control with his proclamation as King, Mediator and Protector

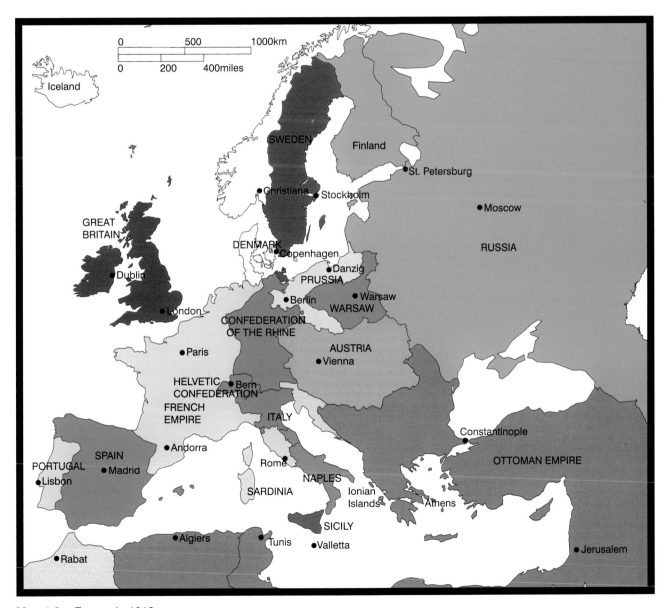

Map 1.3   Europe in 1812

respectively. Poland was revived in much reduced circumstances as the Grand Duchy of Warsaw, while the Free City of Danzig was established under French protection.

Even this map is notable for its lack of correspondence to the nations identified on the continent. The Kingdom of Italy covered only a section of the peninsula, which was dominated by the extensions of the French Empire, which included not only Rome but the eastern Adriatic coastline named the Illyrian Provinces. The extension of France to include the port of Lubeck on the Baltic Sea is maybe one of the more extraordinary territorial rearrangements, which was more dictated by the problems of maintaining the coastal blockade against trade with Great Britain, than any reference to the

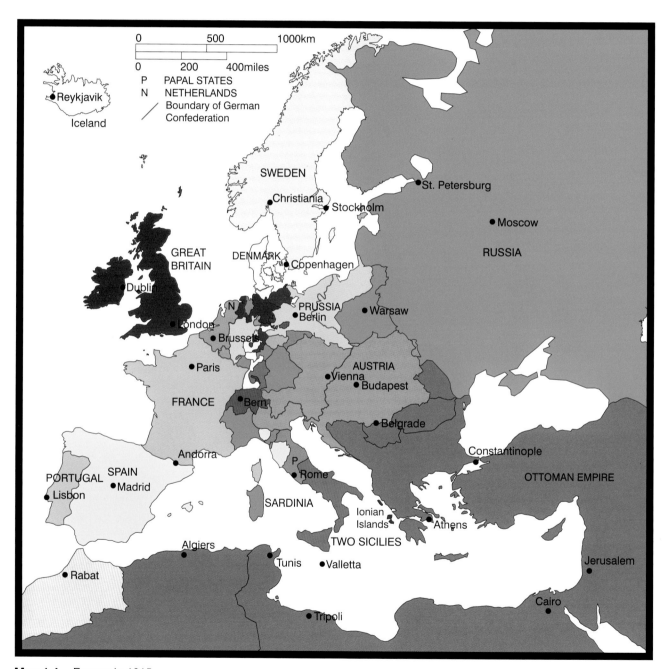

Map 1.4   Europe in 1815

concept of nationality. However, the system offered a sense of pan-European identity and cooperation which had previously been lacking, and it represented a significant attempt to create a dominant European state at the core of the European world system, similar to the position of China in East Asia.

Russia achieved further territorial advances at the expense of Sweden and the Ottoman Empire. The European state system was thus reduced to one of its most simplified situations, with the French Empire and its dependencies surrounded by only eight independent European neighbours, if the surviving mini-states of Andorra, San Marino and Montenegro are excluded.

1.4 EUROPE IN 1815

The final defeat of France by a grand continental alliance at the Battle of Waterloo in 1815 secured the restoration of many of the features of the pre-revolutionary state framework in Europe. However, although the German Confederation appeared as a revived form of the Holy Roman Empire, the more than 350 small states which had been eliminated between 1792 and 1812 could not be restored. In addition, the Italian and Polish states created under Napoleon were eliminated. The ease with which minor states could be established and dismantled was remarkable.

France remained the focus of the European political system, but was bordered by a number of militarily significant states, which could act as barriers to any future attempts by it to dominate the continent. Thus the Kingdom of the United Netherlands was formed to include the territories of the former Austrian Netherlands (modern Belgium and Luxembourg). Prussia was strengthened with the acquisition of substantial Rhineland territories. Sardinia, under the House of Savoy, with several north Italian duchies formed a barrier to French expansion to the south. The German Confederation was formed to replace the defunct Holy Roman Empire, with the Emperor of Austria as its president. Austria, with possessions in both Germany and northern Italy, emerged as the dominant central European power. In the general rearrangement of territories Russia received another part of Poland, Sweden gained Norway and Great Britain retained the strategic bases of Malta, the Ionian Islands in the Mediterranean and Heligoland in the Elbe estuary.

Within the Balkans the long loss of territory by the Ottoman Empire to Russia continued. However, the Serbian revolt of 1804 had been successful to the extent that it had resulted in the establishment of a separate Christian tributary principality in 1815. This represented the first of the incipient nation-states of the Balkans to appear upon the map. It was only with the Greek revolt in 1821 that the nationalist undermining of the Ottoman government from within was to result in the redrawing of the map in very different ways from the earlier imperial expansion of Austria and Russia in the region.

The distinguishing characteristic of the settlement drawn up at the Congress of Vienna in 1815 was the lack of recognition of nationalism and the nations of Europe. The majority of the states which emerged were in some senses multi-national and owed their legitimacy to their sovereign rulers. Thus Italy and Germany were divided into 9 and 38 states respectively, if the Austrian dominions are excluded. A further anomaly was presented by the kings of Great Britain, Denmark and the Netherlands becoming members of the German Confederation, through their external dynastic holdings. Whereas a pan-German 'state' nominally existed in the form of the Confederation, Italy possessed no overarching political structure and was in the terms of the Austrian Chancellor, Prince Klemens von Metternich, no more than 'a geographical expression' (Woolf, 1979: 227).

1.5 EUROPE IN 1900

The evolution of the European state system in the ensuing 85 years was vital for the development of the world state system, at the core of which it lay. It was the more remarkable in that it took place without a general European war. Each war on the continent tended to be fought in isolation, without seriously undermining the stability of the continent as a whole, with the result that the map in 1900 looked similar to that of 1815. Intra-European rivalries were largely fought out elsewhere.

The most significant changes in the map were the national unifications of Italy and Germany. The highly complex diplomatic and military campaigns associated with the formation of these states need not detain the reader here. However, in a certain sense the unifications were incomplete as substantial bodies of Italian and German speakers continued to live outside the new nation-states. In part this was due to the survival of multi-national Austria-Hungary as a major power. Inevitably, as unification had been achieved by the ruling elites, both new governments were involved in creating a sense of common nationality after a long history of regional divisions. The former prime minister of Sardinia, Massimo d'Azeglio, commented: 'We have made Italy: now we have to make Italians' (Seton-Watson, 1977: 107).

The other significant changes involved the further disintegration of the Ottoman Empire, with the emergence of Greece, Romania and Bulgaria between 1830 and 1878 (Turnock, 1989). The constitutional evolution was long and complex, involving such moves as the unification of the previously separate principalities of Moldavia and Wallachia in 1861 to form Romania. The evolution of Bulgaria was similarly tortuous. Elsewhere, the independence of Belgium in 1830 and the consequent independence of Luxembourg sixty years later completed the broad picture. The diplomatic situation, controlled through the close cooperation of the great powers, in the nineteenth century was such as to favour the maintenance of the status quo throughout the continent.

Map 1.5 Europe in 1900

1.6 WORLD POLITICAL STATUS 1900

By 1900 the world had changed dramatically. The military and political dominance of the European powers was overwhelming as a result of the technological, organisational and medical innovations of the nineteenth century (Headrick, 1981). Comparatively few states outside Europe had been able to withstand the assault upon their independence. However, already in the Americas the post-colonial republican successors to the imperial powers dominated the continent. In terms of state raison d'etre the traditional monarchies and the revolutionary republican regimes were complemented by the colonial dependencies and monarchical nation-states, as the clear distinctions between governmental forms were often obscure.

At the beginning of the twentieth century the majority of the population of the world still lived as subjects of an hereditary ruler. Indeed nearly half the global population were subjects of the Emperor Kuang Hsu of China and the British Queen-Empress Victoria. The two represented, in the core of their respective states, two different governmental traditions, with absolutist royal control over the core of the former and democratic institutions over the core of the latter empire. However, on the periphery the distinction between the dependencies of a democratic and an absolutist regime might be slight. The practical constitutional position of the imperial vassals, such as the Nizam of Hyderabad and the Dalai Lama of Tibet, had more in common than the distinction between European (Western) and Asian imperial systems, as depicted upon the map, might suggest.

Although the year 1900 is often considered to be close to the zenith of imperialism and therefore associated with the institution of monarchy, of the 56 sovereign states in being, some 25 were republican in constitutional form. Republics, and with them, the populist or national

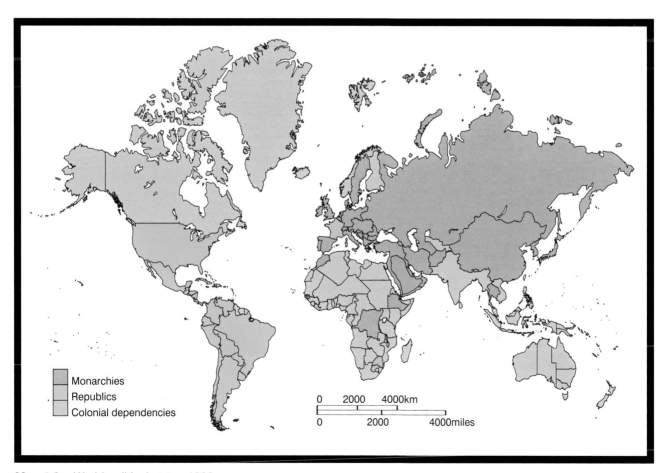

Monarchies
Republics
Colonial dependencies

0   2000   4000km
0   2000   4000miles

Map 1.6   World political status 1900

legitimation of the state, dominated the Americas after gaining their independence from the British, French, Spanish and Portuguese empires. The independence of the Latin American states had been assisted by the United States for suitably revolutionary reasons, and also by Great Britain, which had been concerned to counter the dominance of absolutist monarchist governments in Europe. The British Foreign Secretary, George Canning, suggested that he had: 'called the New World into existence to redress the balance of the Old' (Thomson, 1957: 118). Protected by the isolation bestowed by the American proclaimed Monroe Doctrine and British support, the new republics were able to develop into viable functioning nation-states in the course of the nineteenth century.

In Europe the republican system of government, outside France, had not been as successful as the rise of nationalism. Throughout the nineteenth century the great European powers had successfully imposed monarchies upon nation-states newly gaining their independence. Thus the Greek government had to accept Prince Otto of Bavaria

(1833–1862), and then, following his deposition, Prince George of Denmark (1863–1913) as its monarchs. Similarly Prince Leopold of Saxe-Coburg-Gotha was offered the throne of Belgium in 1831, while that of Romania was presented to Prince Carol of Hohenzollern-Sigmaringen in 1866. The trend continued until the First World War. The other European republics were those of some antiquity such as San Marino and Switzerland.

Colonial dependencies covered a third of the world, and often differed little in constitutional position, whether incorporated into the French Republic or the German Empire. They were regarded as essentially sources of supply of raw materials for the industrial plants situated in the metropolitan country (Rodney, 1974).

1.7 WORLD POLITICAL STATUS 2000

One hundred years later at the beginning of the third millennium, most of the monarchies had been overthrown. Only one emperor, Akihito of Japan, remained upon the

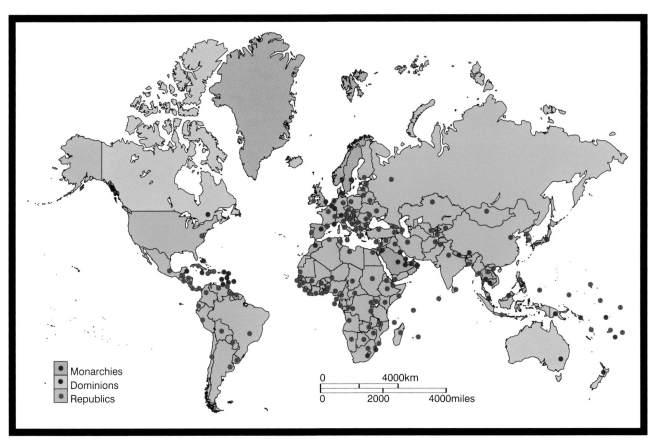

Map 1.7 World political status 2000

throne, compared with ten in 1900. Otherwise the other remaining 26 independent monarchies were mainly limited to western Europe and the Arab states. Few monarchs retained a measure of real executive power, although those that did retained the legitimating raison d'etre of the state, notably the Islamic monarchies, from Morocco to Brunei. A surprising anomaly was the survival of the British monarchy, which following decolonisation enabled Queen Elizabeth II to retain the constitutional thrones of some 16 Commonwealth dominions. Apart from Canada, these dominions were restricted to the Caribbean and Pacific regions. Significantly no African or Asian state retained such a long-term link with the colonial past, although the Queen had been head of state of a further 15 states on a short-term basis immediately after independence.

It is notable that the process of decolonisation resulted in few monarchies being established. Only a few protectorates survived with the institution of an hereditary sovereign intact, and some of these succumbed to revolution after independence. Those in the Arab world were the most notable survivors, but some were overthrown in the nationalist era after the creation of the state of Israel. The disintegration of the Communist system brought no restoration of deposed monarchies. Even King Michael of Romania who had been king twice (1927–1930 and 1940–1947) before, failed to regain his throne after the overthrow of the Communist government in 1989. Only in Cambodia did King Norodom Sihanouk regain his throne in September 1993, some 38 years after his abdication.

Republics formed the virtually universal form of government by 2000, adopted in over three-quarters of states. Their structures varied substantially, ranging from highly centralised administrations and loose confederations. All laid claim to embodying or representing 'the nation' or 'the people'. Their raison d'etre was thus expressed in nationalistic terms, where the state effectively defined the nation. Such universalism of outward form should not suggest uniformity of constitutional outlook. Each was the expression of the history of the particular society involved, with the result that generalisations are difficult to sustain. Indeed the adjectives applied to the republican title often supplies some indication of the form of political system. 'People's Republics' or 'Democratic Republics' were commonly proclaimed by Communist or Socialist governments. 'Federal Republics' were formed by those emulating the United States. 'Islamic Republics' were declared by those governments seeking to follow the precepts of the Koran more closely, and in the expectation that the new fifteenth century of the Islamic era ushered in in 1980, would be more auspicious for believers than the previous century. Some made claims to wider allegiances by, for example, incorporating their Arab character into the official state title. That names may be misnomers is demonstrated by the state which began the twentieth century as 'the Congo Free State' and entered the new millennium as 'the Democratic Republic of Congo', but in reality had experienced a century of repression, whether colonial, military or kleptocratic.

CHAPTER 2

The World in 1900

This chapter, which examines the world map in 1900, must, of necessity, be relatively lengthy as the state system is examined in some detail as the foundation upon which subsequent chapters are based. Many of the countries examined, notably in the Americas, will not be referred to again as they were stable blocks in an otherwise shifting global pattern of sovereignties and dependencies. On the other hand, some states have undergone dramatic changes necessitating their reappearance in altered circumstances in several of the following chapters. Furthermore boundary changes have been dealt with selectively, and only examined where considered significant. Similarly internal boundaries receive limited attention, only where some aspects of state sovereignty are concerned. Thus the still extant federal boundaries of the United States, Argentina and Australia are compared with the centralised administrative structures symbolised by the departments of France. In contrast the constitutional complexities of Austria-Hungary and the British Indian Empire have been dissolved to be replaced by new entities, either on an international level as a result of state fragmentation or through internal administrative reconfigurations.

2.1 THE WORLD POLITICAL MAP IN 1900

The colonial empires of the European powers dominated the world map outside the Americas in 1900. The political partition of Africa was virtually complete as the smaller and militarily weaker societies of the continent were incorporated into the European based technologically advanced empires. Similarly in Asia and the Pacific Ocean most of the major colonial conquests had been effected by 1900 and few remained to be undertaken. The indigenous states which had been able by either their strategic buffer status or physical isolation to preserve their independence from the colonial powers were few. The dangers of the era were aptly described by the British Prime Minister, Lord Salisbury, in 1898, when he stated that:

You may roughly divide the nations of the world as the living and the dying ... the weak states are becoming weaker and the strong states are becoming stronger ... the living nations will gradually encroach on the territory of the dying and the seeds and causes of conflict among the civilised nations will speedily appear.

(Sharp, 1991: 1).

As a result only 56 internationally recognised sovereign states remained in the world by 1900. They differed substantially in form, size and internal relationships. In addition, there were several hundred non-sovereign states locked into various dependent relationships with the independent sovereign states. Many of them were the inheritances of the personal allegiances surrounding the institution of monarchy and the land-based fealties of the feudal system. Others were the result of special treaty relationships between often unequal rulers or societies, as a result of conquest or submission to the threat of force. Some reflected the establishment of federal structures, both monarchical and republican, linking nominally equal partners in joint state structures. Yet others were highly centralised states with few internal spatial peculiarities or local autonomies.

It is therefore scarcely surprising that a remarkably high number (23) of the independent states were to be found in Europe, the seat of the major colonial empires. Even the latecomers to national unification, Germany and Italy, were engaged in the process of seeking out and annexing parts of the world not already controlled by other powers. However, not all the European states possessed colonies outside Europe, although only Belgium, Luxembourg, Switzerland, Sweden, Austria-Hungary and the small Balkan states had failed to acquire territory outside the continent. To this list must be added the mini-states, including Andorra, Liechtenstein, Monaco and San Marino, which had survived through careful diplomacy and by being pliant in eras of territorial aggrandisement.

The considerable range in state forms, reflecting the chequered histories of the ruling dynasties and governments concerned, may be demonstrated in an examination of the territorial structures of a number of the key states. The prime European example of the most traditional dynastic state was the Austro-Hungarian Empire, which still constituted one of the five 'great powers' of the international political and military system. However, despite its prosperity, the Habsburg monarchy was in relative decline and was racked by serious internal dissensions which were deemed capable of destroying the integrity of the structure. The very character and raison d'etre of the state was open to doubt, as loyalty to the Emperor was increasingly questioned in an era of nationalism. The Empire's pedigree was such that its internal administrative structures reflected the course of the history of the Habsburg family over a period of more than 600 years. Significantly the Austro-Hungarian Empire held no colonial territories outside Europe, although the administered province of Bosnia-Herzegovina could have been regarded as a European equivalent of a colony.

If Austria-Hungary was a cumbersome even anachronistic structure, the German Empire, as created in 1871, represented a remarkable compromise between the forces of modernity and historicism, through the welding of traditional monarchies to modern nationalism. In contrast France, or to give it its official title, The French Republic, was a centralised unitary state consisting of some 86 metropolitan departments and one territory, which reflected little of the country's history. Both Germany and France had acquired extensive overseas empires, but only France had attempted to incorporate a significant part, Algeria, into the metropolitan administrative structure.

In 1900 the world was organised in essentially European derived patterns and on European terms. The other countries proffered in this chapter cover a range of state formations which could be identified in the remainder of the state system. However, particular attention must be directed towards the most extensive state of the time, namely the British Empire, and its particularly complex pattern of territorial arrangements and personal relationships to the central government, symbolised by the Crown. The peculiarity of the Indian Empire within the British Empire is particularly worthy of examination. The emerging self-governing dominions in Canada and Australia also deserve attention as the forerunners of the process by which empires could be transformed and dismantled by constitutional rather than revolutionary means. In contrast the Russian Empire, which constituted the largest contiguous state in the world, was held together by an autocratic government intent upon centralisation. Two other empires which were undergoing fundamental change under the impact of modernisation, namely the Chinese and Ottoman Empires, also deserve extended examination. The concentration of this chapter upon empires is inevitable owing to their diversity and because it would be fair to suggest that the republics of the world emulated either the French or American examples.

The United States of America represented a recurring phenomenon in the international state structure, namely a set of colonies which had forcefully gained their independence. In many respects it inherited the attributes of the established state system, with a complex federal constitution preserving the rights for which the colonists had fought against a centralising metropolitan government. However, it also inherited the colonial government's problem of conducting relations with the indigenous peoples who were excluded from access to political power. In addition, the United States had by 1900 acquired an overseas empire, although the term colony was not used in the official terminology. The most nebulous international situation was the constitutional position of Cuba at the end of the Spanish–American War, which was neither a colony nor an independent state.

The remainder of the Americas, outside Canada, Newfoundland, the Caribbean and the Guianas, consisted of independent republics, created in the wake of the disintegration of the Spanish Empire in Central and South America and Brazil. In contrast to the complex history surrounding the disintegration of Spanish colonial rule, the more ordered independence of Brazil was marked by the declaration of the Brazilian Empire by Dom Pedro I, the heir to the Portuguese throne in 1822, preserving the integrity of the Portuguese half of the South American continent. Only in 1889 was the Emperor Dom Pedro II overthrown and the United States of Brazil proclaimed.

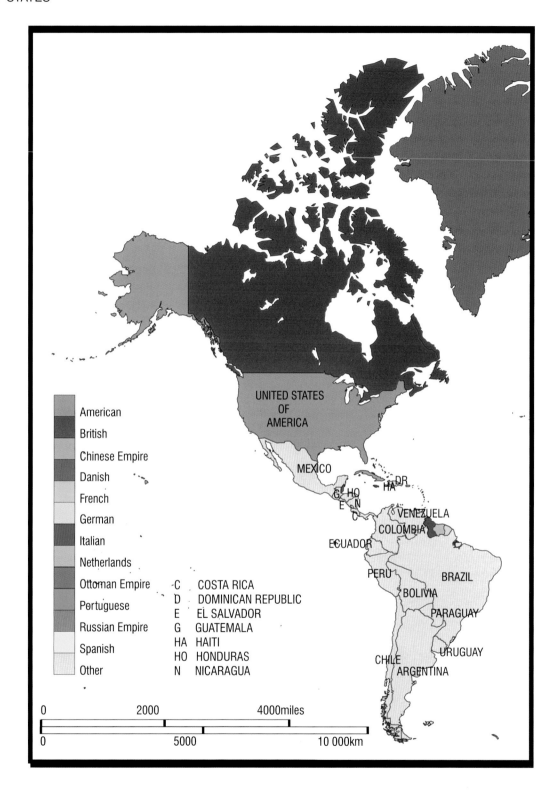

American

British

Chinese Empire

Danish

French

German

Italian

Netherlands

Ottoman Empire

Portuguese

Russian Empire

Spanish

Other

C   COSTA RICA
D   DOMINICAN REPUBLIC
E   EL SALVADOR
G   GUATEMALA
HA   HAITI
HO   HONDURAS
N   NICARAGUA

UNITED STATES
OF
AMERICA

MEXICO

DR

HA

G HO

E   N

C

VENEZUELA

COLOMBIA

ECUADOR

PERU

BRAZIL

BOLIVIA

PARAGUAY

URUGUAY

CHILE

ARGENTINA

0   2000   4000miles

0   5000   10 000km

Map 2.1   The world political map in 1900

After an initial and often prolonged period of conflict the new continental state system established a degree of coherence which was not subsequently disturbed. The first state outside the United States of America to proclaim its independence was Haiti in 1804. The African slaves on the island rose in revolt under the leadership of Toussaint L'Ouverture, overthrew the French colonial government and proclaimed their independence. France was unable to re-establish control, although the Spanish briefly regained the Spanish-speaking eastern portion of the island of Hispaniola before it came under Haitian control. Only in 1844 did the Dominican Republic gain its independence from Haiti.

Significantly Spanish America did not attain independence as a single entity, or even at the level of the four extensive vice-royalties into which the administration of the Empire had been divided. Independence was often attained at the provincial level of the former presidencies and captaincy-generals. Initial attempts to retain the larger units as the basis of the new states were ultimately unsuccessful. Imperial disintegration commenced with the declaration of independence by the United Provinces of La Plata (Argentina) in 1810 and was completed on the mainland with the Spanish surrender in Peru in 1826. Simon Bolivar's attempt to unite Spanish-speaking South America was not attainable and the United Provinces of New Granada, subsequently the United Republics of Colombia, disintegrated into its three component parts in 1830. This virtually completed the state system on the continent which has persisted to the present.

The independence of the Vice-royalty of New Spain as the state of Mexico in 1821 was contested with the secession of the United Provinces of Central America two years later. The five component provinces of Costa Rica, El Salvador, Guatemala, Honduras and Nicaragua subsequently chose to declare their separation in 1839. The resultant states were small, with El Salvador measuring only 18 700 square kilometres and containing a population of only one million in 1900. Attempts by Yucatan to gain a substantial measure of autonomy between 1821 and 1868 were eventually thwarted by the Mexican federal government, but the declaration of independence by Texas in 1836 was sustained with the assistance of the United States of America, which nine years later incorporated the new republic into its own system.

Most of the republics established to the south of the United States adopted constitutions modelled upon that of the United States of America, with the concepts of extensive local self-government and liberal democracy. Thus unions such as the United States of Colombia and the Argentine Republic offered the governments of their constituent states or provinces considerable autonomy. The occupation of the lands of indigenous peoples continued, as in North America, with their incorporation into the new states as areas open for colonisation. Only the autonomous Acre Territory, situated between Brazil, Peru and Bolivia possessed a degree of liberty in 1900. This was subsequently incorporated into Brazil under the Treaty of Petropolis in November 1903. Boundary disputes were to continue throughout the twentieth century.

2.2   THE AUSTRO-HUNGARIAN EMPIRE: POLITICAL UNITS

The Habsburg monarchy possessed a unique position with regard to the evolution of the European state system. It was only in 1648 at the Treaty of Westphalia that the monarchy, still entitled 'The Holy Roman Empire of the German Nation', gave up its claim to the universal allegiance of all Christendom and that the modern European system of fully sovereign and nominally equal states formally came into being. In 1283 Rudolf, Count of Habsburg, was elected Holy Roman Emperor and the Habsburg family held the title more or less without interruption until its abolition in 1806. Napoleon I's coronation as 'Emperor of the French' in 1804 had ended the unique Habsburg imperial claim. The demise of the thousand year empire, founded by Charlemagne in the year 800, had been anticipated in the same year by the Emperor Francis II with the proclamation of the Austrian Empire, named after the most important of the family's archduchies. The final change in state name came with the political compromise of 1867 between the Emperor and the Hungarian nobility whereby the historic Lands of St Stephen were excised from the Austrian Empire to form the kingdom of Hungary. The two states were joined together for purposes of foreign affairs, defence and currency to constitute the 'Dual Monarchy' of Austria-Hungary. In other respects Austria and Hungary operated as two separate states.

The compact block of the Austro-Hungarian Empire measured some 684,286 square kilometres and numbered some 46.6 million inhabitants in 1900. Its component territories reflected the long history of dynastic marriages, inheritances, conquests and losses. As such it was a highly personal empire within which the Emperor Franz Joseph had inherited many titles reflecting the complex history of the family. The 'grand Imperial title' is worth quoting to illustrate the nature of the state:

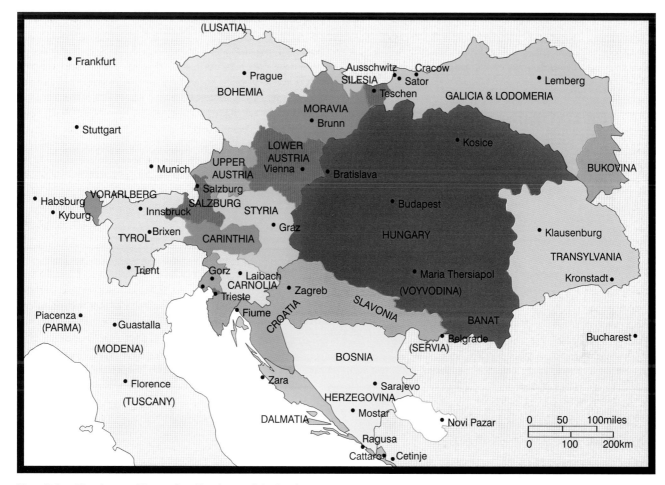

Map 2.2   The Austro-Hungarian Empire: political units

By God's Grace, Emperor of Austria; King of Hungary, of Bohemia, of Dalmatia, Croatia, Slavonia, Galicia, Lodomeria, and Illyria; King of Jerusalem, etc.; Archduke of Austria; Grand Duke of Tuscany and Cracow; Duke of Lothringia, of Salzburg, Styria, Carinthia, Carniola and Bukovina; Grand Duke of Transylvania, Margrave of Moravia; Duke of Upper and Lower Silesia, of Modena, Parma, Piacenza and Guastalla, of Ausschwitz and Sator, of Teschen, Friaul, Ragusa and Zara; Princely Count of Habsburg and Tyrol, of Kyburg, Gorz and Gradiska; Duke of Trient and Brixen; Margrave of Upper and Lower Lausitz and in Istria; Count of Hoenembs, Feldkirch, Bregenz, Sonnenberg, etc.; Lord of Trieste, of Cattaro and above the Windisch Mark; Grand Voyvod of the Voyvodina, Servia, etc., etc.

(Jaszi, 1929: 34)

The title is intriguing not only for the range of territories named and their varying and often overlapping statuses within the Empire, but for the wide range of effectively defunct titles. The town of Habsburg itself is situated in Switzerland, from where the family had been displaced in medieval times. The last remnant of the Crusader Kingdom of Jerusalem had fallen finally to the Moslems in the year 1291. The City of Jerusalem itself had been taken in 1244. Thereafter the title had been no more than a pious hope, which had not inhibited the Emperor Franz Joseph from visiting the City in 1869, thereby personally recognising that it formed an integral part of the Ottoman Empire. Some of the other titles reflected lands in Europe previously held by the family, including Lusatia, lost in 1648 to the Elector of Saxony and subsequently conquered by the King of Prussia. Various Italian, German and French titles were no longer extant following revolutions and annexations. Other titles were more recent. The Duchy of Cracow was the successor to the autonomous Congress Republic of Poland established in 1815 and annexed by Austria in 1834. Furthermore the formal titles where the Emperor did exercise power gave little indication of the relative strengths of the component parts of the Empire. Thus the kingdom of Hungary enjoyed constitutional equality with the Empire of Austria, but the kingdoms of Croatia and Slavonia were dependencies of the kingdom of Hungary.

2.3   THE AUSTRO-HUNGARIAN EMPIRE: PEOPLES

The Austro-Hungarian Empire was often referred to as the 'Dual Monarchy' in contemporary literature, reflecting the constitutional position of the kingdom of Hungary and the remaining territories grouped together as the Empire of Austria. Although German and Hungarian were the official languages of these two states, both the German and Hungarian speakers were minorities within the states they controlled. In 1900 German speakers only constituted 35.1

percent of the population of the Austrian Empire and Hungarian speakers only 45.4 percent of the population of the kingdom of Hungary.

Under the Compromise of 1867, the Emperor had conceded complete internal self-government to Hungary subject only to a personal union with Austria. The kingdom attained its own parliament, with only defence, foreign affairs and currency under the control of joint imperial committees. Within Hungary, a Magyar national state was created where the government sought to promote, indeed impose, the Hungarian language and culture upon the national minorities. This programme the Hungarian authorities appeared to be pursuing with a measure of success. At the time of the 1880 census only 46.7 percent of the population of 'Hungary Proper', (excluding Croatia-Slavonia) was enumerated as Hungarian speaking. By 1900 this percentage had reached 51.4 and indeed at the time of the last Imperial census in 1910, Hungarians constituted

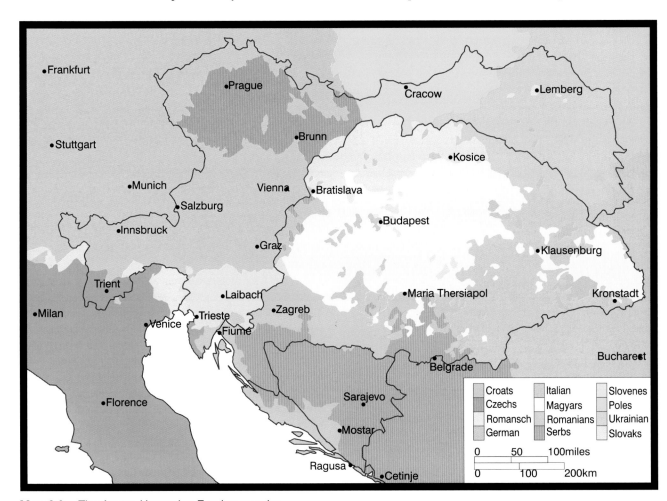

Map 2.3   The Austro-Hungarian Empire: peoples

some 54.5 percent of the population. The policy of 'Magyarisation' or assimilation appeared to be making significant headway. However, this could not disguise the fact that in 1900 within a total population of 19.3 million, five other national groups (Romanians, Germans, Slovaks, Croats and Serbs) each numbered over a million members within the Hungarian kingdom. The linguistic situation in some counties was particularly complex, reflecting the Imperial policies of attracting settlers to the devastated and depopulated frontier districts recaptured from the Turks in the course of the seventeenth and eighteenth centuries. The last of the special military regimes governing such areas (including the Voyvodina) had only been abolished in 1881.

By way of contrast the Austrian state authorities in the rump state allowed for considerable linguistic and cultural autonomy, with the aim of maintaining and indeed fostering the diverse local loyalties of the component kingdoms, archduchies, duchies and counties. In this manner it was considered that local loyalties would be focused upon the dynasty, in the unifying figure of the Emperor, rather than the various nationalist movements seeking separate states. The Austrian government lacked the ability to call upon the spirit of German nationalism, as this would have embittered inter-community relations in other parts of the empire and logically would have led to the demand for political links with Germany to the north. Thus the Czech language (spoken by 22.8 percent of the population) was officially used within the lands of the historic kingdom of Bohemia (including Moravia and Silesia), and Polish (spoken by 16.3 percent), within the kingdom of Galicia, although other languages were permitted for educational purposes. The position of Ruthenian (Ukrainian) in Galicia (spoken by 12.9 percent) was more problematical as its official use came into conflict with the historic interests of the Polish population and so was restricted to the eastern portion of the kingdom. However, the use of Slovene (spoken by 4.6 percent) was permitted in parts of Styria and Carniola, but rising linguistic chauvinism could lead to crisis in areas situated on the language divides. The impasse over the use of Slovene in the grammar school of Cilli in Styria in the 1890s was symptomatic of the tensions induced by the language policies within the Austrian half of the Empire. It also demonstrated the need to maintain the delicate series of compromises which were necessary in order to keep the multi-ethnic complex together, in contrast to the Hungarian nationalist approach.

The two contrasting approaches to harnessing nationalism to the service of the state were also reflected in the administrative structures of the Empire (Magocsi, 1993b). Within the kingdom of Hungary a centralised administration operated. The country was divided into some 71 counties, 24 county boroughs and two cities, Budapest the capital, and the port of Fiume. The sole exception to this uniform pattern was Croatia-Slavonia, which had gained a limited measure of self-government, with its own elected diet, as a result of an agreement with the Hungarian government in 1868. The other claims to autonomy for the Serbs of the Voyvodina and the Romanians of Transylvania were not entertained and such previously autonomous or privileged entities were subsumed into the counties in the years immediately after the compromise of 1867. In contrast the administrative pattern of Austria reflected a high degree of decentralisation to the seventeen provincial diets, with structures as diverse as the Emperor's titles. Surprisingly the historic hierarchies, such as the historic kingdom of Bohemia were not retained, so that the Diet of Moravia meeting in Brunn operated independently of that meeting in Prague.

Despite warnings that such a complex constitutional structure could not survive the national political demands of minority groups, notably the Czechs and the Serbs, for greater autonomy, the Dual Monarchy remained one of the five great powers of Europe. Indeed it had engaged in territorial expansion in the course of the Congress of London in 1878, when it had undertaken to administer the Turkish provinces of Bosnia and Herzegovina, and station a military garrison in the Sandjak of Novi Pazar, which separated Serbia and Montenegro. Bosnia-Herzegovina effectively became Austria-Hungary's sole colony. Its inhabitants were 96 percent Serbo-Croat speaking, but at the time of the 1895 census the population was divided on religious grounds into Roman Catholic (21.3 percent), Serbian Orthodox (42.9 percent) and Muslim (35.0 percent) communities. Administration was undertaken as a joint Austro-Hungarian responsibility, but as a result of the territory's proximity to the Hungarian lands, it was Hungary that sought to settle the territory with its own nationals.

2.4 GERMAN STATE STRUCTURE

The German Empire was proclaimed with great splendour in the Hall of Mirrors at the Palace of Versailles in 1871 following the decisive victory of Prussia and its allies over France. The complex series of wars and diplomatic manoeuvres which had preceded this event had produced the groundwork for the establishment of the new state. Political unification had been anticipated by the establishment of the German Zollverein or customs union, under Prussian leadership in 1834. This structure excluded

Heligoland

SCHLESWIG
HOLSTEIN
OLD
LUBECK

MECKLENBURG
SCHWERIN

STRELITZ

● Hamburg

POMMERANIA

WEST PRUSSIA

● Königsberg

● Danzig

EAST PRUSSIA

● Stettin

OLD ● Bremen

HANOVER

SL

PROV

● Brunswick

BRANDENBURG

● Berlin

POSEN

L

ANHALT

SAXONY

SILESIA

WESTPHALIA

W

SAXONY

● Breslau

● Cologne

HESSE-NASSAU

THURINGIAN
STATES

RHINE
LAND

● Prague

OLD

HESSE

BAVARIA
PALATINATE

BAVARIA

ALSACE-
LORRAINE

WURTTEMBURG

● Stuttgart

BADEN

● Sigmaringen

● Munich

L   LIPPE-DETMOLD
SL   SCHAUMBERG-LIPPE
W   WALDECK
OLD OLDENBURG

| 0 | 100 | 200miles |
| 0 | 100 | 200km |

THURINGIAN STATES

	Saxe Weimar - Eisenach		Schwarzburg - Rudolstadt
	Saxe Coburg - Gotha		Schwarzburg - Sondershausen
	Saxe - Meiningen		Reuss (elder line)
	Saxe - Altenburg		Reuss (younger line)

Gotha   Erfurt   Weimar

● Coburg

| 0 | 10 | 20miles |
| 0 | 20 | 40km |

Map 2.4   German state structure

Austria, which occupied the presidency of the wider German Confederation established after the Napoleonic Wars at the Congress of Vienna.

The more immediate chain of events leading to unification began with the war between Denmark and the members of the German Confederation in 1864, over the issue of the disputed succession to the duchies of Schleswig-Holstein. The defeat of Denmark had strengthened Prussian control in northern Germany. In 1866 the war between Prussia and Austria and its German state allies resulted in the collapse of the German Confederation. In its place a new North German Confederation, under the presidency of the King of Prussia, was established linking the German states situated north of the River Main. Significantly those states in northern Germany that had allied themselves with Austria in the course of the war were directly annexed to Prussia, as was the whole of Schleswig-Holstein. Only the kingdom of Saxony was reprieved in response to a personal appeal by the Emperor Franz Joseph. The result was the physical linking up of the previously separated Prussian territories in the east with those on the Rhine. After 1866 only three states, Baden, Wurttemburg and Bavaria, remained independent, situated between France, Austria and the new North German Confederation. Baden applied for membership of the Confederation, which was clearly unacceptable to the French Emperor Napoleon III, who sought to maintain some territorial buffer between his country and the expansionist German state. The ensuing war between France and Prussia ensured the final unification of the country.

The constitution of the new German Empire provided for 'an eternal union for the protection of the Realm and the care and welfare of the German people' (*Statesman's Year Book*, 1900: 583). The union linked a set of 22 monarchical states, including 4 kingdoms, 7 grand-duchies, 3 duchies and 8 principalities, to the 3 Hansa free cities and the Imperial Province of Alsace-Lorraine gained from France. It covered some 540 867 square kilometres and enumerated some 56.4 million inhabitants in 1900. The kingdom of Prussia dominated the federal structures of the Empire in both political and economic terms. The King of Prussia, Wilhelm I, assumed the title 'German Emperor' and acted as President of the federal structure. Indeed Prussia was the home to 34.5 million (61.2 percent) of the Empire's inhabitants and covered 348 620 square kilometres (64.5 percent) of the national territory. Within Prussia the boundaries of the 14 provinces reflected the historical expansion of the state, most recently the conquest of Schleswig-Holstein, Hanover, Hesse-Nassau and a number

of smaller states in the war of 1866. Many of these provinces were to form the basis of the federal länder of 1949. A small Prussian outlier at Sigmaringen reflected the Hohenzollern dynasty's connections with the south of the country.

The kingdom of Bavaria, with a population of 6.2 million and an area of 75,840 square kilometres, constituted the second largest state in the Empire. It retained a high degree of autonomy after 1871. It also retained control of the Palatinate situated on the western side of the Rhine. Many of the other states were also fragmented, reflecting the long and complex histories of their dynasties. For example, the Grand Duchy of Oldenburg on the North Sea included the Principality of Lubeck on the Baltic Sea, north of the Free City of Lubeck, and the Principality of Birkenfeld in the Rhineland. Some of the constituent states were of considerable antiquity. Thus the Grand Duke Friedrich Franz IV of Mecklenburg-Schwerin traced his family back through 25 generations to Slavonic origins, being descended from Niklot, Prince of the Wends, who died in 1160. However, the greatest complexity was to be found among the eight Thuringian states, which had a combined population of some 1.4 million. The smallest, the Principality of Reuss-Greiz (Elder Branch), covered only 316 square kilometres and enumerated a population of 68 000 in 1900.

It is significant that Alsace-Lorraine, annexed from France, was given the distinctive status of an Imperial Territory. This was done as an alternative to annexation to Prussia, as in the case of previous acquisitions, and indeed in the case of Heligoland after its cession by Great Britain in 1890. One further anomaly was the continued inclusion, until 1918, of the independent Grand-Duchy of Luxembourg within the German Zollverein, which it had joined in 1842.

German unification was comparatively late in terms of European state formation. Thus it was also late in joining the European acquisition of overseas colonies. However, as the Kaiser Wilhelm II stated with pride: 'We have fought for our place in the Sun and won it' (*The Times*, 18 June 1901). Between 1884 and 1900 the country acquired an overseas colonial empire. The largest blocks comprised the four African colonies, which had previously been situated in regions assumed to be within the British sphere of influence, but not possession. Other smaller territories were annexed in the Pacific Ocean, notably New Guinea, again in an area assumed to be within the British sphere of influence, together with the northern Pacific islands which had remained under Spanish control after the Spanish–American War of 1898. Finally the western islands of Samoa were acquired in an Anglo-German-American agreement defining colonial spheres. In China the port of Kiaochow on the Shantung peninsula was gained as part of the general Western encroachment upon that country. It is significant that no attempt was made to include the colonies within the administrative structures of the metropolitan Empire, nor grant any system of local autonomy.

2.5 FRENCH STATE STRUCTURE

France, officially designated 'The French Republic', embodied a very different concept of state sovereignty. This concept was to have a profound impact upon the international state system in the twentieth century. Following the French revolution in 1789, a number of highly significant changes were made to the manner in which the state was organised and the way national sovereignty was perceived. The abolition of the monarchy, which had been based on the concept of divine right of the king and his embodiment as sovereign over the state and its population, was fundamental to the change of concept. Indeed Louis XVI had been executed in 1793 to destroy both personally and symbolically the old feudal bonds between the sovereign and his subjects (Jordan, 1979). Subsequent attempts to recreate such monarchical links, whether under the traditional legitimist restoration of 1814–1830 under Louis XVIII and Charles X, the Orleanist monarchy of 1830–1848 under Louis Philippe or the Bonapartist Second Empire of 1852–1870 under Louis Napoleon, had foundered.

In the revolutionary proclamation of 'liberty, equality, fraternity' embodying the equality of all people before the law, the major principles of universal applicability were enunciated. Thus the complex relationships between different provinces and the king and the royal central government in Paris were abolished and all citizens were deemed to be equal with a right to participate in the government of the country. Just as the old concept of sovereignty residing in the monarch was abolished, so were the old provinces to which old loyalties were attached. In the place of the historic provinces and counties, a set of uniform administrative departments were drawn, named after the local rivers, mountains and other physical features. Two-thirds were in the range of 5000 to 7000 square kilometres in extent. Only Paris, under the guise of the Department of Seine (480 square kilometres), was an exception to the general rule. After the defeat of 1871 the Territory of Belfort (610 square kilometres) became an anomaly as the sole section of the department of Upper Rhine to remain under French control. In 1918, however, it was not reunited with the regained portion. Only in 1964 were the departmental boundaries in the Parisian region redrawn to create five more entities. Otherwise only the division of Corsica into two altered the departmental pattern during the century.

The administrative revolution impacted directly upon sections of the country which had previously retained a measure of local autonomy. Thus Brittany had been united with the kingdom of France through the marriage of Claude, the heiress to the Duchy, to King François I (Ellis, 1985). The treaty of 1532 formalising the personal union had provided for the retention of Brittany's traditional administrative system. This autonomy was abolished at the revolution and the duchy was divided into five departments, with the prefects appointed by the central government, one of whose tasks was to prevent local deviations from national policies. Thus the entire national territory and population was subjected to the same centralising processes, which in the course of the nineteenth century operated to create the modern French nation. The distinct Breton language was therefore suppressed for official purposes and French substituted. The idea that state and nation should coincide in the 'nation-state' became the political programme to which successive governments throughout the nineteenth and twentieth centuries have subscribed. The French approach thus became the model for other countries wishing to attain the same ends of democratic national integration.

France was one of the major colonial powers, although its foremost enterprises in North America and India had been lost by 1815. However, it retained a number of relics of a long history of overseas enterprise. Thus the islands of St Pierre and Miquelon off the coast of Newfoundland were retained as a residual of the country's North American empire and as a base for French fishing fleets on the Newfoundland Banks. Similarly the five towns of the French Indian Settlements survived under French control after the failure of the attempt to displace the British in the subcontinent. Other seventeenth and eighteenth century acquisitions, such as Guadeloupe and Martinique in the West Indies, French Guiana in South America and Reunion in the Indian Ocean, were also regained after British occupation in the Napoleonic Wars. These colonies returned deputies to the National Assembly and were to some extent integrated into metropolitan French political structures. To these 'historic' possessions were added the range of strategic bases and islands dating from nineteenth century expansion, notably in the Pacific Ocean with the acquisition of New Caledonia and the Oceanic Settlements

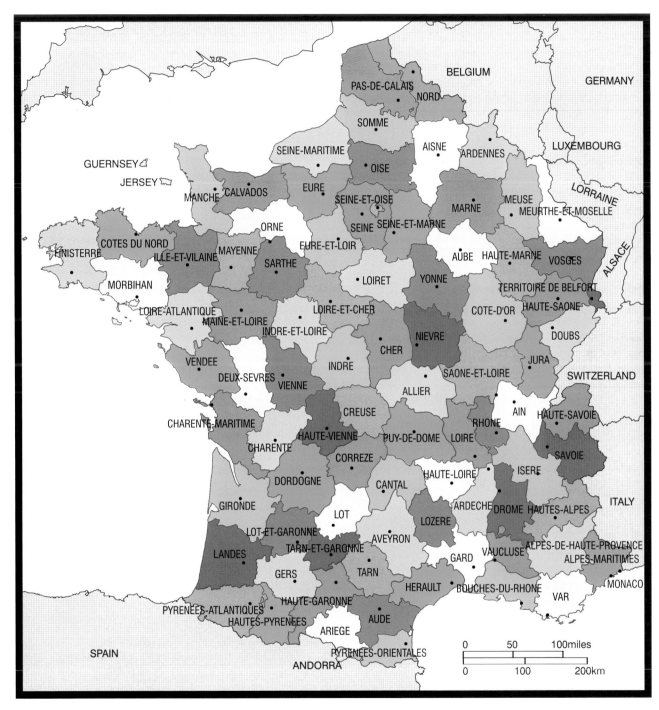

Map 2.5   French state structure

in Polynesia. The New Hebrides were administered jointly by French and British naval officers, an anomaly formalised only in October 1906 with the establishment of a condominium government.

It was in Africa and Indo-China that France acquired in the course of the nineteenth century the extensive colonial empire which featured so prominently on the world map of 1900. The Algerian conquests were integrated into the metropolitan structures where the coastal section of the colony was divided into three departments returning deputies to the National Assembly in Paris. Only in Algeria was overseas settlement by French colonists undertaken on any scale in the nineteenth century. However, political and economic equality was initially solely for Frenchmen. Colonial peoples were not admitted to the franchise. At various stages some of the overseas possessions had sent deputies to Paris, but the numbers had been small. However, the concept of the eventual incorporation of colonial peoples into the nation through assimilation was propagated through the 'civilising mission' of France. Even in 1946 only a few islands and Guiana that had been in French possession since the seventeenth and eighteenth centuries qualified for such incorporation.

2.6   THE EUROPEAN MINI-STATES

Europe also contained a number of small states which had not been conquered or incorporated by their larger and more powerful neighbours. A group of small states, even termed 'bizarre' by some contemporary writers, had escaped the general expansionism of the previous few hundred years and remained upon the political map of the continent (Laroche, 1903). They were a disparate group including Monaco, San Marino, Andorra and Liechtenstein (Catudal, 1975). Two other states, Montenegro and Luxembourg, might also be included.

The Principality of Monaco had been ruled by the Grimaldi family since 1297 and consisted of little more than the old town of Monaco and the more modern suburb

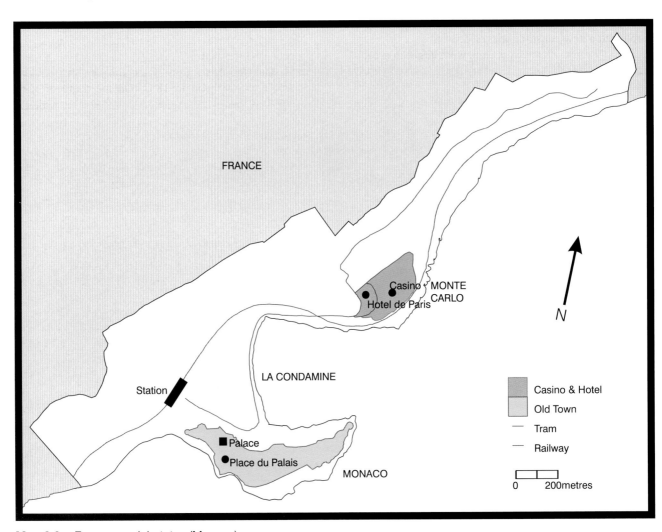

Map 2.6   European mini-states (Monaco)

of Monte Carlo, after the surrender of Mentone and Roccabruna to the French in 1861. It was thus the smallest of the independent states on the world map in 1900 with an area of only 190 hectares. Prosperity was gained through enterprises such as the casino which had been established by Prince Charles III in 1863. His new town of Monte Carlo catered for the leisured classes of Europe (and the Americas), who were encouraged to pass the winter season on the Mediterranean coastline. Thus it was not the smallest country in terms of population, as it was home to some 15 000 inhabitants by 1900. The subsequent development of Monaco in the twentieth century witnessed a doubling of the population. Legal changes came through the July 1918 treaty with France which recognised the latter's reversionary right to sovereignty over the principality, should there be no recognised Grimaldi heir (Duursma, 1996). Latterly, in December 1962 Prince Rainier III renounced the principle of rule by divine right and introduced a new constitutional dispensation.

The other mini-states were somewhat larger in area, but each the subject of a peculiar history enabling it to survive. The Principality of Liechtenstein was one of the minor members of the German Confederation before 1866, which because of its physical isolation from the remainder of Germany, was not included in the unification effected in 1871. The state was linked to Austria-Hungary through a customs agreement signed in 1852 and many other arrangements including judicial appeal to the High Court in Innsbruck. Even the national anthem is ambiguous on the principality's status, referring to: 'This beloved homeland in the German fatherland' (Shaw and Coleman, 1963: 219). In terms of size it covered 168 square kilometres, but enumerated a population of only 9400 souls.

The Principality of Andorra, situated in the Pyrenees between France and Spain, enjoyed the distinction of being governed by two joint rulers, the President of the French Republic (as heir to the counts of Foix and kings of France) and the Bishop of Urgel in Spain. The latter is appointed by the Pope, further internationalising the status of the co-rulers. Effectively control was exercised by the local council. Although in territorial terms it covered some 453 square kilometres, in 1900 it had the distinction of being the least populous state in the world, enumerating only 6000 souls.

The Republic of San Marino, situated in the Apennines, was completely surrounded by Italian territory, as it had been by the Papal States before the unification of the country. The state had a long history of delicate negotiations with its neighbour preserving its independence from the times of St Marinus in the fourth century, traditionally claiming foundation in AD 301. The state

measured only 60 square kilometres and housed 9500 inhabitants. In the three latter cases the physical isolation and relative insignificance of the states aided their governments' policies of self-preservation.

There were two small states which might be considered as contenders for categorisation as mini-states: Luxembourg and Montenegro. Luxembourg had been united with the Netherlands under the settlement at the Congress of Vienna. Following the revolt in 1830, the southern provinces seceded to form the kingdom of Belgium, but Luxembourg was partitioned between the two states. The eastern portion, measuring some 2,586 square kilometres, including the City of Luxembourg, remained under control of the King of the Netherlands. However, he ruled as Grand Duke of Luxembourg, and was a member of the German Confederation until 1866. Furthermore, the state retained a Prussian garrison to guarantee its independence against anticipated French aggression. Dispute over its status following the demise of the Confederation resulted in its international recognition as a neutral state, the demolition of the fortifications and the removal of the garrison in 1867. On the death of King William III of the Netherlands, the Grand Duchy, which at the time was subject to the Salic law, and thus did not provide for a woman to succeed to the throne, did not pass to Queen Wilhelmina, but to her uncle Adolph, thereby constitutionally separating the state from the Netherlands.

Montenegro remained an independent state as it had successfully resisted administrative incorporation into the Ottoman Empire. Although reduced to an Ottoman vassal at one stage it retained its own government and maintained relations with the other powers of Europe, notably Russia, whose flag it adopted in inverted form. Unlike the other mini-states, Montenegro was able to maintain its independence through its own military skills. Indeed it was able to expand its territory in the course of the nineteenth century, a feat which was beyond the means of its smaller contemporaries. Thus by 1900 it covered some 9400 square kilometres and had gained direct access to the sea through the acquisition of the coastal town of Antivari. The principality contained a population of approximately 228 000 people, which was much the same as Luxembourg. It was smaller than any of the states in the other continents and could therefore be included in the anomalies still present in the European state system. Furthermore, a closer link between Montenegro and Serbia, even a common border, had consistently been opposed by Austria-Hungary as a move towards a 'Greater Serbia', with serious implications for the allegiance of the Empire's Serb population.

By 1900 the European mini-states were regarded as anachronisms, but the question of their survival or destruction was generally not considered to be of major importance by their more powerful neighbours. They were not invited to participate in international meetings such as the Hague Peace Conferences of 1899 and 1907 and their sovereignty was considered to be compromised by their size. Luxembourg and Montenegro were invited to international gatherings and to sign international conventions. This suggested that they were of a different character to the true mini-state, which had more specific problems of viability.

2.7   THE UNITED KINGDOM OF GREAT BRITAIN AND IRELAND

The most extensive state or empire in the world in 1900 was the British Empire, which covered nearly a quarter of the surface of globe and incorporated nearly a quarter of the population. The Empire was a complex collection of territories bound together by an allegiance to the monarch. Queen Victoria held among other titles that of Empress of India, taken in 1877 to share the Imperial distinction with the emperors who dominated central and eastern Europe. Her official title, and that by which the empire was held together administratively, remained that of 'Queen of the United Kingdom of Great Britain and Ireland'. It was the government of this state which remained ultimately responsible for the administration of the entire empire. The disparity between metropole and empire in terms of population and area is striking. The population of the United Kingdom was only 41.5 million in 1901, yet the British Empire 'beyond the seas' contained a population of some 354 million. In terms of area the imbalance was even greater, with the United Kingdom covering some 315 100 square kilometres and the overseas possessions more than 28.8 million square kilometres.

The metropolitan state was a unitary state constitutionally created by the successive acts of unions between England and its neighbours, namely Wales in 1535, Scotland in 1707 and Ireland in 1801. The core kingdom of England emerged in the eighth century when the fragmented Anglo-Saxon kingdoms recognised a high king. Following the Danish invasions in the tenth and eleventh centuries, the kingdom of Wessex gained control of the whole of England. It was this state that the Normans conquered and organised and proceeded to expand through conquests in Wales and Ireland.

The kingdom was constitutionally enlarged by the Act of Union with Wales, which represented the legitimisation of English conquests effected between the twelfth and fifteenth centuries. The Principality of Wales was retained as the title bestowed upon the eldest son of the sovereign, but otherwise it had no administrative relevance. For general purposes the country was divided into counties with the same functions as English counties. Even the Church of England incorporated the country directly into the Archdiocese of Canterbury. The Act of Union made no change to the title of the state, which remained the Kingdom of England.

The Act of Union with Scotland represented the legal merging of two separate kingdoms ruled by the same monarch as a result of the inheritance of the English throne by King James VI of Scotland in 1603. The personal union was uneasy as the two separate constitutional systems operated independently. A brief attempt was made to impose English institutions upon Scotland under the Cromwellian republic between 1649 and 1660 and the subsequent restoration of the monarchy between 1660 and 1688. The revolution of 1688 radically changed the basis of state sovereignty from that of monarchical divine right to a shared concept of the 'Sovereign in Parliament'. Countrymen and women did not become citizens, they remained subjects, a concept which by the twentieth century was remarkably at variance with prevailing ideas. The accession of King William III and Queen Mary II enabled Scotland to reassert its nominal independence under sovereigns more to the ruling Protestant elite's liking. Constitutional unification came in 1707, largely as a result of the threat of a Roman Catholic restoration under the exiled Stuart dynasty and the financial crisis following Scotland's unsuccessful colonial venture at Darien on the Isthmus of Panama. The resultant union served the interests of both and retained many aspects of Scotland's distinctive political culture, notably the legally established state Church of Scotland, and the administrative, legal and education systems. Significantly the title of the state was changed to the United Kingdom of Great Britain.

The United Kingdom reached its full extent with the Union of Great Britain and Ireland in 1801. The English conquest of Ireland had begun in 1171 and continued through many vicissitudes until the seventeenth century. The Kingdom of Ireland as a separate entity within the English empire was established in 1538 and a considerable degree of autonomy was granted to the viceroy and parliament in Dublin. However, the majority of the population remained hostile to English rule, a hostility which was reinforced by the Reformation in England, but

1	Nairn	31	Leitrim
2	Elgin	32	Longford
3	Banff	33	West Meath
4	Kincardine	34	Kings County
5	Dumbarton	35	Queens County
6	Stirling	36	Kilkenny
7	Kinross	37	Carlow
8	Renfrew		
9	Clackmannan		
10	Linlithgow		
11	Edinburgh		
12	Peebles		
13	Selkirk		
14	Westmorland		
15	Nottingham		
16	Shropshire		
17	Stafford		
18	Leicester		
19	Cambridge		
20	Huntingdon		
21	Northampton		
22	Bedford		
23	Buckingham		
24	Oxford		
25	Radnor		
26	Brecknock		
27	Monmouth		
28	Londonderry		
29	Armagh		
30	Monaghan		

Map 2.7   The United Kingdom of Great Britain and Ireland

not in most of Ireland. Protestant settlers from Scotland and England in the sixteenth and seventeenth century profoundly affected the balance of population in the northern section of the country, but failed to make much impression in the south. Threats of a French invasion in the 1790s led the ruling Protestant elite to consider that unification with Great Britain was the best way to maintain the status quo. In the nineteenth century opposition to the Union increased, with a substantial block of disaffected Irish members of Parliament sitting in the British House of Commons, committed to the repeal of the Act of Union.

In pursuit of effective internal administration the country was divided into the counties. In extent they ranged from the territories of the smaller Anglo-Saxon kingdoms, such as Essex, Sussex, Kent, and the two divisions such as the Nor(th)folk and Sou(th)folk of the kingdom of East Anglia, to the county divisions established in the extensive kingdom of Wessex and extended to the remainder of the state by the eleventh century. Peculiarities such as the Bishopric Palatine of Durham survived until the Parliamentary Reform Act of 1832, but the reform of national and local government in the course of the nineteenth century removed the many anomalies in the system to produce a uniform series of administrative structures similar to France, although their sizes differed markedly. Thus the county of Inverness covered 10,907 square kilometres, whereas Clackmannan measured only 141 square kilometres. The historic county of Yorkshire (15,774 square kilometres) was larger, but had been divided into its three ridings for administrative purposes. Furthermore, the metropolitan London County Council served a population of 4.5 million, compared with only 6,981 by its counterpart in Kinross.

The United Kingdom government was also responsible for a number of small territorial relics of medieval times. The Bailiwicks of Jersey and Guernsey (including the Lordship of Sark) in the English Channel were the last parts of the Duchy of Normandy to remain in the dynasty's hands after the French occupied the mainland in the year 1204. The Isle of Man had a complex relationship with the English Crown, which resulted in it retaining its own parliamentary government dating from the Norse kingdom of Man in the eleventh century. Significantly none of these islands was represented in the central parliament at Westminster, nor were any of the British colonial possessions. This, however, did not preclude discussion of the possibility of the integration of the Empire into a super-state, rather than its fragmentation (Wyndham, 1904).

2.8 THE BRITISH EMPIRE

The British overseas empire was a vast and complex collection of possessions acquired by England and the United Kingdom since the end of the sixteenth century (Hyam, 1976). In terms of area it covered approximately 28.5 million square kilometres, or a quarter of the surface of the globe, and contained approximately 395 million people. The colonies included a number of regions of European settlement where societies formed in the image of England and Scotland were in the course of evolution. There were also colonies of exploitation where the indigenous population was organised for the economic benefit of the empire. The earliest and clearest examples of such colonies had been the slave plantations of the West Indies, but the trading empire in India and adjacent lands paralleled the development of colonies of settlement and exploitation. In territorial terms the occupation of vast tracts of Africa in the late nineteenth century followed the concept of an empire as a means of international prestige, which might be converted into a profitable enterprise. It could be noted in this regard that the chartered trading companies which took an active part in the conquest of Africa were generally unable to generate substantial revenues. For example, the British South Africa Company was unable to pay a single dividend for the entire 33-year period that it administered Rhodesia, while the Imperial British East Africa Company went bankrupt. It is notable that British economic interests were directed as much towards foreign countries as the Empire. Indeed Argentina could have been regarded as an informal dominion (Platt, 1986). Indicative of this status was the opening of the sole overseas subsidiary of Harrods, the London department store, in Buenos Aires in 1912.

Constitutionally the overseas British Empire lacked the uniform administrative structure of many of its contemporaries. The Confederation of Canada had gained dominion status in 1867 and in most respects, other than control over the conduct of foreign affairs and defence, functioned as an independent state. Other colonies of European settlement, including those in Australia, New Zealand, Newfoundland, the Cape of Good Hope and Natal, had been granted internal self-government and were constitutionally about to obtain dominion status. Certain long established colonies such as Barbados and Bermuda enjoyed varying degrees of local government control. The majority of colonies, however, were directly administered by government officials appointed by the Colonial Office, Foreign Office and India Office in London. India as an Empire was unique in its government structure as the

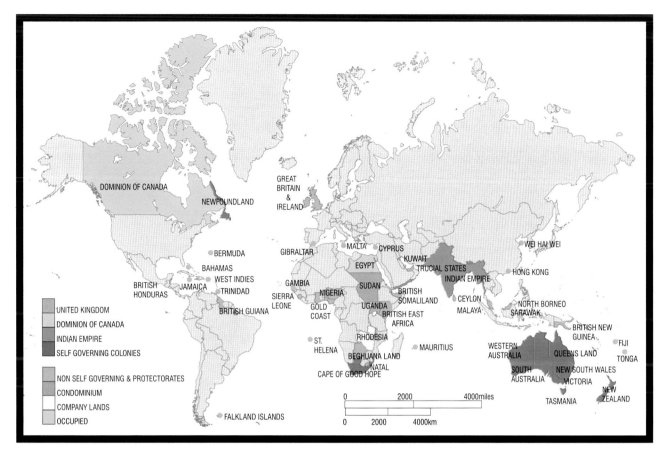

Map 2.8   The British Empire

Viceroy was given a significant degree of discretion, but was still subject to the supervision of the India Office.

Within each of the colonies it was rare for the administrative pattern to be completely uniform in character. Thus apart from the smaller colonies, there were areas subject to different degrees of central government control. In part this reflected the philosophy of 'indirect rule' which was applied to large parts of India, the tropical colonies and the indigenous reservations in the colonies of European settlement. Pre-existing societies were incorporated into the Empire sometimes with a considerable degree of self-government. Indeed in a number of protection treaties the indigenous ruler undertook to conduct external relations only with the British government and accept the appointment to his court of a British 'Adviser' or 'Resident', who would seek to modernise the local administration. Thus directly ruled colonial status regions were included within the same administrative colony as those with protectorate status. As in the United States, the relative strengths of the two sectors varied, not only in time but from continent to continent and from one colony to another.

2.9   THE INDIAN EMPIRE

The largest and most important British overseas possession was the Indian Empire, aptly characterised as 'The Jewel in the Crown'. Indeed Lord Curzon went so far as to describe it as 'the noblest fabric yet reared by the genius of a conquering nation' (Wright, 1987: 347). The Indian Empire, with a population exceeding 294 million in 1900, was second only to China in terms of population. Its territory extended from Aden in the Arabian Peninsula in the West to Burma in the East. Its political and economic influence extended to East Africa and the Persian Gulf, where British influence was exercised through the Indian administration and the rupee circulated as the common currency. The Indian Army, numbering some 140 000 men in 1900, was a large and efficient force, not subject to the

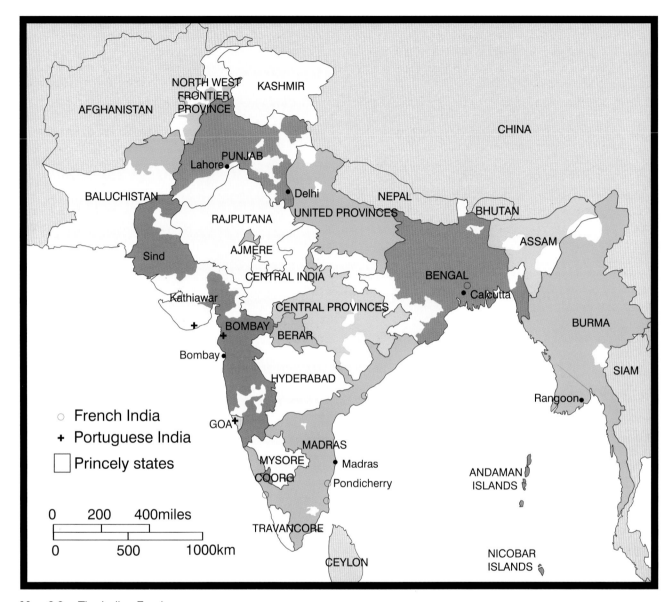

Map 2.9   The Indian Empire

parliamentary restrictions placed upon the metropolitan army. However, after the mutiny and rebellion of 1857, a significant part of the British Army was permanently stationed in India, both for external defence and for the maintenance of internal order. In 1900 this amounted to some 74 000 men out of a total of 232 000. In addition, the princely states maintained approximately 350 000 troops.

Broadly the Indian Empire could be politically divided into two sections: British India and Princely India. The former was administered directly by British officials and covered the most populous two-thirds of the country, which

had been acquired first by the Honourable East India Company and after 1858 by the Government of India. The three extensive historic presidencies, based on Calcutta (the capital), Bombay and Madras, were subdivided into provinces and districts under the aptly named collectors. The demarcation of provinces involved a great deal of political calculation to balance local interests. Administrative reform was ongoing. The amalgamation of the North-western Provinces with Oudh to form the United Provinces was a contemporary case of streamlining the inherited administrative structures, although the resultant unit contained some 47.7 million inhabitants in 1901. The redefinition of the unwieldy Bengal Province with its population of some 74.7 million in 1901 was not to be achieved so easily in the coming decade, leading to political conflict both in India and in London. The partition of the province was the subject of popular protest, which resulted in a further redefinition of boundaries in 1911.

In addition to piecemeal conquest, annexation and the imposition of direct administration, the East India Company and the successor Government of India entered into treaty relations with the indigenous rulers of the sub-continent. In this respect in northern and central India they effectively replaced the Moghul Emperors who had exercised similar systems of suzerainty over the margins of their empire. The more than 500 princes retained virtual independence within their own dominions, but recognised British suzerainty and undertook not to enter into treaty relations with other powers (Ashton, 1982). The degree of British influence over the princes varied from the strict adherence to treaty relations between sovereign states to the concept that the princes represented no more than an Indian variant of the English hereditary nobility and with no more influence over local politics (Gilmour, 1994).

The largest princely state, Hyderabad, covered some 214 000 square kilometres and housed 11.1 million people in 1901. The smallest, Veja-no-ness in Kathiawar, covered only 2 square kilometres and enumerated a population of under 200 people. Hyderabad was in a class of its own, as the next largest state, Mysore, only counted 5.5 million inhabitants. Furthermore the Nizam of Hyderabad had territorial claims against British India in the dispute over the province of Berar (2.8 million inhabitants), which he wished to have restored to his rule. The complexity of the state patterns was remarkable, particularly in the Kathiawar peninsula, reflecting the element of freezing the previously shifting feudal patterns of control by the imposition of British suzerainty. The disparity between the religion of the princes and that of their subjects was not significant under imperial rule, although tensions were sometimes important in local politics.

2.10   THE KATHIAWAR PENINSULA

The Kathiawar peninsula, which formed part of the Bombay presidency, on the west coast presented the greatest complexity of the princely state territories in India. The imposition of British control in the late eighteenth and early nineteenth century had been accompanied by the independent recognition of feudal

rulers previously owing allegiance to other more senior rulers as well as those nominally directly subject to the Moghul Empire. All received the same recognition. Inevitably there was a marked contrast in status between the more powerful and the weakest, distinctions which were maintained by a plethora of honours bestowed by the Viceroy, such as the number of guns fired in a princely salute. The rulers enjoyed a high degree of freedom to pursue their own, often eccentric, policies covering everything from running the railway and postal services to the imposition of taxation and the administration of justice.

One of the major features of the map was the extreme degree of fragmentation. Portions of British India, in this case the district of Ahmadabad, were interspersed with the princely states, which were themselves intricately interlocked with one another, and were usually composed of more than one portion. The complex pattern of divided inheritances and territorial conquests are evident in areas of extreme fragmentation. Even at the scale of the map presented, the smallest states could not be shown. But the map is dominated by a few larger states, although none contained a population in excess of one million at the time of the 1901 census.

One of the largest states in Kathiawar, Junagarh, was ruled by the Nawab who was a Muslim, although the population was predominantly Hindu. There were other smaller states, including Manavadar, which were in the same position. This situation was to assume international significance at the time of the partition of India in 1947, when the two rulers declared a desire for the inclusion of their states in Pakistan. However, the two states were promptly occupied by Indian forces, in support of the claims by the majority of the population for inclusion in the Dominion of India. If the rulers of Junagarh and Manavadar had succeeded in carrying out their intentions of acceding to Pakistan or gaining complete independence, the complexity of international boundaries may be gauged from an examination of the green shadings of the two states on the map.

2.11   CANADA

The Canadian Confederation had been established in 1867 as the first of the British self-governing dominions. It represented the political grouping of the British North American colonies to form a bastion against the feared encroachment by the United States. After the formal recognition of the independence of the

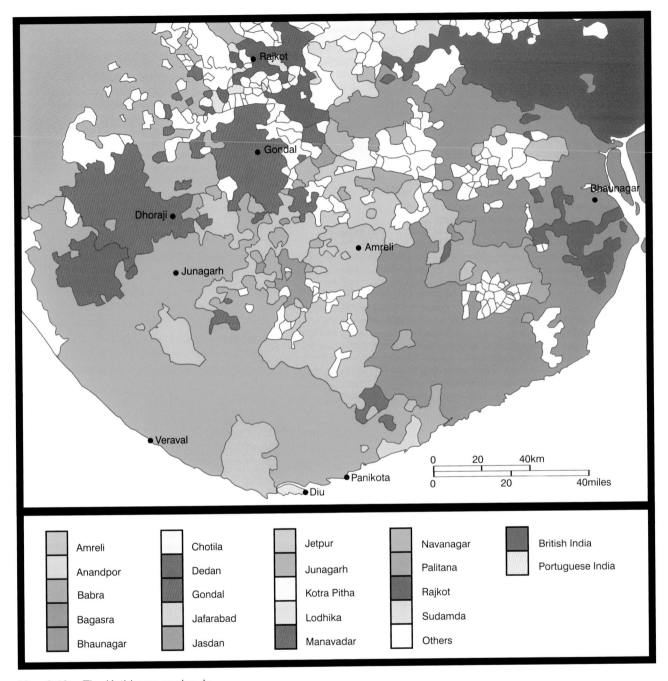

Map 2.10 The Kathiawar peninsula

thirteen American colonies in 1783, the remnants of British North America consisted of a few disparate colonies linked along the St Lawrence valley. The most important was Canada itself, which had been captured from the French in 1759. The Empire Loyalists who had supported Great Britain in the course of the American War of Independence came to settle in Canada and the other colonies following their defeat. In the main, they settled in the Great Lakes region, leading to a major geographical separation between French-speaking settlers in Lower Canada (Quebec) and English speakers in Upper Canada (Ontario).

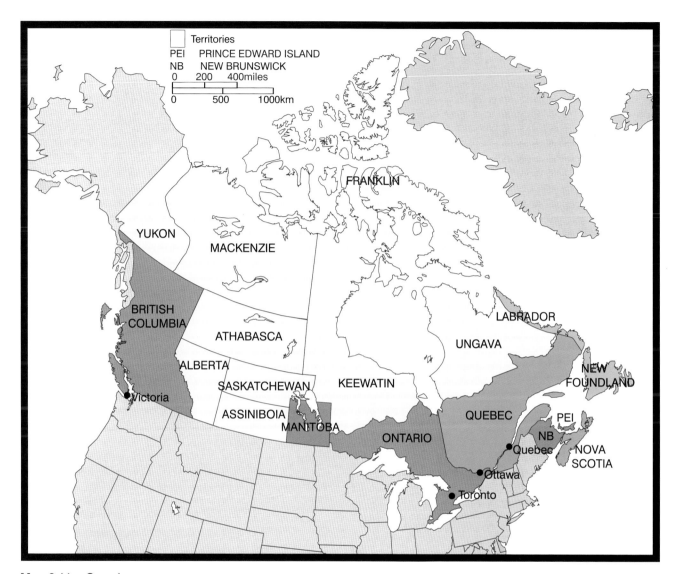

Map 2.11   Canada

Self-government was introduced as a means of attaching the allegiance of the inhabitants firmly to the British Crown. However, political relations between the French and English speakers were not easy. The American Civil War (1861–1865) and the threat of American expansionism forced the colonial politicians to contemplate a closer union, as direct British protection diminished with the removal of the imperial garrisons. Thus in 1867 the colony of Canada was divided into the provinces of Ontario and Quebec, which, together with New Brunswick and Nova Scotia, elected to form a loose confederation under the title of the Confederation of Canada. Significantly the constitution provided for a mechanism for secession should

a province decide that its interests would be better served by separation. Prince Edward Island joined six years later, but Newfoundland, including the Labrador coastline, decided to maintain its separate status until 1949.

The extensive territories in northern and western North America, which had been administered by the Hudson's Bay Company until 1870, were acquired by the Canadian federal government and reconstituted as the North West Territories. The province of Manitoba was established at the same time to cover the area assessed to be most immediately suitable for European colonisation. Within the North West Territories the interests of the indigenous Indians and Inuit population were in large measure recognised by the federal authorities. However, in 1882 a series of new territories were created on the Prairies in preparation for European colonisation. Other sub-divisions covered extensive areas with sparse populations, north of 60°N. Suitable lands were selected and Indian indigenous title was extinguished through a series of some 500 treaties between the individual Indian bands and the Canadian federal government (Dickason, 1992). In return the Indian bands received small reservations, which were excluded from the area open to European colonisation. In 1895 a separate Yukon Territory was established to gain a measure of control over the influx of prospectors associated with the gold rush to the Klondyke.

By 1846 British territory had been formally consolidated as a block extending to the Pacific Ocean, through the partition of the Oregon Territory with the United States. However, the colony of British Columbia was separated from the remainder of effectively occupied British territory by an extensive open and undeveloped region. In order to consolidate the accession of British Columbia to the Confederation in 1870, the federal government undertook to build a railway to link the two sides of the continent, independent of American territory. The completion of the Canadian Pacific Railway in 1886 guaranteed the new province's continued inclusion in the confederation.

In 1901 the Dominion covered some 9.6 million square kilometres with a population of only 5.4 million, mostly concentrated in the east close to the American border. It most closely resembled Siberia in terms of area and population development. The provinces of Ontario (population 2.2 million) and Quebec (1.6 million) dominated the Confederation. In contrast British Columbia enumerated a mere 179 000 inhabitants, smaller than independent Newfoundland (202 000). Manitoba enumerated 255 000 inhabitants, but the remainder of the three Prairie territories were home to only 164 000 people.

2.12 AUSTRALIA

Australia represented the development in relative isolation of a set of exclusively British colonies of settlement. The first, New South Wales, had been settled in 1788 as a convict station in substitution for the lost American colonies. A further convict colony was established on the island of Tasmania in 1803 and free colonies were founded in Western Australia in 1829 and South Australia in 1836. Later New South Wales was divided to establish separate colonies in Victoria 1850

and Queensland in 1859. For administrative convenience, the remaining portion of the continent, the Northern Territory, was placed under the administration of the South Australian government. Queensland embarked upon its own programme of colonial expansion with the annexation of south-eastern New Guinea in 1886, named British New Guinea, as a means of preventing German interests from taking the whole of the eastern half of the island.

All six colonies had achieved internal self-government and sought constitutional advance on the Canadian model. The distances between the various colonial capitals were substantial, necessitating voyages of several days, in the era before the transcontinental railway and air transport. Until the 1890s each colony had preserved its separateness, even to the extent of building railway systems with different gauges. However, the intervention of Germany in the western Pacific and the general colonial alienation from British control resulted in the search for a distinctive Australian identity (Robinson, 1975). The vast area of the continent, nearly 7.7 million square kilometres, contrasted with its comparative emptiness, only 3.8 million inhabitants. Such an image of vacancy was assumed to result inevitably in an Asian, possibly Chinese, interest in colonisation to relieve overcrowding at home. In the xenophobic atmosphere of the period, some form of political unification therefore appeared desirable. During the negotiations between the colonies, the government and electorate of Western Australia, the most remote and therefore most detached, expressed the greatest doubts about the unification of the continent. However, the colony exemplified Australia's problems most acutely with some 183 000 inhabitants spread across an area of nearly 2.5 million square kilometres. Equally remote was the Northern Territory, administered by South Australia, which covered some 1.36 million square kilometres but was inhabited by approximately 4000 people, excluding an un-enumerated number of Aborigines.

The establishment of a confederal Commonwealth of Australia was delayed until January 1901. Significantly, as in Canada, the individual states' right of secession was incorporated into the constitution. After unification the federal government later assumed responsibility for the federal capital territory at Canberra, with its outport at Jarvis Bay, the Northern Territory acquired from South Australia and Queensland's section of New Guinea, which was subsequently renamed Papua in September 1906.

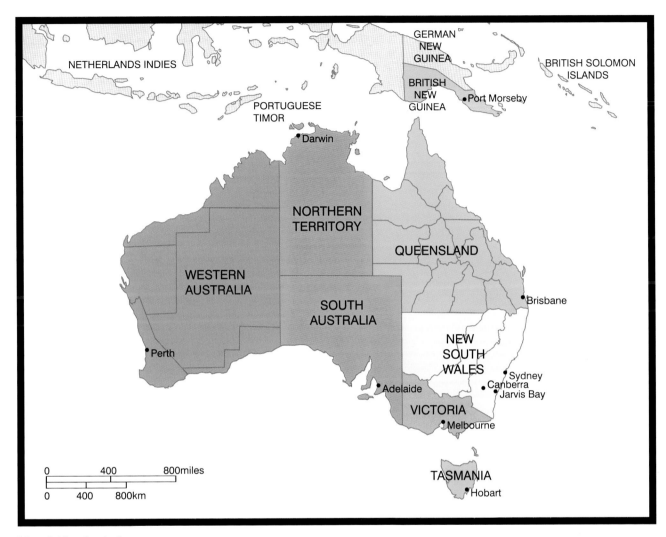

Map 2.12   Australia

2.13 AFRICA

The political map of Africa had been dramatically transformed by the events of the last fifteen years of the nineteenth century (Christopher, 1984). The explorations carried out in the nineteenth century had virtually filled in the missing blank spaces on the maps consulted in the capitals of Europe. The major advances in technology and tropical medical science necessary to effect and sustain the conquest of the continent had been developed. The technological superiority emanating from the discoveries associated with the Industrial Revolution, notably in military firepower, was such that small groups of well trained and supplied European led soldiers could defeat indigenous armies of vastly greater size. The one-sided nature of colonial warfare is illustrated by the outcome of the last major battle of the British campaign in the Sudan at Omdurman in 1898. The Anglo-Egyptian army only lost some 40 men to the Sudanese loss of 11 000 men (Headrick, 1981). The era was evoked in Joseph Conrad's (1993: 8) words in the *Heart of Darkness*:

The conquest of the earth, which mostly means the taking of it away from those who have a different complexion or slightly flatter noses than ourselves, is not a pretty thing when you look into it too much.

At the Berlin conference in 1884–1885 the ground rules had been agreed upon by the European powers engaged in the division of the continent (Brownlie, 1978). It is a

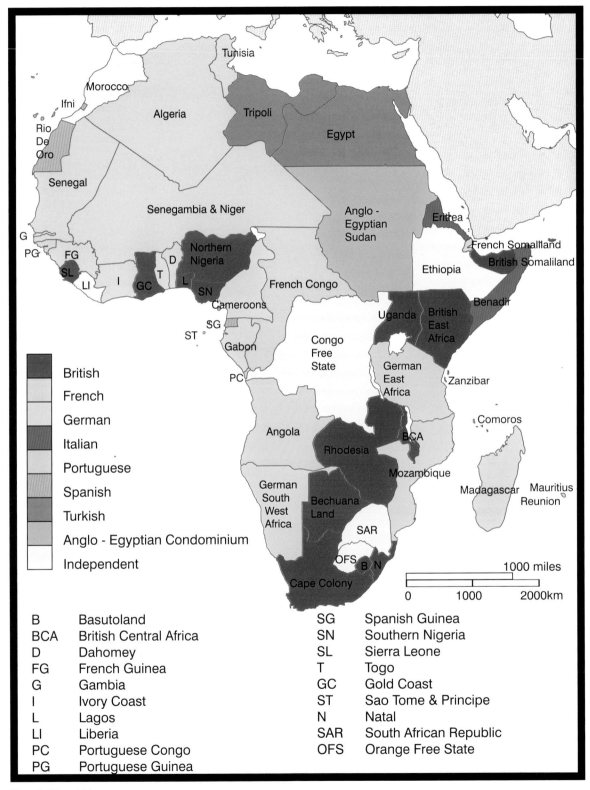

Tunisia

Morocco

Ifni

Algeria

Rio De Oro

Senegal

Senegambia & Niger

Tripoli

Egypt

Anglo - Egyptian Sudan

Eritrea

French Somaliland

British Somaliland

Ethiopia

G

PG

FG

SL

LI

I

GC

T

D

L

SN

Northern Nigeria

Cameroons

French Congo

Uganda

British East Africa

Benadir

SG

ST

Gabon

Congo Free State

German East Africa

Zanzibar

PC

Angola

Rhodesia

BCA

Mozambique

Comoros

Madagascar

Mauritius Reunion

German South West Africa

Bechuana Land

SAR

OFS

B N

Cape Colony

British

French

German

Italian

Portuguese

Spanish

Turkish

Anglo - Egyptian Condominium

Independent

1000 miles

0   1000   2000km

B	Basutoland	SG	Spanish Guinea
BCA	British Central Africa	SN	Southern Nigeria
D	Dahomey	SL	Sierra Leone
FG	French Guinea	T	Togo
G	Gambia	GC	Gold Coast
I	Ivory Coast	ST	Sao Tome & Principe
L	Lagos	N	Natal
LI	Liberia	SAR	South African Republic
PC	Portuguese Congo	OFS	Orange Free State
PG	Portuguese Guinea		

Map 2.13   Africa

measure of the effectiveness of the arrangements and the relatively low priority attached to the continent that the entire enterprise was effected without direct conflict between the colonial powers. The European partition of the continent was rapid and although spheres of influence had been determined by mutual agreement, the definition of fixed boundaries and the establishment of effective administrations were still in their infancies over large parts of the continent in 1900. It is notable that portions of territory were traded between the powers. Thus in 1890, as part of a general settlement, Germany surrendered its interests in Zanzibar and British East Africa in return for the British cession of Heligoland in Europe and sale of British interests in the Cameroons. In this way territories were consolidated, and the many isolated outliers removed. In the course of the nineteenth century the Netherlands and Denmark had withdrawn completely from Africa, selling their possessions in the Gold Coast to the British.

Just six states on the continent retained a nominal independence by 1900. Only two, Morocco and Ethiopia, were historical empires with long pre-colonial histories and nominal acceptance as part of the international community of nations. This did not mean that they were immune to outside intervention. The exception to the general statement in a previous paragraph concerning military power had been the battle of Adowa in 1896, when the Ethiopians, with French armaments, had been able to defeat the Italians. Italy thus had to defer its conquest of Ethiopia for 40 years. Morocco retained a shaky independence as a result of the rivalry of the great powers over the division of the spoils. Agreement on the division was only to come after two international crises in 1905 and 1911 between France and Germany over the status of the country.

The four other independent states owed their origins to colonial intervention on the continent. The freed slaves of Liberia had proclaimed their independence in 1847 and retained it through the benign support of the United States of America, which had initially established the settlement. The Orange Free State and South African Republic (Transvaal) had gained independence in the 1850s after the occupation of the region by Afrikaner settlers who rejected the policies of the British colonial government in the Cape of Good Hope. The South African Republic proved to be the site of the largest gold deposits in the world, giving the state a remarkable degree of economic independence from Great Britain. In 1900 both states were at war with the British Empire in a contest for supremacy in the sub-continent. Their period of independence was about to end as the British government poured in men and materiel from around the Empire. Finally the Congo Free State had been established at the Berlin conference by King Leopold II of the Belgians as an international commercial enterprise to open the Congo River basin to trade and exploitation and therefore it effectively became his personal fiefdom. In a separate enterprise, the Congo Free State leased the Lado Enclave in the south of the Anglo-Egyptian Sudan as an extension of its operations (Collins, 1971).

In terms of territory, the French and the British gained the largest shares of the continent, although the French sector included much of the Sahara Desert. The Portuguese, the first of the European powers to colonise Africa, retained significant holdings, but lost the opportunity to link Angola and Mozambique as they had planned. Germany and Italy obtained a few territories which had not been claimed by others by the 1880s. Although the Germans had been able to expand into the interior, the Italians were unable to occupy their designated sector beyond the coastal belts of Eritrea and Benadir. Spain retained small possessions on the northern coast of Morocco and in the Gulf of Guinea and latterly obtained a section of the Saharan coastline opposite the Canary Islands and the port of Ifni on the west coast of Morocco. Finally the Ottoman Empire retained direct control over Tripoli and nominal suzerainty over Egypt and with it the Anglo-Egyptian Sudan.

Extensive territories were acquired rapidly by the European powers through either agreement or rapid conquest. Pre-existing states such as the Sultanate of Sokoto were forcefully incorporated into the expanding empires, often to become protectorates within the new dispensation. This was particularly true of the governors of the British Empire, who pragmatically recognised the diversity of their new territories, rather than adopting any centralising and assimilationist philosophy. Some of the resultant arrangements were complex. The fate of Zanzibar is instructive in this respect (Bennett, 1978). Zanzibar prior to the 1890s exercised suzerainty over the East African coast between Mozambique and the Gulf of Aden, with troops stationed in the main ports. Zanzibari trading bases had been established elsewhere along the coast and in the interior as far as the Great Lakes. However, in the course of the scramble for Africa, the Sultan was unable to prevent the division of his mainland territories between Germany, Great Britain and Italy. In 1890 he accepted British protection over his remaining island possessions. The Germans and Italians acquired his territorial interests on the mainland, while the British government leased the equivalent strip of territory between Mombasa and Lamu and Kismayo and it was subsequently administered as a protectorate within the larger colony of British East Africa.

As a result of the rapidity of conquest a number of colonies became cumbersome for administrative purposes, while others which had remained viable as small coastal enclaves ceased to have a meaningful role in the changed circumstances of the post-scramble era. Thus the extensive French West African territories, annexed to the French Sudan, were divided to allow the coastal colonies to extend inland, and the rump renamed Senegambia and Niger as a more geographical description of the region included. At the same time the entire area of French West Africa was included in a governor-generalship responsible for general policies of administration. Similarly the French colonies of the French Congo and Gabon were linked under the governor-generalship of French Equatorial Africa.

Internal reorganisation was not confined to the French dominions. Smaller British colonies in South Africa, such as British Bechuanaland and Zululand, were merged with the self-governing colonies of the Cape of Good Hope and Natal respectively in the 1890s. The Niger Coast Protectorate and the lands previously administered by the Royal Niger Company were merged in 1900 and redivided as the separate colonies of Northern and Southern Nigeria.

2.14   COLONIAL STATES IN MOZAMBIQUE

Many colonial ventures had been viewed by the metropolitan government as essentially commercial ventures and so were administered by commercial companies. The chartered companies formed in several European countries to exploit the resources of the West Indies, West Africa, India and the East Indies had often been superseded by direct administrators appointed by the metropolitan governments (Griffiths, 1974). Thus in North America in 1607 the English Virginia Company initiated the settlement of that state until financial constraints forced the government to assume responsibility. Similarly, and more successfully, Ruperts Land and the northern territories in Canada were administered for 200 years by the Hudson's Bay Company, chartered in 1670, before they were transferred to the Dominion government in 1870. The rapid colonial expansion of the 1880s and 1890s was in many cases entrusted to chartered commercial companies as a means of engaging in 'imperialism on the cheap'. Many were not successful, indeed went bankrupt, and had to be taken over by the metropolitan governments. Others were able to call upon investment funds with the promise of returns to follow at some distant date, with the result that the Congo Free State and large parts of British, French, German and Italian Africa were entrusted to commercial

enterprises. Thus the British South Africa Company under the aegis of Cecil Rhodes was able to obtain an interest in and ultimately administrative control of a substantial tract of land in southern Africa and launch a successful colonial administration.

The British South Africa Company's success as a colonisation agency was emulated by the Portuguese in neighbouring Mozambique in the 1890s in an attempt to obtain foreign finance to strengthen the country's tenuous hold on the region. Already in 1898 the British and German governments had reached an informal agreement on the partition of Portuguese Africa between them in the event of a breakdown in administration (Taylor, 1954). A new understanding was to be reached in 1913. Chartered companies were incorporated to administer and exploit extensive tracts of the colony, leaving only sections under the direct control of the Portuguese government (Vail, 1976). In practice Mozambique was fragmented into six separate states. Three companies were chartered to administer and develop the north and central parts of the country. The largest and most important was the Mozambique Company, based on Beira, which controlled a belt of territory linked up to the Rhodesian interior. The Nyassa Company was given oversight of the northern districts along the border with German East Africa and extending to Lake Nyassa. Finally the relatively short-lived Zambesia Company was assigned the Zambezi valley to exploit. The Portuguese government retained control over Mozambique province in the north and Inhambane and Lourenco Marques in the south.

As part of the general reorganisation of the province, the seat of the governor-general was shifted southwards from the traditional centre on Mozambique Island to the new economic hub at Lourenco Marques, which was in the process of development as the premier port for the South African Republic, independent of British control.

2.15   COLONIES IN THE CARIBBEAN

The Caribbean had been one of the first overseas arenas of European colonial enterprise. Christopher Columbus had discovered not the American mainland in 1492, but the West Indies. It was the island of Hispaniola which became the first major Spanish colony, and served as a base for the expeditions of conquest to Mexico and Peru. Furthermore it was in Cuba and Puerto Rico that Spanish rule in the Americas survived after the independence of the mainland colonies in the first half of the nineteenth century. Indeed Spain briefly reoccupied the Dominican Republic during

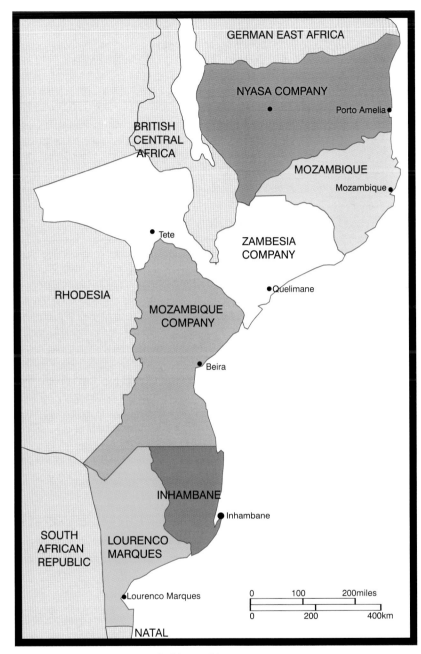

Map 2.14   Colonial states in Mozambique

the American Civil War (1861–1865). However, the Spanish–American War of 1898 brought the country's 400 year presence in the West Indies to a close.

Spain was joined by other European powers in the quest for riches in the West Indies. Until the early seventeenth century no permanent rivals had survived in the region, but thereafter most of the European powers acquired islands for the purposes of producing tropical crops, notably sugar and its derivatives. Often the enterprises were undertaken by private companies chartered by the metropolitan governments. West Indian enterprises proliferated. Eventually, Great Britain, France, the Netherlands, Denmark, Sweden and even Courland (then nominally part of Poland) acquired bases in the region. In some cases this

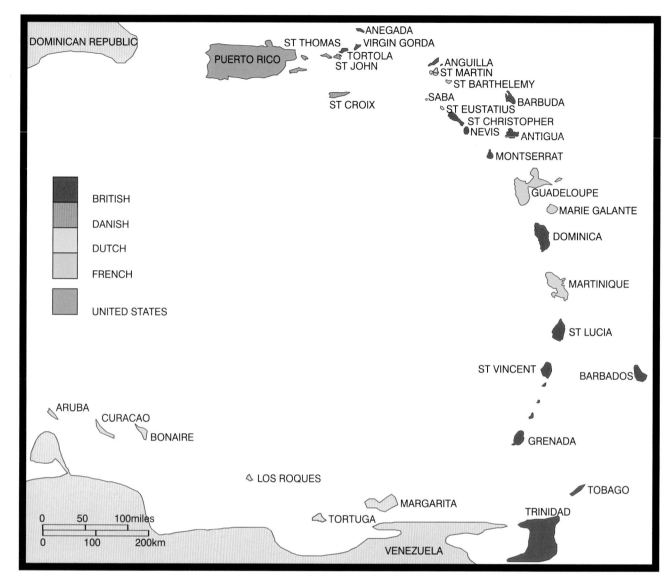

Map 2.15   Colonies in the Caribbean

involved the conquest of Spanish held islands, such as the British conquest of Jamaica in 1655, or the western half of Hispaniola by the French in 1665. However, the smaller, Lesser Antilles had not attracted Spanish attention and following the demographic disaster attendant upon the arrival of European diseases, the unoccupied or lightly occupied islands presented the opportunities for the establishment of plantations, without international complications.

The European wars of the seventeenth and eighteenth centuries resulted in recurring conquests and often destruction of the islands' infrastructures. Barbados, the most

isolated of the islands, was one of the few to remain in one power's hands throughout the colonial period. It is notable that despite the rivalries, few countries were eliminated from the West Indies as the importance to the tropical trade was recognised by all. At the peace gatherings which ended the various conflicts up to 1815, the majority of islands were returned to their previous owners and the conquerors, usually the British, evacuated them. However, Courland's brief enterprise on Tobago lasted only 13 years (1642–1655), paralleling its slave station on the West African coast. Sweden retained control of St Barthelemy for nearly a century (1785–1877) before ceding the island to France.

In 1900 therefore, in addition to the two independent republics of the Dominican Republic and Haiti, the West Indian islands were held by five colonial powers, namely Great Britain, France, the Netherlands, Denmark and the United States. The largest group were held by Great Britain, ranging in size from Jamaica to Anguilla. The problems of administering the islands had resulted in a complex system without any central authority. Thus Barbados retained a measure of self-government dating from the granting of the right to a local General Assembly in 1638, in line with the constitutional development of the other North American colonies on the mainland. The other islands were directly administered Crown Colonies.

In common with many other areas of British imperial endeavour, attempts were made in the second half of the nineteenth century to group colonies together for the sake of economy. The government of the main island of Jamaica thus was responsible for the dependencies in the Cayman Islands and the Turks and Caicos Islands. In addition, the Leeward Islands, comprising the presidencies of St Christopher and Nevis (a merger of two previously separate entities), the Virgin Islands, Montserrat, Antigua (including Barbuda) and Dominica, had been grouped together for certain central functions such as postal services in 1890. Similarly the three Windward Islands, Grenada, St Lucia and St Vincent, were linked for some administrative purposes. Also included in the late nineteenth century administrative amalgamations was the merger of Tobago with Trinidad in 1896. However, inter-island cooperation was always difficult to achieve and tensions within these groupings led to greater decentralisation as the colonies achieved greater measures of self-government.

The French administered two colonies, Guadeloupe and Martinique. Guadeloupe included within its domain the island of St Barthelemy and the French northern half of the island of St Martin. The Netherlands administered a group of six islands as a unit under control from Curaçao, after which island the entire colony was named. The islands fell into two groups. The one adjacent to the coast of Venezuela consisted of the major islands of Curaçao, Aruba and Bonaire, while in the Leeward Islands the Netherlands retained the southern half of St Martin (St Maarten), St Eustatius and Saba. The Danish West Indies, based on St Croix, consisted of a small group of adjacent islands. The United States was the most recent colonial power to intervene in the West Indies with the acquisition of Puerto Rico in 1898. Although the United States also occupied Cuba it was committed to a programme aimed at establishing an independent republic as soon as possible, a mission accomplished in 1902.

The history of the West Indies in the colonial period had been dominated by the institution of slavery and the massive forced in-migration of captives from Africa (Segal, 1995). Thus in virtually all the islands the descendants of the slaves constituted the vast majority of the population. The seizure of independence by the former slaves of Haiti in 1804 was therefore significant for other islands where slavery was only abolished later in the century (it was not until 1888 that Spain finally emancipated its slaves in Cuba). However, cooperation between the various colonial peoples was limited and no pan-Indies movement assumed any significance.

2.16 RUSSIAN EMPIRE

The Russian Empire constituted the largest contiguous state in the world. With an area of 22.6 million square kilometres and a population of approximately 130 million people it was one of the major powers and was viewed as the key to the world political system by some contemporaries (Mackinder, 1904). However, communication between the European heartland and the Far Eastern regions was difficult and time consuming prior to the completion of the Trans-Siberian Railway. This basic weakness was exposed in the course of the Russo-Japanese War in 1905, contributing to the defeat which halted territorial expansion.

The Empire was a vast assemblage of territories acquired by successive rulers through conquest and occupation. The Principality of Muscovy had established its control over the other Russian principalities in the fourteenth and fifteenth centuries. Thereafter, in the period between the conquest of the Khanate of Kazan in 1552 and the foundation of the port of Okhotsk on the Pacific Ocean in 1648, Russian pioneers had encountered little organised resistance to their occupation of Siberia. Russian enterprise in North America ended when Alaska was sold to the United States in 1867. In Europe major expansion took place as a result of the incorporation of the Ukraine in 1654 and the three partitions of Poland between 1772 and 1795. In 1900 the Empire's European boundaries reflected the Congress of Vienna settlement of 1815, which placed the core of the former Polish kingdom under Russian control. In the south territorial acquisitions at the expense of the Ottoman Empire and the various Caucasian states had been completed by 1876. In Central Asia extensive conquests in the course of the nineteenth century had added a substantial central Asian colonial empire as well as more strategic annexations from China. Indeed the central Asian

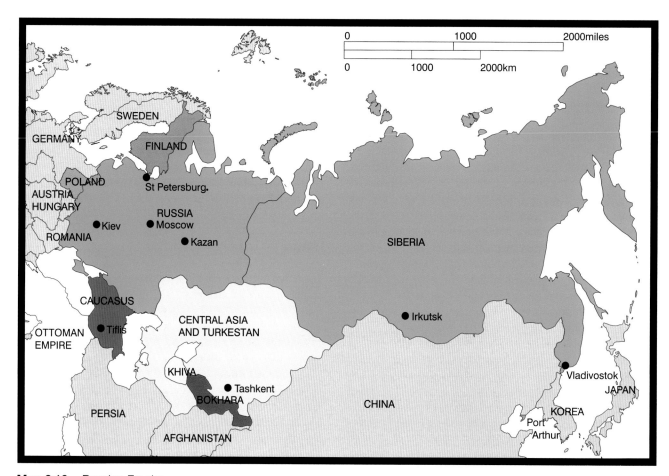

Map 2.16   Russian Empire

boundaries had only been defined in 1895 in the Pamir Mountains in the final apportionment of territory between British India, China and Afghanistan while Port Arthur in Manchuria had been acquired in 1898.

The core of the Russian Empire remained European Russia, which at the time of the first census in 1897 housed 94.2 million people (Parker, 1968). In contrast Siberia, extending over an area of approximately 10.9 million square kilometres, enumerated only 5.7 million inhabitants. It was viewed as a field for internal migration and development akin to North America, but progress in this regard had been limited before 1900. Russian Central Asia with an area of some 4.0 million square kilometres housed a population of 5.7 million people under direct rule and approximately 2.1 million in the protectorates of Khiva and Bokhara. In the Caucasian region some 11.7 million people were enumerated. Finally, the European dependencies of Finland and Poland enumerated some 2.8 million and 9.4 million people respectively.

Although Russia was ruled as a centralised autocratic empire under Nicholas II, Czar of All the Russias, there were a number of administrative anomalies. In Europe, Finland enjoyed a limited parliamentary autonomy with the Czar acknowledged as the Grand Duke of Finland. A small portion of historic Poland had been constituted an autonomous 'Congress Kingdom' in 1815 when the Czar Alexander I assumed the title of King of Poland, but the kingdom had lost that status following the revolt of 1830, a loss confirmed after the revolt of 1863. The Baltic Provinces, Estonia, Livonia and Courland, retained a limited measure of self-government under the German Baltic barons, inherited from the period of rule by the knights of the Teutonic Order. In central Asia the khanates of Bokhara and Khiva had signed protectorate agreements with Russia in 1868 and 1873 respectively and so survived the final Russian conquest and annexation of the region. It is significant that the complex pattern of nationalities within the empire found no other administrative expression as the policies of centralisation and Russification were applied to the population with varying degrees of resistance. Even the Little Russians (Ukrainians), White Russians, Red Russians and Black Russians were subjected to the imposition of the Great Russian language and culture. In the two latter cases success was achieved, but the former encountered resistance from the nascent nationalist movement.

The Russian Empire occupied a unique place in the European state system as the political centre of the Orthodox Church and the Pan-Slav movement. Following the fall of Constantinople and the overthrow of the Eastern Roman (Byzantine) Empire by the Ottomans in 1453, the rulers of Muscovy claimed to be the inheritors of the true, Orthodox, form of Christianity. The dynastic link was established through the marriage of Sophia Paleologue, niece of the last Byzantine Emperor, to Ivan III in 1472. Moscow was presented as the 'Third Rome' and the promotion of Orthodoxy and the protection of its adherents became a significant element in Russian policy, notably as the Ottoman Empire weakened. In 1547 Ivan IV was crowned Czar of All the Russias. Peter the Great in 1721 had assumed the imperial title in pursuit of these aims and in commemoration of the Treaty of Nystad which successfully concluded the Great Northern War and established the country as one of the great powers. The re-establishment of the Byzantine Empire was an element in Russian policy, which coincided with the desire to obtain Constantinople and free passage through the Straits to the Mediterranean Sea for purely Russian national objectives. The Russians were also the largest of the Slavic-speaking peoples and from the mid-nineteenth century the promotion of Pan-Slavism was a means of undermining the stability of states such as Austria-Hungary and the Ottoman Empire which contained substantial numbers of Slavs (Kohn, 1960).

2.17   OTTOMAN EMPIRE

The Ottoman Empire was the only major non-Christian power to maintain a substantial inter-continental territory into the twentieth century. The Sultan was vested with the title of the Calif, the supreme temporal authority in the Islamic world, and protector of the Holy Cities of Mecca and Medina in Arabia. This pre-eminence was such that Turkish national interests had to be considered in all states which incorporated large Moslem colonial populations, notably Britain, France and Russia. The Sultan's prestige and power also derived from the possession of a vast empire which had expanded steadily until the sixteenth century. Turkish forces had laid siege to Vienna in 1529 and 1683, threatening the very core of Christendom. Subsequently, the Empire entered a long period of decline and loss of territory. In the nineteenth century the fragility of the state had been the cause of considerable tension and at times conflict between the European powers, where the country had been dubbed 'the Sick Man of Europe' and the future disposal of its territories labelled 'the Eastern Question' (Anderson, 1966). Effectively the very existence of the Empire had been supported at times by the European powers, as the division of its territories in the case of collapse was considered to be too fraught with potential for conflict.

Nevertheless the Ottoman Empire remained one of the most extensive and populous in the world. In 1900 it extended over approximately 4.1 million square kilometres under direct control and a further 5.5 million square kilometres of nominal control. Some 40 million people lived under direct rule and another 25 million in the dependencies. The state was held together by a remarkably complex pattern of personal and treaty relationships between the Sultan and the European powers and subject peoples. Thus direct Ottoman control extended over only a portion of the nominal Empire. Directly administered provinces encompassed a belt of land from Albania on the Adriatic to Armenia on the Russian Caucasus boundary, and from Anatolia to the Yemen in southern Arabia. Tripoli in North Africa had also been under direct control since the 1830s.

The Ottoman authorities allowed for local peculiarities and extensive autonomy. The Kurdish clans thus exercised considerable freedom in return for recognition of the Sultan's authority and undertaking to defend the boundaries against the Shah of Persia. However, within the Arabian peninsula a number of rulers owed only nominal and occasional allegiance to the Sultan, notably the Sultans of Nejd and their dependencies including Jebel Shammar (Al-Rasheed, 1991). At times this allegiance was repudiated in the convoluted domestic politics of the peninsula, resulting in the usual cartographic device of leaving the heart of the peninsula politically blank on atlas maps. On the Persian Gulf coast the rulers of Kuwait, Qatar, and Bahrain had entered into agreements with the British government and so lay outside direct Ottoman control. However, their international position was the subject of differing interpretations, as traditional concepts of territoriality could not readily be incorporated into the Western state system (Wilkinson, 1983).

The status of Kuwait, which was to exercise the international community at various stages throughout the

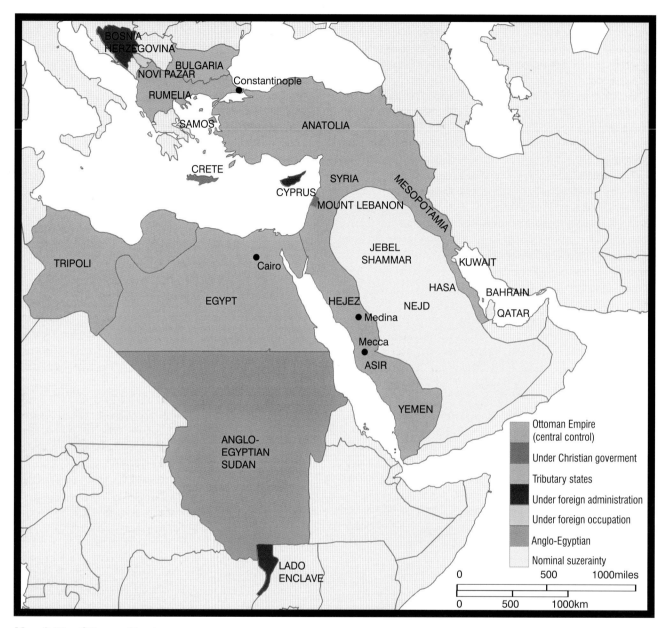

Map 2.17   Ottoman Empire

twentieth century, is particularly important (Mendelson and Hulton, 1994). The al-Sabah family had gained control over the settlement in the eighteenth century. In the 1870s while the Ottomans strengthened their control over sections of eastern Arabia they received assistance from the Sheikh of Kuwait, who was rewarded with property to the north. The Ottoman presence was enforced in three ways: by the Sheikh's appointment as sub-governor of Kuwait, which was regarded as honorific; by flying the Ottoman flag, and

briefly by the establishment of a customs house. However, for currency purposes the Indian rupee and Maria Theresa thaler were in circulation and not the Turkish pound. Into this complex situation the Sheikh signed an agreement in January 1899 whereby Great Britain offered him 'good offices' and a subsidy, which were exercised effectively two years later. The Sheikh's position was clarified under an Anglo-Turkish convention in 1913, which provided for complete administrative autonomy with a sixty kilometre zone around the town and to act as sub-governor in a further zone extended up to 200 kilometres. The Sultan's position was broadly that of a suzerain rather than sovereign. Whether this constituted de facto independence was disputed.

In Egypt the governor, Ismail, had been awarded the title of Khedive or Viceroy by the Sultan in 1867 and operated a virtually independent government. Egypt also pursued its own colonial policy of expansion in the Sudan, which by the early 1880s had resulted in the conquest of territories as far south as northern Uganda and the Somali coast. The drive towards modernisation and associated Europeanisation, together with excessive government spending, resulted in severe strains within the social fabric of the state. Revolts took place in both Egypt and its colonial empire in the Sudan. As a result, in 1881 the country was occupied by Great Britain and a five power international commission was constituted to administer the country's finances. The British government repeatedly gave undertakings to withdraw its forces when the internal security situation improved, but it did not do so. The conquest of the Sudan by Anglo-Egyptian forces in 1898 further complicated the constitutional position. The regained territory was administered by a joint condominium regime, in which the Governor-General of the Sudan also held the position of Commander-in-Chief of the Egyptian army. The appointment to the position was made by the Khedive on British advice and was always an Englishman. The constitutional pragmatism involved worked while Egypt was completely subservient to British control, but opened up possibilities for conflict once the power relationship began to change.

External powers had detached other substantial portions from the Sultan's direct control, while leaving them only nominally under his suzerainty. Thus after the Congress of Berlin in 1878 Austria-Hungary had occupied and administered Bosnia-Herzegovina, and Great Britain did the same for the island of Cyprus. Austria-Hungary, in addition, occupied but did not administer the Sanjak of Novi Pazar, which physically separated Serbia from Montenegro.

The weakness of the empire was also demonstrated by the presence of autonomous Christian administered areas within the nominal fabric of the empire. In all cases this status had been imposed as a result of external intervention. The unfinished contest with Greece over the control of the Greek inhabited areas of the empire had resulted in the creation of two autonomous states, which were legally prevented from joining Greece. The island of Samos in the Aegean Sea was granted the status of a tributary principality in 1832 following the conclusion of the Greek War of Independence in 1830. Similarly the revolt in Crete in 1896–1897 resulted in the intervention of the great powers and the establishment of an autonomous government under Prince George of Greece as High Commissioner.

Particularly unusual was the status of Bulgaria, which remained a Christian principality under the nominal suzerainty of the Sultan and subject to international treaty following the Congress of Berlin in 1878. The separate Christian administered province of Eastern Rumelia (South Bulgaria) created by the same Congress had been incorporated into Bulgaria after a revolt in 1885.

In Asia, French military intervention had been able to secure a substantial degree of self-rule for the Maronite Catholic Christians of Lebanon under an internationally guaranteed Organic Regulation in 1861. The autonomous Sanjak of Mount Lebanon was created to provide security for the Christian population after the massacres of the previous year. The administration was headed by a Christian governor and its citizens enjoyed economic privileges. The special regime was further recognition of a long history (1590–1842) of autonomy from direct Ottoman control for the Lebanon. The city of Beirut, it should be noted, lay outside Mount Lebanon and was directly administered by the Ottoman authorities.

The Empire was also subject to a number of treaties awarding extra-territorial rights to the subjects of the European powers. Thus within the Empire small exclaves were effectively under the control of the European powers. This was demonstrated by the complex arrangements surrounding the management of the Christian religious sites in Jerusalem or the diplomatic quarters in Constantinople. The various powers even ran their own independent postal systems.

2.18 CHINA

The Chinese Empire was the oldest state on the world political map with a continuous pedigree extending back for several thousand years. The Emperor, known as the Son of Heaven and 'Lord of Ten Thousand Years', possessed a special place among the rulers of the world, as the ruler of the last 'world empire' which had successfully resisted integration into the Western dominated world economy until the nineteenth century (Aisin-Gioro, 1987). This insularity was significant as the successive governments of the most populous state in the world belatedly adjusted to

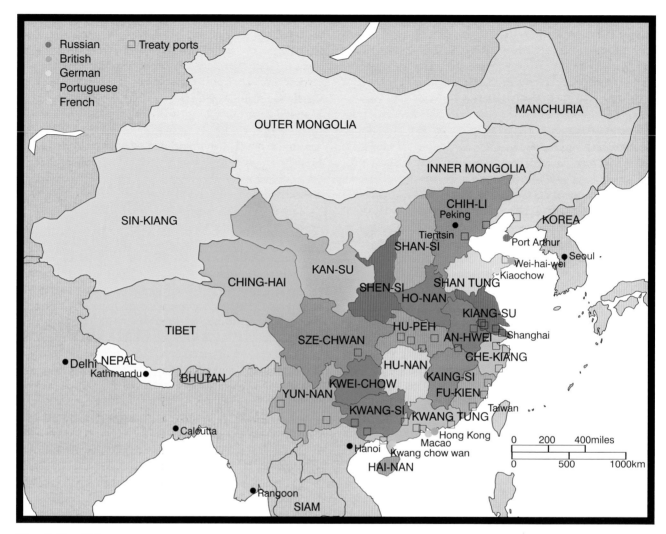

Map 2.18   China

the incursions of other countries in the nineteenth and twentieth centuries. China, which produced approximately one third of world manufacturing output in 1800, compared with only 6 percent a century later, was effectively de-industrialised (Bairoch, 1982). With the loss of economic power went political power.

The Chinese Empire had been substantially reduced in extent in the course of the nineteenth century as outlying tributary states were detached from its sphere of influence. Thus the British detached Burma in 1886, France detached Annam in 1884–1885 and Japan detached Formosa and forced the Chinese withdrawal from Korea in 1895. On the northern frontiers a steady Russian encroachment had significantly changed the map of northern Asia in the course of the nineteenth century. In 1900 Russia occupied, but did not annex, Manchuria, the homeland of the ruling Manchu, Ch'ing dynasty.

Thus by 1900 the Chinese Empire had been reduced to an area of approximately 11.0 million square kilometres with a population estimated at 400 million, still the most populous state or empire in the world. The majority of the population (383 million) lived in China proper, which covered only 3.5 million square kilometres. The 17 historic provinces varied substantially in size, with Szechuan housing some 67.7 million inhabitants. The dependencies, extending over 7.5 million square kilometres, were inhabited by only 6.7 million people. Mongolia was the most significant of these, covering 3.3 million square kilometres and housing approximately 2 million inhabitants.

The Chinese government remained in administrative control of the provinces of China proper, together with the border lands of Inner Tibet (Ching-hai), Inner Mongolia and Chinese Turkestan (Sinkiang). The tributary states of Outer Mongolia, Tibet and Nepal remained nominally under the suzerainty of the Emperor, but enjoying a substantial, though fluctuating, degree of de facto independence over internal affairs. In the main this independence was perceived as the power to exclude foreign influences and so remain isolated, rather than engage in relations with neighbouring or other powers. Chinese control was thus nominal and exercised through representatives and advisers rather than governors possessing coercive and administrative powers.

Chinese isolation from Western influences had been broken by the forcible intrusion of the Western powers. Initially Great Britain, at the conclusion of the first 'Opium War' of 1840–1842 by the Treaty of Nanking, had forced the Chinese government to open five 'treaty' ports on the southern coast for trading purposes to foreigners. At the end of the second Opium War in 1860 a further ten ports were opened in northern China and in the Yangtze valley in central China. Subsequent agreements extended the number of ports to 34 by 1900, creating a country-wide network of commercial centres under European control. The concessions provided for extra-territorial legal regimes and in some cases the establishment of de facto colonial territorial enclaves adjacent to the major Chinese ports. The concessions thus provided for the free trade regimes which the European powers, and particularly Great Britain, sought to establish universally in the nineteenth century.

Shanghai at the mouth of the Yangtze River became one of the major bases of European, and subsequently American and Japanese, activity. The International Concession operated as a virtually independent state, subject to separate laws and guarded by foreign soldiers (Wakeman, 1995). The concessionary regime provided basic economic security for foreign firms operating in China and Shanghai became the financial capital of the country.

At the same time the colonial powers began the process of establishing formal colonies in China. The Portuguese had obtained the right to use the port of Macao on the western side of the Pearl River estuary in 1555. In 1887 the Chinese recognised the Portuguese right to perpetual occupation, limited only by the proviso that the settlement could not be transferred to a third party without Chinese approval.

In 1841 Great Britain acquired possession of the island of Hong Kong on the eastern side of the Pearl River estuary as a base for the supply of the treaty port concession at Canton. A separate Crown colony was created for administrative purposes. In 1860 the settlement of Kowloon on the adjacent mainland was ceded to secure the anchorage. In 1898 the process of territorial acquisition was carried further. Great Britain acquired a 99-year lease on the New Territories adjacent to Hong Kong as a security zone and agricultural extension for the Colony.

In 1898 Great Britain also acquired a lease on Wei-hai-wei as a naval station on the Shantung Peninsula in northern China, complete with an extensive neutral territory. Russia displaced the Japanese from Port Arthur in southern Manchuria as the second and ice-free terminus for the Trans-Siberian Railway. Germany gained Kiaochow also on the Shantung Peninsula and France leased Kwangchow in southern China.

The Chinese reaction to European encroachment wavered between reformist policies seeking to incorporate useful changes into Chinese society and a rejection of outside influences. The outcome was the Boxer rebellion of 1900, which sought to remove the intruders. An international expeditionary force was despatched to support the embattled legations in Peking and the concessions elsewhere. The suppression of the Chinese revolt was accompanied by much speculation in Europe. Kaiser Wilhelm II, in addressing the German contingent bound for China in July 1900, referred to the threat from the 'Yellow Peril', a theme that was taken up by others and contributed to geopolitical thought in the ensuing decade (Balfour, 1964). Significantly the foreign suppression of the Boxer rebellion did not result in a further annexation of Chinese territory, but a general agreement among the participating powers to promote international trade and preserve the integrity of the Chinese state in the absence of any agreement on what should be done in the case of its collapse.

2.19   THE TIENTSIN CONCESSIONS

The port of Tientsin on the Hai-ho River near the imperial capital, Peking, illustrates the extent to which the treaty port system created a colonial enclave within the Chinese Empire. The original treaty port areas, established in 1860, covered only 26 hectares downstream of the Chinese city of Tientsin, also on the western bank of the river. The British, American, German and French governments had obtained concessions covering some 207 hectares by 1899. The construction of the Manchurian Railway spur to Peking passed the settlement on the eastern bank. As a result of the suppression of the Boxer rebellion in 1900, the concessions

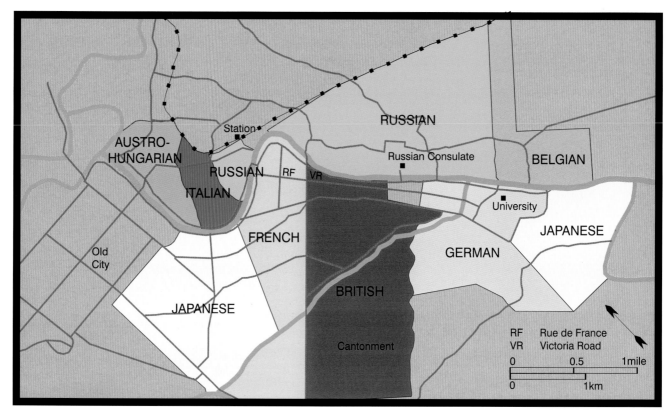

Map 2.19   The Tientsin concessions

were substantially expanded and a number of additional countries accommodated. Thus some 1770 hectares were set aside as concessions for eight countries, namely Great Britain, Germany, France, Japan, Belgium, Russia, Italy and Austria-Hungary. The largest, the Japanese (417 hectares), was strategically divided into two blocks, one adjacent to the walled Chinese city and the other downstream of all the other concessions.

The concessions were developed as colonial enclaves, complete with consulates, post offices, banks, schools and other services. Significantly these, and the accompanying housing, were built in the distinctive architectural styles then popular in the metropolitan powers. Such juxtapositions as Victoria Road becoming Rue de France at the concession boundary were noticeable. Linked strategic road systems were laid out and the civil and military personnel rapidly deployed. The British concession included a substantial cantonment, garrisoned by soldiers of the Imperial Indian Army, until 1922. The extensive Russian concession on the eastern side of the river was essentially related to the control and operation of the railway installations, including the station. Beyond the

concessions, facilities such as the arsenal and the rifle range were common to all the powers and the roads joining them to the concessions had the status of international roads through Chinese territory.

2.20   THE UNITED STATES OF AMERICA (STATES AND RESERVATIONS)

The United States of America came into existence as a result of the forceful assertion of independence from an imperial government situated in another continent. Furthermore, as a political movement for freedom it was inextricably bound up with the notions of local and personal freedom. The concept of an American nation initially was relatively vague and the inherited local particularities were defended once independence had been achieved by powerful state governments. The original thirteen ex-colonies thus formed a loose federation in 1787, with relatively few powers vested in the central government, beyond defence, foreign affairs and currency.

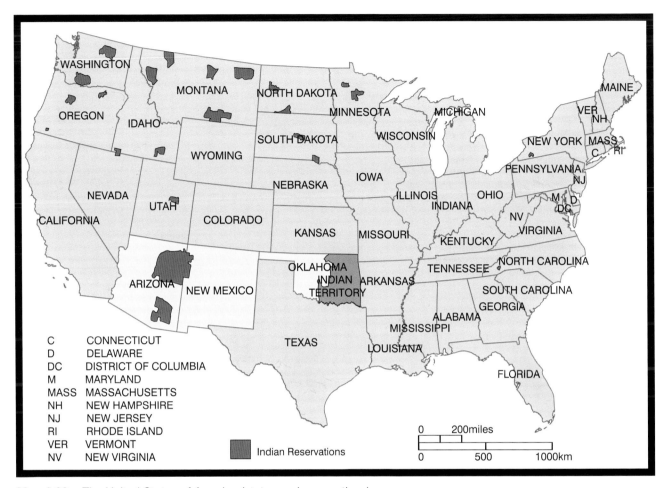

C   CONNECTICUT
D   DELAWARE
DC   DISTRICT OF COLUMBIA
M   MARYLAND
MASS   MASSACHUSETTS
NH   NEW HAMPSHIRE
NJ   NEW JERSEY
RI   RHODE ISLAND
VER   VERMONT
NV   NEW VIRGINIA

Map 2.20   The United States of America (states and reservations)

However, the permanency and power of the Union was tested in the Civil War (1861–1865) when the attempt by eleven southern states to secede was thwarted by military means. Provision was made for other states to be created out of the federally controlled lands and join the Union after demographic developments warranted a territory's admission. In the period from 1800 to 1900, as a result of massive immigration from Europe, the population of the United States increased from 5.3 to 76.0 million. The result was the effective occupation of the vast interior of the continent and the development of the foremost agricultural and industrial power in the world. It could be argued that it was this enterprise which created a distinctive American nation (Webb, 1951).

In 1900 the coterminous United States, covering some 7.7 million square kilometres, was divided into 45 states, three territories and the federal District of Columbia. The three remaining territories, Arizona, New Mexico and

Oklahoma, were constitutionally well advanced on the path to statehood. There was a considerable range in size, both in terms of population and in area among the states. Thus the most extensive, Texas, covered some 684 000 square kilometres, whereas Rhode Island measured only 2740 square kilometres. It is noteworthy that the latter was still larger than the independent state of Luxembourg. The majority lay within the restricted range from 106 000 to 215 000 square kilometres. This degree of uniformity reflected their origins as often arbitrarily drawn cartographic units on the map of the federal lands as settlement took place. The same range of size was evident in terms of population totals. The most populous state, New York, enumerated some 7.3 million inhabitants at the time of the 1900 census, while the least populous, Nevada, only recorded 42 000. The equality of representation between the states in the Senate worked to the benefit of Nevada and other small entities, whereas in the House of

Representatives New York state elected 37 seats to Nevada's one. Significantly the remaining territories all counted populations substantially in excess of 100 000. Indeed Oklahoma and the Indian Territory recorded a combined population of 790 000, and were in the final constitutional stages of achieving statehood, which was gained in November 1907.

Within the Union the indigenous, 'Indian', peoples were linked to the federal government through a series of treaties signed between sovereign peoples. The legal concept of 'sovereign, domestic, dependent nations that have entered into a trust relationship with the United States government' was a complex issue reflecting the long history of interaction between the immigrant Europeans and the indigenous peoples (Sutton, 1976). The recognition of the rights of prior occupation by indigenous peoples was one of the significant developments in the history of the English colonies in North America. Formal treaties between the Indian nations and the federal government became the accepted norm of regulating their relationships, notably the control of land. Thus, although sovereignty was claimed over extensive tracts of North America, whose extent was determined by the international treaties between the European powers, land rights were controlled by treaties between the colonial governments and the indigenous peoples. The balance of power between the two changed through time as the colonists became stronger, and the indigenous peoples became relatively weaker. However, the concept of a treaty survived independence and was significant in determining which parts of the United States were controlled by American federal, state and territorial authorities and which by indigenous authorities, namely the reservations. The reservations thus possessed certain attributes of sovereign states although these were severely prescribed, but they still covered some 308 000 square kilometres in 1900. This status did not prevent wholesale forced removals of Indians, notably the seven civilised tribes of Oklahoma, from the eastern states in the 1830s in an attempt to consolidate Indian territories to the west of the Mississippi River. The resulting map by 1900 indicated that most Indian reservations were situated in the western, more arid areas, which were less desirable for European colonisation. The largest single block was the Indian Territory, which was only to be incorporated into Oklahoma at the attainment of statehood in 1907.

Thus America's colonial empire was in some measure internal. However, the United States had acquired several overseas possessions in line with the European powers. Alaska, covering some 1.5 million square kilometres, had been purchased from Russia in 1867 for $7.2 million. The

Hawaiian Islands had been seized as a result of the overthrow of the islands' monarchy in 1893. The government of these two territories was initially conducted along colonial lines. Although in 1900 they enumerated 64 000 and 154 000 inhabitants respectively, they were not admitted to the Union as states until the late 1950s. Alaska entered the Union in June 1958 and Hawaii as the fiftieth state in August 1959.

After a long period of isolation, the American government by the 1890s was intent upon joining the imperial powers and expanding its influence across the Pacific Ocean and in the Caribbean Sea. In this regard it followed the geopolitical concepts of the significance of naval power of the day. Thus when the Samoan monarchy was overthrown in 1899, the islands were divided between the United States and Germany. A major group of possessions had been acquired under the Treaty of Paris in 1898 which concluded the Spanish–American War. Puerto Rico, the Philippines and Guam were acquired as a series of bases for projecting American naval power in Central America and eastern Asia. Significantly Cuba was occupied by the United States forces in the course of the war, but the rights of the indigenous independence movement were recognised, and provision made for the establishment of a sovereign republic after the peace. This process had not been completed in 1900 and the country remained under American military control.

By contrast, in the Philippines the indigenous independence movement was suppressed and the islands forcibly subjected to colonial rule. The excuse for doing so was couched in traditional imperialist terms. The 1900 Report of the Philippine Commission to the President stated that:

Should our power by any fatality be withdrawn, the commission believe that the government of the Philippines would lapse into anarchy, which would excuse, if it did not necessitate, the intervention of other powers and the eventual division of the Islands among them. Only through American occupation, therefore, is the idea of a free, self-governing, and united Philippine commonwealth at all conceivable... Thus the welfare of the Filipinos coincides with the dictates of national honor in forbidding our abandonment of the archipelago. We cannot from any point of view escape the responsibilities of government which our sovereignty entails.

(Bowman, 1928: 721).

2.21   COLOMBIA

The political confusion in Spain following the French invasion in 1808 offered the opportunity for local leaders throughout the overseas Spanish Empire to assume control

Map 2.21 Colombia

over their own affairs. This first rebellion took place in Colombia in 1810 in the port city of Cartagena and was followed by a revolt in the Viceregal capital, Bogota. The independence movement was not united and some provinces remained loyal to the Spanish monarch, resulting in the failure and defeat of the insurrection by 1816. However, in 1819 Simon Bolivar, advancing from Venezuela, defeated the Spanish and sought to create a single independent government for the entire area covered by the Viceroyalty of New Granada reconstituted as the 'United Republic of Colombia'. Bolivar continued to wage the war of independence in Ecuador, Peru and Upper Peru (Bolivia) in an attempt to unite as much of Spanish-speaking South America as possible. However, the attempt failed and the various provinces proclaimed their separate sovereign statehoods.

In 1830 only the area of the old Spanish Captaincy-General of New Granada remained under the nominal control of the government in Bogota. Conflict over the constitutional relationship between the central government and the provinces was to exercise much debate and exhaust national resources in conflict for the remainder of the century. National and local politics were pursued with a high degree of turbulence and violent party cleavage. Eight civil wars were fought in the course of the nineteenth century, culminating in the highly destructive War of a Thousand Days of 1899–1902. The country's problems were exacerbated by the extreme degree of federalism practised until the 1880s as the nine state governments possessed their own armies and often acted as separate sovereign states. The frequent constitutional changes were reflected in the successive names adopted for the country. The title 'Republic of New Granada' (1831–1857), was followed by the 'Granadine Confederation' (1857–1861), the 'United States of Colombia' (1861–1886) and finally the 'Republic of Colombia' in 1886.

The 1886 constitution provided for the president to nominate the governors of the departments rather than the state congresses. The change of name itself is significant, reflecting a change from American style federalism to French style centralism. The national congress also gained the power to create new departments by fragmenting the existing departments, in order to reduce their power vis-a-vis the central government. However, the powers were not used until after the War of a Thousand Days. Thus the historic province of Cauca (in excess of 650 000 square kilometres) extended over half the national territory including the entire Pacific coastline and much of the Amazonian territory and contained a population of approximately 621 000. In contrast, the department of Magdalena contained only 90 000 inhabitants and the department of Santander covered only 40 000 square kilometres. By 1991 the department of Cauca had been reduced to 29 308 square kilometres.

After 1900 the redefinition of departmental boundaries was a matter of conflict as those favoured by the central government gained at the expense of those that were not. The department of Antioquia's acquisition of its disputed land corridor from the capital to the Caribbean Sea is a case in point (Parsons, 1967). The detachment of the Amazonian territories from individual departmental control was also pursued as a part of strengthening the power of the central government. As a result, the historical provinces which still appeared on the map of 1900 were to be extensively subdivided in the ensuing century, trebling the number of administrative units. Thus in July 1991 the number of departments was increased to 32, with the constitutional advance of all the federal territories to self-government, with the exception of the Federal Capital District of Bogota.

2.22 ARGENTINA

Conflict in Spain during the Napoleonic Wars affected political attitudes throughout the Spanish overseas Empire. In Buenos Aires the Spanish Viceroy of La Plata was overthrown in 1810. This was followed by the establishment of a 'sovereign' United Provinces of the River Plate, although formal independence was only proclaimed in 1816 once the revolution was secure. However, Upper Peru (Bolivia) and Paraguay refused to recognise the new administration and the Spanish colonial authorities attempted to regain control of the region. The complex war of independence which followed resulted in the permanent loss of Bolivia and Paraguay. In addition, the land to the east of the Uruguay River was lost as a result of civil war and finally as a result of a compromise with the Brazilian Empire it became the Eastern Republic of Uruguay in 1828.

Thereafter the country passed through a period of constitutional experimentation marked by civil wars and negotiations as the leaders of the powerful provinces sought some accommodation with the dominant position of the province of Buenos Aires, through federal constitutions. From 1826 the country was named the Argentine Confederation, although briefly the name United Provinces of South America had been used. In 1853 the provinces adopted a closer form of union to overcome the autonomy of local military leaders, but the new constitution was rejected for six years by the powerful province of Buenos Aires, which proclaimed its independence.

In 1862 the country adopted the title 'Argentine Republic' (Republica Argentina) and began a long period of economic expansion and national integration. The political organisation of the national territory paralleled that of the United States of America. The historic provinces, within permanently defined boundaries, enjoyed a substantial measure of self-government including elected assemblies. In addition, a series of poorly developed and lightly populated territories on the northern and southern peripheries were administered by the central government until they had developed sufficiently to be admitted as provinces. The contrast between the provinces and the territories was stark in 1900 as the territories covered some 44 percent of the national territory, but housed only 2.8 percent of the population. The dominant position of the city and province of Buenos Aires, where 40.9 percent of the

Map 2.22 Argentina

national population lived by 1900, was recognised by their effective double representation in the Senate.

Between August 1951 and July 1955 the remaining eight mainland territories attained provincial status. This represented a rare example of continuity where the internal provincial and territorial boundaries drawn on the map of 1900 were maintained for the entire subsequent century. Only Tierra del Fuego retained territorial status until April

1990, when it too was raised to the status of a province. It was nominally expanded to include the Falkland Islands (Ilas Malvinas) and the other islands claimed by Argentina in the South Atlantic Ocean, which were temporarily occupied in April 1982. It is notable that the former (1900) territories had developed to house some 12 percent of the national population by the end of the century.

CHAPTER 3

The Final Phase of Imperial Expansion 1900–1914

The period before the First World War witnessed a number of significant changes in the world political map involving both the creation and destruction of states. Thus the state map of 1914 included Albania, Bulgaria, Cuba, Panama, Nepal and Norway, which had attained independence. In contrast, the Congo Free State, Korea, Morocco, Orange Free State, and the South African Republic had lost their independence. These eleven changes of status represented a substantial alteration in the composition of the list of internationally recognised states in a fifteen year period without a general world war. Yet it is indicative of the attainment of a certain degree of stability in the international system of the period, as the wholesale destruction of states in the nineteenth century had ceased. It should be noted that change was not limited to one particularly volatile region, but was evident in every continent. In Asia the Chinese Empire collapsed and the ensuing Republic was unable to hold its extensive territorial inheritance together, while the Japanese Empire continued its expansion through conquest and annexation. It was the last period when the European colonial empires were able to expand virtually unchecked, notably in Africa, where only two states remained outside the control of the European based empires. In contrast, the United States extended its influence by creating new, nominally independent, states.

3.1 EUROPE IN 1914

The map of Europe in 1914 is one of the most frequently published and cited versions, apart from the modern map. It reflected the culmination of virtually a century of general peace and therefore limited territorial adjustments. No European war involving all the major powers had been fought since 1815 and the main outlines of the territorial settlement drawn up at the Congress of Vienna were still in place. It is notable that the five great powers which entered the First World War in August 1914 were the same as those that had concluded the peace in June 1815. There had been some significant changes in the map. Prussia had been transformed into a united Germany during the period, but politically was still recognisable. Similarly the Italian states had been unified between 1859 and 1870 into a single kingdom. However, the most noticeable cartographic changes had taken place in the Balkans which had been part of the Ottoman Empire in 1815, and where a series of new nation-states had emerged a century later. The final disintegration of the Empire's European possessions was accomplished in the years immediately before the First World War and so warrant particular attention as the forces affecting the Balkans were directly responsible for the upheaval which followed.

The independence of Norway was particularly instructive so far as the development of political thought and especially the concept of self-determination in western Europe was concerned. In 1814, Norway had been ceded to Sweden by Denmark, under whose control the country had been since medieval times. In 1815 the formal Act of Union between the two countries took place with the establishment of only minimal joint organisations, mainly related to the monarchy, diplomatic and defence matters (Derry, 1973). The joint services were maintained largely

Map 3.1   Europe in 1914

under Swedish supervision as the more populous and influential state. In common with other European countries, Norwegian national awareness increased markedly in the nineteenth century. The parliamentary franchise was widened in the 1880s, leading to more populist politics. The apparent Norwegian subservience to Sweden in the conduct of foreign affairs became an issue of conflict between the two parliaments precipitating the constitutional crisis of 1892–1895. On this occasion the Union was preserved and joint control of foreign affairs maintained.

However, the constitutional crisis over the appointment of separate Norwegian consuls resurfaced in 1905, resulting in the Norwegian parliament unilaterally voting in favour of the dissolution of the Union. The Swedish government chose to negotiate with the Norwegians, but insisted upon a referendum as a means of measuring the support for or against the continuation of the Union. The referendum held in August 1905 recorded over 99.9 percent support for the dissolution of the Union by the Norwegian electorate. King Oscar II thereupon renounced the Norwegian throne in October 1905, thereby formally ending the constitutional link. The peaceful outcome was the result of the concern of the political leaders in both countries to achieve future conciliation, while no great power was interested in fomenting conflict.

The peaceful independence of Norway was markedly in contrast to the bloodshed that had previously surrounded the creation of the majority of sovereign states. The contrast with the fate of the autonomous Grand Duchy of Finland within the Russian Empire is particularly instructive in this respect. Russification, military integration and increasing repression followed the attempts by the Finnish government to secure greater independence. This culminated in the Russian government assuming control of most affairs in the Grand Duchy in June 1910 and a policy of integration being practised, as had been previously applied to Poland.

3.2   OVERLAPPING NATIONAL CLAIMS IN THE BALKANS

The Balkans was one of the most complex regions in Europe so far as conflicting national territorial claims were concerned. If the situation prior to 1912 is examined, each of the Balkan kingdoms had unresolved national claims dating back to the period before the Ottoman invasion of the continent in the fourteenth century. The outlines of medieval Greater Serbia, Greater Bulgaria, the Byzantine Empire and other entities were studied, together with the ethnographers' maps to establish the future map of the region (Marriott, 1917).

Historical pedigrees over a period of 2500 years were examined and used to promote current national interests. The most venerable was the Greek. Prior to the disastrous Fourth Crusade (1200–1204), much of the Balkans had been under the control of the Byzantine Empire, which had waged a fluctuating struggle for control with the other Balkan powers. This political and cultural hegemony could be traced back to classical times and linked to the development of Greek civilisation in the millennium before Christ. Furthermore, the Patriarch of Constantinople was the first among equals of the spiritual leaders of the Eastern Orthodox Church, which provided the continuing impetus towards the usage of the Greek language and the adoption of Greek or Byzantine systems of organisation and thought within the Church and the states influenced by Orthodox Christianity. Thus Greek politicians looked back to their Classical Greek and Byzantine heritages for national revival and sought to re-establish some semblance of an illustrious past. Indeed the initial War of Independence in the 1820s had brought forth considerable support through tapping widespread philhellenic sentiments elsewhere in Europe, based upon the prevailing classical foundation of the education of the continent's ruling elites. The much publicised involvement of Lord Byron in the struggle for independence is a case in point. The Greek territorial claims on ecclesiastical and historical grounds were, as a result, usually far in excess of the area occupied by speakers of modern Greek.

The leaders of the other Balkan states had to rely more closely upon the historical record following their migration into the region after the break-up of the Roman Empire, of which only the briefest account can be given. The main body of South Slav settlers, the Serbs and Croats, occupied a substantial area adjacent to the Adriatic Sea soon after the fall of the Roman Empire. Their subsequent conversion to Christianity by missionaries from both Rome and Constantinople was to have permanent results as the language was written in Latin script by those who came to identify themselves as Croats and in Cyrillic, derived from Greek, by those who came to identify themselves as Serbs. The histories of the two groups diverged markedly, with the Croats largely absorbed into the Hungarian sphere of influence. The Serbs emerged from the collapse of Bulgaria and assumed their greatest extent in the fourteenth century under Stephen VIII (1331–1355), who sought to replace the Byzantine Empire as the major Balkan power. However, Serbia was defeated by a combination of Byzantine and Ottoman forces. In 1389, at the battle of Kosovo, the Serbs were defeated and the heartland of the Serbian kingdom came under Turkish control. In the late sixth and early seventh centuries the Bulgars migrated into the eastern Balkans. Two significant developments took place, namely their assimilation of the Slavic language and conversion to Orthodox Christianity. They proceeded to create an independent state between the Adriatic and Black Seas. It reached its height under Simeon the Great (893–927) but

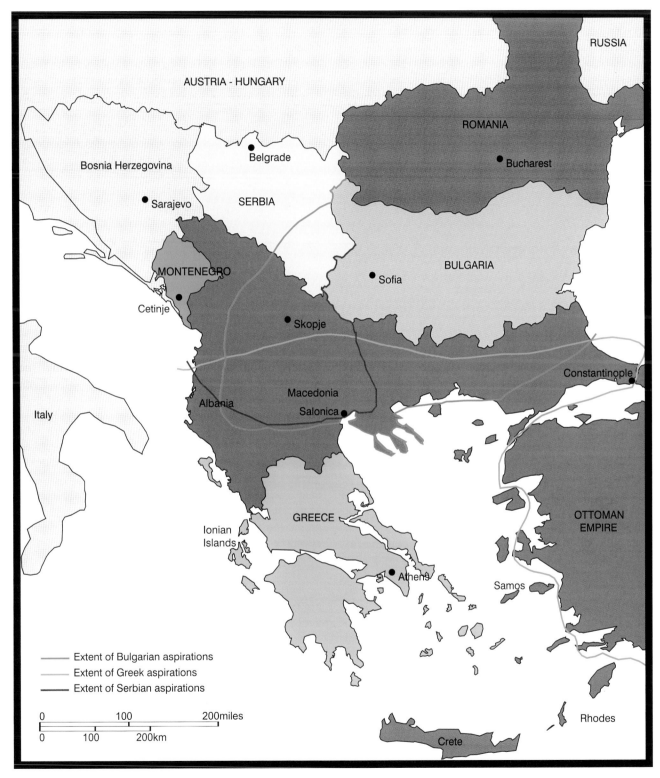

Map 3.2   Overlapping national claims in the Balkans

was subsequently conquered by the Byzantine Empire. A later revival was highly ephemeral and the area was conquered by the Turks.

Turkish colonisation and the conversion of some of the Balkan populations to Islam, notably in Bosnia and Albania, followed to further confuse the picture. The volatile sequence of overlapping empires and states made any clear and uncontested claims based on historic claims extremely difficult to support. However, they provided an indication of national perceptions and ambitions which in turn influenced events in the first half of the twentieth century.

3.3   ETHNIC DISTRIBUTIONS IN THE BALKANS

Mapping the ethnic characteristics of the inhabitants of the Balkans before 1912 was an area of academic contention between the ethnographers of many countries (Wilkinson, 1951). This was all the more important in an era when increasingly ethnicity and language were assumed to define the nation and therefore the nation-state. The distribution of linguistic and cultural groups, even the existence of some, was highly disputed in the Balkans. Maps from the 1820s onwards sought to show the distribution of the various nations or linguistic groups. Many were taxonomic studies akin to the scientific studies undertaken throughout the world by European ethnographers exploring and documenting the newly discovered regions. The Balkans, because of their proximity to the major scientific centres of the continent, were particularly intensively studied. Other investigations were of a more overtly political nature, indicating the bias of the writer, and more particularly his nationality. Until the twentieth century there was a remarkable lack of official data on the subject, notably within the Ottoman Empire, and what there was, was often open to differing interpretations. Lacking official information, the ethnographers played a significant role in the development of the Balkan states in the nineteenth and early twentieth centuries.

The early ethnographic maps attempted to draw broad lines to distinguish the areas occupied by the major groups. With time more detailed and complex maps appeared and a shift was noticeable from religious affiliation to language as the national identifier. The first 'modern' map was compiled by the Czech, Pavel Safarik, in 1842, based on his detailed knowledge of Slavic languages. His map indicated that the greater part of the Balkans were occupied by Slavs, not Greeks and Turks as had previously been believed.

Furthermore, he amalgamated many of the smaller sub-groups such as Montenegrins, Illyrians, Bosnians and Winds, in favour of two, namely Serbo-Croats and Bulgarians. Amongst his innovations was the grouping of the Albanians and the restriction of the Greeks to all but the Aegean coastline. This map was to be remarkably influential in the manner that later generations and particularly politicians perceived the nations of the Balkans.

This view was modified in detail by later maps but not confounded. The French geographer, Ami Boue, in 1847 elaborated Sarfarik's map in expanding the Albanian area and reducing yet further the area of the Greek influence. He also recognised the noticeable degree of overlap between groups, suggesting that simple lines could not be used to distinguish between homogeneous linguistic areas. This trend was continued in both French and German maps, culminating in that of Heinrich Kiepert in 1876, which recognised a substantial Turkish presence, particularly in the eastern part of the Balkans. His map was particularly influential in that it was used at the Congress of Berlin in 1878 and was considered to be politically neutral and thus a scientific depiction of the distribution of languages. The Russians, in concluding the war with Turkey in 1878 at the Treaty of San Stephano, had included most of the areas depicted on Kiepert's map as inhabited mainly by Bulgarians within the proposed Bulgarian state. The state had been reduced in size at the subsequent Congress of Berlin for political, not ethnographic, reasons.

There followed intensive national ethnographic investigations as the Balkan countries sought to support their claims to Turkish territory on the basis of nationality. Thus a school map produced in Serbia in 1891, and widely propagated, indicated that much of Macedonia was not occupied by Bulgarians but by Serbs. However, most maps continued to show most of Turkish Macedonia as occupied by Bulgarians. Jovan Cvijic, the Serbian geographer, investigated the linguistic characteristics of the Macedonian population and came to the conclusion in 1906 that they had sufficient distinctive traits to be classified separately as 'Macedo-Slavs'. His subsequent revision of the ethnographic map was highly detrimental to Bulgaria's interests, even if not to Serbia's obvious immediate advantage, although the pure Serb area was extended into northern Macedonia and northern Albania. In the First Balkan War of 1912–1913 ethnographic maps and historic claims were largely irrelevant as the states pursued their own strategic objectives. They were of greater significance in the Second Balkan War of 1913, when the Macedo-Slavs were assumed to be incipient Serbs when the final boundaries were drawn. Cvijic's 1913 map was influential

Map 3.3   Ethnic distributions in the Balkans

as portraying the Macedo-Slavs occupying a strategic section of the Balkans and so legitimising the Serbian occupation. The maps left a legacy of a vast body of 'scientific' material for use in the later territorial disputes in the two world wars, and the subsequent creation and destruction of the Yugoslav federal republic.

3.4 THE OTTOMAN EMPIRE IN THE BALKANS

International diplomacy in the nineteenth and early twentieth centuries had been frequently directed towards solving the unfolding crises associated with the 'Eastern Question'. The disintegration of the Ottoman Empire accelerated in the early twentieth century. A short-lived revolt took place in Macedonia in August 1903 and general discontent among the Sultan's Christian subjects continued. In April 1908 Sultan Abdul Hamid II was overthrown and a reformist 'Young Turk' government took power in Constantinople, with the aim of revitalising the Empire and converting it into a Turkish national state. In response Austria-Hungary unilaterally annexed Bosnia-Herzegovina, while Bulgaria renounced Ottoman suzerainty, and Prince Ferdinand assumed the title of Tsar of Bulgaria as the ruler of a fully independent state. In both cases these declarations did little but convert a de facto situation into de jure terms. The new Turkish government was forced to recognise both reductions in the nominal extent of the Empire. The one consolation it was able to secure was the withdrawal of the Austro-Hungarian garrison from Novi Pazar.

Turkish attempts to reform the administration and particularly to enhance the Empire's military capability, in alliance with Germany, achieved some highly publicised successes. As a result, the governments of countries which coveted Turkish territory became more anxious to seize it while the opportunity still existed. In September 1911, without any prior warning or preliminary crisis, Italy declared war on Turkey and invaded Tripoli in North Africa. Tripoli had been viewed by successive Italian governments as falling into the Italian sphere of influence for eventual annexation. The war in Africa was inconclusive and in May 1912, the Italians proceeded to occupy the twelve islands of the Dodecanese Archipelago including the island of Rhodes in the Aegean Sea as a means of threatening its opponent more directly. The war was only concluded in October 1912 when the wider Balkan war broke out. Under the Treaty of Lausanne, Turkey surrendered Tripoli and Italy undertook to evacuate the Dodecanese islands – a promise that was not kept.

The four Balkan countries, Bulgaria, Greece, Montenegro and Serbia, had generally been too divided by their mutual rivalries to make a combined assault on Turkey. Thus the last Greco-Turkish war in 1898 had been a disaster from a Greek point of view as it had received no external support. However, the diplomatic situation was such that in the course of 1912 the four governments were able to agree upon a joint programme to destroy the Ottoman Empire in Europe through the formation of the Balkan League. The League's intervention in October 1912 was prompted by the revolt in Albania against Turkish rule, which appeared to threaten its members' territorial interests. Within two months of the declaration of war the forces of the League had occupied virtually the whole of European Turkey. The interplay of great power rivalries and Austro-Hungarian hostility towards Serbia were such that the great powers played a significant role in drawing up the peace terms. At the Treaty of London in May 1913, which concluded the First Balkan War, the four countries of the League made impressive territorial gains, but most significantly an independent Albania was also created, with the object of denying Serbia direct access to the sea. Turkey in Europe was restricted to the immediate vicinity of Constantinople. The autonomous governments of Crete and Samos were formally incorporated into Greece in December 1913, with only the Dodecanese islands remaining in Italian hands.

The Bulgarian government was highly dissatisfied with the outcome of the war and sought to obtain a larger share of the territory than it had been able to occupy in the First Balkan War. In June 1913 therefore Bulgaria attacked Serbia and Greece, precipitating the Second Balkan War over the division of Macedonia. Subsequently Romania and Turkey entered the war against Bulgaria, resulting in substantial losses for the latter at the concluding Treaty of Bucharest in September 1913. Significantly no thought of an independent or autonomous Macedonian state for the 'Macedo-Slavs' had been entertained by any of the parties involved in the war. The international community was too concerned with the establishment of the buffer state of Albania to intervene on behalf of another nationality.

3.5 ALBANIA

The Balkan crisis of 1912 had been initiated by revolts in Albania. This country had in many respects been one of the more politically and culturally assimilated regions of the European sector of the Ottoman Empire. The presence of a

Map 3.4   The Ottoman Empire in the Balkans

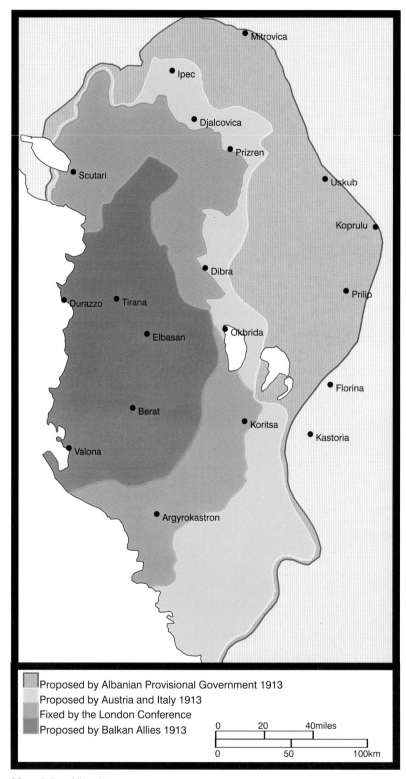

Map 3.5   Albania

substantial Moslem population, amounting to approximately 70 percent of the total, was a factor which favoured the maintenance of the status quo. This was illustrated by the establishment of the first Albanian League in June 1878, which had been formed specifically to oppose the Treaty of San Stephano, which had consigned sections of the Albanian-speaking area to Bulgaria. The end of the immediate external threat led to the dissolution of the League (Jelavich and Jelavich, 1977).

Furthermore, there had been no history of national cohesion and Christian–Moslem enmity had tended to reinforce the latter's loyalty to the Sultan. Historical research and folk memory could not call upon an extensive 'golden age' kingdom, which had been so noticeable a feature in the propaganda of the other nations. The fifteenth century conquests of Skanderberg were quoted in support of an Albanian state, but not its territorial extent. Literary references to the ancient Illyrians supplied some linguistic if rather spurious historic continuity (Wilkes, 1992). Even within the Moslem population the divide between the Gegs of northern Albania and the Tosks of the south was of significance and usually precluded pan-Albanian cooperation. No standard form of the written language had been devised until the formal adoption of the Latin alphabet in November 1908. This development was regarded as subversive by the Ottoman authorities who promoted the use of Arabic script and were equally intent upon the imposition of Turkish as the national language. Any sense of Albanian national awareness was thus a comparatively late development.

The successes of the Balkan League prompted the incipient Albanian national movement to declare independence in November 1912, as a means of preventing the country being partitioned between the four allies. However, the establishment of an independent Albanian state was essentially the successful outcome of Austro-Hungarian and Italian diplomacy, and was imposed upon Greece, Montenegro and Serbia. The Austro-Hungarians sought to secure their passage through the Straits of Otranto at the entrance to the Adriatic Sea, while the Italians sought to control the Straits. The governments of both countries wished to prevent the area falling into the hands of the Serbians and the Greeks. The lack of any other great power's vital national interest in the issue resulted in the Italian and Austro-Hungarian solution being accepted. In December 1912 the great powers decided that Albania should become an independent state and employed sufficient military force to ensure that this was done. Indeed in April 1913 an international blockade of the coastline had been imposed to force Montenegro to withdraw from the fortress of Scutari, which was defined as falling within the new state's boundaries.

The definition of an Albanian state proved to be a matter of negotiation between the great powers. The Albanian national delegation, at the conference in London concerned with ending the First Balkan War in May 1913, had limited input into the project and their rather extravagant plans were ignored. It was rare however, for the great powers, particularly Austria-Hungary, to apply the principle of national identity so effectively in the creation of a nation-state which had not fought for its own independence. The significant religious and cultural divisions between the Roman Catholic, Orthodox and Moslem populations were ignored as language was taken as the indicator of nationality, a perception disputed by the Serbians and Greeks, who wished to annex the areas inhabited by their co-religionists. As such Albania has some claim to be the first 'quasi-state' to be established in the twentieth century, which obtained its independence as a result of the intervention of the international community, and whose continued existence was dependent upon continued international support.

An International Control Commission was established by the great powers in October 1913 which sent an international police force to assist in the establishment of the national administration. Further, the German, Prince William of Wied, was selected to become the Prince of independent Albania and arrived in March 1914. Antagonistic factions, including influential pro-Turkish forces, made the task of government building extremely precarious. As a result, soon after the outbreak of the First World War, Prince William and the international force were compelled to leave the country in September 1914. The key routeways and towns were duly occupied by its neighbours, while much of the interior reverted to the control of local tribal groupings. Albania ceased to exist as a state for the duration of the war. The contrast between Albania and Norway with regard to the processes of state formation was startling, reflecting the different degrees of national cohesion and the significance of the role of the great powers prior to the First World War.

3.6   THE FINAL PHASE OF THE PARTITION OF AFRICA

Four states in Africa lost their independence between 1900 and 1914, leaving Liberia and Ethiopia as the only fully sovereign countries on the continent. In South Africa the conflict between the British government and the two

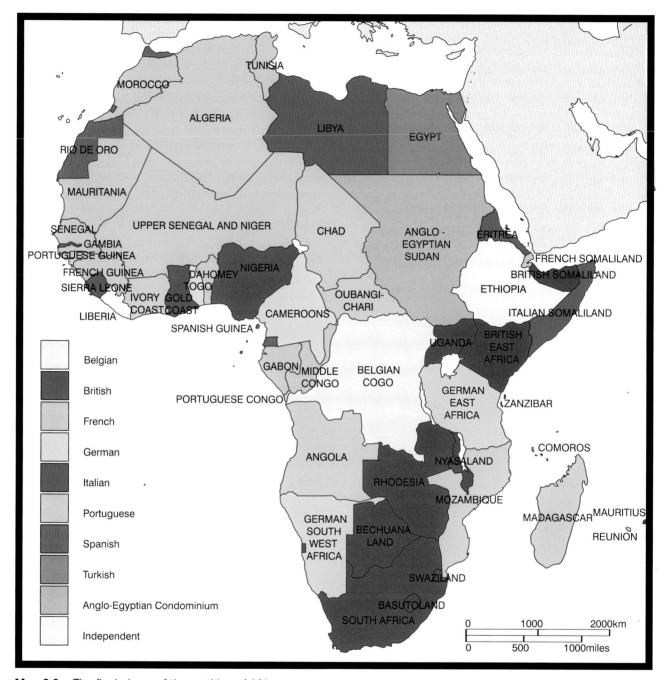

Map 3.6   The final phase of the partition of Africa

Afrikaner Boer republics for hegemony in the sub-continent reached crisis point in October 1899 with a declaration of war by the latter. Inevitably the mobilisation of the massive resources of the British Empire, including the deployment of forces from Canada, Australia and New Zealand, resulted in the defeat of the Boer forces. The war was prolonged for two years after formal British annexation, as the Boers refused to recognise the end of their independence and engaged in a guerrilla war. However, in May 1902 at the Treaty of Vereeniging, the representatives of the governments of the Orange Free State and South African Republic (Transvaal) formally recognised the British annexations of 1900 and their loss of independence.

The two states became British Crown colonies. However, the grant of self-government four years later prepared the way for the unification of South Africa. In May 1910 the colonies of the Cape of Good Hope, Natal, Orange River Colony and the Transvaal joined to form the Union of South Africa, which was granted dominion status by Great Britain (Christopher, 1976). Provision was made for the possible future incorporation of Southern Rhodesia and the three High Commission territories of Basutoland, Bechuanaland Protectorate and Swaziland into the Union (Hyam, 1972). Significantly the loose confederal structures adopted in the constitutions of the earlier British dominions of Canada and Australia were not emulated by the delegates to the South African constitutional convention. The resultant state was a highly centralised union with no right of secession, and few powers delegated to the four provinces.

Morocco which had retained a precarious independence as a result of the rivalry of the great powers over its future in the nineteenth century, eventually fell prey to an agreement between the very same powers in the early twentieth century. In March 1912 France and Spain assumed protectorate powers over the country, whose nominal unity was maintained with Sultan Mulai-Abd-el-Hafid's position retained, but his powers reduced to largely ceremonial levels by the protecting powers. The French took the major part of the country, while in November 1912 the Spanish acquired a northern zone adjacent to Ceuta and Melila and the other Spanish towns on the Moroccan Mediterranean coast, and a southern zone adjacent to the colony of Rio de Oro. Significantly the Spanish exclave of Ifni remained isolated from the remainder of Spanish territory.

The special status of Tangier derived from its peculiar history and strategic location on the Straits of Gibraltar. Tangier had been assigned as the place of residence for the foreign diplomatic representatives and merchants in Morocco in order to prevent their interference in the country's domestic affairs. In 1880 the extra-territorial rights of the foreign population had been codified. In the face of increasing lawlessness, the resident diplomatic corps assumed greater control over the affairs of the city. Its special status, lying outside the French and Spanish zones, was recognised in 1912, but it was only in December 1924 with the signing of the Tangier Convention that international status was legally conferred upon the city. The international administration was headed by a French official, with a Spanish deputy, and assisted by a Legislative Assembly. Tangier remained one of the seats of the Sultan of Morocco who retained a palace in the city.

The fourth state to lose its independence was the Congo Free State, which was annexed by the Belgian government in October 1908 following the exposure of gross humanitarian abuse of the indigenous people by the agents of the independent state. It was renamed the Belgian Congo. The Lado enclave reverted to the administration of the Anglo-Egyptian Sudan following King Leopold II's death in December 1909.

The various colonial empires continued the process of reorganising their holdings in more convenient forms for administration. Thus in French West Africa, the colony of Mauritania was established in October 1904 to administer the coastal belt north of the Senegal River. Its viability was doubtful as its administrative headquarters remained in the Senegalese capital of St Louis. Aptly the colony was described as 'one more administrative solution created by France during her colonial venture in West Africa' (Gerteiny, 1967: 11).

The British possessions in Nigeria underwent a significant reorganisation and rationalisation of administrative structures. First the colony of Lagos was incorporated into Southern Nigeria in February 1906 and then Northern and Southern Nigeria were united in January 1914 to create the most populous state on the continent. In similar vein, the four Comoro Islands of Grande Comoro, Mayotte, Moheli and Anjouan were attached to Madagascar in February 1914.

3.7   MALAYA

Between 1900 and 1914 the Malay peninsula underwent a number of changes as a result of the British acquisition of territory from Siam and the internal reorganisation of administrations. The extension of British control in the region had been a slow process, beginning with the acquisition of the island of Penang by the English East India Company in 1786. Province Wellesley on the mainland opposite was acquired from the Sultan of Kedah in 1811 and incorporated into Penang. The strategic island of Singapore was ceded to the Company by the Sultan of Johore in 1819. In the general exchange of territorial holdings in the region with the Netherlands in 1824, the British withdrew from Sumatra and the other islands but in return acquired Malacca on the mainland. Two years later the administration of the three possessions on the Straits of Malacca were grouped together and aptly named the Straits Settlements. In 1826 a tract of coastal land, the Dindings, was ceded by the Sultan of Perak in order to develop a port between

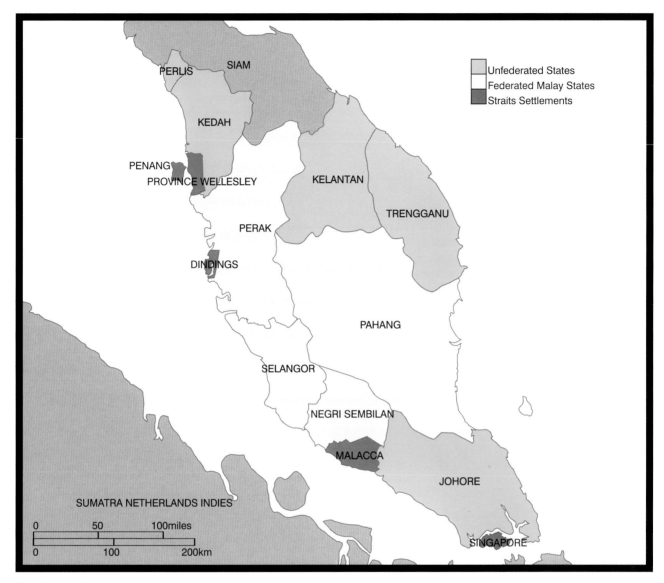

Map 3.7   Malaya

Penang and Malacca. The project was never undertaken and the area reverted to Perak in February 1935.

With the loss of the China trade monopoly in 1833, the British East Indian Company and its successor the Government of India lost interest in the region. As a result, in 1867 the Straits Settlements were detached from India to form a separate Crown Colony. In October 1906 the British colony of Labuan off the coast of North Borneo, which had previously been administered by the British North Borneo Company, was also attached to the Straits Settlements. The political linkage between Malaya and northern Borneo thus anticipated the political unification of Malaysia nearly 60

years later. Additional rationalisations of the Imperial administrative map resulted in Christmas Island and the Cocos-Keeling Islands in the Indian Ocean being attached to the Straits Settlements in 1900 and 1903 respectively.

British influence amongst the Malay sultans increased in the second half of the nineteenth century. In 1874 the Sultans of Perak, Selangor and Sungei Ujong accepted British protection, followed by the remaining states of Negri Sembilan (incorporating Sungei Ujong) in 1886 and the Sultan of Pahang in 1886. The rapid economic development and the official perception of the need to make the administration of the four states more effective resulted in the formation of the Federated

Malay States in 1895. The four northern states of Kedah, Kelantan, Perlis and Trengganu were transferred from Siamese suzerainty to British protection in March 1909. They together with Johore, which only formally became a British protectorate in May 1914, remained as the 'Unfederated States'. Thus although 'British Malaya' was the term used by cartographers, the administrative pattern was far more complex.

3.8   THE DISINTEGRATION OF CHINA

Revolution broke out in Wuchang in Hupeh province in October 1911 and quickly spread throughout China. In February 1912 the Ch'ing dynasty was overthrown, the Empire abolished and a republic declared. The new

government attempted to hold the territories of the previous Empire together, but many of the more remote and loosely held provinces sought greater autonomy if not independence. Furthermore, within the eighteen provinces of China proper the government's hold on power was often precarious and dissension, even military revolts, reduced the central government's effectiveness. It was a measure of the Empire's political and military weakness in its final years that the Russo-Japanese war of 1905 had largely been fought in Manchuria, which was still nominally a part of China. Three years later Nepal had ended its tributary status and was recognised as an independent state.

By 1914 Tibet and Mongolia had effectively achieved administrative independence of the central government, although the republican authorities were no more inclined

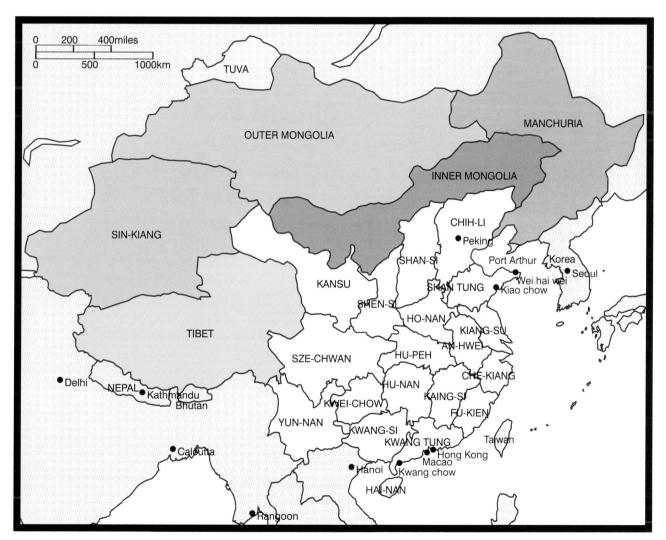

Map 3.8   The disintegration of China

to recognise the legal disintegration of the country than the emperors had been before them.

The affairs of Tibet had been thrown into confusion by the arrival of a British expedition in the country in August 1904 with the demand for it to be opened to trade and closed to the influence of other powers, notably Russia. This move represented another move in the contest between Great Britain and Russia for security and advancement in central Asia, 'The Great Game' (Hopkirk, 1990). It was only in August 1907 that the two powers sought a rapprochement and agreed effectively to divide the areas of contention between them into informal spheres of influence. The Dalai Lama, the spiritual and political leader of Tibet, had fled to Peking in August 1904 and had reaffirmed Chinese suzerainty on his return in December 1909. The following year the Chinese sought to impose administrative control over the country and the Dalai Lama again fled, this time to India. By April 1913 the Chinese forces had withdrawn following the Dalai Lama's declaration of independence. A conference was held at Simla, the summer capital of India, between delegates from China, India and Tibet to regulate the affairs of the region in July 1914 (Mehra, 1974). It was agreed that Tibet proper should be a separate province with an autonomous government and only nominally under Chinese suzerainty. However, it was also agreed that Inner Tibet (Ching-hai) would be under a greater measure of Chinese administrative control with only the spiritual authority of the Dalai Lama recognised. That section of Tibet south of the Himalayas was to be transferred to the control of the Indian government, although again the jurisdictions of the local authorities were to be respected. The Chinese government subsequently refused to ratify the agreement. Tibet thus gained effective independence, but was unable to obtain legal recognition of that status.

The Mongolian leaders similarly made a bid for independence following the Chinese revolution in November 1911 (Friters, 1951). In this case Russia was the supportive power. The complex interaction between the Chinese and Russian governments and the Mongolian authorities resulted in 1913 in the recognition of the autonomy of Outer Mongolia. Inner Mongolia remained under Chinese control and was subject to continuing Chinese agricultural colonisation. Manchuria was more closely integrated into China and no independence movement was encouraged by either the Chinese or the Japanese, who were in effective control. The remaining province of Chinese Turkestan (Sinkiang) remained under the control of a Chinese governor, although subject to Russian influence (Forbes, 1986). Until July 1928 Sinkiang

remained relatively peaceful and unaffected by events elsewhere in China.

Nepal's relationship with China had rested upon its enforced acceptance of Manchu suzerainty after the defeat of 1792. Thereafter Nepal sent a tribute mission to Peking every five years. The last mission was sent in May 1908. With the overthrow of the monarchy, Chinese suzerainty was rejected. Incorporation into the new, nominally multi-racial, Republic of China was also rejected by the Nepalese Prime Minister, Chandra Shamsher, in September 1913 in the following terms: 'With regard to the question of Union with the Five Races of China I am sorry that as Nepal is an ancient Hindu Kingdom, desirous of preserving her independence and her separate existence, she cannot entertain the idea of such a union with the Five Affiliated Races said to constitute the Republic of China' (Husain, 1970: 280). The Chinese authorities did not pursue the matter any further. Under the Anglo-Nepalese Treaty of Friendship signed in December 1923, any lingering doubts as to the independent status of Nepal were removed.

3.9   JAPANESE EXPANSION

The Japanese Empire had been expanded as a result of the successful war against Russia in 1904–1905. At the Treaty of Portsmouth concluding the war, Japan exacted territorial gains that included Port Arthur in northern China and the southern section of the island of Sakhalin. Port Arthur and the Liao-tung peninsula had been secured by Japan in 1895 but it had been forced to withdraw under international pressure. They represented the first incorporation of territory on the mainland of Asia as opposed to the acquisition of islands. In addition, Japan replaced Russia as the occupying power in southern Manchuria, with control of the Manchurian Railway.

The war had wider international implications. Korean independence proved to be short-lived. The country had been released from Chinese suzerainty in 1895 at the conclusion of the Sino-Japanese War and its isolation was ended. The country became the scene of economic and political rivalry between Russia and Japan, which the Emperor of Korea was initially able to exploit to his country's advantage, through the grant of concessions to the former power. However, following the Treaty of Portsmouth in September 1905, Russian interests were expressly excluded and the Japanese army was placed in effective control of the country. In November 1905 Korea was forced to accept a Japanese Resident-General in Seoul to take charge of the conduct of the country's external affairs.

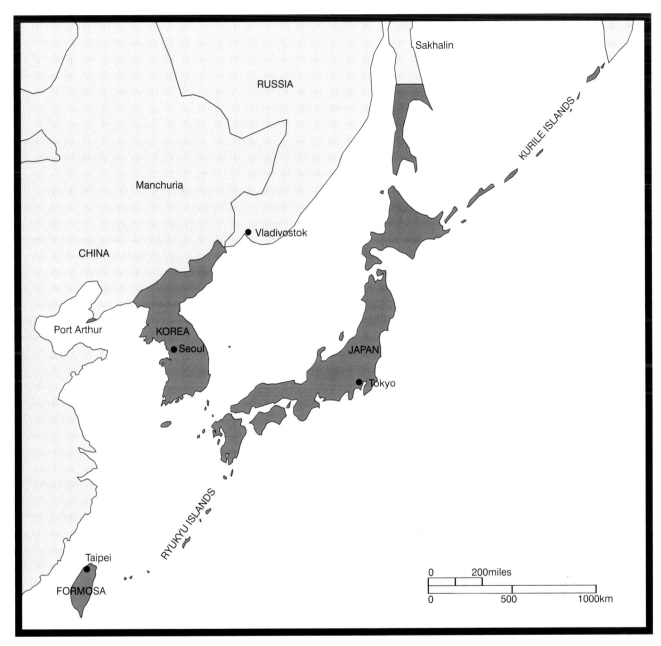

Map 3.9   Japanese expansion

Effectively the country became a Japanese protectorate, although the outward trappings of the Korean Imperial court and administration were maintained. No opposition was encountered from the great powers, which recognised the country as falling within the Japanese sphere of influence. Control over sections of the internal administration were transferred from the Korean to the Japanese governments under protocols between the two countries. From 1907 Japanese diplomacy was directed towards the outright annexation of the country. Significantly it was able to prevent the acceptance of the credentials of the Korean delegation to the Hague Peace Conference of that year. Following the deposition of the Emperor Kojong, a new Japanese–Korean agreement of July 1907 provided for the judiciary to be taken over by Japan and for Japanese vice-ministers to be appointed in all ministries and in various key security positions such as chief of the Police Bureau. The disbandment of the Korean Army followed in August 1907. Thereafter Japanese control tightened steadily. Under the Korean–Japanese Treaty of August 1910 the last Korean Emperor, Sunjong, ceded all his rights of sovereignty to the Japanese Emperor. He noted that for the solution of the nation's problems, it was necessary for him to 'entrust Our great task to abler hands than Ours' (Kim and Kim, 1967: 215). Korea was thus annexed to the Japanese Empire and administered by a Governor-General under military control.

3.10   THE CREATION OF PANAMA AND THE PANAMA CANAL ZONE

The considerable length of time taken by United States warships to pass from the Atlantic and the Pacific Ocean in the course of the Spanish-American War emphasised the need to pursue the construction of a canal between the two oceans. French efforts to open the route through Panama in the 1880s and 1890s had been unsuccessful. The Colombian government was not amenable to American pressure to pursue the project during a period of internal turmoil. As a result, the American government supported a secessionist revolt in Panama in November 1903 by preventing the Colombian central government from sending forces to suppress it. The new Panamanian government took control of the area of the former department and was immediately recognised by the United States, although not by Colombia, which withheld recognition of the secession until December 1921, upon receiving American compensation for the loss. It was only in May 1924 that Colombia and Panama established diplomatic relations, over 20 years after the proclamation of the new state.

In return for a guarantee of Panamanian independence, the United States acquired a strip of land measuring 1680 square kilometres, and approximately 16 kilometres wide, across the country through which the projected canal would pass. The coastal cities of Panama and Colon were specifically excluded from American jurisdiction. The Panama Canal Zone became an American territory, with its own administration and border posts and guarded by a strong garrison. The Panama Canal was completed in August 1914 and represented the major American strategic asset in the region. It also represented a major feat of engineering, breaching the continental divide (see dashed red line).

As with all territorial advances the new acquisition needed to be secured, with the result that the protection of the approaches to the newly constructed Panama Canal became one of the major security concerns for the American government. Thus countries in Central America and the Caribbean came increasingly under American forces of supervision, including at times military occupation. However, unlike the European colonial powers, the United States annexed little additional territory. Power was exercised through military occupation and the financial supervision of nominally independent governments. Thus Nicaragua came under American supervision in 1913, as a prelude to the granting of canal construction rights and naval bases three years later. Intervention in the Dominican Republic (1907) and Haiti (1915) extended the chain of defensive bases around the Caribbean.

At the same time the final resolution of the status of Cuba was essential to the American position in the region. The attainment of formal independence by Cuba was a remarkably lengthy affair (Hitchman, 1971). The Treaty of Paris in December 1898 had indicated that the United States did not intend to annex Cuba but rather to administer the island until the population could govern itself. The prerequisite for American withdrawal was the establishment of an independent republic whose stability would pose no threat to the security of the United States. It was only in May 1902 that the American military government concluded its task and the sovereign independence of Cuba was gained. The national convention framed a constitution, but was required to satisfy the United States as to its stability. This was secured through the Platt Amendment, defining relations between the United States and Cuba. Restrictions on the conduct of foreign affairs were imposed, while the rights of intervention by American forces in cases of internal disorder or financial mismanagement were written into the Cuban constitution. In addition, a major naval base at Guantanamo Bay was reserved to the United States Navy. Effectively Cuba became an American protectorate in all but name.

For the sake of completeness one further event should be noted. The perceived threat to the region during the First World War was such that the American government purchased the Danish West Indies in April 1917 for $25 million, ostensibly to prevent their acquisition by Germany. This effectively brought to an end one of the historic European colonial ventures in the Caribbean and completed the territorial chain of islands defending the American position in the region.

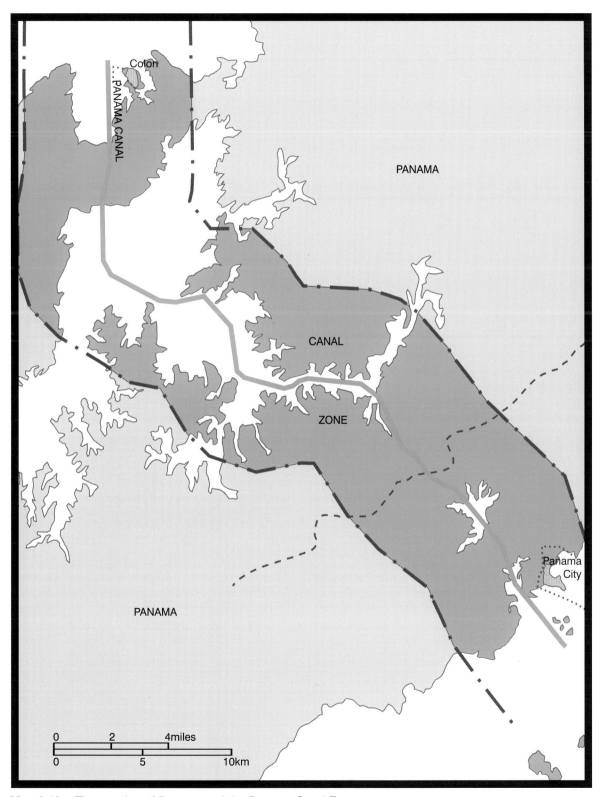

Map 3.10   The creation of Panama and the Panama Canal Zone

CHAPTER 4

The Struggle for Mastery in Europe 1914–1918

The First World War broke out in August 1914 as a result of national rivalries in Europe, which governments were neither willing nor able to control. The initial dispute erupted between Austria and Serbia over responsibility for the assassination of the heir to the Austro-Hungarian throne, the Archduke Franz Ferdinand, and his wife, Sophie, in the Bosnian capital, Sarajevo on 28 June 1914. It developed into a general world-wide war as a result of the interaction of the mutually hostile and interlocking alliance systems of the great powers in the Triple Alliance and the Triple Entente. The mobilisation and battle plan timetables set by these systems prevented any reconsideration of the consequences of the actions involved. The alliance system was such that once the first national military mobilisation orders had been given, the remainder of the declarations of war were virtually automatic.

There was general popular nationalist rejoicing at the outbreak of war throughout Europe and so restraint was not on the political agenda. The immensity of the disaster was only foreseen by a perceptive few. Sir Edward Grey, the British Foreign Secretary, observed at the outbreak of the war: 'The lamps are going out all over Europe; we shall not see them lit again in our lifetime' (Thomson, 1957: 507). It was only in retrospect that the war was generally assessed as a disaster for the European powers (Tuchman, 1967). Indeed the period before the war assumed the status of a golden age in contrast to the carnage which was to follow (McLeod, 1983). On both sides governments thought the war would be short and understandably every combatant country considered that it would be victorious. The French defeat of the Germans

before Paris and the German defeat of the Russians at Tannenberg in East Prussia in the first month of the war indicated that the war was not to be short and Europe settled down to more than four years of mass slaughter and attrition. In contrast the war in most of Germany's colonies was relatively brief with occupation effected by the British, French and Japanese allies within a month or two of the outbreak of war.

Germany occupied a considerable extent of territory in the first weeks of the war as the General Staff put the Schlieffen Plan into operation and conquered Belgium and occupied Luxembourg as a means of defeating France. The violation of the neutrality of these two states had been the ostensible cause of the British entry into the war and so their occupation remained as German bargaining blocks for negotiating the eventual peace settlement. As a result, the status of these two states remained an unresolved question throughout the war. Dissident Flemish and Walloon political movements in Belgium were encouraged to seek German support and annexation plans were examined but with little serious purpose. The creation of an integrated continental economic block, dominated by Germany, appeared to be the main objective of the occupying power, as propounded by the Chancellor, Theobald von Bethmann-Hollweg, in September 1914 (Stirk, 1996). However, the promotion of the Council of Flanders and the Flemish language was to have disruptive effects upon the restored Belgian state after the war. The Grand Duchy of Luxembourg remained nominally independent, although its future was considered to lie as a German federal state in the event of a German victory.

Germany's wider plans only unfolded as the war continued and the conquest of Russia began. The allied powers remained uncertain about effecting any major changes to the map until 1915, when the need to entice Italy to join the war and decide upon the future of the Ottoman Empire seemed necessary. It was only with the entry of the United States of America into the war in April 1917 that President Woodrow Wilson's 'Fourteen Points' presented a programme for the organisation of the post-war world in the event of an allied victory. Significantly America described itself as an 'Associate Power', not an ally, because it rejected the system of secret treaties between the allies providing for the disposition of territory at the end of the war. However, the collapse of Russia enabled German war plans to be put into action at an earlier date. On both sides there was an increasing willingness, even eagerness, to change the existing international order radically and in doing so change the state pattern dramatically, to ensure the total and permanent defeat of the enemy.

4.1   A NEW MAP OF EASTERN EUROPE

The gradual collapse of Russia in the course of the war enabled Germany to impose its own political settlement upon eastern Europe (Fischer, 1967). The policy unfolded gradually as German armies penetrated deeper into Russia and greater use was made of national independence movements and various anti-Czarist émigré groups. In many respects the German and Austrian leaders followed historical precedents rather than appeals to popular self-determination in redrawing the map of the region. The capture of Warsaw in August 1915 raised the future of Poland as a matter of immediate concern for the two Central Powers. The Congress Kingdom, established in 1815, came under German and Austro-Hungarian control. In November 1916 the kingdom of Poland was revived but neither its boundaries nor constitution were finalised as the territories remained under the occupation and administration of the General Government of Poland established by the two imperial armies. Disagreements between the two empires over the country's relationship to the existing Austro-Hungarian Empire and its possible incorporation of Galicia were still unresolved in November 1918. As the war progressed, so the Austro-Hungarian position vis-a-vis Germany weakened and effectively Poland was increasingly administered as a German dependency.

By late 1916 German armies had penetrated deeply into the Baltic provinces. Initially all were considered suitable for annexation and incorporation into the German Empire. However, upon greater reflection it was appreciated that Lithuania constituted a distinctive national society unlikely to be Germanised and so the medieval Grand Duchy was revived. Lithuania's independence was finally proclaimed in December 1917 by the local parliament, while the country remained under German military occupation and before Russia had signed a peace treaty. The area assigned to the country was relatively small compared with the extent of the state in medieval times, but it was strategically placed between East Prussia, Poland, Courland and the anticipated rump Great Russian state. The Lithuanian government was unable to effect any independent policies until after the German defeat as the extent of independence was highly circumscribed.

The Baltic provinces of Courland, Livonia and Estonia, with their substantial German-speaking landowner and merchant classes, were considered to be suitable for colonisation by German settlers and eventual direct incorporation into the German Empire. Historically the provinces, together with Prussia proper, had for a long period been subject to the Military Order of Teutonic Knights and thus possessed a highly symbolic place in German and particularly Prussian history and mythology. Indeed German speakers still constituted some 7 per cent of the total population. Furthermore, the Baltic German nobles controlled the local governing Knights' Estates through agreements reached with the Czar upon the Russian annexation in the eighteenth century. They urged German military and political intervention, particularly after the revolution in Russia and the start of land nationalisation seizures. The independence of the three provinces was recognised by the German government in the course of 1918, but within very tightly prescribed circumstances, which were linked to the offer of the thrones of those states to the King of Prussia and German Emperor.

The March 1917 revolution in Russia had weakened the control of the central government to the extent that it was forced to acknowledge the independence of the Ukraine in July 1917. This was confirmed at the Treaty of Brest Litovsk in March 1918. Following the signing of the treaty the Ukraine was occupied by German forces, which proceeded to stage a coup d'etat and install a more pliable government in Kiev. For the remainder of the war the country was effectively run by the German military authorities for the exploitation of its agricultural and mineral resources for the benefit of the wider war effort.

Finland, which had maintained the highest degree of autonomy within the Russian Empire, delayed formal secession and only declared its independence in December

Map 4.1   A new map of Eastern Europe

1917, following the revolutions in Russia and the outbreak of civil war throughout the country. Complete independence from Soviet intervention was finally secured with the aid of German forces in April 1918. As a means of consolidating the state, Prince Friedrich Karl of Hesse was elected to the vacant throne in October 1918, but the end of the war the following month resulted in the proclamation of a republic and renewed embroilment in the civil war in Russia.

The Treaty of Brest Litovsk did not set an effective eastward limit to German plans for the redrawing of the map of Europe. The continued advance of its armies in the summer and autumn of 1918 involved the occupation of lands beyond the boundaries of the Ukraine as stipulated in the treaty. The Crimea, a part of Great Russia, was occupied in May 1918 after the collapse of a short-lived Crimean Tatar Republic and its subsequent occupation by Soviet forces. The Crimean Tatars, who amounted to only 13.5 percent of the population of the peninsula, had appealed to the Ottoman Empire for support, a request which was at first favourably entertained on the basis of historic ties. However, this proposal was rejected by Germany, which wished to establish its own regime in the Crimea and Kuban Territory, so blocking Russian access to the Black Sea. The Ukrainian government similarly staked its claim to the Crimea, which was acknowledged by the German military occupation forces as a means of rewarding it for assistance with the war effort. German influence was expanded into the Don Cossack Republic, east of the Ukraine and the North Caucasian state, as part of a drive to secure the mineral resources of the region. These entities were all regarded as part of the complex relationship between Germany and the rump Russian state. Their interests were essentially dependent upon the final agreement between the two states, as the supplementary treaties of August 1918 demonstrated (Fischer, 1967).

Direct German military intervention was extended to the Transcaucasian lands as a potential source of petroleum supplies. The situation in the Caucasus was highly confused as the Ottoman Empire continued to prosecute the war in order to regain territories lost in the nineteenth century. In addition, the local nationalist movements were in conflict with the local Soviet forces supported by the Russian government. Initially a Federated Transcaucasian Republic was established in April 1918. However, the strains between the three constituent states and between Germany and the Ottoman Empire were such as to cause its disintegration the following month. Christian Georgia and Armenia received German support while Moslem Azerbaijan was supported by the Turks. Inevitably German intervention resulted in fresh involvement in the Russian civil war and was complicated by the need to prevent their allies, the Turks, occupying the region, yet secure control of the Baku oilfields. This was accomplished in September 1918.

The Central Powers achieved military successes in the Balkans, but were unable to make any significant advances elsewhere. Thus by the end of 1915 Serbia, Montenegro and northern Albania had been occupied by Austro-Hungarian armies. The Austro-Hungarian authorities were, however, uncertain as to what to do with the territories and deferred a decision until the end of the war. Annexation was ruled out as this would have increased the Serb population of the Empire and with it the potential for disruption. In contrast to Germany, the Austro-Hungarian Empire possessed no workable war aims in an era of rising nationalism. Germany's other allies had specific war objectives. Bulgaria seized Macedonia and the Dobruja, while Greece occupied southern Albania. Turkish attempts to retake Egypt were unsuccessful as British and Indian forces repulsed the attack on the Suez Canal in April 1916.

In the course of the First World War Germany had the opportunity to redraw the map of eastern Europe with almost exclusive reference to its own perceived national self-interest. Its allies Austria-Hungary and the Ottoman Empire played little part in the exercise. Although the legal basis of the settlement, notably the Treaty of Brest Litovsk, was repudiated at the end of the war, many of the state entities established by Germany in this period survived as part of the subsequent peace settlement.

4.2 THE ALLIED RESPONSE

The Allied powers initially also had few clearly defined war aims. In August 1914 the Czar of Russia issued an appeal to the Poles for support in return for the promise of the creation of a united autonomous state, including the Congress Kingdom, Austrian Galicia and the Prussian section of Poland, under the Russian crown. Only the eastern portion of Austrian Galicia came under Russian control and was effectively incorporated into Russia for the duration of the two periods of occupation (September 1914 to June 1915 and July 1916 to June 1917). France regarded the recovery of Alsace-Lorraine as an indispensable part of any peace settlement and a measure of security against renewed German invasion, but the wider territorial implications of securing its position in Europe were not clear.

With the prolongation of the war and the need to extract some compensation for the vast toll of men and money which the prosecution of the war placed on them, the formulation of specific territorial aims ensued. Promises

Map 4.2 The Allied response

were made in a series of secret treaties to attract more allies into the war against Germany. Thus the British and French agreed in April 1915 to substantial Italian demands against Austria, in the Tyrol, Istria and Dalmatia, to attract the country into the war. Similarly Romania was enticed into the war in August 1916 with the promise of gaining extensive Austro-Hungarian lands, in Transylvania, Banat and Bukovina. Such agreements were about advantageous territorial changes, not the establishment of new sovereign states. Even a much reduced Albania was only to be revived as an Italian protectorate, with most of the country divided between Serbia, Montenegro and Greece. France had envisaged the establishment of an independent Poland, but even this emotional commitment to that country was abandoned in return for the promise of Russian support for establishment of the Rhine frontier in negotiations held in February 1917. The latter proposal provided for the creation of an autonomous and neutralised state on the west bank of the Rhine, garrisoned by French troops (Taylor, 1954: 556).

It was the entry of the United States into the war as an 'Associated Power', not linked to the secret agreements alluded to above, that changed the Allied position. President Woodrow Wilson wished to introduce some concept of morality into the conduct of foreign affairs and abandon the system of secret treaties and territorial enrichment that had characterised the conduct of the war diplomacy until that time. In January 1918 the President laid down a plan for a peace settlement in the 'Fourteen Points'. The first five provided for the regulation of international affairs and the establishment of a legal and organisational framework for doing so in 'a general association of nations'. The remaining nine points concerned specific territorial issues required for the stable settlement of Europe. They included the evacuation of Russia, the restoration of Belgium and the occupied French provinces and of Alsace-Lorraine, an adjustment of the boundaries of Italy along clearly recognisable lines of nationality, autonomy for the peoples of Austria-Hungary, independence for the Balkan states, including the evacuation of Romania, Serbia and Montenegro and access to the sea for Serbia, autonomy for Turkey itself and for the nationalities under Turkish rule and finally independence for Poland with secure access to the sea. Clarification of the issues of self-determination came in further speeches in 1918 as the various leaders of the nationalities staked their claim to recognition. Such points were only enforceable after the complete defeat of Germany and Austria-Hungary.

In more immediate terms, the Allies had effectively driven the Germans from their colonies which they divided between them. The division was close to that finally effected at the peace settlement in 1919. In Africa, the French and British divided Togo and Cameroon between them, German East Africa was occupied by Great Britain, although the mountainous kingdoms of Ruanda and Urundi were taken by Belgium. Belgian claims to a larger piece of territory were rejected. Finally South West Africa was occupied by South African forces. In the Pacific, Australia occupied German New Guinea and some of the adjacent islands, including Nauru. Its wider expectations of gaining all the North West Pacific Islands were thwarted by the immediate Japanese entry into the war and its occupation of the

Caroline Islands, Mariana Islands and most of the Marshall Islands that lay north of the equator. Japan also occupied Kiaochow in China. Finally New Zealand occupied German Samoa. Effectively these territories were administered by the occupying powers for their own gain for the duration of the war. German plans for the expansion of its colonial empire, notably in central Africa, in the event of victory had no basis in the reality of the military situation.

4.3   THE ALLIED PLANNED PARTITION OF TURKEY

The Allied response to the war involved a number of complex sets of mutual negotiations concerning both the immediate disposition of territory and eventual plans for the peace. The most significant concern was the final demise of the Ottoman Empire. Turkey joined Germany in November 1914 and the Allies proceeded to anticipate its final collapse. Great Britain deposed the Khedive, Abbas Hilmi, and declared a formal protectorate over Egypt and annexed Cyprus, both of which had been nominal parts of the Ottoman Empire, although under British occupation and, in the case of Cyprus, administration.

Negotiations between the Allies in March 1915 resulted in Russia gaining approval for the post-war occupation of Constantinople and the Straits linking the Black Sea and the Mediterranean Sea. This had been one of the country's major long-term strategic and emotional goals as perceived heir to the Empire of Byzantium. This was probably the most important secret treaty of the First World War as it involved the reversal of more than a hundred years of French and British diplomacy and even the Crimean War in the 1850s to prevent such an eventuality. In January 1916 the Sykes–Picot agreement between France and Great Britain provided for Syria, including Mount Lebanon, to be allotted to France and Mesopotamia (Iraq) to Great Britain at the end of the war. Later, in September 1916, an agreement was reached that Russia was to obtain Armenia and Kurdistan, while in April 1917 Italy was to obtain the promise of a substantial portion of Asia Minor, adjacent to the Dodecanese Islands. These promises were to conflict with Greek aspirations to take the Greek inhabited Smyrna region of Anatolia and Constantinople if possible. In addition, France, Great Britain and Italy were to receive extensive spheres of influence adjacent to their acquisitions. Finally under the Sykes–Picot agreement, Palestine, including Jerusalem, was to become an international territory. The resultant rump Turkish state was

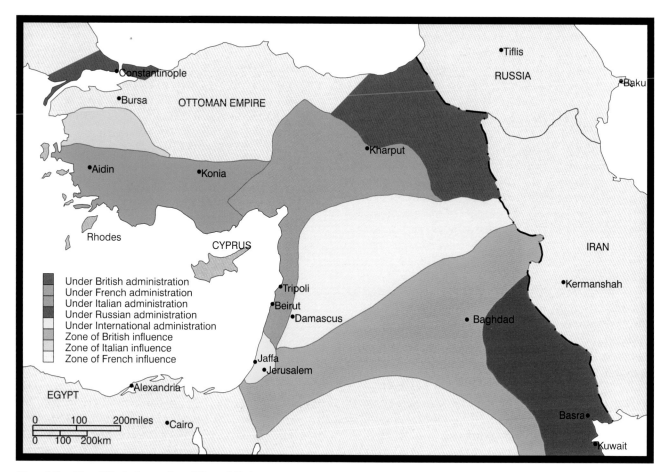

Map 4.3   The Allied planned partition of Turkey

reduced to a remarkably small portion of the pre-war Empire. The secret agreements also contradicted the concept of national self-determination enunciated by President Wilson.

The secret treaties, particularly the Sykes–Picot agreement, were at variance with other agreements concluded in February 1916 with the Sharif Hussein of Hejez and the Arab nationalists for the independence of Syria and adjacent lands. In June 1916 the revolt in Mecca began and in December the independence of Hejez was recognised by Great Britain. In December 1915 Great

Britain had recognised the independence of the Emir Ibn Saud of Nejd, which ran counter to the wider pan-Arab ambitions of the Sharif Hussein. Finally, in November 1917, the Balfour Declaration committed Great Britain to the establishment of a Jewish 'National Home' in Palestine. Some of these agreements were carried out after the war, but others remained completely unfulfilled in the light of the events which followed. The unscrambling of the many promises made anticipating the demise of the Ottoman Empire was to dominate the politics of the region for the remainder of the century.

CHAPTER 5

The Springtime of the Nations 1918–1923

The First World War had a profound effect upon the political map of the world. Defeat in the war shattered a number of the multi-national empires that had been significant building blocks of the political system for centuries. The era can be described as the 'springtime of the nations', as President Wilson's principle of national self-determination was applied to areas previously under the control of the empires. Eastern Europe in particular underwent a dramatic transformation as a result of the collapse of the Austro-Hungarian, German and Russian Empires, while the final demise of the Ottoman Empire led to the re-emergence of independent Arab countries on the world map. The German colonial empire also disappeared from the world map as its possessions were divided among the conquerors. Even the victorious powers were not immune to the forces of self-determination. The British Empire was affected by anti-British nationalism, as events in Ireland and Egypt demonstrated, while the increasing and wide-ranging autonomy of the dominions strained the fiction of a unified Empire. However, for a brief period (1919–1922) the British Empire expanded yet further to cover 35.6 million square kilometres with a population of approximately 450 million (Christopher, 1988). The Empire was territorially the largest empire ever constructed and the only remaining world military superpower, even if ambition and the resources to effect those ambitions were mismatched.

5.1 THE WORLD IN 1923

The First World War had resulted in some six million deaths and war damage of the order of £3000–5000 million. The Allied war costs amounted to over £24 000 million. The Allied leaders had made the promise that it had been 'a war to end all wars'. The peace settlement was thus a vital part of giving effect to the ideals propagated during the war and making it permanent. The establishment of the League of Nations, to oversee the conduct of international affairs, and the Permanent Court of International Justice, to adjudicate in cases of conflict between states, were the cornerstones of the new, more open and democratic world to emerge from the war.

The five years after the end of the First World War were ones of turmoil for the states within the world system, both internally and internationally. The process of concluding the peace was far lengthier than the victorious allies could have imagined in November 1918. The peace conference opened in January 1919 in Paris and continued until January 1920, followed by a Conference of Ambassadors appointed to complete the negotiations (Sharp, 1991). The treaties were named after the various locations around Paris where the treaties were signed. The most significant was the Treaty of Versailles between the Allies and Germany in June 1919. This was followed by that with Austria at St Germain, Bulgaria at Neuilly, Hungary at Trianon and finally the Ottoman Empire at Sevres in August 1920. The latter required complete revision as a result of the Turkish military revival and the subsequent final peace treaty between Turkey and the Allies was only signed at Lausanne

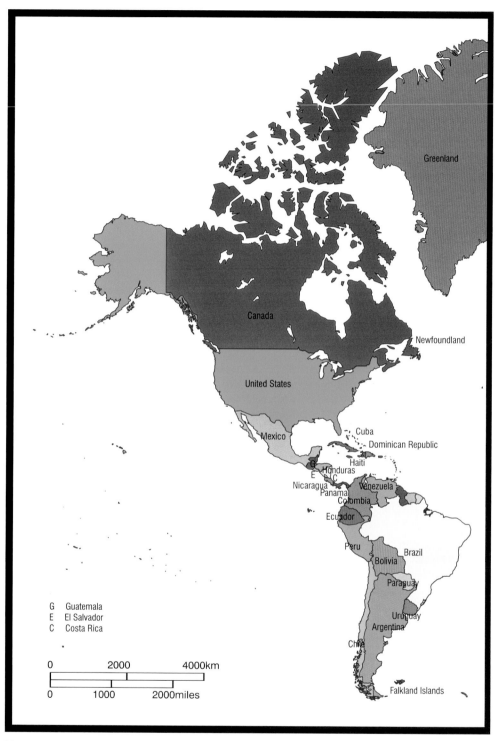

Map 5.1   The world in 1923

C   Czechoslovakia
H   Hungary
Y   Yugoslavia

in July 1923. This treaty ultimately demarcated the national boundary between Greece and Turkey and provided for the exchange of minorities identified on the basis of religion rather than language (Beeley, 1978).

In the course of the period 1918–1923 some eleven new states gained international recognition, while one pre-war state, Montenegro, was merged with its more powerful neighbour. At the same time at least a dozen bids for independence proved to be ephemeral as peripheral provinces were reincorporated by revived central governments.

On the world map the Americas experienced only one change in the course of the war, the transfer of the Danish West Indies (Virgin Islands) to the United States. This degree of stability is remarkable in an era of dramatic change in Europe and Asia. In Africa and the Pacific the German colonies had been apportioned amongst the victors. Elsewhere internal reorganisation of territorial holdings resulted in the emergence of new colonies, notably in Africa. Of particular importance for the political development of the world in the twentieth century was the emergence of the Soviet Union (Union of Soviet Socialist Republics) on the territory of the previous Russian Empire.

5.2 EUROPE IN 1923

The impact of nationalism was most forcefully demonstrated in Europe, where the cultural and political movements associated with minority nationalisms had been operative in the nineteenth and early twentieth centuries. Higher levels of education and government supervision of people's lives resulted not only in the reinforcement of dominant nationalisms but also in the fostering of those of minority groups not reconciled with the ethos of the state. The disintegration of previous loyalties through revolution and the abolition of traditional monarchies had a profound effect upon the perceived identities of many groups during a period of turmoil and uncertainty associated with the First World War and its aftermath. It is worth noting that none of the new European states adopted a monarchical form of government after the war; all became national republics.

The Paris peace settlement and subsequent treaties in Eastern Europe involved a massive rearrangement of territory on the continent. The central feature so far as the security of the continent was concerned was the position of Germany as determined by the Treaty of Versailles. At the settlement Germany lost 12.4 percent (72 500 square kilometres) of its area and approximately 12 percent (7.2 million) of its population. It should be noted that of this lost

7 million people, 58 percent were German speakers. The Allied military occupation of the Rhineland, which remained in place until June 1930, was designed to prevent any resurgence of German offensive military capability. The German Republic was racked by political tensions immediately after the war as revolutions had swept away the traditional monarchies and the new state administrations sought a new constitutional relationship, based on a centralised and unified state. A Bavarian Soviet republic was proclaimed in April 1919, but the central government was able to suppress the secessionist movement. Separatism was also present in the Rhineland, but the new central government was able to re-establish control. The French occupation of the Ruhr industrial area between January 1923 and July 1925 was a last attempt to undo the results of the German unification of 1871.

Austria, the major territorial loser of the war, was reduced to a small mountainous state with only 6.5 million inhabitants. The raison d'etre of the state was abruptly ended with the abolition of the monarchy. The personal union with Hungary was broken as the latter became a fully independent state with the abdication of the Emperor Charles II in November 1918. The rump Austrian state effectively became a second German national entity. Indeed the name adopted briefly in 1918–1919 was German-Austria. The new government sought to unite Austria with Germany, and the new constitution declared German-Austria to be a part of the German Republic. This was blocked by the Allies who had no desire to see Germany increase in area after the war. Austria was thus denied its first choice of opting to end independent status.

Even the unity of the rump Austrian state was challenged. The government of the province of Vorarlberg, with its population of approximately 140 000, sought to secede from Austria and join Switzerland. In a referendum held in May 1919 some 80.3 percent of the electorate supported union with Switzerland (Jelavich, 1987). However, the Allied powers, notably France, resisted the move as it had the potential to upset the delicate religious and linguistic balance within the Swiss Confederation and further destabilise the rump Austrian state. The Tyrol declared its independence in May 1919, in an attempt to preserve the integrity of the German-speaking region, but the Italian occupation of the whole of the area south of the Brenner Pass resulted in a reconsideration of the move. Subsequently both the Tyrol (April 1921) and Salzburg (May 1921) voted to join Germany with 98.6 percent and 99.3 percent support respectively. Both demands were resisted internally by the Austrian government and externally by the Allied powers as contrary to the Versailles settlement.

Map 5.2   Europe in 1923

The position of Luxembourg was particularly precarious after the war as Germany had occupied it during the war and Belgium demanded its incorporation afterwards (Newcomer, 1984). The Grand Duchess Adelaide abdicated in favour of her sister Charlotte and a referendum on the future of the country was held in September 1919. Some 77.8 percent of the citizens voted for continued independence and retention of the monarchy. Only 19.7 percent opted for a republic. At the same time 73.3 percent approved economic union with France, following withdrawal from the German Zollverein. However, France declined and following further negotiations, economic union with Belgium was effected in December 1921. Liechtenstein similarly left the Austrian customs union in

August 1919 and joined the Swiss union in March 1923.

The creation of Czechoslovakia was the solution to a number of political problems attendant upon the dissolution of the Empire. The Czechs of Bohemia and Moravia, astutely led by Tomas Masaryk, sought independence and gained Allied support. They claimed and received their historic boundaries, which included three million German speakers. This was not thought to be an insuperable problem for the new state. Within the former Hungary the Slovaks and the Carpetho-Ukrainians presented different issues. The Slovaks were linguistically related to the Czechs and their leaders were attracted to the political link as a means of resisting what was regarded as the continuing threat from Hungary. The Slovak National Council therefore opted for unification with the Czechs as the 'Czechoslovak nation', rather than separate independence. The parallel with the other Slav union, Yugoslavia, is relevant to the concept of gaining political and military strength from membership of larger groupings rather than recognising small weak nationalities.

The question of the status of Carpetho-Ukraine was more complex and demonstrates the problems of defining nations and states and drawing political boundaries (Magocsi, 1993a). The dissolution of the Austro-Hungarian Empire offered the Ukrainian-speaking population of the region a range of choices. The territory was too small to opt for independence, although the mountainous Hutsul Republic, to the east, maintained its independence from January to July 1919. Initially, in December 1918, the government of the Hungarian Republic assumed it would retain its historic links and granted the Ruthenian Lands a special autonomous status. At the same time the Western Ukrainian National Republic declared in November 1918 in Lwow (Lemberg) sought to incorporate all the Ukrainian lands of the former Empire, including Galicia, Trans-Carpethia and northern Bukovina, into one state. The complex history of the Ukraine culminated in the Polish occupation of the whole of Galicia by July 1919, effectively cutting the region off from the main block of Ukrainian lands.

The continued Ruthenian constitutional link with Hungary was severed with the seizure of power by the Communists under Bela Kun in March 1919. The Allies supported international military intervention against the Communists. Following their defeat the Romanians occupied Hutsul and Czechs the remainder of the Ruthenian lands in June–July 1919. The driving force for the incorporation of the region into Czechoslovakia came from an unexpected source. The Transcarpathians (Hungarian Russians) in the United States had a profound influence upon the development of the area. The community chose a Pittsburgh lawyer, Gregory Zhatkovych, to find a solution for their compatriots still in Europe. Initially opinions had favoured independence, but their size suggested this was not a viable proposition. However, Tomas Masaryk, while on a visit to America, urged the community to join the future Czechoslovakia where their civil rights and autonomy would be respected. In November 1918 a referendum among Ruthenians living in the United States on the proposal resulted in 68 percent voting to join Czechoslovakia (Magosci, 1996). The Czechoslovak government based its occupation upon this endorsement by the diaspora nation.

5.3   THE DEFINITION OF POLAND

One of the most remarkable features of the new map of Europe was the re-emergence of Poland as an independent country. The resurrection of Poland had been one of President Wilson's 'Fourteen Points' for the promotion of a lasting peace in the post-war world issued in January 1918. His Thirteenth Point read: 'An independent Polish State should be erected which should include the territories inhabited by indisputably Polish populations, which should be assured a free and secure access to the sea, and whose political and economic independence and territorial integrity should be guaranteed by international covenant' (Levine, 1973: 9). It is worth noting that Germany alone signed an armistice with the Allied and associated powers on the basis of President Wilson's Fourteen Points. It had done so in the expectation of using the negotiations to exploit such concepts as self-determination in retaining as much territory as possible. However, the negotiations did not take place as anticipated. The subsequent terms of the Treaty of Versailles, notably the provisions concerning Poland, were regarded as unacceptable to the leaders of the new German Republic. They had expected a reward for dismantling the militaristic Empire and instituting a democratic regime. The terms had to be imposed by the Allies through an ultimatum to renew the war.

Inevitably after such a long period of partition under foreign control, the leaders of the new Polish state sought at the Paris peace conference to gain as much territory as possible. They planned to re-establish the boundaries of Poland as they had been before the first of the partitions that had eliminated the country from the map of Europe at the end of the eighteenth century. These demands inevitably impinged upon the claims to national self-determination of other nations. Most problematically they involved gaining recognition of these demands by neighbouring countries.

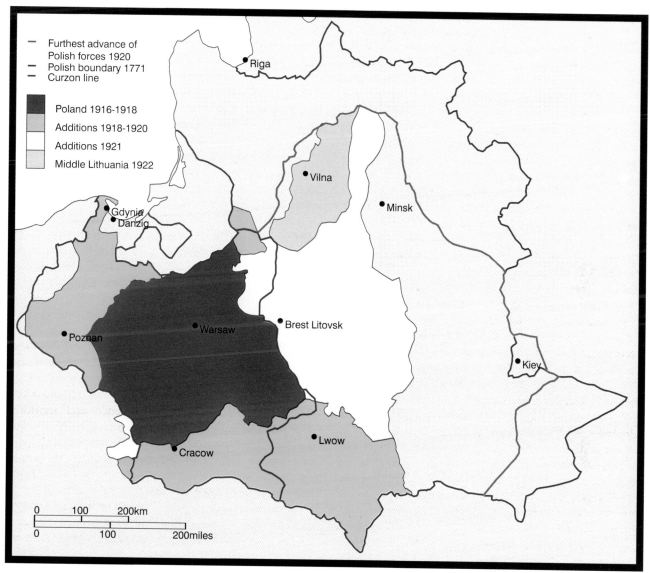

Map 5.3   The definition of Poland

The result was a period of warfare of fluctuating fortunes during which Russian forces reached the outskirts of Warsaw and the Poles occupied Kiev.

The demarcation of the area inhabited by Polish speakers was an alternative point of departure for establishing the new state as a nation-state. The western boundaries with Germany were defined in the Treaty of Versailles with the areas still disputed by Poland subject to plebiscite. However, the key to national viability, access to the Baltic Sea through the 'Polish Corridor', was problematical as the territorial corridor included large numbers of German speakers, and the main port at the mouth of the Vistula River, Danzig, was overwhelmingly German in character and population (see Section 5.7). Despite strong French support for Poland, Danzig was constituted an international territory under the control of the League of Nations. The corridor remained a matter of intense controversy. The identification of a separate ethnic group, the Kaschubes, in the north, confused the issue and was exploited by treaty revisionists in the period up to 1939 (Herb, 1997).

Poland's eastern boundaries presented far greater problems of definition and it brought the state into conflict with Russia, the Ukraine and Lithuania.

Historical and ethnic claims diverged markedly. Polish speakers only formed a majority of the population in much of the old Congress Kingdom and West Galicia. Indeed in an attempt to create an equitable boundary following the linguistic divide, Lord Curzon, the British Foreign Secretary, had proposed a line in December 1919 similar to that drawn in 1945. It was rejected by the Polish government in favour of historic precedent. Polish claims to the extensive eastern territories rested upon the personal union of the crowns of Poland and Lithuania in 1386 and the subsequent closer union of 1569. In the subsequent partitions of the late eighteenth century most of these eastern territories had been seized by Russia and administered as integral parts of the Empire.

Eastern Galicia, which had been part of Austria prior to the war, was inhabited by Ruthenians or Ukrainians. Many people adhered to the Uniate Church, which acknowledged Papal supremacy but retained Orthodox liturgy and organisation. They had also achieved greater economic prosperity than Ukrainians living in the former Russian lands. This distinctiveness led to the establishment of the Western Ukraine National Republic for a short post-war period (November 1918 to January 1919). The subsequent merger of Western Ukraine with the Ukraine was brief as the Polish population, particularly of the towns, were able to prevail in securing the region's adhesion to Poland in July 1919. The wider Polish claim to the Ukraine had been thwarted in the war with first the Ukraine and then Russia, but by the Treaty of Riga in March 1921, Poland was able to secure a substantial part of the area of the pre-1772 state area (Dziewanowski, 1977).

The Polish government also wished to re-establish the union with Lithuania, but this was rejected by the Lithuanian leaders as they had the brief Lithuanian–Byelorussian Soviet Republic of 1919. In the struggle between the two countries, the Lithunian capital, Vilnius, and eastern Lithuania were occupied by Polish irregular forces under General Lucjan Zeligowski in October 1920, proclaiming the establishment of a separate state of Middle Lithuania. Subsequently in April 1922 the transitional government requested incorporation into Poland, which was then effected (Dziewanowski, 1969). This act was not recognised by Lithuania and the border between the two countries remained closed. Poland as it emerged after the First World War thus included substantial minorities, which were to be a source of weakness in the 1930s.

5.4   THE CREATION OF YUGOSLAVIA

In view of the origins of the First World War in Sarajevo, the settlement of the Serb national issue was of prime importance for the Paris peace conference. The defeat and disintegration of the Austro-Hungarian Empire afforded the South Slav leaders a unique opportunity to unite all those lands inhabited by Serbs, Croats and Slovenes into a single state. Such a union had been envisaged by exiled leaders in a pact agreed upon at the seat of the Serbian government-in-exile on the island of Corfu in July 1917. In recognition of the multi-ethnic origin of the new state it was named the Kingdom of the Serbs, Croats and Slovenes. King Peter of Serbia was invited to become the first constitutional monarch of the new state. In practice the new state was a Greater Serbia, with the attendant strains that such a centralisation of power entailed. Indeed the first national elections were only held in November 1920. The brief attempt in July 1919 to establish a separate Croatian republic was symptomatic of the unease which centralisation inspired, and the fact that most Croats and Slovenes had been loyal subjects of the Austro-Hungarian Empire until its final collapse.

In November 1918, with the defeat of Austria-Hungary, the constituent parts began to disintegrate and the majority of South Slav political leaders recognised that their future lay with victorious Serbia. The authorities in Bosnia-Herzegovina sought an accommodation as the Empire disintegrated. The Croat Diet declared its willingness to join the Serbs and end the link with Hungary. Finally the Slovene political leaders similarly sought rapprochement with the victors. There remained the question of the future of the independent kingdom of Montenegro. After the Serbian occupation, King Nicholas was deposed in November 1918 and the Montenegrin government also sought inclusion within the new state. This represented one of the few losses to the state system from the pre-war era. Conflict with Italy over the control of Dalmatia was resolved largely in Yugoslavia's favour, through reciprocal concessions over the port of Fiume. The rulers of the new state had achieved virtually all the aims of the most ardent Slavophile of 1914.

Following the royal coup d'etat in January 1929 the country was renamed Yugoslavia, as part of the programme to emphasise the creation of a new united South Slav nation. However, Croat resistance to the policy of centralisation was increasingly violent, leading to instability and ultimately the assassination of King Alexander in October 1934. Only in August 1939 was a

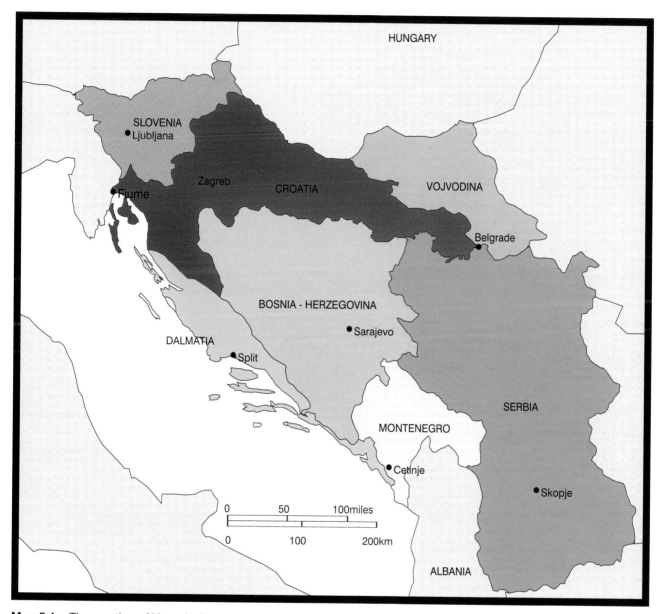

Map 5.4   The creation of Yugoslavia

significant measure of internal self-government awarded to a newly defined Croat province, which included both Slavonia and Dalmatia. The granting of this limited measure of autonomy was insufficient to unite the country in the face of external pressures in the Second World War.

Closely linked to the creation of the South Slav state was the fate of Albania. In January 1920 a National Congress had been convened to re-establish the Albanian state, within its 1913 boundaries. The Italians agreed to abandon their claim to the country, based on the secret treaty of London, in return for the establishment of the Free City of Fiume, and evacuated the country in August 1920. This had the added result that the Serbians and Montenegrins and Greeks were also forced to surrender their gains for Albania to be reconstituted (Jelavich and Jelavich, 1977). The process was only completed in 1922 when Greece, after the debacle in Anatolia and the defeat of its attempt to gain territory in western Turkey, was forced to abandon Northern Epirus to the reconstituted Albanian state.

5.5   THE PARTITION OF IRELAND

The partition of Ireland represented the emergence of another nation-state, albeit somewhat restricted in terms of sovereignty. The long history of English and later British colonisation in Ireland dating back to the twelfth century had resulted in an equally long history of conflict, bloodshed and hostility (Pringle, 1985). Modern Irish nationalism revolved around the emergence of a Celtic cultural revival allied to a strong sense of Roman Catholic separatism from the Protestant ethos of the United Kingdom government. Land seizures, political exclusion and the traumatic effects of the potato famine of 1845–1850 added to the resentment of the majority of the population of the island. However, in the north and indeed thinly scattered across the whole of the country was a Protestant minority which sought to preserve its British identity and the United Kingdom as constituted. Even the solution of the land question at the end of the nineteenth century did nothing to diminish the rise of Irish nationalism (Bull, 1996).

The British Liberal government elected in January 1906 sought to introduce a measure of self-government to Ireland as a means of solving the Anglo-Irish conflict yet preserving the Union. Initially this move was blocked by the House of Lords, but between 1912 and 1914, following constitutional reforms, the projected imposition of home rule appeared to be leading to civil war. The Irish Home Rule Act was finally passed in September 1914. However,

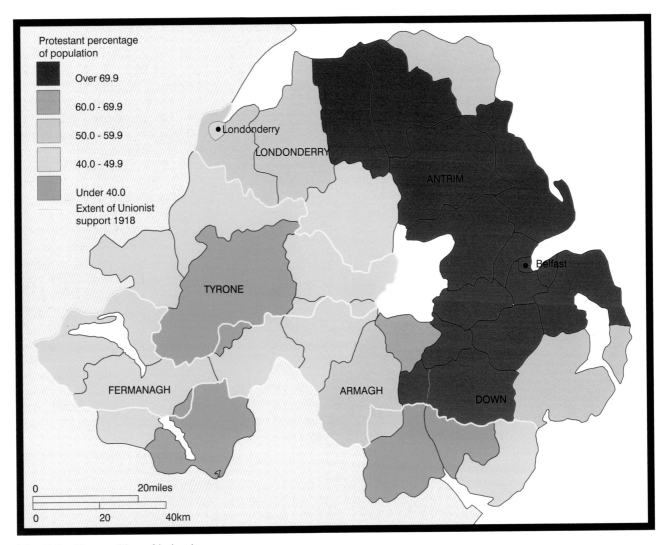

Map 5.5   The partition of Ireland

the introduction of home rule was postponed for the duration of the First World War. The wartime emergency, particularly the demands for manpower, was such as to exacerbate the situation.

In April 1916 the Irish Republican Brotherhood staged an attempted coup d'etat in Dublin and declared Ireland an independent republic. The Easter Rising was ruthlessly suppressed but it symbolically created the political climate for a more radical break with the past. In the British General Election of December 1918, Sinn Fein, the political wing of the Irish Republican Brotherhood (later Army), won 73 of the 105 Irish seats in parliament (Walker, 1978). Rather than take their seats in the Westminster parliament, they constituted themselves as the Provisional Government of Ireland and met in Dublin in January 1919 (Younger, 1970). However, the Irish delegation to the Paris peace conference failed to obtain recognition.

The inconclusive nature of the ensuing civil war, between the two governments contending for control of the island, forced the British government to reach a compromise agreement with the Irish nationalists in December 1921. The Anglo-Irish Treaty provided for the partition of the island between the Irish Free State and Northern Ireland, which would remain part of the United Kingdom. The former was granted dominion status, but not republican status, and was accorded membership of the League of Nations, while Northern Ireland obtained internal self-government with its own elected government. A significant republican faction did not accept the Anglo-Irish Treaty but was defeated in the subsequent civil war, which dragged on from June 1922 to May 1923. The divide between the two factions was to dominate Irish politics for the remainder of the century.

Significantly British forces evacuated the Irish Free State, emphasising its political and military separation from the British Empire. This alienation was furthered in the Second World War by the Irish declaration of neutrality. However, the country when admitted to the League of Nations did so under the same conditions as the other British dominions. Ireland only formally left the British Empire and Commonwealth in April 1949, long after any thought of common political purpose by its members had been rejected.

The concept of partition had been accepted by the British government in April 1914 as a temporary measure as a means of assuaging the opposition of the northern Unionists to a united Ireland. Massive Unionist support for the British war effort strengthened their position after the war to include as many Protestants as possible in the section to remain as part of the United Kingdom. Thus the physical partition of the island was based largely upon the distribution of religious affiliations, which broadly converted into political support. The six counties of Ulster which constituted Northern Ireland had been colonised by Scottish settlers in the seventeenth century, creating contiguous blocks of Protestant settlement, whereas the smaller scale colonisation in the south had failed to achieve a majority anywhere outside ephemeral control of the towns and cities.

The partition inevitably left minorities behind, particularly as Northern Ireland was drawn to include two counties with overall Roman Catholic majorities, in order to incorporate the Protestant areas of Fermanagh. Subsequent attempts to redraw the boundary in November 1925 failed as the exercise was considered to give an added appearance of permanency to the line (Andrews, 1960). Thus nearly a third of the population of Northern Ireland was Roman Catholic, with a high measure of identification with the republican cause and the Irish state to the south. Further, the final Irish constitution promulgated in December 1937 claimed the whole of the island of Ireland as its sovereign territory, thereby refusing to recognise the legitimacy of the Northern Ireland government.

Irish Gaelic was declared the official language of the Irish Free State and its constitutional successors. Gaelic had been superseded by English in most areas of the country. Only a few scattered areas in the western counties continued to use Gaelic as a mother tongue (Johnson, 1993). These areas were declared the Gaeltacht region in 1926 with various political and economic incentives offered to promote the use of the language as a means of converting the country back to the use of Gaelic. Attempts to introduce Gaelic-speaking colonists from the western counties into the east were not successful in re-establishing the language as a spoken means of communication (Nolan, 1988). The use of Gaelic, and the requirement of a measure of proficiency in the language for appointment to civil service posts, remained more a political issue to emphasise the differences between the Irish State and Northern Ireland than a full-scale revival. It was the influence of the Roman Catholic Church which was crucial in projecting an Irish identity, while the marked decline in the size of the Protestant minority in the State resulted in a high degree of homogeneity (Keogh, 1996).

5.6 PLEBISCITE AREAS

One of the unusual features of the peace settlement was the recourse to plebiscites to settle the future of particularly contentious areas. These were mostly related to the final disposition of German and Austrian territory. As such the

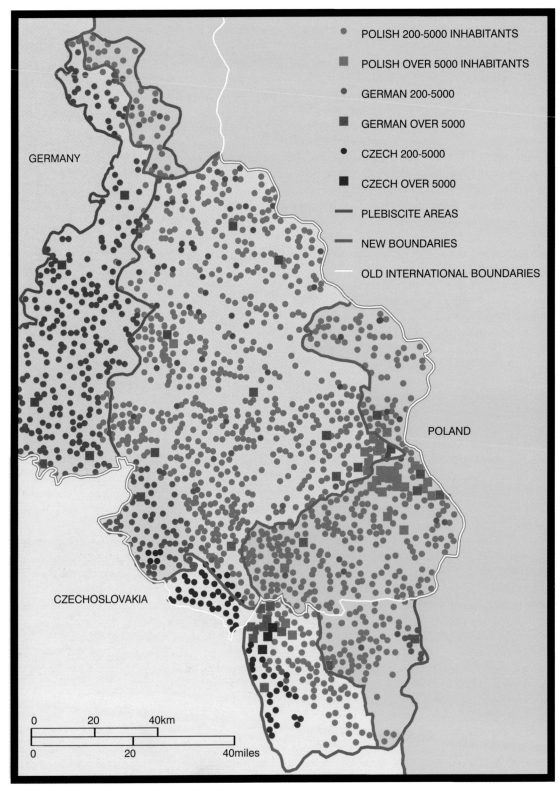

Map 5.6   Plebiscite areas (Upper Silesia)

territories were administered by international commissions prior to and immediately after the plebiscites. In some cases, notably Upper Silesia, an international regime continued to regulate specified affairs of the region for some years thereafter.

Upper Silesia was the largest and most important area to be subjected to a plebiscite to determine its future. The conflict between Germany to retain and Poland to obtain control was dominated by the resources of the coalfield, which offered to provide a degree of economic viability to the new state. The area had not been part of pre-1772 Poland, but contained an overwhelming Polish population majority. The province of Upper Silesia had been established by Germany late in the war as a means of preventing the Allies from possibly transferring the whole of historic Silesia to Poland. However, the Allies realised that to transfer even the smaller province to Poland would so weaken Germany that it probably would not be able to pay reparations and would also lead to the creation of a substantial irredentist problem for the new Polish state. Invoking the holding of a plebiscite was considered the best option in order to defer a final decision on Silesia's future, and so prevent a popular rejection of the treaty terms in Germany. After the signing of the Treaty of Versailles in June 1919, an international allied commission administered the province in preparation for the plebiscite which was held in May 1921. The final international boundary line was only drawn in October 1921, and the formal cession only took place in May 1922, over three years after the end of the war.

Despite the presence of a large Polish-speaking majority, some 63 percent of the electorate voted for the security of remaining part of Germany. The province was then partitioned by the commission between the two countries and a complex convention was signed between the two countries for the regulation of the coalfield and its infrastructure. A mixed commission was appointed to administer the convention and a procedure for arbitration over disputes was established, with ultimate referral to the Council of the League of Nations or the Permanent Court of International Justice at The Hague.

The two plebiscite areas in East Prussia at Allenstein and Marienwerder were designed to offer Poland the opportunity to widen the corridor of land to the Baltic Sea. However, despite the Polish linguistic majority in both areas, the largely Lutheran population voted to remain part of Germany in July 1920.

The plebiscite in Schleswig was particularly significant as Denmark had been neutral in the war. It represented the implementation of a clause in the Treaty of Prague ending the Austro-Prussian War in 1866, which had provided the inhabitants of North Schleswig with the option of reunion with Denmark if they should so decide in a free vote. Prussia did not implement the promise and it was formally abrogated in 1878, while a thorough-going Germanisation programme was implemented in the Danish-speaking areas. After the war Denmark was able to gain support for its claim to the area from the allies. The plebiscite area was divided into two zones, roughly separated by the linguistic divide. In February and March 1920 the plebiscites were held and the northern zone returned to Denmark and the southern zone to Germany.

Two plebiscite regimes were established to determine the final borders of Austria. On the Austro-Hungarian boundary the linguistic line was accepted as the basis for the new inter-state boundary, resulting in the transfer of a section of Hungary, the new province of Burgenland, to Austria. However, the main town Sopron (Odenburg) voted in December 1921 to remain in Hungary. The second plebiscite area in Carinthia was contested between Austria and the new South Slav state. The southern portion was largely populated by Slovenes and so considered likely to join Yugoslavia, while the northern portion was predominantly German, but economically integrated with the south. The international commission divided the plebiscite area into two and in October 1920 the southern zone voted to remain under Austrian control. No vote was therefore required in the northern sector which automatically reverted to Austria. Again the plebiscites demonstrated the basic conservatism of the populations polled and the disaffection towards the nationalist policies of the new states. In most cases the results were an endorsement of the pre-war status quo.

It is worth considering those areas that might have been subject to an internationally supervised plebiscite but were not. Thus under the terms of the armistice the Germans had to evacuate Alsace-Lorraine within 15 days. No test of support for restoration to France was contemplated as French national pride could not accept the possibility of rejection. Similarly Belgium acquired the strategic towns of Eupen and Malmedy and the previous neutral territory of Moresnet following a nominal plebiscite in September 1920. At first glance the results are surprising as the 60 000 inhabitants were virtually all German speakers. However, the plebiscite was conducted under Belgian supervision and most significantly took the form of public declarations. As a result, the procedure was boycotted by the great majority of the inhabitants, who were unreconciled to the change. In other areas, notably Teschen, and Zips on the Polish-Czechoslovak boundaries, projected plebiscites were cancelled and disputes settled by inter-governmental agreements. Elsewhere force rather than public opinion determined boundary definition.

5.7 INTERNATIONAL TERRITORIES

Another of the innovative features of the Paris peace settlement was the practical introduction of the concept of international territories, administered under the auspices of the League of Nations. In its most expansive manifestation the League acted as the guarantor of the mandatory regimes of the territories of the previous German and Turkish empires. However, it was as a solution to the smaller problem territories, which could not be settled by means of a plebiscite, that the concept of an international territory was most useful.

Again the international territories were mostly associated with the Treaty of Versailles and the disposition of German territory. The most important was the Free City of Danzig at the mouth of the Vistula River. The original proposal to include the city in Poland was rejected by the peace conference as flouting the principle of national self-determination, as the population was overwhelmingly German. In order to provide a guarantee for Polish trade in transit through the port, an international regime was selected as a compromise solution. The demarcated city of some 1914 square kilometres had contained a population of 330 000 inhabitants before the war. Danzig had enjoyed a high degree of autonomy under Polish rule from 1454 until the Prussian annexation in 1793, and again as a Free City between 1807 and 1814 under the French, so the proposed regime had historic precedence.

Danzig was only occupied by the Allies in February 1920 and formally proclaimed a Free City in November 1920 (Kimmich, 1968). It was governed by a League of Nations appointed High Commissioner and local Popular Assembly. The Danzig government did on occasion claim that it enjoyed sovereign status, but in reality the Polish presence imposed substantial limitations upon that status. The system worked well until May 1933 when the German National Socialist Party came to power in Danzig and pressed for the end of the special Free City status (Levine, 1973). The destruction of the Free City regime as part of the German invasion of Poland in September 1939 was the ostensible cause of the Second World War.

The Saar basin was the only other significant case of internationalisation in February 1920. An area of 1927 square kilometres covering the coalfield was detached from Germany and placed under an international regime for 15 years. Its final status was then to be determined by a referendum. The complementary resources of the Lorraine iron ore fields and the Saar coalfield had been developed during the period of German rule in Lorraine after 1871. Following the return of Lorraine to France, this economic unity was to be maintained by French control of the coalfields under the international regime. The arrangement was initiated as a substitute for annexation which would have been counter to the principle of self-determination.

The remaining free territories proved to be ephemeral. The port of Memel (Klaipeda) and that part of East Prussia which lay north of the River Niemen were occupied by an international force after the war and an international regime established in February 1920. The area, covering 2657 square kilometres, had a pre-war population of only 141 000 inhabitants. However, in January 1923 the Lithuanians fermented a revolt against the French dominated international regime and the local Diet voted for union with Lithuania. In May 1924 the League of Nations agreed to the incorporation under the Memel Convention. However, the territory was subject to a measure of international control and guaranteed a measure of autonomy.

The Free City of Fiume on the Adriatic coast was also short-lived. Under Hungarian rule it had gained special status as the national port. Its population was predominantly Italian, but the surrounding countryside was inhabited by Croats. Under the secret Treaty of London in 1915, which provided for Italian territorial gains after the war, the Italian negotiators had assumed that the Hungarian state, including Croatia, would survive the war and so Fiume was not included in the Italian zone. However, the Italians refused to recognise Yugoslav control and an international regime under Italian supervision was installed. In September 1919 Gabriele D'Annunzio seized the city to secure Italian interests. In November 1920, under the Treaty of Rapallo, which resolved Italo-Yugoslav disputes, the boundaries of the Free City of Fiume were changed to include a coastal corridor link with Italy and the surrender of the suburb of Susak to Yugoslavia. Finally in January 1924 the Free City was incorporated into Italy.

Although the concept of international or free territories was highly suitable for solving the problem posed by contentious areas, it had severe limitations and few areas were administered by the League of Nations. The nation-states tended to negotiate for the incorporation of such territories, even if it required surrendering much of a claim in order to achieve some national expansion, as in the case of Yugoslavia over Fiume. However, a number of regions

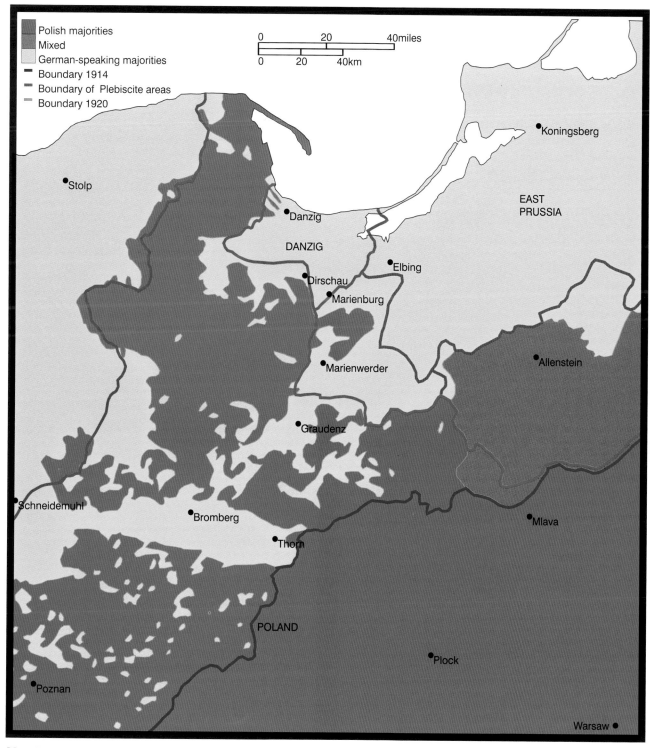

Map 5.7   International territories (Danzig)

did become subject to international regulation. Thus the Aland Islands of Finland at the entrance to the Gulf of Bothnia were demilitarised and received autonomy for the Swedish-speaking population in June 1921 (Barros, 1968). Significantly self-determination was not offered as an option. A special regime for Constantinople under the Treaty of Sevres (August 1920) was relaxed under the subsequent Treaty of Lausanne and the Straits Convention (July 1923). International supervision of the straits between the Black Sea and the Mediterranean Sea was abolished under the Montreaux Convention in 1936.

5.8 NEW STATES IN THE MIDDLE EAST

The destruction of the Ottoman Empire resulted in significant territorial rearrangements in the Middle East. Both the colonial powers and the local populations were involved in a struggle for power and territory. In the Arabian peninsula the end of Ottoman influence and rule resulted in the emergence of a number of independent states. The traditional chieftaincies achieved a degree of independence. Thus the rulers of Nejd (1916) and Jebel Shammar were freed of external interventions, while those in Yemen (1919) and Asir (1917) seized independence (Peterson, 1982). The most significant was the Sharif Hussein of Hejez who rose in revolt against Turkish rule and proclaimed himself King of Arabia in October 1916. He was recognised as King of Hejez and Protector of the Holy Palaces of Mecca and Medina by the British. At the end of the war his son, Faisal, occupied Damascus in October 1918 and was proclaimed King of Syria in March 1920, further extending the influence of the Hashemite family, and the independence of most of the Arab lands of the former Ottoman Empire appeared imminent.

However, the secret agreement between the Allied powers provided for a different disposition of territory. British forces were in control of Mesopotamia, subsequently renamed Iraq, and the Mediterranean coastal region from Palestine to northern Syria. The French took control of Lebanon, where an autonomous Christian administration had been under their influence before the war. The concept of directly administered territories interspersed with spheres of influence of the wartime was dropped in favour of greater direct intervention. Thus France secured a mandate to administer both the Lebanon and Syria, while Great Britain acquired mandates for Palestine and Iraq, which were made contiguous. No attempt was made to create an international regime for Jerusalem and vicinity as envisaged by the Sykes–Picot agreement of 1916.

The Middle Eastern settlement was complicated by the withdrawal of Russia from the war, thereby negating the substantial gains that had been promised under the secret wartime agreements. The subsequent recognition of Armenia and its claims in eastern Anatolia by the Allies had resulted in the definition of a large area for the country at the Treaty of Sevres. An autonomous Kurdistan was also placed on the map, with the prospect of independence, and the inclusion of Mosul in Iraq (Ahmad, 1994). However, the revival of Turkey under the republicans resulted in many of the grander plans for the region being curtailed. Armenia was partitioned between Russia and Turkey in December 1920. Kurdistan dissolved into civil war and was abandoned to Turkey and the northern boundaries of Syria were redrawn in favour of the Turks, while the French conquered the short-lived Hashemite kingdom of Syria in July 1920.

The British mandated area was divided into two sections, Iraq and Palestine. Iraq was administered as a kingdom, the throne of which was occupied in August 1921 by King Faisal as compensation for the loss of Syria. The mandate was terminated in October 1932 when the country was granted independence, following the policy of establishing client states rather than maintaining formal colonial control. The military revival of Turkey led to the abandonment of the plan to create an autonomous Kurdistan, with the result that in June 1926 the Sanjak of Mosul was formally attached to Iraq.

The Palestine mandate was the subject of one of the most controversial decisions of the war. In November 1917, Lord Balfour, the British Foreign Secretary, issued the declaration that bears his name, which affirmed British support for 'the establishment in Palestine of a national home for the Jewish people' (Biger, 1994). Under the League of Nations mandate granted to Great Britain in April 1920, the British government undertook responsibility for 'placing the country under such political, administrative and economic conditions as will secure the establishment of the Jewish national home'. Yet it also undertook to 'safeguard the interests of the community', more especially their land rights. Such undertakings were in reality mutually exclusive as subsequent events were to demonstrate.

The mandatory area was divided for administrative convenience in April 1921, between Transjordan, which was granted autonomy under the rule of the Emir Abdullah, King Faisal's brother in May 1923, and Palestine proper, within which the contradictory duties imposed by the League of Nations were carried out with resultant conflict. The two incompatible objectives have bedevilled the

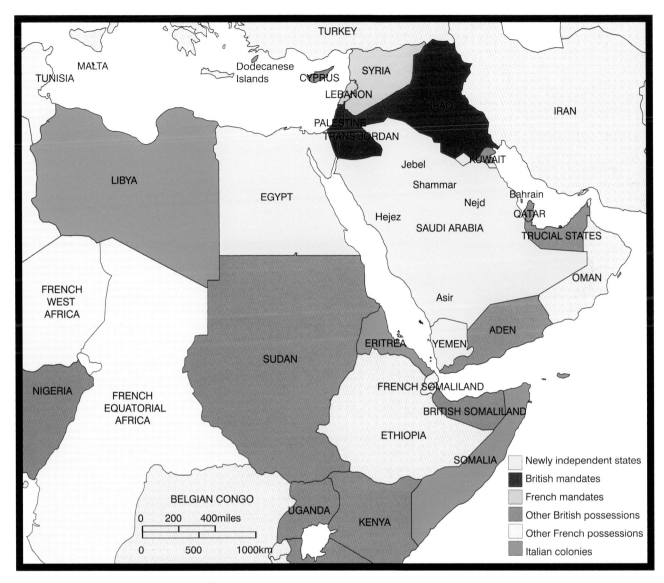

Map 5.8   New states in the Middle East

history of the territory ever since. The Palestine mandate, including control of the Christian holy sites and the City of Jerusalem, had been assumed by Great Britain as a matter of national prestige, as the greatest of the imperial powers.

Within the Arabian peninsula the forces unleashed by the removal of Ottoman influence led to a major realignment of power and the demarcation of a new set of international boundaries (Schofield, 1994). Sultan Ibn Saud of Nejd was able to extend his sovereignty over Jebel Shammar in November 1921 and the other interior rulers by 1922 (Al-Rasheed, 1991). In addition, the Persian Gulf coastline between Kuwait and Qatar was gained as the

Turks withdrew. This brought the Saudi state into potential conflict with Great Britain, which had assisted it against the Turks in the First World War. As a result, neutral zones were demarcated between Nejd on the one hand and the British authorities in Kuwait and Iraq on the other. On the Red Sea coast, partial control of Asir was gained by Nejd in 1920, but the shifting patterns of alliances and allegiances of the various tribal groups made any firm drawing of boundaries problematical.

In December 1925 the forces of Nejd completed the conquest of Hejez and united most of the Arabian peninsula under the Saudi Sultan (Kostiner, 1993). In January 1926 the unified Kingdom of Hejez and Nejd was proclaimed and in September 1932 it was renamed Saudi Arabia. Yemen was able to retain its independence, although neighbouring Asir was completely absorbed into the Saudi state. Otherwise only the ring of British protectorates and the independent Sultanate of Oman remained outside the Saudi sphere.

5.9   SYRIA AND THE LEBANON

The French received the League of Nations mandate for Syria, including the Lebanon, with a requirement that the mandatory power facilitate the development of the territories with a view to the granting of independence. The French interest in the region was based on the link with the Maronite Catholic Christian community of the Lebanon, which it had supported politically and culturally. The autonomous Turkish Sanjak of Mount Lebanon, established in 1861, had been a recognition both of the long history of Lebanese separatism and, on this occasion, of French military support. However, the boundaries of Mount Lebanon had been drawn by the international commission to include only those areas with a clear Christian majority, estimated at 83 percent in 1914 (Winslow, 1996). It covered some 4000 square kilometres and excluded Beirut and a

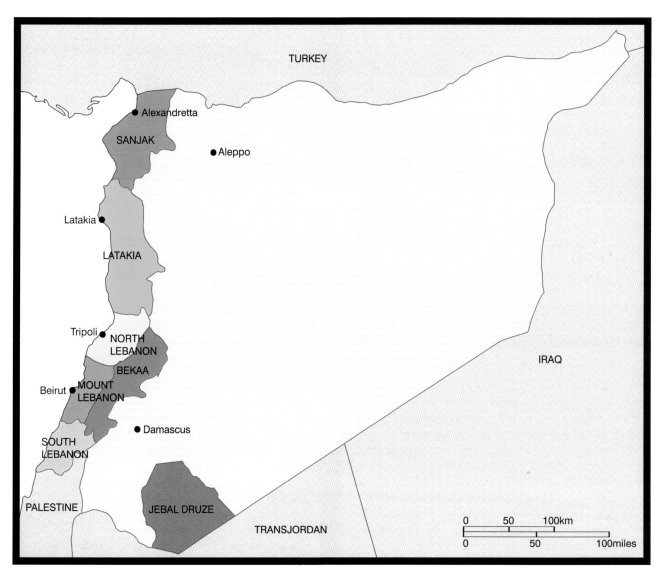

Map 5.9   Syria and the Lebanon

number of districts which had been part of the historic Lebanon. In the immediate post-war period Christian leaders claimed not only a separate state but the restoration of the historic boundaries, and at times the 'natural' geographical boundaries, of the Lebanon (Zamir, 1985).

In the crucial period between 1918 and 1920 the French administration of the coastal Western Zone of Syria supported this expansion, although it was opposed by the Moslem community and the Syrian Arab authorities in Damascus which controlled the interior Eastern Zone. In August 1920 the Lebanon's boundaries were extended to encompass some 10 400 square kilometres and the resulting Greater Lebanon was separated administratively from Syria. These moves took place in the context of the conflict of the period, where the security afforded the Christians by religious numerical superiority was sacrificed for greater territorial extent and the prospect of agricultural development and sustainability. The Bekaa Valley, with its extensive arable lands but Shiite Moslem majority, was one significant addition, which it was expected would provide agricultural self-sufficiency to the state, which Mount Lebanon had so noticeably lacked. The other was the port of Tripoli with its economic importance for the whole region, but an overwhelming Sunni Moslem majority. Thus although the autonomous Mount Lebanon in 1911 had recorded 79.5 percent of its population as Christians, the census of Greater Lebanon in 1921 enumerated only 55.1 percent (Zamir, 1985: 98–100). The more accurate census of 1932 indicated a figure of only 50.7 percent. In all the districts annexed to Lebanon in 1920, Christians were in a minority. Subsequent French suggestions that areas with large Moslem populations be detached in order to safeguard the country's Christian character were rejected by the Maronite leaders. Moslems in general rejected the separate state and continued to look for the unification of 'Greater' Syria, including not only the entire French mandated area, but also Palestine and Transjordan.

The remainder of Syria was constituted a separate administration under a French High Commissioner in Damascus (Khoury, 1987). Two autonomous regimes were established within Syria by the French authorities to serve the distinctive Druze and Alawite minority communities in the country. First, in the south the Franco-Druze treaty of March 1921 established the autonomous Jebal Druze state. The Druze were a highly concentrated community with 87 percent of the population of the state adherents to the sect. Secondly the Territory of the Alawites (renamed Latakia in 1930) was set aside for the Alawite community in March 1923. The Alawites constituted 62 percent of the population of the territory, but only 11 percent of that of Syria as a whole. The autonomous administrations of Latakia and the Jebal Druze were suppressed by the central Syrian authorities in February 1942.

In November 1937, as part of French diplomatic moves to gain allies in the region, the coastal Sanjak of Alexandretta was granted special status in view of its mixed population and significant Turkish interest. Under the Franco-Turkish Treaty of July 1938, Alexandretta was reconstituted a separate Republic of Hatay in September and transferred to Turkey in June the following year.

5.10   REDRAWING AFRICAN COLONIES AND MANDATES

The war between Germany and the Allies had lasted longer in Africa than that in Europe. Count von Lettow Vorbeck, the governor of German East Africa, only surrendered fourteen days after the armistice in Europe after a wide-ranging campaign through neighbouring British and Portuguese possessions. The four German colonies were distributed among the victorious powers. With the exception of the Koinga triangle, which went to Portugal, the remainder were subject to international supervision through the League of Nations mandatory system. Thus Britain and France partitioned Togo and Cameroons between them. Only the larger French portions continued to be administered as separate colonies, the British sections were incorporated into neighbouring Gold Coast and Nigeria respectively. German East Africa, with the exception of Ruanda-Urundi, was assigned to Great Britain and renamed Tanganyika Territory. The twin kingdoms of Ruanda and Urundi were assigned to Belgium. Finally, South West Africa was assigned to South Africa, and was effectively governed as an integral part of the mandatory power. This was so pronounced that the South African territorial outlier of Walvis Bay was included in South West Africa for ease of administration.

The aftermath of the war resulted in the independence of Egypt. At the outset of the war with Turkey, Egypt had been annexed by Great Britain and the Khedive had assumed the title of Sultan. At the end of the war the nationalist movement expected independence to follow as part of the national self-determination programme. The British resisted and rioting ensued, emphasising the problems of maintaining a wartime regime in peacetime. Lacking any clear negotiating partners, the British government unilaterally decided to accede to some of the demands of the independence movement, while not jeopardising vital British interests (Mansfield, 1971). In March 1922, the

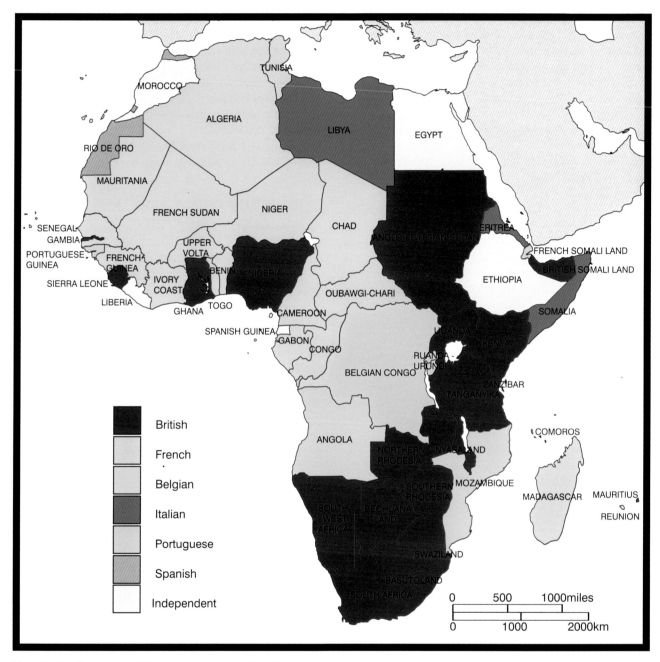

Map 5.10   Redrawing African colonies and mandates

country was declared independent, and the Sultan Fuad became King, although British troops retained control of key areas of the country, including the Suez Canal. Effectively a broad informal protectorate regime was in place, similar to the American relationship with Panama. It was only in August 1936 that an Anglo-Egyptian treaty regularised the situation. The British evacuated all but the Suez Canal Zone, although the right to reoccupy the country in case of war was included in the terms of the treaty. The Canal Zone though was not subject to a separate regime and remained an integral part of the country. The other major feature of the independence proclamation of 1922 was the assignment of complete control over the Anglo-Egyptian Sudan to the British. This was reinforced by the removal of Egyptian officials and army units two years later.

Other changes resulted from the perceived Anglo-French obligation to compensate Italy for its lack of colonial gains from the war. The boundary of Libya was redefined to extend its area, while the territory of Jubaland was detached from Kenya in July 1924, and after a brief separate existence, subsequently incorporated into Italian Somalia.

Elsewhere on the continent the internal administrative structure of the French and British empires were again redrawn. In French West Africa, the extensive colony of Upper Senegal and Niger was divided between a rump French Sudan, Upper Volta (constituted in March 1919) and the colony of Niger (December 1920). In French Equatorial Africa, the northern territories of the Middle Congo were detached to form the descriptively named colony of Ubangi-Chari-Tchad in July 1904. Subsequently in March 1920 Tchad was detached to form a separate colony. In Rhodesia the Charter of the British South Africa Company expired and the Crown assumed control in September 1923. Its extensive territories were divided along the Zambezi River with Northern Rhodesia coming under the direct control of the Colonial Office in London. The electorate of Southern Rhodesia had been offered the choice of joining South Africa or becoming a self-governing colony. The electors chose the latter course in a referendum in October 1922. At the same time some name changing took place to denote new constitutional statuses. Thus British East Africa Protectorate became Kenya Colony in July 1920.

5.11   THE SOVIET UNION

One of the most significant events of the First World War was the second Russian Revolution of November 1917, which brought the Bolsheviks under Lenin to power. The new government was constituted as the Russian Socialist Federated Soviet Republic (RSFSR) based on tightly organised Councils or Soviets, which gained absolute power. Following the first March 1917 revolution, which had overthrown the Romanov dynasty, the new government had sought to democratise the country while continuing to prosecute the war against Germany. The task proved to be impossible and the Bolsheviks were willing to make peace on any terms. The Treaty of Brest Litovsk was imposed by Germany in March 1918. The subsequent armistice and Treaty of Versailles abrogated the Treaty of Brest Litovsk and a new political dispensation of the lands of the former Russian Empire had to be worked out. The concepts of

world-wide workers' revolution propagated by the new Soviet authorities were exported to other parts of Europe, and achieved some initial success, notably in Hungary, Bavaria and Slovakia. These Soviet republics were however, soon overthrown. In consequence the new Russian Soviet state was forced to attempt to achieve 'Socialism in One State', while still adhering to its agenda of world-wide revolution.

In eastern Europe the political disintegration attendant upon the collapse of both Russian and German imperial power was enormous. The states which had emerged in the course of the war initially remained in place, although pressures were exerted in the ensuing civil war to overthrow them. Thus between 1918 and 1921 Poland, Finland, Latvia, Lithuania and Estonia were able to achieve Russian recognition of their complete independence and exclusion from the Soviet system. However, the internationally recognised republics of the Ukraine, Georgia, Armenia and Azerbaijan were unable to prevent reincorporation into the Russian successor state, the Soviet Union. Initially the various Soviet Socialist Republics assumed all the prerogatives of the national governments they had overthrown. Treaty relations were established with the Russian federal government which recognised them to be 'independent and sovereign' states. Thus the Soviet government of Azerbaijan established full diplomatic relations with foreign countries and despatched its representatives to Turkey and Persia and accredited diplomatic representatives of Germany and Finland. The Azerbaijan government, through its support for the Soviet cause, was able to extract significant territorial concessions, gaining both Nagorno-Karabakh and Nakhichevan. However, for military and economic purposes they were integrated into the Russian Republic and were administered by Communist Party officials. Azerbaijan also promoted the use of the Latin alphabet as part of the literacy campaign in June 1924 – a measure adopted by Turkey in November 1928, both as a means of emphasising the break with the past. However, in 1940 Cyrillic was introduced as 'the alphabet of the great geniuses of mankind – Lenin and Stalin' (Swietochowski, 1995: 128). The move was also aimed at reducing the influence of pan-Turkish movements.

In Central Asia, the Emirates of Khiva and Bokhara were overthrown in April and September 1920 respectively and People's Republics established in their place. The treaties between these states and the Russian federal government were similar to those signed with the Soviet Socialist Republics, but internal control was less rigidly enforced, making the substance of independent status more recognisable. Another People's Republic, that of the Far

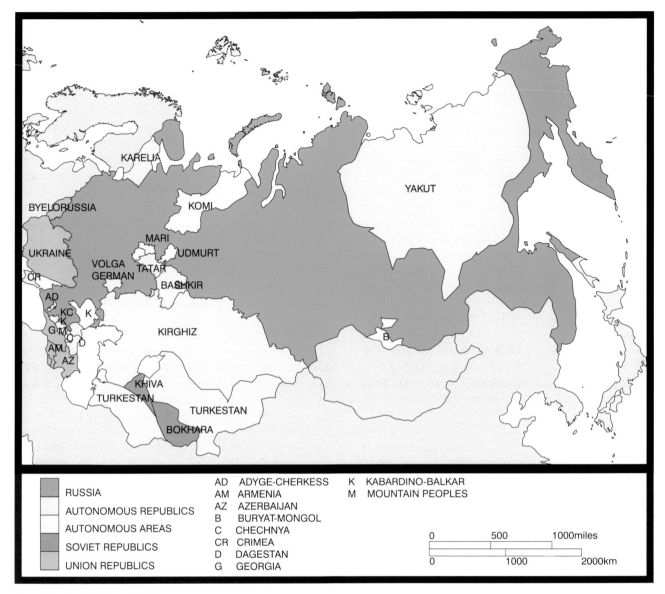

Map 5.11   The Soviet Union

Eastern Republic was established in April 1920 as a buffer against Japanese expansion, but it was reincorporated in October 1922 (Forsyth, 1992).

Other ephemeral states including Karelia and Ingermanland on the Finnish border, the Crimea, and the Don Cossacks were reincorporated into Russia, often with some recognition of a special status. Thus Karelia became a Workers' Commune in August 1920 and an Autonomous Soviet Socialist Republic (ASSR) in July 1923. Its autonomous status was guaranteed under the Treaty of Dorpat in October 1920, which ended the Finnish War of

Independence. However, the guarantee could not be enforced under international law. Significantly the first nationality to receive recognition was the Volga German which gained Workers' Commune status, before the German defeat, in October 1918 and ASSR status in December 1923. The Crimea gained ASSR status in October 1921 as part of Russia, not the Ukraine. In May 1934 the Jewish Autonomous Area was established at Birabidzhan, on the Manchurian border, as a homeland for the Jewish population of the country. It was intended to be an alternative for the Jewish population of the Soviet

Union, who were denied participation in the Zionist project in Palestine.

The new Russian government recognised that the nationalities question was one of the most problematic issues requiring a solution if the Party's far ranging social and economic transformation programmes were to be put into effect. Thus a remarkably open nationalities policy was devised with acceptance of language as a means of communication intrinsically devoid of national content. Accordingly a Marxist curriculum or political programme could be presented irrespective of the language medium. Lenin distinguished between oppressor-nation nationalism (great power chauvinism) and oppressed-nation nationalism (nationalism proper). The first was considered to be bad and could be overcome by proletarian effort. The second was an over-reaction to oppression and could be overcome by sensitivity. Thus 'the gift of national self-determination was a gesture of repentance that would eventually lead to national forgiveness and therefore the end of nationalistic paranoia and therefore the end of national differences' (Slezkine, 1994: 142).

Lenin considered that having transformed capitalism into socialism, the proletariat would force the total elimination of national oppression. This was only possible after the democratisation of society and the establishment of state borders according to the sympathies of the population, including the complete freedom of secession. Lenin concluded that: 'This in turn, will lead in practice to a total abolition of all national tensions and all national distrust, to an accelerated drawing together and merger of nations which will result in the withering away of the state' (Slezkine, 1994: 143). The result was an appeal to national movements to support the Soviets. Thus in December 1917 the Soviet government issued an appeal:

Organise your national life in complete freedom. This is your right. Know that your rights, like those of all the peoples of Russia, are under the mighty protection of the Revolution and its organs, the Soviets of Workers, Soldiers and Peasants.

(Pipes, 1964: 155).

It is therefore remarkable that the two major influences upon the world after the First World War, namely American liberal democracy and Soviet communism, both emphasised national self-determination and the creation of the nation or national state as a means towards the solution of the world's political problems. It was the Soviet experiment which was the most closely followed model in other multi-national states of the twentieth century (Motyl, 1992). Indeed the idea that it offered a model for the creation of 'a new historical community of people' was attractive to other countries experiencing ethnic tensions (Zevelev, 1972: 60).

As a preliminary to this workers' future stateless society, the Soviet government pursued a policy of recognising existing nationalities and developing national organs of administration, education, etc. This involved the establishment of autonomous republics for minor nationalities. Russia thus became the RSFSR composed of the Russian inhabited areas and a myriad of small autonomous republics and autonomous territories for the national minorities. These varied from the peoples of northern Russia and Siberia such as the Komi (August 1921) and Yakut (April 1922), which were small in numbers, to the major nations of Central Asia and the middle Volga such as the Bashkir (May 1919), Tatar (May 1920) and Kirgiz (August 1920). Significantly the Turkish-speaking peoples were disagregated according to comparatively minor linguistic and cultural differences, to prevent the emergence of pan-Turkism, which was considered to be detrimental to the survival of Soviet control. The process evolved throughout the Soviet period as nationalities were granted status within an ordered hierarchy. However, even the Tatars on the Volga could not achieve Union republican status as they were surrounded by Russian territory and thus would have constituted an enclave within the Russian state should the clause guaranteeing the right to secession been exercised.

Those states recognised as independent but which were conquered by Soviet armies in the civil war had been proclaimed Soviet Socialist Republics, nominally independent of Russia. However, the need for some formal centralised coordinating body was deemed essential to link these states. The Soviet Union or Union of Soviet Socialist Republics was formed in December 1922 to link together Russia (RSFSR), the Ukraine, Byelorussia, and the Transcaucasian SFSR (Armenia, Azerbaijan and Georgia). Provision was made for the adhesion of additional states, either through the constitutional evolution of autonomous national republics already within the Soviet Union, or through the incorporation of states beyond its boundaries. The first promotions to full Union republican status were Turkmenistan and Uzbekistan in October 1924 following the incorporation of the nominally independent People's Republics of Khiva and Bokhara into the Soviet Union and the reorganisation of the Central Asian region on linguistic lines. Others were to follow, notably upon the proclamation of the 1936 Constitution, which amongst other matters disbanded the Transcaucasian Socialist Federal Soviet Republic increasing the number of Union republics to eleven. Expansion beyond the 1922 boundaries only began in 1939 during the Second World War.

CHAPTER 6

The Era of the League of Nations 1923–1939

Following the First World War and its immediate aftermath, the Allied powers looked forward to an era of peace and prosperity, free from the scourge of war. The Franco-British rapprochement with Germany and its admission to the League of Nations indicated a greater willingness to achieve the goals of the League. The Soviet Union was absorbed in its own internal transformation of society and apart from the wide-ranging attempt to foment world revolution played little part in the international politics of the period before 1939. This was not to suggest that the era had no effect upon the state system. Several significant events affected the world map. The Arabian peninsula and its neighbours underwent major changes, notably the creation of Saudi Arabia. The smallest state in the current system came into being with the formal recognition of the Holy See or Vatican. In the 1930s the Axis powers, Italy, Japan and Germany, began to refashion the world in their own image. The crises which ensued resulted in the outbreak of the Second World War and the major conflagration affecting a wider sphere than that involved in the First World War. There is as a result a tendency to regard the era of the League of Nations as an interlude between two wars, even merely a truce in one long war. For many of the Western politicians of the period it was an era of attempting to return to the stability of the pre-1914 world. Such an aim proved to be impossible as the essential passivism of the generation which survived the war was confronted by the 'revisionists' who wished to transform the world, by force if need be.

Thus although between 1923 and 1939 four new states came into being, namely The Holy See, Iraq, Manchuria and Slovakia, a total of six states were erased from the map, namely Albania, Austria, Czechoslovakia, Ethiopia, Asir, and Hejaz. In most cases the changes were effected by force or the threat of force. This indicated the continued lack of security in an era where the first important steps had been taken to establish the rule of law and the principle of non-aggression in international relations. A significant exception to this statement was the constitutional transformation of the British Empire into an association of independent states. The separate statehood of the six dominions was recognised in 1931, although one (Newfoundland) had to relinquish that status three years later.

Symbolic of the age was the demise of Ethiopia. The Italian army had been defeated by the Ethiopians at Adowa in 1896. No further attempt had been made to occupy the sector assigned to it in the course of the partition of Africa. So far had plans for the projected conquest been abandoned that in 1922 it was Italy that sponsored Ethiopia's membership of the League of Nations against British objections. However, in October 1935 the Italian government decided to occupy the country as part of the establishment of a greater Italian Empire. The League of Nations imposed sanctions against Italy but was unable to preserve the independence of one of its members. The concept of collective security embodied in the League's charter was proved to be grossly inadequate. In May 1936 Ethiopia was annexed and King Victor Emmanuel III assumed the title Emperor of Ethiopia. The proclamation was flamboyantly greeted as 'a restoration of an empire to the hills of Rome after fifteen centuries' (*Keesing's Contemporary Archives*, 1936: 2100). Later in 1936

Ethiopia, Eritrea and Italian Somalia were merged to form the Empire of Italian East Africa.

6.1   VATICAN CITY STATE

One of the unresolved issues of the nineteenth century had been the territorial extent of the temporal power of the Pope. The Papacy had since medieval times held substantial territories in central Italy, which it had lost in the course of Italian unification between 1859 and 1870. The final portion of the Papal States, Rome and surrounding Latium, had been incorporated into the new Italian kingdom only in 1870. Relations between Italy and the Papacy were apparently irreconcilable over the issue of the latter's territorial sovereignty. The Italian Law of Guarantee of May 1871 recognised Papal sovereignty over the Vatican but the Pope refused to accept the position.

However, in June 1929 the Italian government under Benito Mussolini was able to persuade Pope Pius XI to accept the compromise Lateran Treaty whereby The Holy See, restricted to the area of the Vatican, was established as a separate sovereign state and the loss of the pre-1870 Papal States was acknowledged as permanent in return for suitable compensation. The new Vatican City State with an area of 44 hectares and a population of under 1000 was the smallest entity to join the state system in the twentieth century (Toscho, 1931). Other properties covering approximately 70 hectares, notably the Papal Summer Palace at Castelgondolfo (40 hectares), were accepted as virtual extensions of the sovereign state, and communications between them are governed by diplomatic protocols. The Villa Gabrielli and its environs on the Gianicolo Hill were reserved for future extension of the Vatican administrative buildings.

The admission of The Holy See to full sovereign status made little difference to the actual conduct of international affairs, as a number of states had maintained full diplomatic relations with the Papacy between 1870 and 1929. It was therefore in a class of its own, as it represented the last of the universal empires, with a universal claim to the spiritual allegiance of all men and women in all temporal states and to that extent could function without the normal administrative apparatus of a state, through the world-wide ecclesiastical hierarchy. The state's primary function was to facilitate the administration of the Roman Catholic Church, which in 1929 counted some 330 million adherents. As such it was constituted as a neutral state, which 'will remain

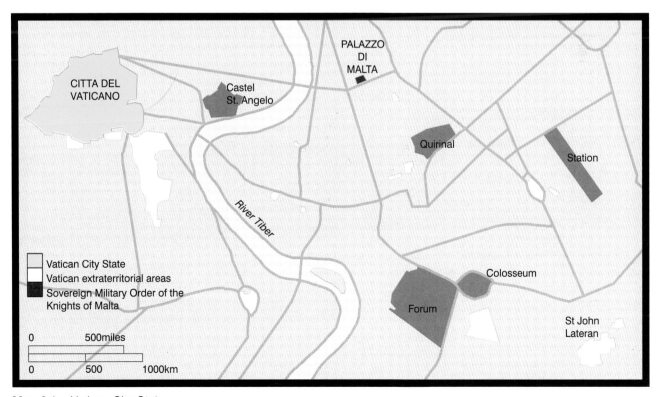

Map 6.1   Vatican City State

outside the temporal rivalries among other states and also apart from international meetings called for such purposes' (Toscho, 1931: 537).

It was also unique in the fact that it possessed no permanent population which might spend its entire life within its boundaries as even the Monegasques of Monaco might do. There is therefore no such concept as Vatican nationality. The citizenry holding Vatican passports, which numbered 532 in 1929, were the nationals of other countries and reverted to their former citizenship when they ceased to hold an office in the Vatican administration. The citizens were mainly Italians (the Secretariat) and Swiss (the Papal Guard). Furthermore, the sovereign was elected from among an international College of Cardinals. Although the sovereign had normally been Italian, the century was to witness the election of a Polish national, Pope John Paul II, to this office. It is a remarkable feature of the State and limitation upon its international status that any citizen can be expelled from the national territory (Duursma, 1996).

Discussion of the Vatican City State raises the question of the smallest European sovereign entity, the Sovereign Military Order of Malta. The Order of Saint John of Jerusalem had initially been formed to establish and maintain hospitals for the care of soldiers and pilgrims to the Holy Land. It had been formally constituted by the Pope in 1113 after the First Crusade (Seward, 1995). Under the pressure of the Crusades the Order gained a military function under a body of knights recruited from all over the Christian world. Upon the fall of the Kingdom of Jerusalem the Order found refuge in Cyprus and later the island of Rhodes, where it was recognised by the Pope as the fully sovereign ruler in 1306. Following the capture of Rhodes by the Ottoman Empire in 1523, the Order moved to Malta, from where it was finally dislodged by the French in 1798. The Order remained in possession of landed property in Rome, where it continued to be recognised as a sovereign power by the governments of the Papal States and the subsequent Italian kingdom. The Palazzo of the Knights of Malta, at 68 Via Condotti, thus constitutes the smallest state, with many of the features of the Vatican City State, including diplomatic recognition by over 80 states.

The Sovereign Order of Malta, the last of the medieval knightly orders, is led by the Grand Master and the Sovereign Council drawn from the knights, who can demonstrate sixteen quarters of nobility, that is that all sixteen great-great-grandparents were nobles. The officers of the Order guard its aristocratic heritage closely. For example, the Order was willing to forgo a substantial Argentinian aid donation in 1949, rather than admit Eva Peron, the President's wife, to the Order as a Dame of Honour and Devotion, to which her non-noble pedigree did not entitle her (Sire, 1994: 258). The sovereign status is primarily retained to facilitate the humanitarian work of the Order, which maintains hospitals and medical services around the world and renders emergency assistance in times of crisis.

In this respect the major international organisations such as the International Committee of the Red Cross and the League of Nations at Geneva and the Permanent Court of International Justice at The Hague possessed some of the features of the extra-territoriality of the Holy See and the Sovereign Military Order of Malta, but were unable to secure recognition of their sovereignty (Moorehead, 1998). Subsequently the United Nations, the European Union and other supra-national organisations assumed similar characteristics, but without formal recognition.

6.2   THE BRITISH COMMONWEALTH

The most significant development in the sphere of imperial reorganisation was the Statute of Westminster in 1931, which recognised the separate and independent statehood of the British dominions. Although they had been recognised as founder members of the League of Nations in 1919, the dominions' diplomacy had been exercised through the British Foreign Office in London. Even at the signing of the Paris peace settlement only one signature on the peace treaties was necessary for the British Empire as a whole. Only in the 1920s had this been changed with the move towards separate diplomatic and consular representation. This had most notably been the case in Canadian–American relations, where Canada also adopted a more neutralist approach by refusing to become involved in British problems in Europe. In 1923 the successful conclusion of the Halibut Treaty between the United States and Canada effectively recognised this separate diplomatic entity (Lower, 1959). In April 1928 the British and Canadian governments exchanged High Commissioners, tacitly acknowledging the need for inter-governmental links superseding the traditional link through the Governor-General as the King's representative.

Under the Statute of Westminster, which came into force in December 1931, six new sovereign states came into being, namely Canada, Australia, New Zealand, South Africa, Newfoundland and the Irish Free State. King George V thus became the sovereign of seven independent states, which were linked only through a personal union. The new dispensation was most clearly illustrated over the

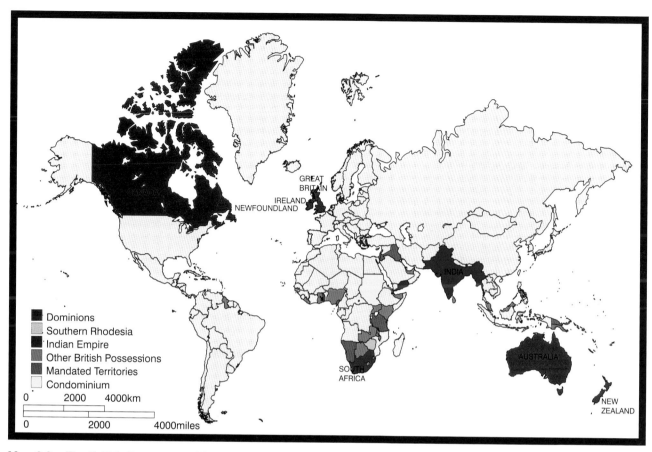

Map 6.2   The British Commonwealth

abdication of King Edward VIII in December 1936 when the Irish and South African parliaments passed their own separate Abdication Acts on different days to those enacted by Great Britain and the other dominions.

The extent of Irish independence was to be illustrated even more clearly when in September 1939 Ireland declared its neutrality. Indeed the 1937 Irish constitution was in most respects a republican document and in conflict with the British imperial ethos. In addition to acknowledging the state's special relationship with the Roman Catholic Church, the constitution laid claim to the sovereignty of Northern Ireland, which remained an integral part of the United Kingdom. This ambiguous position was illustrated in April 1941. Following a severe air raid on Belfast, fire engines were sent from southern Ireland to assist in putting out the blaze. When the German government protested, Eamon de Valera, the Irish Prime Minister, pointed out that Northern Ireland was part of the Irish state.

Newfoundland had become a dominion only in 1917, mainly in recognition of its valuable contribution to the war effort. After the war it had embarked upon a major public works programme, financed from its natural mineral and fishing wealth. In May 1927 the Privy Council awarded Newfoundland the interior territory of Labrador which it had disputed with the Canadian province of Quebec. However, the island was unable to maintain that status financially during the Great Depression and faced bankruptcy. By December 1931 the $90 million debt was beyond the Dominion's capacity to service. The attempt to sell Labrador to Canada for $110 million in February 1932 failed. Only surrender of its independent status offered a means of lifting of the debt burden. In February 1934 Newfoundland reverted to the status of a British Crown Colony, administered by an appointed commission, which supervised the economy (McIntyre, 1977). The island had proved to be too small to sustain financial independence and this must therefore be one of the remarkable cases of the government of a sovereign state voluntarily having to give up its independence to avert bankruptcy. In the 1930s the surrender of independence did not appear as serious as it might to later observers. The island's population still retained a strong sense of British identity, which was reinforced by the presence of French-speaking Quebec as a neighbour. Only in April 1949 did the island join Canada as its tenth province, a constitutional route it had rejected in the 1860s.

The Indian Empire, despite its position as a founder member of the League of Nations, was still administered from the India Office in London in 1931. Constitutional changes were enacted with a view towards the introduction of dominion status, but there was a reluctance on the part of the British government to relinquish ultimate control. However, as part of this projected change of status, the peripheral Indian dependencies of Burma and Aden were detached in April 1937 to became separate colonies. The other significant anomaly of Empire, Southern Rhodesia, retained the status of a self-governing colony and so participated in the Imperial Prime Ministers' conferences but lacked dominion and thus sovereign status.

6.3 MANCHURIA

The confusion in China following the revolution and the civil wars which ensued provided ample opportunity for its neighbours to embark upon plans for territorial aggrandisement. Japan emerged from the First World War as the dominant power in eastern and north-eastern China. The Japanese had captured the German settlement of Kiaochow in November 1914 and proceeded to occupy the zone between that port and Tientsin in 1915. This was followed by the occupation of extensive areas of Manchuria (and adjacent areas of Siberia) in 1918. However, all these territories were evacuated in 1922 and returned to China under pressure from the United States as part of a general settlement of foreign claims against that country. Limited numbers of Japanese troops remained to protect the Manchurian railway system and the base at Port Arthur. British interest in North China ended with the return of the Wai-hai-wei leasehold territory in October 1930.

China was rent by a complex civil war, further complicated in Manchuria by the local regime's declaration of independence from the central government in January 1926. The capture of Peking by the Nationalists in July 1928 led to the restoration of nominal Chinese sovereignty, but not peace. In September 1931 the situation in China was such that the Japanese government decided to occupy the whole of Manchuria. To legitimate its position it further created a separate state, Manchukuo, in February 1932, much as Russia had done in Outer

Mongolia and appeared to be attempting to do in Chinese Turkestan. The state was enlarged with the incorporation of the province of Jehol, previously part of Inner Mongolia in February 1933. In March 1934 the former Emperor of China, Pu-Yi, was formally installed as Emperor of Manchuria (Aisin-Gioro, 1987).

China refused to recognise the independence of the new state, as it had refused to do in the cases of Mongolia and Tibet. Furthermore, the new state was condemned by a commission of enquiry conducted by the League of Nations, which reported in October 1932. However, it was recognised by a number of small countries, which were supportive of the other Axis powers, commencing with El Salvador in April 1933. In practice the Japanese army ran Manchuria as a protectorate, exerting ever greater control over day-to-day administration, until even the official language became Japanese and Japanese flags flew alongside those of Manchukuo. Indeed in March 1942 Japan was officially declared to be Manchukuo's 'Parental Country' (Aisin-Gioro, 1987: 302).

The basic ideological problem for the new state, beyond its reliance upon Japanese military support, was the lack of any recognisable surviving Manchu national identity. The Manchu peoples who had overthrown the Ming Dynasty in China in 1644 had been acculturated and colonised. Despite the attempts by the Ch'ing Emperors to prevent colonisation, substantial Chinese settlement in the nineteenth and early twentieth centuries had resulted in the dominance of Han Chinese in the 'Three Eastern Provinces'. The Manchu clans had been reduced to no more than ten percent of the total population of the country (Joerg, 1932). There was therefore a notable lack of support for what in effect was a Manchu national state, among the majority of the country's predominantly Han Chinese population.

In July 1937 Japan invaded China and succeeded in occupying extensive sections of the north and east of the country. The Japanese government left unresolved the future government of the country and installed local administrations for the areas it occupied. No attempt was made to restore the Emperor Pu-Yi to any territories outside Manchuria, despite his aspirations to regain the whole of his inheritance. Local separatist insurgencies were supported in Inner Mongolia and elsewhere, with a view to divesting the Chinese state of its remaining dependencies, which could then be more readily controlled and exploited by Japan. In November 1937 the autonomous government of Meng-kiang (Mongolian Marches) was established. Governments for North China and Shanghai and Nanking followed (Li, 1975). It was to

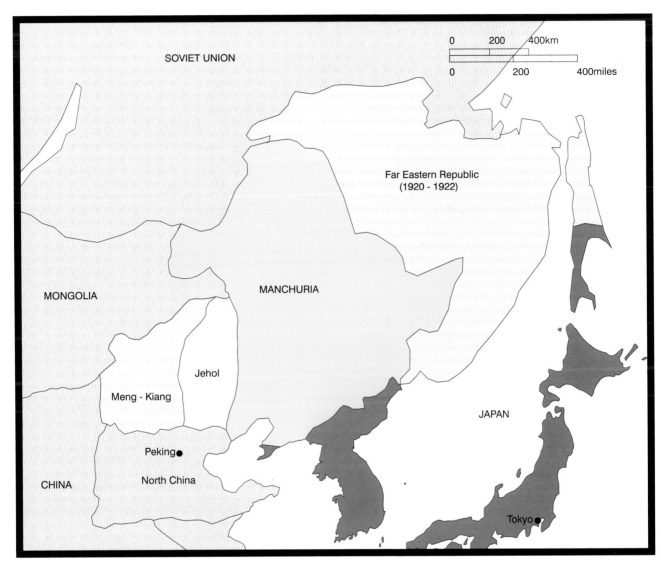

Map 6.3   Manchuria

these governments that Japan handed over its concessions, and those of its enemies in August 1943.

Even Sinkiang was caught up in the turmoil affecting the rest of China. The remaining semi-autonomous khanates were suppressed, giving rise to a series of secessionist movements beginning with that at Hami (April–November 1931). Subsequently the Republic of Eastern Turkestan was proclaimed in September, which became the Turkish-Islamic Republic of Eastern Turkestan in November 1933. Both China and the Soviet Union had interests in the suppression in February 1934 of such a challenge to the status quo in central Asia (Forbes, 1986).

6.4   REVISING THE TREATY OF VERSAILLES IN EUROPE

It was in Europe that the most significant changes to the map took place. In January 1933 the National Socialist Party under Adolf Hitler came to power in Germany, with a programme to destroy the Versailles settlement and create a strong German state. The Munich school of geopolitics had provided a scientific programme to achieve these aims, and the significance of the nation as a united entity was paramount in the events which followed (Paterson, 1987). The first opportunity came in March 1935 when the fifteen-

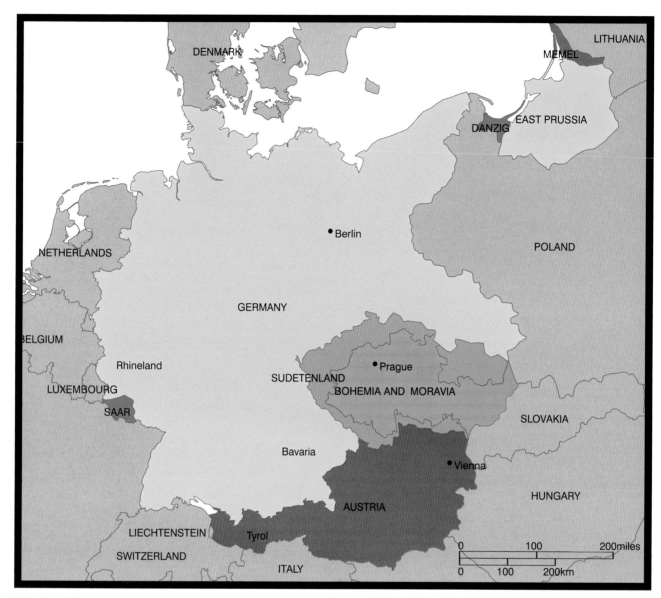

Map 6.4   Revising the Treaty of Versailles in Europe

year League of Nations administration of the Saar terminated. In the plebiscite on the territory's future, conducted in January 1935, the electorate voted overwhelmingly (90.4 percent) to reunite with Germany, rejecting any continuing League of Nations or French presence. In March 1936 the Rhineland, which had been demilitarised in 1919, was reoccupied by the German army, without any hostile reaction from the guarantors of the Versailles settlement, France and Great Britain. The German government therefore considered the prospects for more drastic changes to be promising.

The repudiation of the clause in the Treaty of St Germain which prevented Austria from joining Germany offered the best opportunity for national advancement. Italy, which had acted as the guarantor of Austrian independence, was reconciled to the prospect of German expansion as Italy and Germany moved closer together diplomatically and eventually militarily. Austria had failed to achieve a recognisable raison d'etre in the post-war period. The German unification programme thus found widespread support. The slogan of 'one people, one state, one leader' proved to be emotionally beguiling. German diplomatic and military pressure on the Austrian government in support of unification increased. In March 1938 the Austrian government made the counter offer of conducting a referendum on the state's continued independence. The electorate was to indicate whether they supported 'An Austria, Free and German, Independent and Social, Christian and United' (Wagner and Tomkowitz, 1971: 15). The offer was rejected, as not guaranteeing unification, and the country was occupied by the German army, without resistance. In the April 1938 referendum 99.73 percent of the 4.5 million electorate voted in favour of union with Germany. The country remained an integral part of Germany until the end of the Second World War. The apparent overwhelming support at the time for this course of action is remarkable in suggesting that states can be removed from the world map if there is a lack of support for their continuation as well as the threat of force.

Following its success in Austria, the German government sought to incorporate other areas inhabited by German speakers. The first such zone was the Sudetenland in Czechoslovakia. This area was the peripheral zone of Bohemia and Moravia and had been a part of the Austrian Empire prior to 1918. The Czechoslovak administration had allowed extensive cultural autonomy as well as the benefits of the only free and democratic government in central and eastern Europe. This degree of freedom had been sufficient to maintain ethnic peace in the state, when repression of minorities had become general throughout the region in the 1930s. However, the rising level of German anti-Czech propaganda and the spread of virulent nationalism by the National Socialists resulted in the local population increasingly adopting a pro-German stance. In October 1938, with the agreement of the British and French governments at Munich, the Sudetenland was occupied and incorporated into Germany. The partition involved its other neighbours. Poland took the western section of Teschen denied it in 1919–1920, while Hungary regained the southern strip of Slovakia which was predominantly inhabited by Hungarians.

The rump Czechoslovak state lost its entire defensive capability based upon the mountainous perimeter of the Bohemian Diamond. Internal and external pressures to reform and neutralise the state had an immediate effect. Decentralisation was pursued with the establishment of autonomous governments for Slovakia and the Carpetho-Ukraine later in October 1938.

The next stage of German expansion was not based upon the concept of national unification, but on strategic and economic considerations. In March 1939 Germany occupied the Czech portion of the rump state and declared it the protectorate of Bohemia and Moravia. It was declared part of the German national space and German possession was essential to 'the foundations of reasonable order in Central Europe' (Shirer, 1964: 548). At the same time the governments of Slovakia and Carpetho-Ukraine declared themselves independent, but the latter was occupied by Hungarian forces one day later.

Thus another state established under the 1919 peace settlement was removed from the map, this time as a result of direct military intervention and occupation. The international regime which was essential for the maintenance of smaller states had been destroyed and big power expansionism took its place once more. The smaller Slovak state appeared as a separate entity in its place. Its survival reflected the fact that Hungary had been unable to annex it as part of its programme to re-establish the Kingdom within its historic pre-1918 boundaries. It was, however, able to prevent Carpetho-Ukraine from achieving its independence through annexation.

In April 1939 Italy occupied Albania, a state which, because of its strategic position at the entrance to the Adriatic Sea, successive Italian governments had sought to control either directly or indirectly since the break-up of the Ottoman Empire. King Zog was deposed and King Victor Emmanuel of Italy added 'King of Albania' to his list of titles. The Albanian state had thus been created twice and been occupied twice in a matter of only 25 years. This was a matter of extreme instability and underlined its 'quasi-state' position and dependence upon the positive intervention of the great powers to maintain its independence.

Elsewhere, following an ultimatum, Lithuania returned Memel to Germany in March 1939 and the residual international status of the territory was terminated. The remaining League of Nations territory, Danzig, clearly had only a limited life left as Germany redrew the map of Europe to remove all trace of its defeat in 1918. Its seizure precipitated the Second World War.

CHAPTER 7

The World at War 1939–1945

The Second World War nominally began in Europe in September 1939 and two years later merged with the Sino-Japanese conflict to engulf much of the globe until its conclusion in 1945. As a longer, technologically more sophisticated and more widely dispersed conflict, the casualties were higher and extent of destruction greater than in the 1914–1918 war. Because of the technical innovations in the conduct of war, culminating in the atomic bomb, the narrowly defined killing fields of the trenches of the First World War were more widely spread with more mobile armies and hence a far greater extent of territory changing hands in the course of the conflict. The administration of conquered lands thus became a greater problem for both sides than had been the case in the First World War.

The war opened with a series of sweeping victories for Germany, which left the country by July 1940 in control of much of western and central Europe. Reorganisation took place on the assumption that these victories were permanent as only the British Empire remained hostile. The German invasion of the Soviet Union in July 1941 radically changed the world conflict, leading to the intervention of Japan and the United States in December 1941. Germany and Japan were able to redraw the boundaries and rearrange the state system over wide areas of eastern Europe and South-east Asia. The sole Allied conquests were the Italian colonies in Africa which resulted in the imposition of British and French military governments and the resurrection of Ethiopia.

In the course of the initial phase of German conquest, before the invasion of Russia, most of the remaining states created by the Paris peace settlement were removed from the map of Europe, namely, Poland, Latvia, Lithuania and Estonia, together with Luxembourg. A large number of others were occupied but retained their legal status. The main features of the 1939–1943 European settlement were undone by the German defeat in May 1945. In South-east Asia the Japanese viewed themselves as freeing the local peoples from colonial rule, a view which met some positive response. As a result, Burma, Malaya and the Philippines gained independence, followed at the end of the war by Vietnam, Cambodia, Laos and Indonesia. Again the Japanese defeat in August 1945 undid this settlement as the colonial powers returned, if briefly or with great difficulty. With the exception of the Italian colonies, Allied campaigns were largely aimed at re-establishing the pre-war situation.

7.1   A NEW MAP OF EUROPE 1939–1941

The Soviet–German pact of August 1939 paved the way for the partition of Poland between the two countries and the dismantling of one of the major features of the 1919 Paris peace settlement. In September 1939 the two countries rapidly conquered Poland and divided it between them. At the same time the Free City of Danzig was occupied and reincorporated into Germany. The German sector of Poland was divided between territories reincorporated directly into the German state and those assigned to a newly created General Government based on Cracow. The latter was most certainly not considered to be the nucleus of a future Polish state, but as an area to be ruthlessly exploited for the benefit

Map 7.1   A new map of Europe 1939–1941

of the German state. It was administered by the German army and the National Socialist Party, without even the nominal concession of the protectorate government accorded to Bohemia and Moravia.

The Soviet Union embarked upon the creation of a cordon sanitaire with Germany. The Soviet sector of Poland was incorporated into the Byelorussian and Ukrainian Soviet Socialist Republics. Latvia, Lithuania (including the Vilnius region regained from Poland in October 1939) and Estonia were incorporated into the Soviet Union as Union republics in August 1940. In all three cases the Soviet army occupied the countries in June 1940, following the fall of France. The following month elections took place for new parliaments, on single party lists producing new governments which received apparently between 92.8 and 99.2 percent of the vote. At the request of these new administrations the three states were admitted to the Soviet Union as Soviet Socialist Republics in August 1940. Also in July 1940 tracts of territory were seized on the Finnish and Romanian borders and incorporated into the newly established Union Republics of Finno-Karelia and Moldavia.

In western Europe between April and June 1940 the Germans occupied, but did not annex, Norway, Denmark, the Netherlands, Belgium and France. In Norway and the Netherlands special interim administrations were established as King Haakon and Queen Wilhelmina formed governments-in-exile in London. In Belgium and Denmark most existing structures and personnel, including the monarchs Leopold III and Christian X, were retained with, at first, minimal interference with internal affairs. France capitulated in June 1940 and was divided into two, with the north and west occupied by the German army and the remainder unoccupied until November 1942. The new government, under Marshall Philippe Petain, moved to the city of Vichy in the unoccupied sector. Where possible existing administrative and political structures remained in place. The British Channel Islands of Jersey and Guernsey were occupied and remained under German control until the end of the war. Again little change in status took place, although proposals for annexation by Germany at the end of the war may have been no more than a part of the propaganda surrounding the conflict.

In terms of territorial adjustments, Eupen and Malmedy were regained from Belgium and Alsace-Lorraine from France, reversing the seizures of 1918 and 1919. Significantly that part of northern Schleswig where a plebiscite had been held to test public support in 1920 remained in Danish hands, further demonstrating the German attempt to effect conciliation with the existing states in western Europe.

The future of the Grand Duchy of Luxembourg presented an unusually sensitive issue for Germany. Following its invasion in May 1940, the Grand Duchess Charlotte had fled and a German military regime was installed. Incorporation into Germany was the avowed aim, as the local population spoke a distinctive dialect of German, Letzteburgesch (Newton, 1996). Thus a more accommodating approach was adopted by the occupation forces, although the use of the official language of the Grand Duchy, French, was banned and standard German introduced as a part of a Germanisation programme. Even such peculiarities as the use of the circumflex accents in the

written form of the local dialect were prohibited. No rapprochement with the Grand Duchess could be reached and in October 1941 a plebiscite on union with Germany was held. Some 97 percent of the electorate rejected union. A far more severe regime was installed and in August 1942 annexation was effected, and the use of Letzteburgesch banned (Dear and Foot, 1995).

The disposition of the Danish, French, Dutch and Belgian overseas possessions became of immediate concern to Great Britain and Germany. Governments-in-exile, based in London, were established which took over control of most possessions. Within the French Empire a struggle for control between the Vichy government and the Free French under General Charles de Gaulle began with the adherence of Felix Eboue, the governor of Chad in French Equatorial Africa, to the London based government-in-exile in August 1940. However, the majority of the French colonies initially adhered to the Vichy government. This presented Great Britain with potential threats throughout the world and a systematic programme was undertaken to secure the adherence of the colonies to the Free French. In Syria and Lebanon a British and Free French expeditionary force displaced the Vichy mandatory governments in June 1941 in order to secure Egypt and the Suez Canal. As a result, the Lebanon declared its independence in November 1943 and Syria in January 1944. A similar expedition to secure Madagascar for the Free French and forestall a Japanese occupation in April 1942 did not result in any Allied commitment to independence for the island. French Indo-China was occupied by the Japanese and remained under nominal Vichy control until April 1945. Elsewhere the Belgian government-in-exile administered the Belgian Congo, which effectively was integrated into the British war effort.

The German occupation of Denmark was particularly problematical for the British due to the Danish dependencies' strategic position on the shipping routes between North America and Europe. Great Britain occupied the Faroe Islands in April 1940 following the Danish surrender and retained them for the duration of the war under a special military regime. At the same time the two governing sheriffs of Greenland joined the Free Denmark movement and ran the territory independently, inviting United States military protection for the war period. Iceland presented a more intractable problem. Effectively the country became virtually independent in April 1940. Initially the Icelandic government refused to accept British occupation, but the island was occupied the following month to pre-empt a German occupation. In July 1941 the United States declared it to be a part of the Western

Hemisphere and took over military control. Finally in June 1944 Iceland formally declared itself an independent republic and severed its links with the Danish crown.

Thus by July 1940 the map of western and central Europe had been redrawn substantially in German favour. Only Great Britain remained to dispute the outcome of nine months of war. Indeed until the summer of 1941 the possibility of a peaceful settlement with the British Empire remained high on the German agenda, which precluded as radical a redrawing of western European boundaries as those in the eastern half.

7.2   A NEW MAP OF EUROPE 1941–1945

The apparent stability achieved in June 1940 was not to last. Italy launched an independent campaign against Greece from its bases in Albania in October 1940. It was a failure and the Greeks were able to invade Albania and occupy Northern Epirus (Capps, 1963). In April 1941 Germany went to Italy's assistance, but its way was blocked by Yugoslavia. However, both Greece and Yugoslavia were rapidly defeated by June 1941. Yugoslavia was fragmented with portions annexed by neighbouring Germany, Italy, Hungary and Bulgaria. A substantial Croatian state was established, including Bosnia-Herzegovina and sections of Dalmatia. The remainder was assigned to the revived states of Serbia and Montenegro, which, however, remained under military occupation regimes. Although Queen Elena of Italy was the daughter of the last king of Montenegro the attempt to revive the kingdom failed.

The German invasion of the Soviet Union began in late June 1941. Unlike the campaigns of 1914–1917, that of 1941 was highly successful in conquering territory, but failed to achieve a final victory. The recently acquired Soviet cordon sanitaire was overrun within a few weeks and German armies had advanced to the outskirts of Moscow by December 1941. In the following year another campaign extended the German zone almost to the Caucasus, but following the battle of Stalingrad in January 1943, the Russians began the reconquest of territory lost. It was ironically only after this date that the word 'Greater' was added to the German state name (GrossDeutches Reich) in official documentation, such as postage stamps (August 1943).

The administration of the extensive eastern lands was entrusted to the German state commissions (Reichskommissariats) of Ostland, covering the Baltic states and Byelorussia, and the Ukraine (Freeman, 1987).

A wide zone behind the fronts was maintained under direct military and police control. No serious attempt was made to revive the governments of Latvia, Lithuania and Estonia, which had been incorporated into the Soviet Union in August 1940, less than a year beforehand (Joesten, 1943). For example, the Provisional Government of Lithuania declared its independence in June 1941 but was forced to resign under German pressure in August 1941. The attempt to recreate an independent Ukrainian state in Lviv was suppressed by the German military authorities and the area was incorporated into the General Government. The considerable popular goodwill engendered by what appeared to be liberation from Joseph Stalin's repressive government, which, amongst other acts of terror, had induced famine in the Ukraine in order to eliminate nationalist movements, was rapidly dissipated.

Germany incorporated the Bialystok district on the East Prussian border and enlarged the General Government to include the whole of Galicia. Romania had reincorporated Bessarabia and northern Bukovina and went further to annex a substantial block of Transnistria, including the port of Odessa. Finland invaded the Soviet Union independently of Germany and regained the territory lost in 1940 and continued its advance to occupy much of Karelia with a view to either establishing a separate state after the war or incorporating it into Finland. Karelia occupied a particularly emotional place in the Finnish development of a national sense of identity in the nineteenth century, through the construction of a powerful national mythology (Paasi, 1996).

The German National Socialist perspective on eastern Europe thus took little account of the aspirations of the local populations or their histories, in contrast to the historicism of the Imperial German government in its dealings with the region during the First World War. Plans for the future government of Russia never progressed beyond the concept of a series of Reichkommissariats administered by Germans, mainly from the ranks of the National Socialist Party elite guard detachments, the SS. The political restructuring of the region thus involved colonial expansion not popular self-determination. In large measure this was a reflection of the Party's official view that the Slavic peoples of eastern Europe were not worthy of survival, but had to be reduced to the level of workers for the racially superior Nordic races. Thus the destruction of the societies and states of the region was viewed as an essential precondition for colonisation by ethnic Germans. The prevailing attitude was expressed by Erich Koch, German Commissar for the Ukraine in March 1943:

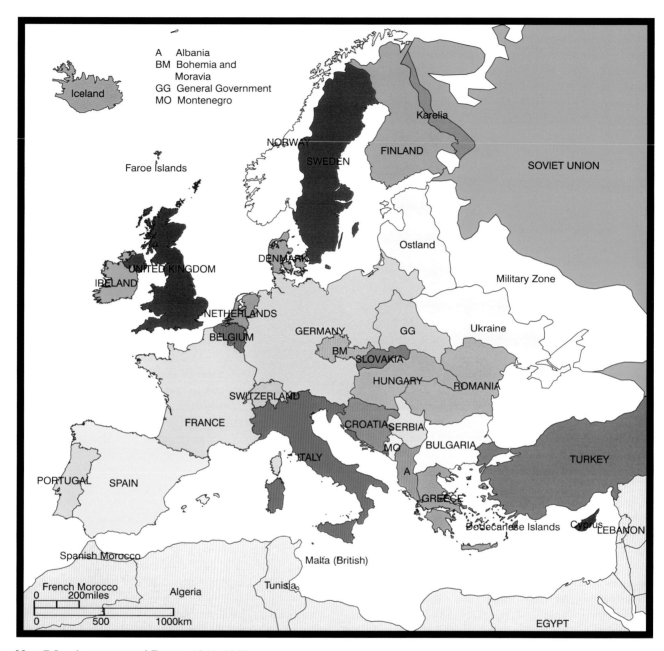

A   Albania
BM Bohemia and
    Moravia
GG General Government
MO Montenegro

Map 7.2   A new map of Europe 1941–1945

We are the Master Race and must govern hard but just ... I will draw the very last out of this country. I did not come to spread bliss ... The population must work, work, and work again ... We definitely did not come here to give our manna. We have come here to create the basis for victory. We are a master race, which must remember that the lowliest German worker is racially and biologically a thousand times more valuable than the population here.

(Shirer, 1964: 1118)

The Soviet reaction to the invasion was the withdrawal of autonomy from several of the nationalities, beginning with the Volga Germans in June 1941. Deportation, death and imprisonment followed. Towards the end of the war, the Crimean Tatars, Chechens, Kalmyks and others were deported from their homelands in retaliation for perceived collaboration with the invaders. In most cases the members of these nations were dispersed across central Asia. Only in

February 1957, following the posthumous denunciation of Joseph Stalin, was the return of the Caucasian people, including the Chechens, permitted together with the restoration of their autonomous institutions. The Volga Germans were rehabilitated in January 1965, but were given no right of resettlement or the restoration of the autonomous republic. The Crimean Tatars had to wait until June 1988 for rehabilitation, again no right of resettlement or restoration of the Crimean republic was granted.

In Siberia, the Soviet Union strengthened its position by incorporating the nominally independent Tuvinian People's Republic in October 1944. The government applied for admission to the Soviet Union as: 'The Soviet State has become mightier under the sun of the Soviet Constitution and has attained the flowering of the material and spiritual strength of large and small peoples in a unified Socialist family. To live and work in this family is the solemn desire of the whole Tuvan people' (Rupen, 1971: 146).

In the final stages of the war further adjustments to the map of Europe were made. Thus with the collapse of Italy in September 1943, Albania was proclaimed independent by the Germans. Areas such as the Dodecanese Islands, Ionian Islands, Gulf of Kotor, Zara (Dalmatia) and the Province of Laibach (Slovenia) were occupied and administered by Germany pending the final outcome of the war. In September 1944, Macedonia was declared independent following the surrender of Bulgaria to the Soviet armies, but the new state collapsed upon the German withdrawal three months later.

7.3   THE NEW MAP OF EAST AND SOUTH-EAST ASIA

The Japanese entered the Second World War with the simultaneous attack on the American naval base at Pearl Harbor in Hawaii and the invasion of British Malaya in December 1941. Within six months the Japanese army had conquered most of South-east Asia, with India and Australia under threat of invasion. Thailand and French Indo-China remained on the map but were forced into military alliances with Japan. Thailand indeed was augmented with the acquisition of territory from French-Indo China, British Malaya and Burma. Although the Portuguese settlement of Macao was not invaded, that on Timor was occupied as a frontline base against Australia. The whole complex was economically and politically integrated as the Greater East Asian Co-Prosperity Sphere. Representatives of the six founding members (Japan, China, Manchuria, Thailand, the Philippines and Burma) met in Tokyo in November 1943 to agree upon a charter.

The newly conquered lands were initially administered by the Japanese Imperial military and naval authorities. Indeed strategic bases such as Hong Kong and Singapore were effectively annexed and administered as integral parts of the Japanese Empire. The Pacific Islands, New Guinea and the outer islands of the Netherlands Indies and the three British states in northern Borneo were viewed in essentially colonial terms open to direct Japanese economic exploitation. However, elsewhere attempts were made to present the conquest as liberation from White colonial rule for the indigenous peoples. Japanese policy on granting political independence remained ambivalent throughout the war. Communities regarded as possibly sympathetic to the former colonial regimes, such as the Indians of Burma and the Chinese of Malaya, were either expelled or viewed with suspicion as potentially hostile national minorities. Otherwise attempts were made to secure support from the indigenous peoples of the region through the promotion of anti-colonial solidarity campaigns.

As an indication of the liberationary nature of the Japanese conquest of South-east Asia, the Philippines was promised independence. The Americans had granted internal self-governing Commonwealth status to the islands in November 1935, with the promise of independence within ten years. The Japanese proceeded to grant independence to the Philippines in October 1943. In August 1943 Burma had been declared an independent state in recognition for the assistance Japan had received from the Burmese National Army against the British. The separately administered Shan States were reincorporated into Burma in December 1943 as a further token of support. In both these cases popular indigenous independence movements were able to cooperate with the Japanese to secure their political ends.

The future of the Netherlands Indies presented a particular problem for the Japanese, as control of their resources, notably oil, was viewed as essential for the maintenance of the war effort. Thus the administration of the Indies was fractured, with Java as a separate command, Sumatra attached to Malaya, while the Imperial Japanese Navy exercised control over the remainder from Makassar in Celebes. The whole was referred to as 'the Southern Regions' rather than the Indonesia of the independence movement. Within this edifice freedom was to be 'different from an independence based on the idea of liberalism and national self-determination' (Dahm, 1969: 223). However, to gain public support a measure of self-government for Java and Malaya was introduced in August 1943, but in

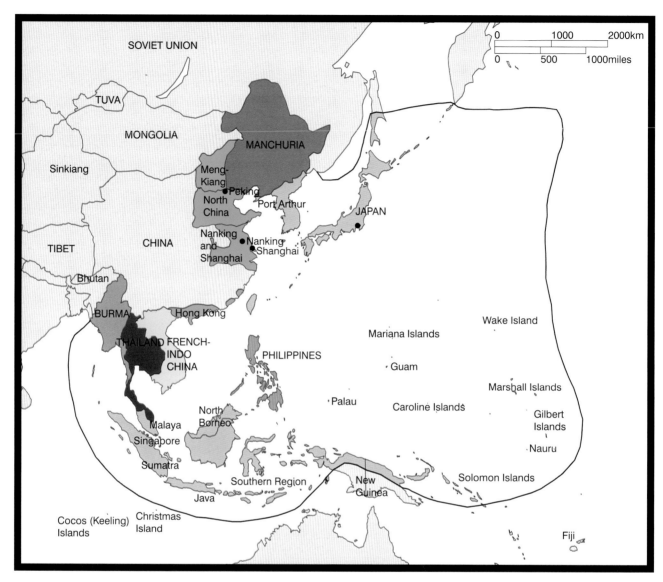

Map 7.3   The new map of East and South-east Asia

secret negotiations independence was rejected in favour of incorporation into the Japanese Empire at the end of the war.

An appreciation of the worsening military situation, following the fall of Saipan in the Mariana Islands to the Americans in July 1944, meant that the Japanese administration sought to enlist Indonesian independence movements more closely in the war effort and involve all the islands in the promotion of the war effort not just in Java. In August 1944 it was acknowledged 'that the Japanese Empire announces the future independence of all Indonesian peoples and thus the happiness of the Indonesian peoples may be forever secured' (Dahm, 1969:

276). This was a major departure for the Japanese authorities as it indicated a willingness to envisage not just Java and maybe Sumatra gaining independence, but the whole of the former Netherlands Indies. A Committee of Investigation was formed to secure these aims but it was only in August 1945, after the Japanese surrender, that Indonesia declared its independence.

In March 1945, following the Allied liberation of metropolitan France, the pro-German Vichy French colonial administration in Indo-China was deposed and dismantled by the Japanese. In its place the independence of the three kingdoms of Annam, Cambodia and Laos was

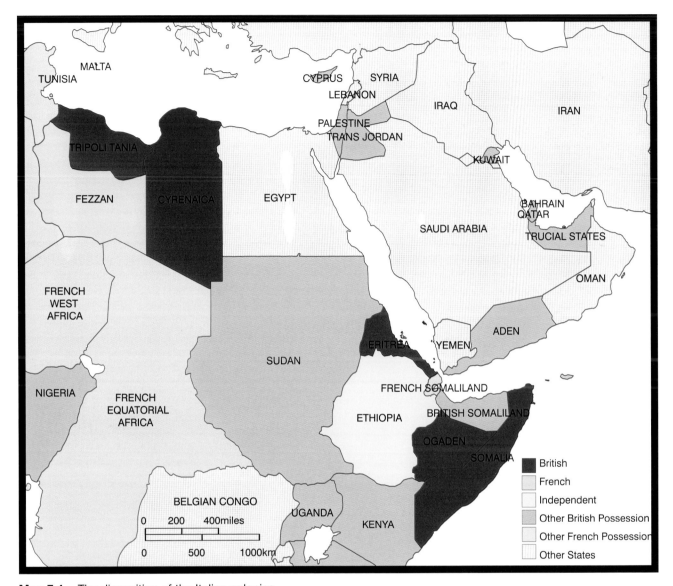

Map 7.4   The disposition of the Italian colonies

proclaimed (McAlister, 1970). Tonkin was attached to Annam but initially Japan retained direct control over Cochin China. However, in August 1945, just before the end of the war, Cochin China also was attached to Annam and the independence of Vietnam was proclaimed.

Owing to the exigencies of the conduct of the war, the newly established governments were unable to achieve any significant degree of autonomy, but they provided the training ground for the post-war anti-colonial national independence movements in the region. The end of the war in August 1945 was remarkably sudden and the political situation throughout much of South-east Asia

was in turmoil, which the returning colonial powers had difficulty in controlling.

7.4 THE DISPOSITION OF THE ITALIAN COLONIES

Italy entered the war, as an ally of Germany, in June 1940 at the time of the fall of France in an attempt to gain political advantage. Its one military success was the conquest of British Somaliland in August 1940, which was incorporated into the Italian Empire of East Africa.

Between February and May the following year, British forces conquered the whole of the Empire and in the process re-established British Somaliland. Italian Somalia and Eritrea came under British military administration until 1950 and 1952 respectively. The colonial government in French Somaliland preserved its status through careful diplomacy, recognising the pro-German Vichy government in June 1940, thereby preventing an Italian occupation and then joining the Free French in December 1942 in order to avoid occupation by the British.

Emperor Haile Selassie returned from exile in May 1941 and the Empire of Ethiopia was re-established. This constituted a dilemma for Great Britain, which was in effective military control of the whole of East Africa. The British government considered that it had defeated the Italians and was entitled to govern those conquests, even through some informal protectorate arrangement. The Ethiopians were able to extricate themselves from this predicament through gradually expanding their room for manoeuvre and appealing to American anti-colonial sensibilities (Marcus, 1983). For the time being, however, the Ogaden region between British and Italian Somaliland remained under British administration. The British plea for the establishment of a Greater Somalia in 1946 was rejected by the other great powers who were suspicious of British expansionist intentions (Laitin and Samatar, 1987). Only in October 1948 was the Ogaden formally returned to Ethiopian sovereignty, although not military control.

The conquest of the Italian colony of Libya presented a greater problem for the British. Egypt had been reoccupied at the beginning of the war to prevent possible German or Italian moves against the Suez Canal in terms of the Anglo-Egyptian Treaty of 1936. Egypt remained nominally neutral and did not officially declare war on Germany until February 1945. The country's declaration of neutrality did not prevent the initial Italian invasion of Egypt in September 1940. This was repulsed, as were the subsequent attacks by the German Afrika Korps in April 1941 and June 1942. Following the defeat of the German and Italian armies in North Africa in May 1943, Libya was apportioned between the French and British. France occupied the interior province of Fezzan together with the Ghadames oasis on the Tunisian border, while the British occupied the coastal provinces of Tripolitania and Cyrenaica.

CHAPTER 8

The Era of the United Nations 1945–1950

The Allied victory in the Second World War ended the German and Japanese military challenge for world supremacy and resulted in the emergence of a new set of superpowers. Indeed the rearrangement of international structures which followed resulted in the emergence of a bipolar world, East and West, dominated initially by the Soviet Union and the United States. Great Britain and France were exhausted and bankrupted by the war, while China slid into civil war. The apportionment of the world into two hostile spheres followed as the spoils of war were divided. The geopolitical transition that this involved was largely in place by March 1946 when Winston Churchill delivered his famous speech in Fulton, Missouri, claiming that an 'Iron Curtain' had fallen across Europe from Stettin in the Baltic to Trieste in the Adriatic (Taylor, 1990). The Cold War had begun and was to last over forty years. It is scarcely surprising that the era was one in which partition as a solution to intractable internal state conflict was particularly prevalent (Waterman, 1987).

However, in the initial post-war period the Allies looked towards a better world and to the establishment of a system of collective security which would prevent the outbreak of another world war. The United Nations was established in October 1945 to supersede the League of Nations and more actively to oversee the maintenance of world peace, through joint military intervention if necessary. All the countries that had taken part in the war against Germany and Japan were invited to join the Organisation and provision was made for others to join, subject to the approval of the membership. The Security Council, which could authorise wide-ranging activities, comprised the five permanent or great powers, the United States, Soviet Union, Great Britain, France and China, in addition to others elected by the General Assembly composed of all member states.

The United Nations was to play a significant role in the coming era, although not quite as its originators had anticipated, as a result of the frequent conflict of interests between the Soviet Union and the United States. Furthermore, the United Nations became involved in the next stage of world political development, namely the dismantling of the overseas colonial empires.

The Atlantic Charter agreed to in August 1941 by American President Franklin Roosevelt and British Prime Minister Winston Churchill had laid out the basis of the Allied war aims, although at the time the United States had not yet entered the war. The basic objectives had been the liberation of countries overrun by Germany and Italy and the self-determination and freedom of subject peoples. The key passage in the Atlantic Charter, affirming 'the right of all peoples to choose the form of government under which they will live', was subject to two very different interpretations. The British War Cabinet considered that: '... the Atlantic Charter... was directed to the nations of Europe whom we hoped to free from Nazi tyranny, and was not intended to deal with the internal affairs of the British Empire...' (Kissinger, 1994: 401). On the other hand, the American government considered the Charter to be universal in application. The American Undersecretary of State, Sumner Welles, offered the interpretation of basic war aims: 'If this war is in fact a war for the liberation of peoples it must assure the sovereign equality of peoples throughout the world, as well as in the world of the Americas. Our victory must bring in its train the liberation of all peoples... The age of imperialism is ended.' (Kissinger, 1994: 402). This policy was pursued after 1945, notably in pressurising Great Britain to grant independence to India (Clymer, 1995).

The twin themes of the Cold War and Decolonisation dominated world politics for the period until 1989. In the initial five years some fundamental lines were drawn on the world map, within which both processes were enacted in the ensuing four decades.

8.1   THE WORLD IN 1950

The world which emerged from the Second World War was more like its predecessor before the war than was the case with the post-First World War settlement. The temporary territorial settlements effected by Germany and Japan were dismantled. In the latter case, however, several of the

Japanese client states were to re-emerge soon afterwards, but Manchuria was permanently erased. In Europe states such as Austria, Czechoslovakia, Albania, Poland and Yugoslavia were reconstituted. Significantly the Baltic states of Latvia, Lithuania, and Estonia were not and the Soviet annexation of 1940 was tacitly recognised. Soviet–American disagreement over the future of Germany prevented any permanent settlement and no general peace treaty was signed. As a result, the military occupation zones demarcated at the end of the war assumed international significance as two German states emerged in 1949.

However, changes were dramatic elsewhere, notably in the Middle East, where the independence of Syria and the Lebanon was confirmed, and that of Transjordan and Israel followed. The Second World War had resulted in a major reappraisal of the British imperial capabilities and the recognition that India could not be retained by force. The outcome was the granting of independence to most of Great Britain's Asian possessions, notably the transformation of

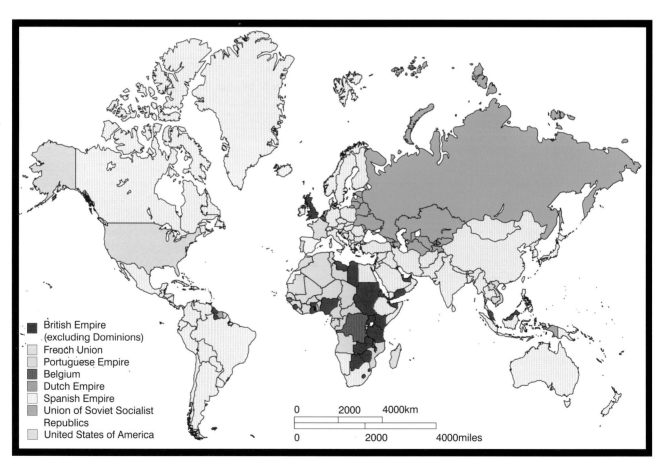

British Empire
(excluding Dominions)
French Union
Portuguese Empire
Belgium
Dutch Empire
Spanish Empire
Union of Soviet Socialist
Republics
United States of America

0   2000   4000km

0   2000   4000miles

Map 8.1   The world in 1950

the Indian Empire into the two dominions of India and Pakistan in August 1947. Independence for Burma and Ceylon followed quickly. The Philippines, so expensively reconquered from the Japanese by the Americans, was granted independence in July 1946 in line with promises made when the islands achieved Commonwealth status in November 1935. In contrast, the French and Dutch sought to re-establish their South-east Asian colonial empires by force. Initially this was done with the assistance of British and Allied armies. However, the reconquest of both the Netherlands Indies and French Indo-China was beyond the means of the colonial powers concerned and complex wars ensued, leading to Dutch withdrawal in 1949 and French withdrawal five years later. Only the British in Malaya and northern Borneo were able to re-establish themselves in effective control of their South-east Asian colonies.

One of the Allied war aims had been the restoration of independence to Korea. However, the peninsula had been occupied by the forces of the Soviet Union and the United States at the end of the war, with the object of establishing a new government. Agreement between the two countries proved to be impossible once the Cold War had begun and the military demarcation line along the 38th parallel between the two armies was consolidated into an international state boundary. Two Korean governments were established in the south and north in August and September 1948 respectively. Both regarded the division as temporary and sought the reunification of the country under its own flag.

The Americans conquered the Ryukyu Islands, which lay between Taiwan and the main Japanese islands, between April and June 1945. The maintenance of the military base on Okinawa was considered to be vital to the preservation of American strategic interests in the region. As a result the islands were placed under American administration, which remained in control until May 1972 when they were returned to Japan.

Significantly independence movements scarcely affected Africa. The French Empire created under the Third Republic was converted into the French Union of the Fourth Republic. However, overseas representation in the National Assembly in Paris was limited, although it did provide opportunities of personal political participation for a number of future African leaders denied their continental compatriots in other colonial empires. France also undertook the political integration of its West Indian possessions of Martinique, Guadeloupe and its dependencies, French Guiana, together with Reunion in the Indian Ocean into the French Republic as departments in March 1946. Again this administrative and political

solution to the constitutional development of small colonies was not emulated by other empires.

The immediate post-war era therefore resulted in the addition of some eleven new states to the world map. The era constituted one of the most significant expansions of the state system in the century as representing the beginning of the end of the European based colonial system. Thus by 1950 some 85 independent states were in existence, a remarkable change from the situation at the beginning of the century, or indeed that at the outbreak of war in 1939.

8.2   EUROPE IN 1950

The meeting of the victorious leaders at Potsdam in July and August 1945 resolved most of the major issues. The subsequent Peace Conference which met in Paris between August and October 1946 determined the conditions of the peace treaties for the defeated European countries, Italy, Romania, Bulgaria, Hungary and Finland. The idealism instilled by President Wilson at the 1919 peace conference was lacking and the prior resolution of most of the problem issues reduced the significance of the event. Germany and Austria were excluded from the settlement as their future could not be agreed upon. The new map of Europe was dominated by the Iron Curtain separating the Soviet dominated sphere of influence from that of the United States and its allies.

In western Europe the map was not dissimilar to that of 1939. Only the independence of Iceland from Denmark materially changed the pattern. The attempted secession of the Faroe Islands and the formation of an independent republic following a referendum in September 1946 was thwarted and an increased measure of autonomy introduced instead. The Grand Duchy of Luxembourg was resurrected following its liberation by American forces in September 1944. The temporary French occupation of the French speaking Val d'Aosta in Italy in May–June 1945 was not the prelude to annexation, only to the granting of autonomy.

It was in eastern Europe and on the interface between the two halves of the continent that the major changes had taken place. The new western boundary of the Soviet Union incorporated virtually all the land taken in 1939 and 1940 under agreements with Germany. In addition, the northern half of East Prussia was acquired from Germany and Transcarpathia from Czechoslovakia. Poland was redefined with a substantial westward movement, surrendering territory to the Soviet Union and gaining compensatory areas from Germany to reach the Oder-Neisse Line. The two major conglomerate Slavic states created in 1918,

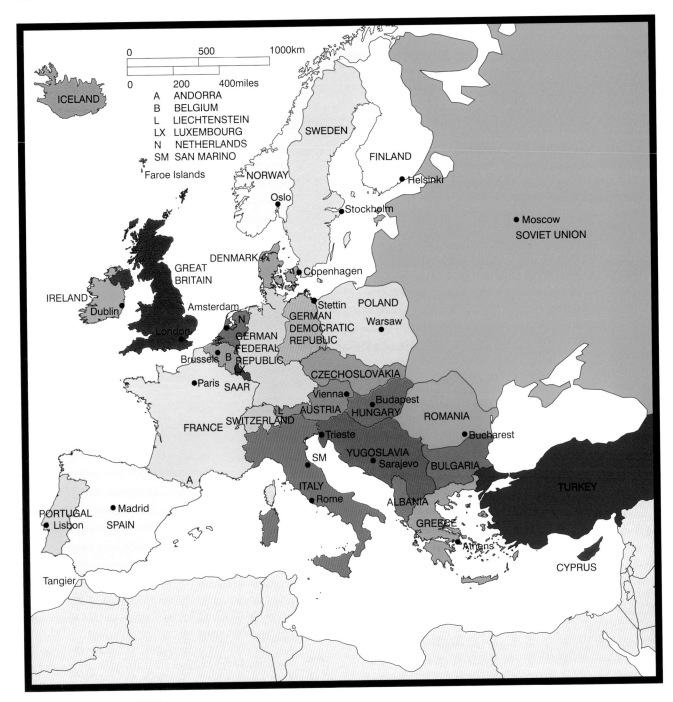

Map 8.2   Europe in 1950

Czechoslovakia and Yugoslavia, were reconstituted. In the former case the German population of Sudetenland, which had constituted over 20 percent of the state total in the 1930s, was deported, changing the ethnic balance in the country markedly in favour of the Czechs.

Indeed the post-war settlement was accompanied by massive population deportations and forced removals as the historic ethnic patterns were changed to fit the new boundaries drawn on the map of the continent. Ethnic cleansing, which had been a significant feature of the continent in the twentieth century, was most rigorously enforced during and immediately after the war (Kosinski, 1969). Some 31 million people were involved in the population transfers, which simplified the ethnic patterns of eastern Europe, effectively eliminating most of the more numerous minority groups between 1944 and 1948 (Magocsi, 1993b). Added to this was the organised mass murder of unwanted people, whether members of ethnic minorities or political rivals. The most significant was the systematic slaughter of six million Jews by the Germans in the course of the Second World War. Further purges took place after the war, notably of those who had opposed, or were thought likely to oppose, the new communist regimes installed throughout eastern Europe by the Soviet Union. The last was the coup d'etat in Prague in February 1948, which brought the Communists to power, only nine years after the Germans had staged their coup against the rump Czechoslovak state.

Where minorities survived and were acknowledged, the Soviet system of autonomous administrations was introduced. Yugoslavia emulated the system most closely, with six national republics constituted in April 1945 for the major national populations and historic entities. It included for the first time a recognition of the distinctive nature of the Macedonians, separate from both the Serbs and the Bulgarians. In addition, two autonomous regions, within the Serbian Republic, were established in Kosovo for the Albanians and the Vojvodina for the heterogeneous population of the former Austro-Hungarian frontier districts.

In Romania the bilateral treaty in February 1948 with Hungary over Transylvania provided for the establishment of an Autonomous Magyar Region. Eventually the region was constituted in September 1952. As a result of the hostility engendered by the Hungarian uprising against Soviet control in October 1956, the region was redefined and reduced in area in December 1960. Finally it was abolished in August 1965 under the new constitution of the Socialist Republic and a period of centralised Romanianisation was imposed upon the Hungarian minority. Elsewhere in eastern Europe governments assumed the minorities had been expelled or assimilated.

An exception to that statement was the peculiar status in east Germany of the Lusatian Sorb population. In May 1945 the Soviet occupying forces were greeted as liberators after an oppressive period of coercive Germanisation, by this the smallest of the Slavonic nations in Europe (Stone, 1972). In the same month a Sorbian National Council was established and the use of the Sorb language encouraged under Russian aegis. In March 1948 the Saxon assembly passed a Law for the Protection of the Sorbian Population's

Rights. It was subsequently copied by the Brandenburg authorities and the main points were incorporated into the constitution of the German Democratic Republic. However, after November 1949 direct Soviet protection was withdrawn and economic development, with attendant inflows of German speakers, undermined the Sorbish character of the area. In the section of Lusatia which fell to Poland in 1945, the Sorbian language had virtually disappeared by the 1960s and the minority was absorbed by the Polish immigrants.

8.3 GERMANY AND AUSTRIA: OCCUPATION ZONES

At the end of the war the four Allied powers were in occupation of Germany and Austria. Unlike the situation at the end of the First World War, the German armies had been completely defeated and Allied armies occupied the whole of the two countries. No national or local governments survived with which the occupation forces might deal so that a military government was initially established. This was followed by the introduction of increasing levels of local government which were entrusted to individuals and groups regarded as non-Nazi.

Austria was detached from Germany and run by a separate four-power Allied Council. The provisional government signed a declaration of independence in April 1945, declaring the unification with Germany in 1938 to be null and void (Brook-Shepherd, 1996). A unified administration under the Socialist leader, Dr Karl Renner, was installed and ratified by general elections. In Vienna some semblance of Allied unity was maintained with four-power military patrols within the sectoral divisions. In certain respects Austrian politicians could claim that the country had been liberated from German occupation in the same manner as Poland and Czechoslovakia. However, it was only in May 1955 that an Austrian State Treaty was signed ending four-power occupation and providing for a fully sovereign, neutral, state government and the withdrawal of all occupation forces.

The division of Germany into four zones of occupation and Berlin into four sectors was to have long-lasting results. Initially the four powers envisaged the formation of a demilitarised, neutral and deindustrialised country that would pose no future threat to its neighbours. Indeed, with the exception of the French zone, common services such as currency, posts and communications were maintained until June 1948. The introduction of currency reform by the Western powers in their zones in that month resulted in the

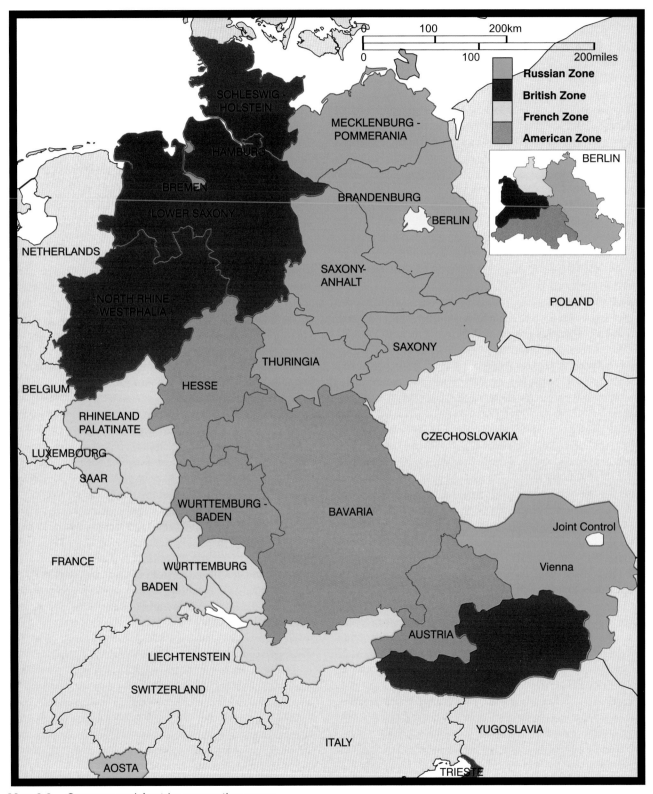

Map 8.3   Germany and Austria: occupation zones

Russian Zone administration issuing a separate currency, emphasising the markedly divergent social and economic reform programmes being undertaken by the occupying powers. In the Western zones economic revival took place and a major reconstruction of the country began, aided by American generosity through the Marshall Plan, launched by the Secretary of State, George Marshall, in June 1947 to facilitate the economic recovery of Europe. The Soviet Union and its allies rejected the Plan and sought to undermine its effectiveness. The Cold War intensified over control of Berlin where the Western powers were protecting their sectors some 160 kilometres inside the Russian Zone. The Russians blockaded West Berlin from June 1948 to May 1949, but failed to extract any concessions from the three occupying powers.

With the failure of the victorious Allies to agree upon the future of Germany, they proceeded to partition the country into two separate states. In October 1949 the three Western zones were merged to form the German Federal Republic, while the following month the Russians established the German Democratic Republic. In both cases the states, or lander, were constituted from the previous system of separate states and Prussian provinces. The name 'Prussia' itself was purged from the map in March 1947, as it was considered to be 'the bearer of militarism and reaction in Germany' and particularly responsible for the two world wars (Magosci, 1993b: 160). Some ingenious administrative innovations, such as the large and dominant North Rhine–Westphalia, emerged in order to unify the administration of the Ruhr industrial region. Baden and Wurttemburg were united, while the Rhineland Palatinate emerged as an administrative solution for government of the remainder of the previous French Zone. As a result, Bavaria lost its lands to the west of the Rhine. In East Germany the states were abolished in July 1952 and replaced by 15 smaller districts designed to promote central control.

The division of Berlin was reinforced, with the Western sectors attached, in all but name, as a land or state of the Federal Republic, while East Berlin became the capital of the German Democratic Republic. Significantly, international recognition for the two states was only forthcoming from the countries allied to either the United States or the Soviet Union. Both German governments refused to recognise even the de facto existence of the other until June 1973. Full recognition of each other's legitimacy and sovereignty was never extended. The fiction of joint four-power occupation and control was to persist until the Treaty of Final Settlement was signed in September 1990 at the end of the Cold War.

A temporary peculiarity in the post-war period was the status of the Saar Territory. In October 1947 the Saar was detached from the French Zone of Occupation. Under a new constitution the territory became politically independent of Germany and economically united with France. The new status was formalised in January 1948 with incorporation into the French customs and franc zones. This special status was ended with reincorporation into Germany in January 1957 as a move towards Franco-German reconciliation and the economic integration of the continent.

8.4   TRIESTE

At the end of the war the Yugoslavs, backed by the Soviet Union, demanded substantial boundary rectifications with Italy to include all the Slovene and Croat populated areas as well as the largely Italian populated coastal settlements of Istria, Trieste, Gorizia and Dalmatia. These included the city of Trieste, which had been the main Adriatic port for the Austro-Hungarian Empire and the hinterland before 1914. However, between 1918 and 1945 the city had stagnated as Yugoslavia directed hinterland trade to its own outlets. The potential economic links after 1945 resembled the position of Fiume after 1918. Close parallels with the earlier Yugoslav–Italian confrontation followed, complicated by the Cold War. Trieste was occupied at the end of the war by both Anglo-American and Yugoslav forces. In June 1945 a division of the territory into military occupation zones resulted in Anglo-American forces retaining possession of the city, although the immediate countryside was assigned to the Yugoslavs.

At the Treaty of Paris in February 1947 a final decision on the future of the city was deferred and as a compromise the Free Territory of Trieste was established to be placed under the control of the United Nations. In the interim period, before the international regime was installed, the Free Territory was divided into two zones. Zone A, including the city itself, was to be controlled by the Americans and British and Zone B by the Yugoslavs. The failure to agree on any long-term regime resulted in the partition of the Territory in October 1954. Zone A reverted to Italy and Zone B to Yugoslavia with a small rectification of the boundary in Yugoslavia's favour. Internationalisation as a long-term solution to territorial problems after the First World War had failed and no permanent United Nations territories emerged from the Second World War.

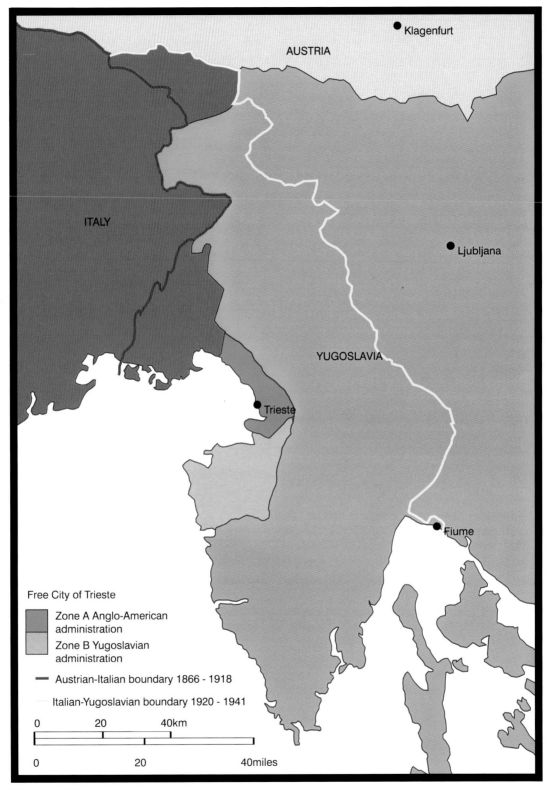

Map 8.4   Trieste

8.5 THE MIDDLE EAST

The Second World War had been partially fought over the Middle East. The formal French presence in the Lebanon and Syria had been brought to an end and expectations for the independence of other Arab countries under colonial rule were raised. The League of Arab States was established in May 1945 in Cairo to coordinate the policies and promote the interests of the Arab states. Initially this grouping was fairly traditional in approach with the majority of members being monarchies. Transjordan achieved independence in March 1946, but little movement took place thereafter, as attention was directed towards the future of Palestine. Indeed Palestinian representatives had attended the initial Cairo meeting.

The Cold War directly affected the region as the Soviet Union sought to exploit its military position in Iran. Soviet forces had been sent to the country in August 1941 in order to prevent Reza Shah Pahlavi joining Germany in the war.

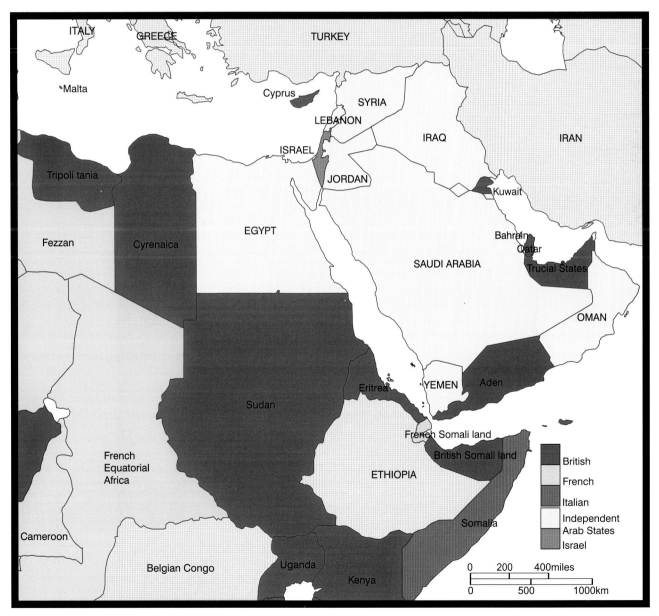

Map 8.5   The Middle East

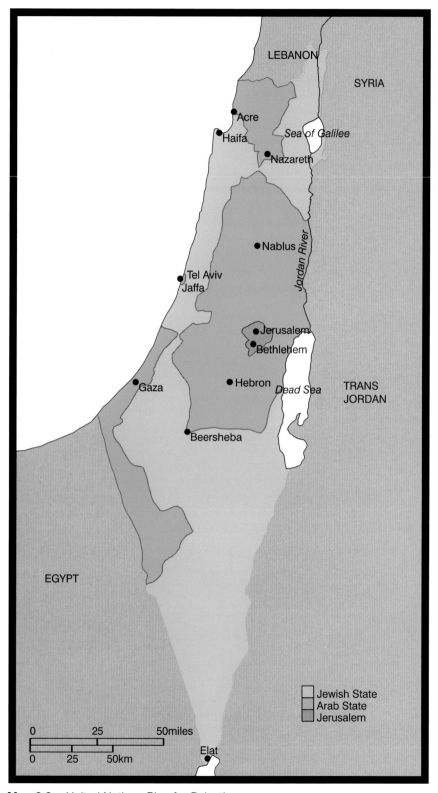

Map 8.6   United Nations Plan for Palestine

After the war the Soviet government promoted the secession of two sections of the country. First, an Azerbaijan Republic was proclaimed in Tabriz and then a Kurdish Republic in Mahabad in December 1945. The republics were short-lived as the withdrawal of Soviet forces following pressure from the United States resulted in the collapse of both in December 1946. Neither state was able to establish effective control over their state areas, nor overcome the tribal dissension which was exploited by the Iranian government in the reimposition of control.

8.6   UNITED NATIONS PLAN FOR PALESTINE

One of the most contentious political issues of the twentieth century has been the future of Palestine. In 1920 the British government had assumed the League of Nations mandate for Palestine, with the aim of establishing a 'national home' for the Jews. Jewish immigration was substantial and the population of the territory changed markedly in ethnic composition (Lehn, 1988). The Jewish population increased from approximately 58 000 in 1918 to 650 000 by 1948. Conflict with the indigenous Arab Palestinian population was inevitable as two distinct peoples sought to live in one territory. The British authorities sought to reduce conflict levels, which in 1939 meant severely curbing Jewish immigration, just at a time when the exodus of those fleeing Nazi persecution and ultimately the Holocaust in Europe was increasing dramatically.

Jewish settlement in Palestine had been based upon the premise of agricultural colonisation. Most Jewish communities in eastern Europe, from where the majority of the settlers came, had been denied access to rural land. The creation of a modern nation as opposed to a religious community therefore incorporated the idea of land settlement and agricultural self-sufficiency. The Jewish National Agency purchased land in Palestine with agricultural potential notably in the coastal plain and other areas requiring land reclamation and so rarely encroached upon the more densely settled hill regions of the interior where the majority of the Palestinian population lived. The pattern of Jewish land ownership thus reflected this activity and constituted the territorial basis for a viable nation-state (Stein, 1984). Approximately 200 000 hectares had been acquired for Jewish settlement, although this constituted only eight percent of the surface area of Palestine.

Partition of the country as a solution to ease Arab–Jewish conflict had been a part of official British thinking from the 1930s onwards. The British Palestine Partition Report in 1938 had envisaged the creation of Jewish and Arab states and a continuing mandated area centred on Jerusalem. Various modified plans were devised to secure the interests of both communities. However, the rejection by the Arab majority of any form of partition meant that the plans were not implemented. After the war increased flows of Jewish immigrants from newly liberated Europe presented practical and moral problems which the mandatory power was unable to solve. Jewish refugees were held in camps outside Palestine in an attempt to stop the flow, resulting in American condemnation. An Anglo-American Commission of Enquiry devised another partition plan, but the British requirement that the two sides be disarmed led to rejection.

The United Nations then took over responsibility for finding a solution. The Special Commission for Palestine opted to divide the country into two autonomous states, which were to remain integrated in economic terms. The plan was approved by the United Nations in November 1947 and formed the basis for the establishment of the Jewish state. It is noticeable that the plan provided for the Negev Desert to be included in the Jewish state, although few Jews lived within it. The boundaries were highly complex, allowing for territorial bridges between the various sections of the two states. In order to overcome the religious complexities of the capital, Jerusalem was to become an international city. Because this was the last internationally sanctioned plan for Palestine, the fiction of the international status of Jerusalem persists after half a century, with most countries stationing their ambassadors to Israel in Tel Aviv, not the city claimed by Israel as its capital.

8.7   THE PARTITION OF PALESTINE

The United Nations plan was rejected by the Arab states and the Arab leaders of Palestine. Hostilities began as both sides sought to improve their position before Great Britain terminated the mandate over the country. In May 1948 Britain evacuated Palestine and the State of Israel was proclaimed. At the same time the regular forces of the Arab League states invaded Palestine in support of the Arab community. The disconnected battles for local control at the beginning of the war were transformed into a conflict with regular front lines. The war was punctuated by ceasefires until the final armistice in April 1949. International attempts at mediation failed. Count Folke Bernadotte, the United Nations mediator, proposed a redrawing of the lines to consolidate the two states in July 1948. These terms were rejected and his assassination in September indicated that

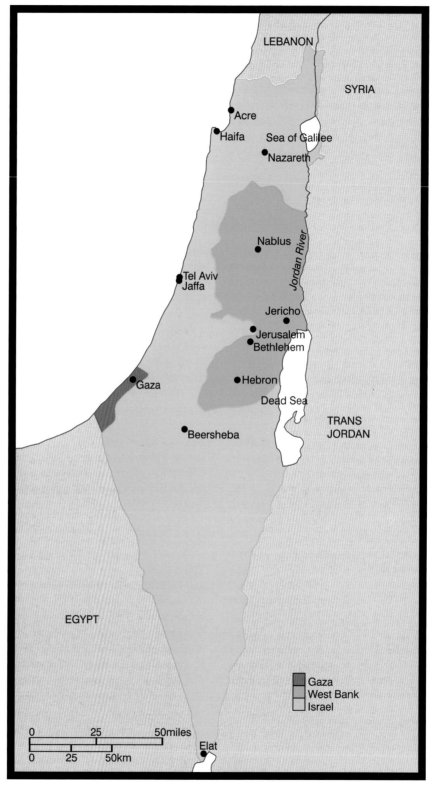

Map 8.7   The partition of Palestine

the military solution was inevitable. The Arab armies were defeated and the Arab states were unsuccessful in their aim of eliminating Israel and securing the establishment of an independent Arab state of Palestine, coincident with the former British administered territory.

At the end of the war Israel secured some 20 700 square kilometres (78 percent) of pre-war Palestine, including a corridor to link the coastal belt with the New, Jewish, City of Jerusalem. Egypt occupied some 363 square kilometres in the Gaza Strip on the Mediterranean coast. Transjordan occupied the hill country including the Old City of Jerusalem. The area subsequently referred to as the 'West Bank' covered some 5505 square kilometres. The status of these territories has changed according to the phases in the wider Arab–Israeli dispute. Egypt did not annex Gaza, but administered it as a dependency, awaiting the recreation of a greater Palestinian state. A nominally independent kingdom of Palestine was proclaimed in the Transjordanian occupied sector in December 1948. The parliament of this entity then offered the Crown to King Abdullah, leading to the union of Transjordan and Palestine as the Hashemite Kingdom of the Jordan in April 1950 (Smith, 1984). This move still did not preclude the future constitutional settlement in the event of a successful Arab war to eliminate Israel.

The armistice did not solve many of the questions raised by the war, most noticeably the Palestinian refugees (Morris, 1990). Approximately 150 000 Arabs fled to Gaza and 300 000 to the West Bank and Transjordan, while smaller numbers went to Syria and Lebanon. In all, approximately 720 000 Palestinians fled or were expelled from the territory that became the Israeli state. Most were housed in refugee camps under the humanitarian supervision of the United Nations. No attempt was made to integrate the refugees into the host communities, as had been the case after the Second World War in Europe. The Palestinian refugees thus effectively became a nation without a state, awaiting the opportunity to return to the homes from which they had fled in 1948–1949. The lack of any recognition of the Jewish state by its Arab neighbours until the Egyptian peace treaty of March 1979 was a severe drawback to the stability of the region as the wars of 1956, 1967 and 1973 illustrated. The presence of a large number of Palestinian refugees expecting to return home added to the problems as they provided the recruits for the numerous liberation movements which sought to reverse the outcome of the 1948 war.

8.8   THE PARTITION OF INDIA

Although the Second World War had left Great Britain victorious, it was also effectively bankrupt and no longer able to invest in maintaining the coercive control systems over its more politically volatile overseas possessions. India had been placed on the constitutional route to dominion status in 1935. The process was halted by the war and by the complex politics of the period. For example, India had been involved in the war in 1939 without due consultation between the British and Indian governments, even though it was a separate member of the League of Nations. At the end of the war the interests of the Moslem League, led by Mohammed Ali Jinnah, proved to be incompatible with those of the main independence movement, the Indian Congress Party, led by Jawaharlal Nehru and Mahatma Gandhi. Hindu nationalists reminded the Moslems that 'minorities must live by the grace of the majority' (Akbar, 1985: 23). This view Moslem leaders finally rejected and sought separate statehood.

The failure to secure agreement on independence for a united India led to the formulation of the plan of partition. The basis of the plan was the excision of the Moslem majority areas to form a separate state of Pakistan. The plans as drawn up envisaged the division of British India according to population preference and the accession of the princely states to one or other of the new dominions. Briefly the option of even greater fragmentation through the separate independence of the princely states was contemplated (Hodson, 1969). The division of British India was entrusted to a boundary commission under Sir Cyril Radcliffe (Spate, 1947). Partition lines had been suggested by the two sides, but they bore little relationship to one another. Finally the division of the Punjab and Bengal into Indian and Pakistani sectors was done with reference to population numbers according to the 1941 census, the canal systems or irrigation schemes and lines of communication. It was the latter consideration which led to the inclusion of the Chittagong Hill Tracts in Pakistan although only 2.8 percent of the population had been enumerated as Moslem. The resultant compromise was acceptable to both sides, which have not sought to redefine the lines in the subsequent wars over the fate of the princely state of Jammu and Kashmir.

As B.L. Sukhwal (1971: 75) noted, 'The Indian Independence Act left the Indian states completely free and so created not two but 564 independent countries of which two, India and Pakistan, were dominions'. In practice the princely states were not given the option of recognised

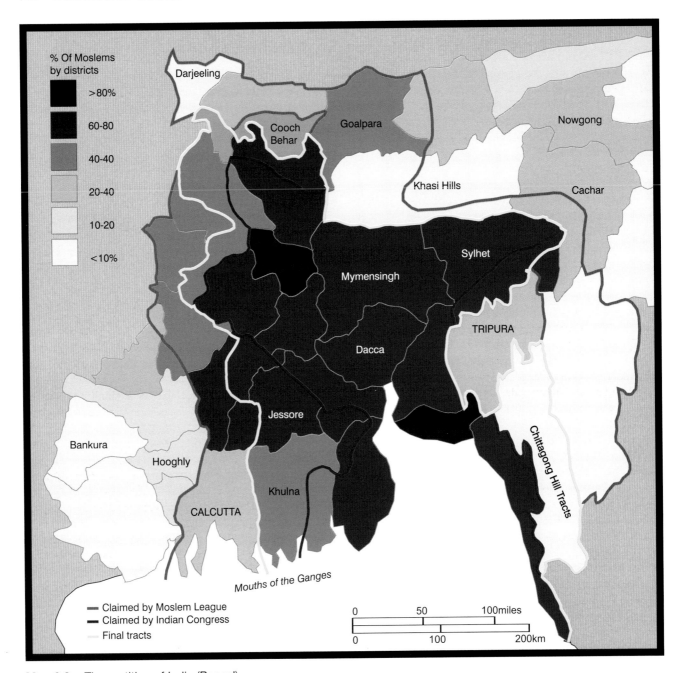

Map 8.8   The partition of India (Bengal)

independence and all had to agree to a treaty of accession to either India or Pakistan. Owing to the spatial distribution of the states and their relationship with the Indian or Pakistani sections of British India, the majority had little difficulty in arriving at a decision. Three states deserve particular mention as other options did appear open (Mahajan, 1983). It should be noted that in a number of states the religion of the ruler was not that of the majority of his subjects. Thus in the Kathiawar peninsula the Nawab of Junagarh, Maharajah Mahabat Khan, acceded to Pakistan in August 1947, although the majority (80 percent) of his subjects were Hindus. The Nawab of Junagarh, together with the Khan of Manavadar, held out against rising levels of popular discontent until the states were eventually was occupied by

Indian forces in November 1947. The subsequent plebiscite in February 1948 overwhelmingly endorsed accession to India. The spatial significance of the act of accession to Pakistan could be appreciated from the intense fragmentation of territory involved as shown in Map 2.10.

Some princely states, notably Hyderabad and Travancore, sought to claim complete independence with the ending of the British paramountcy. However, the Maharajah of Travancore reconsidered his position and acceded to India before independence. The constitutional position of Hyderabad was more complex as the ruler, the Nizam, Nawab Mir Osman Ali Khan Asaf Jah VII, was a Moslem, but the majority of his subjects (85 percent) were Hindus. Moreover, with a population of 18 million and a state area of 214 000 square kilometres, it was larger than many recognised independent states. The state was severely restricted in its options as it was completely surrounded by Indian territory and lacked a coastline. Negotiations to secure transit rights through Portuguese Goa were still confronted with this basic problem. In November 1947 a 'standstill' agreement was reached postponing a decision on accession. Disturbances and riots followed and in September 1948 the Indian army intervened and the state was placed under military rule. Only in November 1949 did the Nizam formally recognise the constitutional incorporation of his state into the Dominion of India and military rule was ended.

Other states retained a nominal independence for varying periods. Kalat on the borders of Afghanistan and Iran declared independence in August 1947 and was only occupied by Pakistani forces in April 1948. In contrast Bahawalpur, adjoining Indian Rajputana, retained independence for a matter of seven weeks before the Emir voluntarily acceded to Pakistan. In both cases the apparent options offered by the states' situation on international boundaries proved to be extremely limited.

Partition was a vast undertaking and the authorities had little appreciation of the magnitude of the disaster which then ensued. Some 15 million refugees moved between the two states, while an estimated 500 000 were killed in inter-communal fighting. The Hindu minority in Pakistan was virtually eliminated, although a substantial Moslem community remained in the secular state of India. The two states that emerged were large by world standards. India, with 361 million inhabitants at the time of the 1951 Census, was the second most populous state in the world, while Pakistan, with 76 million, occupied sixth place. Both states were also spatially large, with India nominally extending over 3.2 million square kilometres and Pakistan over 944 000 square kilometres.

Pakistan at independence possessed the peculiarity that it consisted of two sectors separated by 1500 kilometres of Indian territory. East and West Pakistan were united only by a common religion, as in linguistic and economic terms they differed markedly. The tensions of that situation were such that the secession of East Pakistan to form the state of Bangladesh was proclaimed in March 1971. After Indian military intervention the new state received Pakistani recognition in December 1971.

8.9   KASHMIR, CREATION AND PARTITION

The most intractable political problem to emerge from the partition of India was the fate of the princely state of Jammu and Kashmir (Schofield, 1996). The culturally complex and strategically placed state had been constructed by the Dogra Maharajah Gulab Singh in the nineteenth century. Beginning from a territorial base in Jammu, which he obtained in 1822, he was able to extend his power northwards into Ladakh in 1834 and then the Vale of Kashmir and Baltistan in 1846. Later in the century Kashmiri control was extended over Gilgit to the north-west. Although the Maharajah was a Hindu, as was his dynastic base in Jammu, his conquests had been mostly of Moslem populations, with the exception of Buddhist Ladakh. Thus at the time of partition, over three-quarters of the population was Moslem.

At independence the Maharajah, Hari Singh, was placed in a similar position to the Nizam of Hyderabad. He and his population differed over the issue of accession and the preferred option of independence had not been sanctioned. The outbreak of rebellion amongst sections of the Moslem population in the western areas in favour of joining Pakistan resulted in the establishment of a government of Azad (Free) Kashmir in October 1947. Confronted with this threat to his position, the Maharajah sought military protection and acceded to India later in the month. The Indian government accepted the accession, subject to a vague provision for ascertaining the wishes of the population. Indian concessions to attain accession included a high degree of autonomy and the provision (in January 1957) of a separate constitution for the state, the only one in the country. The war between India and Pakistan which followed was indecisive and the armistice in January 1949 resulted in the partition of the state. Although the agreement provided for a plebiscite to settle its future, such a test has never taken place. Subsequent wars, notably that from August to September 1965, did not change its status. Some local politicians proposed the establishment of a separate

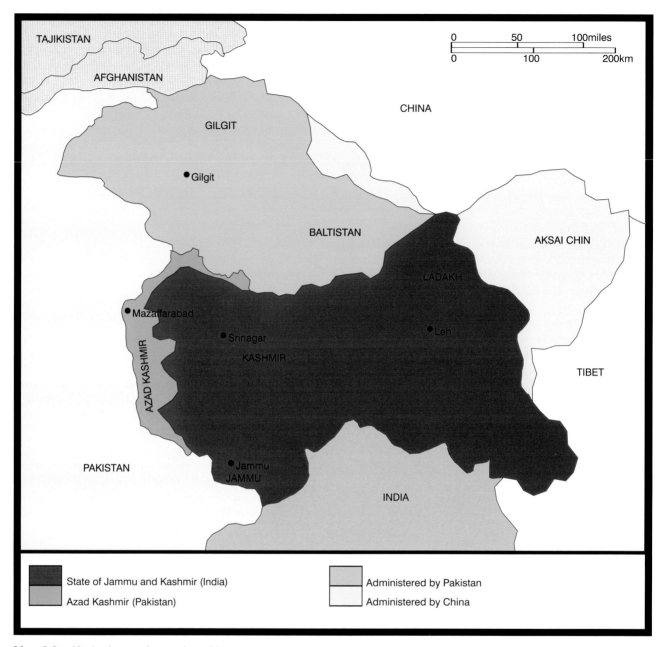

Map 8.9 Kashmir, creation and partition

independent state, but neither of the occupying powers wishes to relinquish its hold on the state.

Kashmir was divided into four zones. The major part of the state, including Jammu, the Vale of Kashmir, together with western Ladakh, became a state of the Indian Union. Its special status is indicated by the dominant role of the central government in maintaining its adhesion to the Union. A small section of western Kashmir is held by the Azad Kashmir government, which is supported by the Pakistani government. Baltistan and Gilgit were taken under the direct administration of the Pakistani government immediately upon the outbreak of hostilities in October 1947. Subsequently eastern Ladakh was occupied by China, which successfully disputed the boundaries between Ladakh and Tibet and between Kashmir and Sinkiang.

8.10   THE INDIAN UNION

The government of India adopted a dominion style constitution in August 1947, with the Emperor assuming the status of King of India. However, this was only a transition phase, with the introduction of a republican constitution in January 1950. Intriguingly the new state remained within the Commonwealth, whereas previous states rejecting the monarchy had left the organisation, including Burma in 1948 and Ireland in 1949. The new constitution of the Indian Union was federal in character with considerable powers devolved upon the states. However, no right of secession was granted and the constitution provided for the imposition of a limited term of direct presidential rule where state governments came into unresolvable conflict with the central government or proved to be incapable of fulfilling their functions.

The highly complex administrative pattern inherited by the new Indian government was tackled with a major rationalisation of the state structure. Thus states were grouped into new units to simplify the administrative map, while the old princely states were merged into the administration of the remainder of the country. New states such as Rajasthan thus emerged through the unification of the previous Rajput states and ex-British Ajmere. Some 200 states in the Kathiawar peninsula were formed into the ephemeral Union of Saurashtra in February 1948 and then merged with Bombay. However, the results of such ad hoc arrangements were clearly at variance with the need to establish viable states for the Indian Union, where local patriotism could be harnessed for national development.

In 1955 the States Reorganisation Commission embarked upon the systematic redrawing of the ad hoc pattern that resulted from these amalgamations. In doing so the members were guided by four broad principles, namely: the preservation and strengthening of the unity and security of India; a regard for areas of linguistic and cultural homogeneity; financial, economic and administrative considerations; and the successful working of the national plan. In reaching a new administrative dispensation the Commission considered that the regional languages had developed into 'rich and powerful vehicles of expression creating a sense of unity among the peoples speaking them' (India, 1955: 35). The Commission hoped to steer a middle course between the promotion of potentially separatist ethnic 'homelands' and 'the conflict and discord ... inherent in administrations in which diverse elements are forcibly held together' (India, 1955: 37).

The major linguistic groups therefore became the building blocks for the new states (Breton, 1997). Existing districts and in some cases states were left untouched, notably in the Hindi-speaking north of the country. The major issue was the position of the Hindi-speaking population, which constituted 40 percent of the total population. A single Hindi state would have dominated the Union. Historic boundaries in the north were retained to fragment the Hindi region. Thus the old United Provinces was renamed Uttar Pradesh and with a population of 63.2 million in 1951 was the largest state in terms of population. Jammu and Kashmir also remained as a special case pending the final resolution of its status. In other parts of the country the old system was ignored as new lines were drawn upon the map. The former princely state of Hyderabad, for example, was partitioned between three new states on a linguistic basis.

Fourteen new states initially emerged from the process with a number of federal territories including the capital at Delhi and smaller groupings unable to support full statehood. With the exception of Jammu and Kashmir (3.2 million), and Assam (9 million), which were constituted as a result of their historic and geographical peculiarities respectively, the newly defined states contained large populations. Based on 1951 census figures, seven states possessed populations in excess of 25 million, while a further five exceeded 13 million inhabitants.

The sheer size and diversity of the states led to reappraisals and the demands for new states right from the inception of the new state map. Thus Bombay State was divided as a result of Gujerati demands for a separate state in May 1960. The new unit, Gujerat, was still large and contained over 16 million inhabitants in 1951, as opposed to the 32 million remaining in Bombay, which was renamed Maharashtra. However, it was in Assam that the greatest demands for secession, whether for separate statehood within or outside India, took place. The Nagas, after a lengthy secessionist war, compromised by accepting separate Union status for their homeland in July 1960. However, with only 200 000 inhabitants at the time of the 1951 census, it represented a completely new concept in state size in India. Other separatist groups as well as the inhabitants of the Union territories sought full statehood.

The Union territories included several of India's sensitive international areas of dispute. At independence, both Portuguese and French India remained under colonial rule. However, the Indian government sought to incorporate them into the Union. Chandernagore, situated in the Calcutta conurbation, was incorporated first. The municipal assembly voted to join India in December 1948.

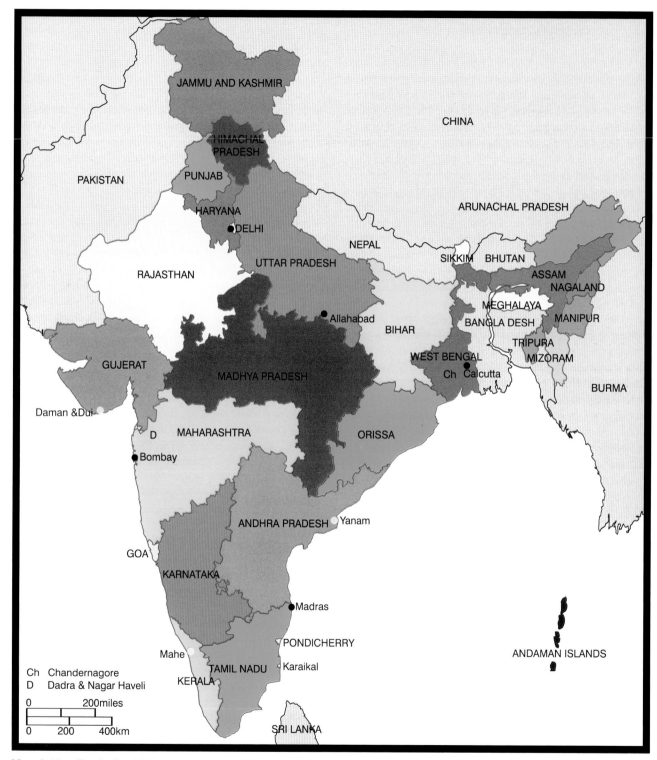

Map 8.10   The Indian Union

The subsequent referendum in June 1949 favoured union with India. The formal handover took place in April 1950, although the treaty of cession was only ratified in February 1951. The French withdrew from the other four settlements in November 1954, following the outcome of a plebiscite.

The Portuguese government resisted the loss of territory. In December 1955 the enclave of Dadra and Nagar Haveli was occupied by a 'People's Congress' and India refused to allow Portuguese police to cross its territory to re-establish colonial authority. This autonomous government was, however, committed to incorporation into India, not separate statehood. Finally in December 1961 Indian forces occupied the remaining Portuguese possessions (Dui, Daman and Goa). Portuguese recognition of this step only came after the revolution in Lisbon in April 1974. Owing to their distinctive historical and cultural background these territories were initially administered as Union territories, and Goa was later raised to full statehood.

Two areas on the border with China presented diplomatic and administrative problems. The position of the princely state of Sikkim was confirmed by treaty in 1950, leaving the state effectively as an Indian protectorate but not a Union territory. The Chogyal retained internal control but the state effectively became more dependent upon India as development projects were undertaken and militarisation occurred under threat from China in the 1960s. Finally in May 1975 Sikkim was incorporated into India with the status of a separate state, as a means of thwarting moves to declare independence. The other contentious area was the Northeast Frontier Agency, the sovereignty of which was disputed with China. It had been administered by the British before independence with minimal interference with established local practice. Indeed any outside influences were discouraged as leading to the destabilisation of the existing society. The post-independence Indian administration began a process of modernisation as a Union territory. Progress was such that the territory assumed full statehood as Arunachal Pradesh in February 1987, a constitutional advance which was denounced by the Chinese government.

The partition of the Punjab in 1947 left the Indian sector still severely divided (Ahmed, 1996). The Sikhs who had dominated the region prior to its conquest by the British sought to establish their own administration. Agitation led to the further division of the Indian state in November 1966, when the mountainous tracts were added to Himachal Pradesh and a separate Hindi-speaking state of Haryana was established, leaving the Sikh Punjabi-speaking population dominant in the rump state. Sections of the Sikh population then wished to establish an independent state of Khalistan in the Punjab State, which was supported by a militant campaign and opposed by the Indian government.

8.11 SECESSIONISM IN BURMA

The British had reconquered Burma from the Japanese by August 1945 but they lacked the power or determination to retain control once the war was over. The interim government drafted a republican and centralised constitution. The Union of Burma at independence in January 1948 therefore left the Commonwealth and embarked upon a programme to enforce central control over the disparate communities of the country.

Under the 1923 constitution the British administration had effectively divided Burma into two sectors, central 'ministerial' Burma and the 'scheduled' or 'excluded' areas. This basic diarchy had been exacerbated by the Japanese occupation between 1942 and 1945 (Selth, 1986). It remained as the various frontier communities sought independence or autonomy in the post-independence era. The constitution was modelled upon that of the Soviet Union, but probably the extensive rights offered to minorities were also not meant to be exercised in practice (M. Smith, 1991). Indeed the independence constitution provided for the right of secession of the Shan State after a ten-year trial period. The Shan, because of their remote but strategic situation, were considered to constitute the most significant minority in the country and had preserved the thirty historic principalities until independence. Although speaking a separate language they had been linked to the former Burmese kings, as had other nationalities, through the observance of Therevada Buddhism. The modern concept of linguistically based nationalism had not been involved. The Karenni received a similar promise. Initially only the Kachin, Karenni (Kayah) and Shan attained statehood. The Chins were administered as a 'Special Division'.

In October 1951 the Karen received the right to a separate state, but within a much restricted territory. The Karen occupied an extensive tract extending from the Irrawaddy delta to the Thai border, but their core area had been disrupted by Burmese land settlement in the colonial period. As a result, much of the area that the Karens claimed was assigned to the Burman section of the country and so fell under the direct control of the central government. The Karen were to fight the longest and most determined war for independence. Limited agreements were reached with the seven peripheral communities, including the Mon and Arakanese, for some degree of

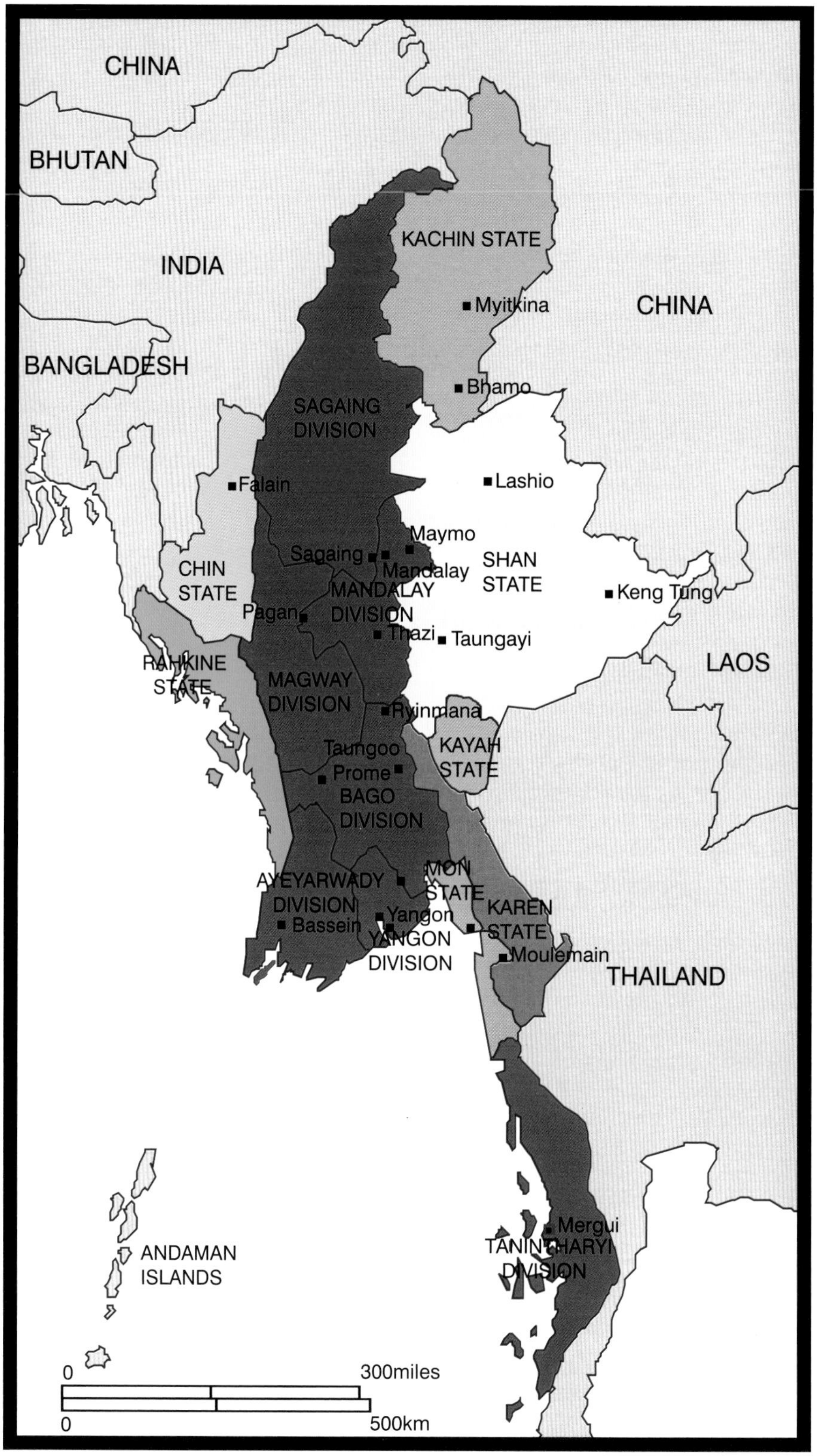

CHINA

BHUTAN

INDIA

BANGLADESH

KACHIN STATE

■Myitkina

CHINA

■Bhamo

SAGAING
DIVISION

■Falain

■Lashio

Maymo

Sagaing■ ■Mandalay

SHAN
STATE

CHIN
STATE

■Keng Tung

Pagan■ MANDALAY
DIVISION

RAHKINE
STATE

■Thazi ■Taungayi

MAGWAY
DIVISION

LAOS

■Pyinmana

Taungoo■

KAYAH
STATE

Prome■
BAGO
DIVISION

AYEYARWADY
DIVISION

MON
STATE

■Yangon

KAREN
STATE

■Bassein   YANGON
DIVISION

■Moulemain

THAILAND

ANDAMAN
ISLANDS

■Mergui
TANINTHARYI
DIVISION

0   300miles

0   500km

Map 8.11   Secessionism in Burma

autonomy, although no uniformity of the extent of devolution was agreed upon. Indeed central government authority was often tenuous in the years which followed as the Communist insurrection and the Chinese civil war also spilled over into the country to destabilise it. The military government, installed by the coup of March 1962, sought to abolish the concessions to the non-Burman ethnic groups, but did not immediately achieve a unified state.

The January 1974 Burmese constitution sought to bring a more uniform approach to the governance of the country as a means of promoting the 'Burmese Way to Socialism'. The state was divided into seven Union republics for the minorities and seven administrative divisions for the Burman population. The republics provided for the seven major minority groups to be afforded a measure of autonomy while enforcing the political and social objectives of the government. Within the administrative divisions no autonomy was envisaged. The Burman population accounted for some 60 percent of the total and none of the individual minorities totalled more than 10 percent. Furthermore, the definition of identity was remarkably difficult with the result that attempts to enumerate minority numbers were often contradictory as colonial and post-colonial concepts of nationality were fused with pre-colonial concepts related to religious observance, upon which the government increasingly called to unite the modern nation (Thomson, 1995). The problems posed by the multiplicity of local dialects within the main linguistic families prevented any over-arching minority cohesion. As a result, the government by the 1990s was able to achieve some success in enforcing its policies of assimilating minorities into a Burmese nation. In military terms, between 1994 and 1996 the government reasserted its control over most of the national territory and the open secessionist movements, which had numbered twelve in 50 years, were largely defeated. It was symbolic of the centralisation undertaken under military rule that in June 1989 the State Law and Order Restoration Council changed the name of the country to Myanmar.

8.12 INDONESIA

The confused political situation in the Netherlands Indies at the end of the Second World War was not resolved for another five years. The Republic of Indonesia, proclaimed by Achmed Sukarno in August 1945 at the end of the Japanese occupation, was confronted by the British military occupation the following month. In the course of 1946 the Dutch reoccupied the outer islands and key points in Java

and Sumatra. The weakened colonial power found itself having to cooperate with the forces of the Indonesian Republic. Negotiations between the two ensued with intermittent agreements and military confrontations. The Dutch sought to use their position controlling the outer islands to force the Republic holding most of the populous parts of Java and Sumatra to accept a form of Dutch Commonwealth, modelled on the British precedent. The Republican authorities sought to extend their rule over the whole of the Netherlands Indies in a centralised state. In November 1946 a provisional agreement was reached for the establishment of the United States of Indonesia, based on federal principles. The Dutch subsequently improved their military position and sought to increase their influence, but they lost international legitimacy as the pressures of anti-colonialism gained strength.

In December 1949 the United States of Indonesia was established and granted international recognition. It involved the creation of a federal structure between the Republic, based in Java and Sumatra, and the outer islands, held by the Netherlands. The government, under President Sukarno, proceeded to undermine the inherited constitution and incorporate the federal states into a unitary structure. The choice for the states was thus between integration and unilateral declarations of independence. Only the predominantly Christian, South Moluccan Republic chose the latter course in April 1950. It was suppressed by force in November 1950. Elsewhere Christian communities, such as Minahasa in northern Celebes, recognised the wider Indonesian claim upon their loyalties and accepted incorporation (Henley, 1995). In August 1950 the Indonesian Republic was re-proclaimed and the federal structure was repudiated.

The Dutch retained administrative control of West New Guinea on the grounds that the territory was inhabited by a markedly different ethnic Papuan population. It was to remain a major source of international conflict as the Indonesian government claimed the whole of the former Netherlands Indies and refused to recognise Dutch retention of the territory. International pressure was such as to force the Dutch to surrender the territory to an interim United Nations Temporary Executive Authority in October 1962. This body administered the territory to facilitate the Indonesian takeover in May 1963 as the province of Irian Jaya.

Japan had occupied Portuguese (East) Timor during the Second World War, but afterwards the colonial power was able to effect a swift return. Portuguese control was maintained until 1975 over the predominantly Roman Catholic population. The Portuguese revolution in April 1974 prompted the rapid decolonisation of the country's

Map 8.12   Indonesia

overseas empire. East Timor was set on the course to independence, but the colonial government lost control of events. A referendum was promised for March 1975, but was abandoned in favour of elections. In June 1975 a provisional government composed of the liberation movements was established, which accepted continued colonial control until October 1978 in order to facilitate political development. In August 1975 a coup resulted in the withdrawal of the Portuguese from much of the country and a civil war. The major pro-independence movement, Fretelin, declared independence in November 1975. Indonesia invaded and established a provisional government in December 1975. The last Portuguese officials were evacuated later in December 1975. The Indonesian backed East Timorese government rejected a test of public opinion and sought incorporation into Indonesia, which was effected in July 1976. The annexation was not recognised by the international community, and the war of independence on the island resulted in the death of approximately a third of the population of the former Portuguese colony. The East Timorese question remains one of the major international issues for resolution in the twenty-first century (Lagerberg, 1979).

8.13   THE REUNIFICATION OF CHINA

China underwent a major transformation following the defeat of Japan. The country was admitted to the United Nations as one of the five permanent members of the Security Council as worthy of the status of a superpower. With a population estimated at approximately 500 million, it was by far the most populous in the world. The immediate results of victory were the regaining of control over the areas occupied by Japan during the war. Manchuria was restored to Chinese control, although the Soviet Union remained in occupation of the country until April 1946. In addition, Formosa (Taiwan), ceded to Japan in 1895, was regained. The French leasehold territory of Kwangchow, which Japan had incorporated during the war in February 1943, was also occupied by Chinese forces. However, swift British action prevented the Chinese occupation of Hong Kong in August 1945.

The Nationalist government, under General Chiang Kai-Shek, however, was confronted by the revived Communist insurgency, which gained strength from Soviet support on

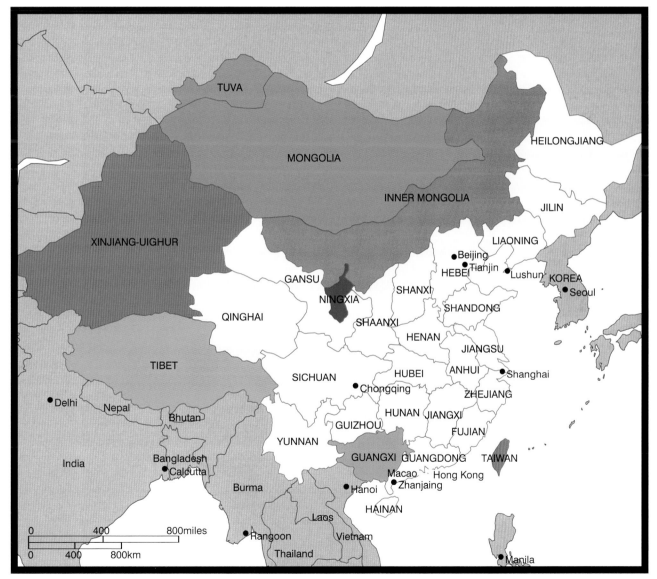

Map 8.13   The reunification of China. (Names have been transliterated into the Roman alphabet according to the 'Pinyin' (phonetic spelling) system adopted by the Chinese government in 1958)

the northern boundaries. Civil war broke out in Manchuria upon the Soviet evacuation. The Nationalists lost their remaining positions in Manchuria by late 1948 and thereafter defeat in the rest of China took place in the course of 1949. The People's Republic of China was proclaimed by Mao Tse-tung, Chairman of the Chinese Communist Party, in October 1949, and the Nationalists were confined to Taiwan. The existence of two governments, both claiming to be the legitimate government of China, persisted for the remainder of the century.

The new central government, which established itself in the old Imperial capital of Peking, sought to re-establish control over all the peripheral parts of the country which had achieved de facto independence since the overthrow of the monarchy in 1912. The agreement with the Soviet Union resulted in the recognition of the independence of Mongolia and the Soviet incorporation of Tanna Tuva. In return, Soviet support for the ephemeral Republic of Illi in Chinese Turkestan (Sinkiang) established in November 1944 was withdrawn and the Chinese Communists took over in September 1949. Following the Communist victory in the civil war, Port Arthur was handed over to the Chinese under the Sino-Soviet Treaty of Friendship and Alliance in March 1950.

In May 1951 the government forced the Tibetan government to accept Chinese suzerainty. This was followed in September 1951 by the military occupation of Tibet and its integration into the People's Republic after nearly 40 years of de facto independence. In March 1959 a revolt took place and the Dalai Lama fled to India. The local government was replaced by the Autonomous Region of Tibet regime, which instituted far-reaching reforms and integration into the Chinese economy. Only in December 1964 was the Dalai Lama formally stripped of his titles by the Chinese government. The Tibetan community in exile in India remains bound together by religious ideals and seeks to return to its homeland (Grunfeld, 1987).

China proceeded to reorganise the administrative structures of the country and provide nominal autonomy, on Soviet lines, to the ethnic minorities. Within China proper the historic provinces survived, albeit with some significant boundary modifications, demonstrating a remarkable historic power of survival. For the larger minorities, the Soviet system of linguistically defined autonomous regions was instituted. The implications of this were limited by the fact that ethnic Han Chinese accounted for 94 percent of the population, but the national minorities occupied 60 percent of its surface area. Most were in a minority in their historic homeland compared with the Chinese speakers, resulting in the promise of only cultural autonomy.

Of the fifty identified minority groups only five achieved significant territorial autonomy: the Mongols (Inner Mongolia), the Huis (Ningxia), the Uighurs (Sinkiang-Uighur), Chuangs (Kuangxi Chuang) and Tibetans (Tibet). Significantly Manchu speakers, then numbering approximately two million, did not gain regional status as they constituted only a small minority within Manchuria (Crossley, 1997). Even their homeland was renamed the 'Northeast' in order to eliminate any reference to the Ch'ing dynasty and the Japanese sponsored war-time state of Manchukuo. After 1950 the twin processes of Chinese colonisation and acculturation which had proved so successful in Manchuria were adopted in other parts of the country, notably Inner Mongolia and Tibet. The end result was the establishment of Han Chinese majorities throughout most of the country, thereby undermining any future attempts to divide the Chinese state. The Cultural Revolution of 1965–1969 was particularly destructive of the cultural heritage of minority groups, which were seen as not conforming to the national revolutionary ideal (Sneath, 1994). The Moslem Uighurs of Sinkiang proved to be the most resilient to cultural pressures as a result of their greater numbers, Islamic background, and distance from the core of the Chinese state (Barnett, 1993). Secessionism or pan-Turkism, particularly following the independence of the former Soviet republics in central Asia in 1991, has been severely repressed.

CHAPTER 9

The Cold War and Decolonisation 1950–1990

The Cold War intensified with the Communist victory in the Chinese civil war, as the American government considered itself and its allies threatened by the advance of Russian inspired global revolution. In order to overcome the perceived threat the United States developed the policy of 'containment'. To effect this a series of comprehensive military alliances, beginning with the North Atlantic Treaty Organisation in August 1949, linked the Western powers together with others in Europe and Asia. As a counter measure the Soviet Union linked its allies together in the Warsaw Pact. Contention between the two blocs, although initially confined to the contact zone between them, later spread to the Middle East, Africa and Latin America as the Cold War was waged on a global scale (Smith, 1998).

The first direct challenge by the Communist powers came in Korea, where in June 1950 the North Koreans invaded South Korea intent upon the reunification of the peninsula. The American response was rapid with the despatch of an expeditionary force to resist the invasion. Owing to a miscalculation on the part of the Soviet Union delegation, the force was despatched under the United Nations flag. Subsequent United Nations victories were partially undone by the intervention of the Chinese on the side of North Korea. The war continued until July 1953 and ended with an inconclusive armistice, where the ceasefire lines did not differ markedly from the initial 38th parallel division before the war. After this experience the politics of decolonisation in Asia in particular was viewed in Cold War terms. Thus, whereas the Dutch in Indonesia had been internationally condemned for attempting to re-establish their empire in the period 1945–1949, the French in Indo-

China were supported by the Americans in the early 1950s, as were the British in Malaya. The former resulted in one of the major conflicts of the Cold War, while the latter was resolved relatively peacefully.

Decolonisation took place in Africa remarkably rapidly and certainly far faster than the colonial powers had anticipated in the immediate post-war period. The end of empire in the Caribbean and the Pacific later in the century was equally unanticipated. Thus by the termination of the Cold War the colonial empires which had dominated the map of the world earlier in the century had been dismantled. The practical application of the ideals enunciated in the 1941 Atlantic Charter encountered severe problems, not least the emergence of a host of states brought into being not as a result of struggles for self-determination, but as a result of administrative decisions by the colonial powers. Many states lacked a basic national raison d'etre and could only be maintained through the intervention of the international community (Jackson, 1990). Such 'quasi-states' were the product of the rivalries of the Cold War and their survival was initially dependent upon its continuation.

9.1 DECOLONISATION IN INDO-CHINA

The Japanese surrender in Indo-China was accompanied by the assertion of independence on the part of the three constituent states of Vietnam, Cambodia and Laos. To add to the confusion, in order to oversee the Japanese surrender, northern Indo-China had been occupied by Chinese forces

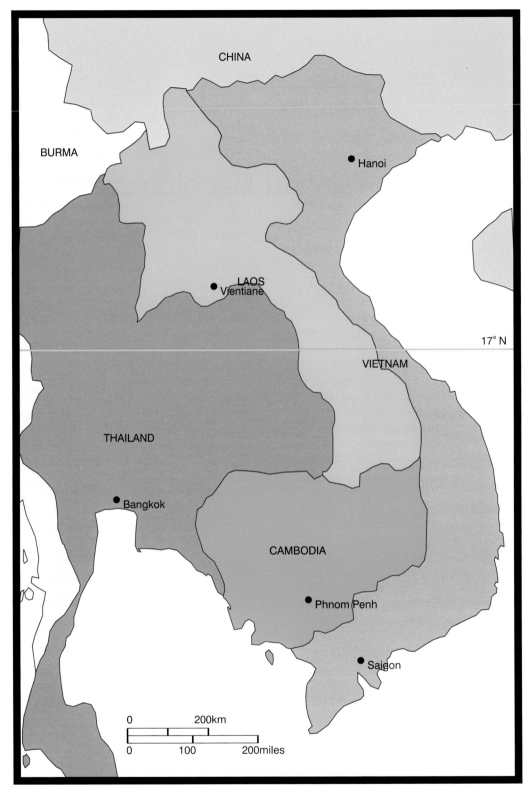

Map 9.1   Decolonisation in Indo-China

and the south by British forces. Thereafter the re-establishment of French control was accomplished through a combination of force and diplomacy from an initial base in Cochin China. Even the Democratic Republic of Vietnam proclaimed by the Communist leader, Ho Chi Minh, in Tonkin in September 1945, acknowledged the French right to station forces in the province in March 1946. Initially Ho Chi Minh also accepted participation in a projected Federation of Indo-China, which would remain a part of the French Union. Disagreement over the character of the Federation and the extent of Vietnam resulted in the outbreak of hostilities in November 1946. Although the French army was able to conquer parts of Tonkin including the capital, Hanoi, it could not displace the Vietminh supporters of Ho Chi Minh from the countryside.

As a way out of the constitutional impasse, the French sought to involve the Annamese Emperor Bao Dai, who had abdicated in August 1945 under pressure from the Vietminh. Independence within the French Union was granted in February 1950 to the 'State of Vietnam' and recognition came from the United States the following month. China and the Soviet Union formally recognised the Vietminh dominated 'Democratic Republic of Vietnam' in January 1950. Both sides proceeded to assist their nominees with military aid and training, but not with direct intervention as had taken place in Korea. The global Cold War confrontation and containment policies thus were linked to the struggle between the forces of colonialism and national liberation. This was not an outcome that the Americans had hoped for, as A.J. Stockwell (1992: 368) perceptively commented: 'Of the three options in Indochina – colonialism, communism or monarchy – the Americans relished none, though they were persuaded to stomach the last when it was garnished with the rhetoric of self-determination.'

Two governments thus claimed the same national territory and the conflict between them was fought to an effective stalemate, with neither side able to defeat the other. However, the major French defeat at Dien Bien Phu in May 1954 ended that country's resolve to remain embroiled in the affairs of Indo-China. The result was the compromise agreement reached at the Geneva Conference in July 1954. The agreement provided for Vietnam to be temporarily partitioned between the two governments along the 17th parallel. The Vietminh were to withdraw their forces from the South and the French were to withdraw completely from Indo-China. Furthermore, an election was to be held throughout Vietnam in July 1956 to reunify the country. At the same time the complete independence of Laos and Cambodia was underwritten by the international community. In the former case this represented a major change in policy as Laos had been regarded in the colonial period as little more than an area for Vietnamese colonisation (Stuart-Fox, 1995).

The Geneva agreement did not prove to be the end of the Indo-Chinese war. In South Vietnam the monarchy was overthrown and an American backed republic was established in November 1955. However, the new regime refused to hold the agreed elections in 1956 for the reunification of the country and a North Vietnamese backed insurgency commenced in the South in 1959. A rival National Liberation Front government gradually gained control of sections of the countryside, while the towns and often daytime control of much of the countryside was retained by the American backed government. Direct American military support for the South grew following the proclamation of a state of emergency in October 1961, as the struggle was viewed as an essential part of the containment of global Communism. The Vietnamese war spread into Laos and Cambodia, leading to the overthrow of the monarchies and the installation of Communist governments. The domestic political impact of high American personnel losses in the war were such as to force their withdrawal from the country under the Paris Peace Agreement of January 1973. A nominally South Vietnamese civil war ensued.

In April 1975 the southern capital, Saigon, fell to the Communists and a Provisional Revolutionary Government of the Republic of South Vietnam was established. As a measure of its international standing it established diplomatic relations with 82 countries and sought membership of the United Nations. Initially unification was viewed as a long-term process, recognising the South's need for post-war reconstruction and particular means for building socialism in a formerly capitalist economy (Beresford, 1989). However, North Vietnam had no desire to see the preservation of a separate South Vietnamese state and pressed for the unification of the country, which was accomplished in July 1976 following country-wide elections.

9.2   DECOLONISATION IN MALAYSIA

The British re-establishment of colonial control in Malaya and northern Borneo at the end of the Second World War was more effective than either the Dutch or the French return to South-east Asia. The British had the numbers of troops available to make a swift return and found sufficient support among the local communities and traditional rulers to establish a more secure political base. At the conclusion

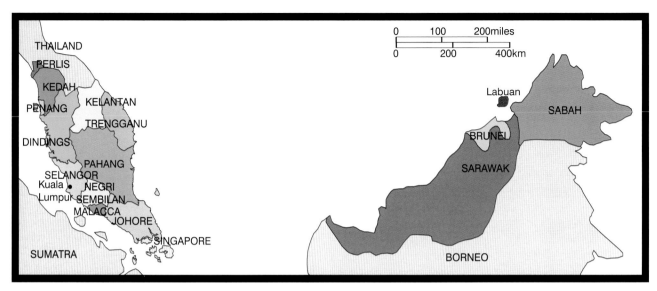

Map 9.2   Decolonisation in Malaysia

of the military administration regime, the Malayan Union was inaugurated in April 1946. It linked together all the Malay states including the former Straits Settlements of Penang and Malacca in a centralised state. Unanticipated strong opposition from the Malay sultans to a perceived diminution of their roles and the implied strengthening of the Chinese community's position resulted in the establishment of a looser Federation of Malaya in February 1948. Singapore, the site of Great Britain's major Far Eastern military and naval base, became a separate Crown Colony. In northern Borneo, Sarawak and North Borneo were annexed by the Crown, replacing the administrations of the Rajah Sir Charles Vyner Brooke and the British North Borneo Company with direct colonial rule in July 1946. As part of the territorial reorganisation, the island of Labuan was attached to North Borneo. Finally the protected Sultanate of Brunei remained unaffected by the constitutional changes taking place elsewhere.

The Malayan Communist Party embarked upon an armed insurgency against the British authorities in June 1948, with the aim of establishing an independent republic. It was to last twelve years, but by 1953 the counter-insurgency measures had begun to succeed as a result of the support of the predominantly Malay rural population for the government. At the same time the communally based political parties reached a broad measure of accommodation in the face of an essentially Chinese backed Communist insurgency. The inter-communal compromises necessary for national government resulted in the constitutional grant of independence to the Federation

in August 1957. The sovereignty of the sultans remained intact, while the position of head of state was rotated amongst them, in marked contrast to the loss of status and power by the Indian princes at independence.

The Federation remained closely allied to Great Britain and played a significant role in the further decolonisation of the region. Indeed the Federation cooperated with Great Britain in the internal maintenance of security in Singapore after 1957. The Federation had been established as a predominantly Malay state, in which the Malay majority community dominated politically, although economically the Chinese community was in the ascendant. In contrast, the Chinese formed approximately three-quarters of the population of Singapore. Malay politicians were thus not convinced that the accession of over one million Chinese would not compromise their privileged position within a combined state. In July 1959 the State of Singapore was proclaimed which enjoyed internal self-government, but was not offered independence as a separate state as no viable raison d'etre could be established.

The British and Malayan governments sought to overcome the problem of the final status of Singapore with the propagation of the Malaysia programme. Brunei and the colonies of Sarawak and North Borneo housed a significant Malay population, together with an indigenous population which the British government considered to be susceptible to assimilation to the dominant Moslem Malay culture. Malay politicians calculated that the incorporation of northern Borneo into the Federation would therefore counterbalance the anticipated effects of including the predominantly Chinese population of Singapore. In the negotiations over the wider Federation, Brunei withdrew as neither the special status of the Sultan in the proposed Council of Rulers nor a special dispensation over the Sultanate's oil revenues was accepted by the Malayan delegation. Thus in August 1963 the Federation of Malaysia was established comprising the eleven states of the old Federation of Malaya, together with Singapore, Sarawak and North Borneo (renamed Sabah). Subsequent internal reorganisation included the declaration of Kuala Lumpur as a separate federal territory in February 1974 and the detachment of the island of Labuan from Sabah and its administration by the federal government in April 1984.

The establishment of Malaysia faced considerable opposition from its neighbours. Indonesia embarked upon a programme of 'confrontation', which involved limited military action, to prevent Brunei, Sarawak and Sabah from joining the Federation. This formed part of President Sukarno's general expansionist programme aimed at the creation of a Great Indonesia including the whole of Malaysia and the Philippines. In addition, the Philippines claimed Sabah as its territory. Neither threat achieved any success and were dropped in the ensuing years. In December 1962, following the success of anti-Malaysian parties in Brunei's first elections, a short-lived attempt was made to establish an independent North Borneo state (Kalimantan Utara) incorporating Sarawak and North Borneo and reviving the pre-colonial sovereign status of Brunei.

Subsequently the government of Singapore decided to withdraw from the Federation in August 1965. In very general terms, conflicts of approach between the monarchist Moslem Malay central government and the secular urban Chinese state government over a host of economic and language issues assumed unbridgeable proportions. The federal government realised that any attempt to impose central government control would raise more problems than it would solve and so the split was accepted. Singapore then pursued a particularly active policy of nation building to accommodate the various communities and promote economic development following the running down and closure of the British base. It was officially recognised that there was a need 'to evolve and anchor a Singaporean identity, incorporating the relevant part of our varied cultural heritages, and the attitudes and values which have helped us to survive and succeed as a nation' (Chua, 1995: 32). Multi-culturalism, based on shared values, together with the constant emphasis upon the nation and society resulted in a remarkable degree of cohesion and prosperity in the ensuing decades.

The remaining British responsibility in the region was Brunei. The Kalimantan Utara revolt and the failure of the Malaysia negotiations prompted the Sultan to embark upon a different programme of nation building. The powers previously exercised by the British Resident to the protectorate were effectively transferred to the Sultan in 1959. After the 1962 revolt this concentration of control was intensified as the country was developed within the prescribed form of an Islamic sultanate. External threats and the need to retain the protection of the British army delayed the acceptance of formal independence, which was only assumed in January 1984.

9.3   DECOLONISATION IN AFRICA

Africa was the last continent to experience decolonisation. In 1950 only four states (Ethiopia, Liberia, South Africa and Egypt) were independent; the remainder were under colonial control. Despite the rhetoric of self-determination, the colonial powers still viewed their tenure of control as stretching for decades if not permanently, in spite of the decolonisation of South and South-east Asia. Independence movements essentially fell into two sections divided by the Sahara, including the countries influenced by the Arab world and the remainder of the continent. For a long time, a third area, White-ruled southern Africa, filled a space on the pre-1994 map of the continent.

The first post Second World War issue faced by the international community was the final disposition of the former Italian colonies. Ethiopia had resumed its independent status and sought to extend its influence. The remainder were the matter of negotiation between the victorious powers, who handed the issue over to the United Nations. The wartime occupation settlement remained in place until 1950. In April that year Great Britain gave up its plans for the creation of a British administered Greater Somaliland, and the United Nations awarded Italy a trusteeship with the task of preparing its former colony, Somalia, for independence in ten years. In Libya the Emir Idris el-Sennusi was installed as ruler of Cyrenaica in September 1949. Finally in December 1951 the three occupation zones of Cyrenaica, Tripolitania and Fezzan were reintegrated as an independent United Kingdom of Libya under King Idris. In September 1952, after minimal consultation, the United Nations voted to ignore the call for independence and transferred Eritrea to Ethiopia as a federal territory nominally enjoying a measure of autonomy. Ten years later the federation was unilaterally terminated and

Eritrea was incorporated as a directly administered province into Ethiopia.

In October 1951 the Egyptian government abrogated the Anglo-Egyptian Treaty of 1936 and the 1899 Sudan Condominium Agreement and proclaimed King Farouk, 'King of Egypt and the Sudan'. The military coup d'etat in July 1952 paved the way for the revision of the Anglo-Egyptian treaty in February 1953, which resulted in an agreement to end the condominium status of the Sudan. A three-year transition period provided for the election of a Constituent Assembly which would exercise the right of self-determination as to whether to opt for independence or forge some link between the Sudan and Egypt. The pre-independence elections recorded a victory for the National Unionist Party which had campaigned for unity with Egypt. However, with the favourable prospects of sovereign independence, election pledges were ignored and the Assembly opted for independence and the withdrawal of all forces from the Sudan in January 1956. Effective constitutional guarantees for the special status of the non-Moslem southern regions of the country did not materialise.

Elsewhere in northern Africa movements for the independence of the protectorates of Morocco and Tunisia gained strength and were acceded to in March 1956. Between March and August 1956 the Spanish and French zones of Morocco were reunited under Sultan Mohammed V and the international status of Tangier was abolished. Morocco, though, still claimed extensive areas which it had lost in the colonial period both to France in the Sahara and Mauritania and to Spain in the Western Sahara and Ifni. Morocco thus remained one of the states permanently hostile to the post-colonial acceptance of colonial borders on the continent. In North Africa only Algeria remained under colonial control by 1956, albeit as an integral part of France, as a result of the presence of one million French settlers. It is significant that the major war of independence on the continent was launched in that country in November 1954, which was waged with great ferocity on both sides until independence was attained in July 1962 (Horne, 1977).

These developments, together with the prevailing anti-colonial sentiments in the international community, encouraged independence movements elsewhere on the continent. They were countered by colonial economic development programmes and either the promotion of self-government or increased participation in metropolitan affairs. In the former category the independence of the Gold Coast in March 1957 was a major step as representing the first decolonisation in 'Black Africa'. The country was regarded as a special case and no general British decolonisation was planned at this stage. Significantly the new state took the name Ghana, as a reminder of the great pre-colonial West African empires. In September 1958 the electorates of the French colonies were called upon to approve the constitution of the new Fifth Republic and their autonomous status within the newly formed French Community. All but French Guinea approved the new constitution, with overwhelming majorities. The colony was immediately expelled from the French Union and assumed independence as the Republic of Guinea in October 1958. These two forerunners were to have a powerful influence upon the subsequent course of events (Hamdan, 1963).

The sense of dramatic change was captured by the British Prime Minister, Harold Macmillan, in his 'wind of change' speeches, first in Accra in January 1960 and subsequently his far more highly publicised version to the South African parliament in Cape Town the following month (Macmillan, 1972). In the course of 1960 some seventeen African states assumed independent status in the largest exercise in state making in any single year in the century. By the end of the year, comparatively few states remained under colonial control outside southern and eastern Africa. All the constituent republics of the newly formed French Community opted for full independence, with membership of the United Nations and other international organisations, rather than the qualified status they enjoyed under the 1958 constitution. Thus all the constituent states of the former French West Africa, French Equatorial Africa and Madagascar became independent. The last, Mauritania, was subject to a territorial claim by Morocco, which was not resolved until October 1961. In a rather different category Belgium decided to grant independence to the Belgian Congo in July 1960. No previous Congolese government had been established and the whole exercise was carried out with the utmost haste. Finally Nigeria was granted independence as a federation in October 1960. After a lengthy process of constitutional development driven by the politicians of Western and Eastern Nigeria, the demographically dominant Northern Nigeria had attained internal self-government in March 1959, thus paving the way for independence.

Territories under United Nations trusteeship agreements also achieved independence. The previously mandated territories of Togo and Cameroon were the first to obtain sovereign status. The British section of Togo had gained independence as an integral part of Ghana in 1957 following a plebiscite in May 1956. The British Cameroons were given the option of joining either Nigeria, of which they had been administratively a part, or joining the ex-French Cameroon. The plebiscite was delayed until February 1961,

Map 9.3   Decolonisation in Africa

and resulted in the northern sector opting to remain in Nigeria and the southern to join Cameroon in a federal constitutional structure. Somalia became independent in July 1960 and joined the former British Somaliland, which had become independent the previous month.

Decolonisation continued at a slower pace thereafter. In the three years 1961–1963, a further eight African states received independence. They included the three trusteeship territories which had previously constituted German East Africa. No attempt at reintegration on the Cameroon model was attempted. Indeed, following the overthrow of the monarchy in Ruanda in November 1959, the United Nations had to accept that two states, not one, would emerge from the Belgian sector. Rwanda and Burundi achieved independence in July 1962. The remaining British East African territories achieved independence. Decolonisation in Kenya was delayed until December 1963 as a result of the presence of a substantial White settler interest. Zanzibar attained independence at the same time, but following the overthrow of the sultanate the following month, the new revolutionary government sought to join Tanganyika to form the United Republic in July 1964, which was renamed Tanzania in October 1964.

The pace of decolonisation slackened as the future of the remaining colonies was more contentious and involved a greater emotional commitment on the part of the metropolitan powers. Initially, international attention was focused upon the British possessions in Central Africa. The Federation of Rhodesia and Nyasaland, established in October 1953, had aimed at the development of a multi-racial society based on 'partnership' as a counter to the segregationist apartheid policies pursued in South Africa. Indeed the White controlled government of Southern Rhodesia had rejected independent dominion status in favour of the formation of the larger entity, which included Northern Rhodesia and Nyasaland (Welensky, 1964). The African political leaders of the latter colonies sought to secede and achieve independence once internal self-government had been attained. The British government reviewed the situation in 1960 and came to the pessimistic conclusion that:

Federation cannot, in our view, be maintained in its present form. On the other hand, to break it up at this crucial moment in the history of Africa would be an admission that there is no hope of survival for any multi-racial society on the African continent, and that differences of colour and race are irreconcilable. (Great Britain, 1960: 111).

Support for the Federation collapsed, with the British and finally the Southern Rhodesian governments rejecting it. Following its demise in December 1963, the two northern states achieved independence as Malawi (July 1964) and Zambia (October 1964).

There followed one of the more remarkable episodes in the decolonisation of the continent. Following the impasse in the constitutional negotiations (Southern) Rhodesia made a unilateral declaration of independence (UDI) in November 1965. The White settler community of approximately 250 000 out of a total population of approximately four million sought to avoid African majority rule. Despite the imposition of international sanctions by the United Nations it was only in March 1978 that compromise with the internal African leadership was reached. This led to the establishment of the short-lived state of Zimbabwe-Rhodesia in January 1979, which remained unrecognised. Only with the conclusion of the Lancaster House conference in London in December 1979 and the reimposition of British colonial rule were internationally recognised elections possible. In April 1980 a recognised African majority government was installed and the country renamed Zimbabwe.

Portugal resisted the grant of independence to its overseas provinces. After 1961 liberation movements began to challenge continued colonial rule and major counter insurgency campaigns were launched, accompanied by intensified White settlement schemes. However, the rising costs and death tolls of the wars and the general international opposition to the Portuguese stand led to revolution in Lisbon in April 1974 and the subsequent grant of independence to the five colonies between September 1974 (Guinea-Bissau) and November 1975 (Angola). It is significant that although the anti-colonial war in Portuguese Guinea and in the Cape Verde Islands had been waged by a single political movement, Partido Africana da Independencia de Guine e Cabo Verde, independence was taken separately and negotiations for union foundered. The coup d'etat in the Cape Verde Islands in November 1980 ended even this tenuous link.

Many of the smaller colonial territories only received independence after the main body in the early 1960s. This reflected the colonial power's assessment of the questionable viability of small states and the possibility of annexation by a more powerful neighbour. The most precarious were Botswana, Lesotho and Swaziland, which were dominated economically by South Africa and were only granted independence in 1966–1968, when the threat of South African annexation had receded. Djibouti only received independence in June 1977 as a result of French concern over the expansionist intentions of both Ethiopia and Somalia. The Comoros, which had been detached from Madagascar in May 1946 and granted administrative autonomy, gained independence in December 1975, without resolving the status of the island Mayotte, which remained under French control. In the case of Equatorial Guinea the Spanish combined the autonomous island of Fernando Póo with the mainland territory of Rio Muni in an uneasy amalgamation for administrative convenience in October 1968 (endorsed by 63 percent of the electorate). The last (March 1990) and most contentious colonial possession, South West Africa–Namibia, will be examined later (Section 9.8).

9.4   FEDERATIONS IN AFRICA

The African continent is divided into some 54 states, more than any other comparable part of the world. Despite the size of many of these entities, the perception that political groupings in federations would be advantageous has been evident in both colonial and post-colonial times. In the colonial era the major federations of French West Africa and French Equatorial Africa allowed for the supervision of common services such as communications and trade at one level and closer supervision of justice and taxation at another. Federations also offered savings in reducing the size of colonial administrations by centralising some

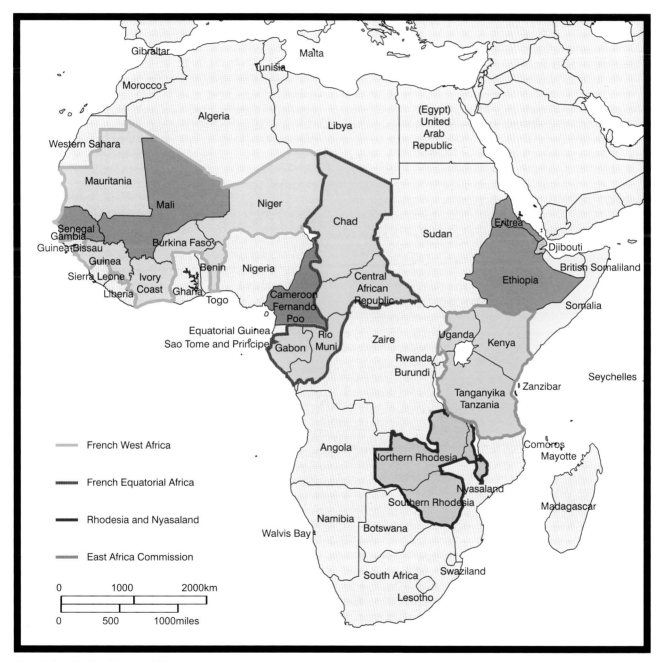

Map 9.4   Federations in Africa

facilities in the federal capital. Other colonial federations included the short-lived Italian Empire of East Africa, the British East African Community and the Federation of Rhodesia and Nyasaland.

Almost without exception at the time of independence the individual colonies sought independence as separate entities. Political activities had generally been based upon the smaller units with the result that the independence leaders were often rivals within the larger grouping. Only in the case of French West Africa was an attempt made to retain the beneficial links between inland and coastal colonies. Within the French Community the French Sudan, Senegal, Upper Volta and Dahomey sought to retain links as the Federation of Mali in January 1959. However, the latter two states withdrew in April 1959. Finally, Senegal sought full independence separately in August 1960, leaving the French Sudan to take independence under the style of the Republic of Mali.

Following independence many plans were proposed, but few progressed beyond the agreements establishing them (Griffiths, 1995). Several initiatives were proposed by President Kwame Nkrumah of Ghana initially to link Guinea and Mali. However, physical separation and lack of long-term political planning did not lead to any lasting success. The political idealism was subsumed in the concept of continental unity with the formation of the Organisation of African Unity (Cervenka, 1977).

Those unification schemes which did succeed were linked to more specific and often local objectives. Thus former-Italian Somalia and former-British Somaliland united at independence on the basis of a common language. Tanganyika and Zanzibar did so soon afterwards, following the overthrow of the ruling Arab dynasty on the islands (Clayton, 1981). The British and French Cameroons joined on the former's attaining self-determination. More disastrously Eritrea was federated with Ethiopia as an alternative to independence following a highly dubious test of opinion in the former Italian colony. The institution of a confederation between Gambia and Senegal to form Senegambia in February 1982 was based on common languages and a shared cultural inheritance. However, the scheme came to nought as a result of the incompatibility of the two states' colonial heritage, more particularly the official languages and the differing legal systems. It was dissolved by mutual agreement in September 1990.

Mergers were actively discouraged once the Organisation of African Unity came into being in May 1963. The founding fathers of the Organisation considered that unity should be striven for on a continental scale and that the rival regional groupings, which had developed

before 1963, hindered the interests of African development. Thus the attempts to create limited mergers largely ceased. Indeed the maintenance of the existing state pattern necessitated increased levels of coercion as the tensions created by demands for self-determination within a European defined 'nation-state' system became apparent (Davidson, 1992).

An exception to this generalisation was the Moroccan effort to expand its rule in the Sahara and West Africa. At independence Morocco claimed Mauritania, but was forced to recognise its independence in 1961. After a long campaign the Moroccans were able to force the Spanish to relinquish the Spanish (Western) Sahara to it and Mauritania in January 1976. The local independence movement, the Polisario Front, refused to recognise the move and began a war of independence. Mauritania was forced to abandon its section of the Western Sahara in August 1979, which was duly occupied by Morocco. The war became stalemated, with the Polisario Front in control of sections of the desert, but the population centres and the phosphate mines under Moroccan control. Compromise over the implementation of self-determination through an internationally supervised referendum has not been forthcoming, as the dispute over the entitlement to vote has not been resolved.

9.5   LINGUISTIC GROUPS IN AFRICA

One of the major features of the African continent is its linguistic diversity (Ajayi and Crowder, 1985). Several broad linguistic families are divided into a myriad of mutually unintelligible languages and more closely related dialects. Many of these have developed over a long period of time in relative isolation, while others have undergone major changes as a result of cultural and political interaction (Ehret and Posnansky, 1982). Few had been written down by the beginning of the colonial period. In the northern parts of the continent, influenced by Islam, Arabic was widely used, although it might have been the home language of comparatively few south of the Sahara. The colonial period resulted in the standard-isation and the written recording of the African languages. Christian missionaries in the pre- and early colonial periods were particularly influential in standardising languages and giving them literary form, with the objective of bringing the Bible to each group in its own language. Significantly the Koran remained in its original Arabic, thereby facilitating the extension of the use of the language.

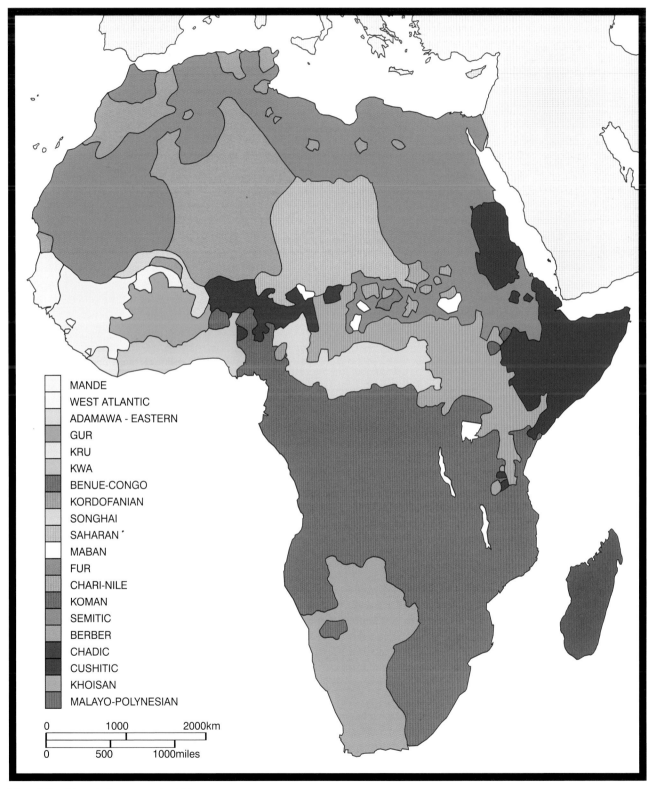

MANDE
WEST ATLANTIC
ADAMAWA - EASTERN
GUR
KRU
KWA
BENUE-CONGO
KORDOFANIAN
SONGHAI
SAHARAN
MABAN
FUR
CHARI-NILE
KOMAN
SEMITIC
BERBER
CHADIC
CUSHITIC
KHOISAN
MALAYO-POLYNESIAN

Map 9.5   Linguistic groups in Africa

The picture presented in the early colonial period was one of the utmost complexity. In practical terms the apparent isolation which this inheritance imposed was limited by the widespread multi-lingualism of many Africans and the detachment of language from the concept of ethno-nationalism so prevalent in Europe. Indeed it is on the African continent that official state languages diverge from home languages most widely (Kidron and Segal, 1995).

In the former Belgian Congo (Zaire, Congo-Kinshasa) some 365 separate spoken languages were identified in the colonial period (Laclavere, 1978). Several broad families were discerned as well as individual forms which had no close relations. Virtually all were grouped into the wider Bantu language family, which extended from west Africa to the extreme south. Upon this detailed picture was superimposed a network of four 'national languages' (Kikongo, Kiswahili, Lingala and Tshiluba), which acted as the linguae francae for wide regions of Zaire (Congo) and whose use was promoted in schools. These, as with the local languages, overlapped the national boundaries. Kiswahili, which was widely understood in the eastern section of the country, originated in the coastal regions of Kenya and Tanzania and was transferred inland along the pre-colonial trade routes. The indigenous Kikongo was also widely spoken in the adjacent states of Congo and Angola. Superimposed upon the national languages was the official language of French, which was used by the state bureaucracy. As an added complication, during the Belgian colonial period, Flemish was also an official language.

One of the major features of the broad map is the lack of coincidence with the political boundaries drawn by the colonial powers. Linguistic groups were divided by the lines drawn by the European treaty makers and colonial administrators, as well as being included in multi-linguistic entities which bore little relationship to the patterns of the pre-colonial period. However, because of the multi-linguistic nature of the colonial states few indigenous languages assumed national status and therefore defined the nation. Multi-lingualism has been generally accepted as inevitable and not necessarily detrimental to the cohesion of the states. The limited role of language in ethnic conflict is illustrated in Rwanda and Burundi, where the Hutu and Tutsi groups speak the same language, yet in 1994 the Hutu led government carried out some of the most far-reaching and systematic acts of attempted genocide on the continent against the Tutsi (Prunier, 1997). The conflict spilled over into the neighbouring Zaire (Congo), resulting in the desta-bilisation of that country.

9.6   LINGUISTIC GROUPS IN SOUTH AFRICA

South Africa has been a special case in African political development throughout the century. It was the scene of the largest European settlement programme on the continent, with one million people of European descent resident in the country by 1900, out of a total of approximately five million. Politically the conquest of the Dutch, Afrikaner republics in 1900 paved the way for the establishment of a British dominion in May 1910, which achieved complete international recognition with the ratification of the Statute of Westminster in December 1931. For a section of the Afrikaner population this was not a sufficient degree of independence from Great Britain. Following the election of the National Party government in May 1948 significant changes were effected, symbolised by the declaration of a republic and withdrawal from the Commonwealth in May 1961.

The White electorate was faced with the problem that it remained a minority and so the introduction of majority rule inevitably involved the loss of control of the state to the African majority. This the government was not willing to accept. Thus in an era of decolonisation the government embarked upon a unique variant, aimed at retaining White control over most of the country. Only in very limited urban areas were Whites in a numerical majority. Even in the environmentally poorer western section of the country, which did not have an African majority, people of mixed racial origins, and classified as Coloured, significantly outnumbered Whites. However, to achieve the perpetuation of White rule the government adopted the policy of partition as a component of 'grand apartheid' (Christopher, 1994a).

The policy makers considered that each African indigenous ethnic or linguistic group should possess its own state, in order to reduce ethnic tensions and develop nation-states in the classic European mould. The identification and distribution of the various linguistic groups thus became of prime importance for the development of the policy. Although all spoke variants of the broad Bantu family of related languages, several broad groupings, such as Sotho and Nguni, had been distinguished. Then sub-divisions had been encountered and standardised on the introduction of literacy in the nineteenth century by the missionaries. These distinctions were accentuated in determining the 'nations' for political purposes. Finally some nine African languages were defined and promoted as the basis of ethno-linguistic nations. The number of speakers of each language varied

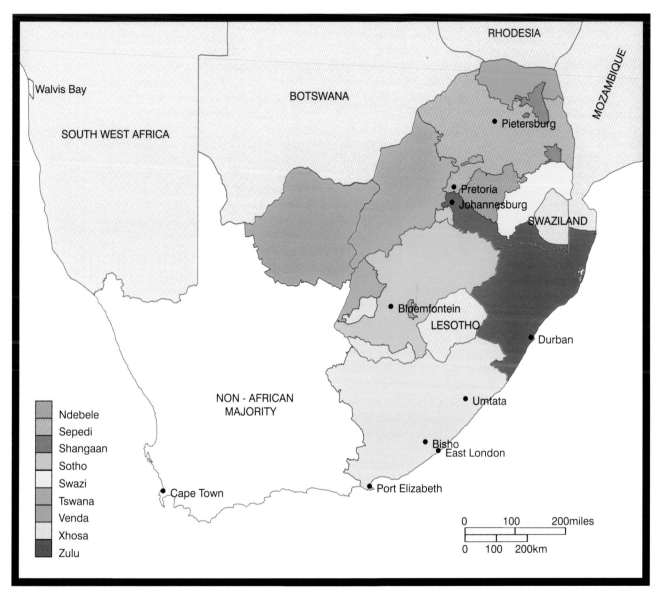

Map 9.6   Linguistic groups in South Africa

from under 500 000 to over four million in 1970 (Christopher, 1994b). The distribution of language groups as indicated in Figure 9.6 therefore might have provided a basis for the determination of either new federal maps as in the case of the Soviet Union or the Indian Union, or partition plans as in the case of the Balkans. In fact it did neither. The South African government was intent on the establishment of nation-states on a different territorial basis.

The linguistic distribution pattern is noticeable for a number of almost homogeneous blocks, where the major 'nations' still lived in their historic homelands. However, in other parts of the country areas of considerable interdigitation were also apparent, where no group was in a clear majority. This was particularly true of the industrial heartland of the country. The Witwatersrand region, centred upon the Johannesburg metropolitan area, had been on the frontier zones of several indigenous societies prior to the colonial period. The burgeoning industries, associated with the discovery of gold in 1886, had attracted workers from all over southern Africa, leading to a remarkably cosmopolitan population by the mid-twentieth century.

9.7   SOUTH AFRICAN HOMELANDS

Intent upon permanently removing the African majority from the political process in South Africa, the National Party government devised and elaborated the policy of apartheid. The object was to provide a political home for every African in one of the defined homelands or Bantustans. In this manner there would be no African citizens of South Africa and the Whites would become a majority of citizens. At a later stage (1984) it became possible to incorporate the Coloured and Indian populations into the segregated political structures without endangering White supremacy.

The process of defining the territories of the states began in 1959. The starting point was the pattern of scattered tribal reserves. These had been set aside in the nineteenth and early twentieth centuries for the exclusive use of the African population, usually under the control of traditional leaders. However, the area so set aside amounted to only 13 percent of the country, although Africans constituted 70 percent of the population at the time. Clearly the authorities which had defined the extent of the reserves had not contemplated the establishment of the nation-states for the groups concerned. Except in the Transkei and parts of Natal the reserves had been highly fragmented with little contiguity. Often no more than a few thousand hectares had been assigned to a local chief for his people, while the remainder of the land had been taken by White settlers. An added complication had been the purchase of land by the African population, often not contiguous with an existing reserve. Such individual or group purchases had been tightly restricted in 1913 and were prevented entirely in 1936, but added to the highly dispersed character of African land holdings.

The apartheid planners assigned each block of land to a particular linguistic group and the fragmented blocks became the basis of the nation-state. However, the blocks housed only a third of the African population of the country by the middle of the twentieth century. In order to make the resultant states more viable politically, the government embarked upon two programmes aimed at the physical consolidation of the fragmented blocks and the movement of population into the homelands. Changes to the initial concept took place as the programmes developed. From the beginning the Xhosa population was divided in two on historic grounds into the Transkei and Ciskei homelands. The promotion of a separate Ciskeian nationality proved to be a remarkably difficult, if not impossible, task (Peires, 1995). In addition, the Ndebele group was only awarded a

separate homeland in January 1975 as members of the group were removed or fled from other homelands, which in pursuit of the nation-state ideal, began to impose their own language upon ethnic minorities.

The consolidation programme was directed at the removal of isolated farms and reserves, labelled 'black spots', and the linking together of the larger blocks through the purchase of intervening White owned land. Expropriation and forced removal followed. In addition, large numbers of Africans resident in both the urban and rural areas of rump 'White South Africa', but considered surplus to White needs, were forcibly removed to the homelands. At least 3.5 million people were moved in the process (Platzky and Walker, 1985). However, the rump White state continued to house an African majority and the homelands did not take on the desired characteristics of nation-states, housing most of the nation within a single, consolidated and clearly defined territory.

In October 1976 the first homeland, Transkei, was granted independence and was followed by three more Bophuthatswana (1977), Venda (1979) and Ciskei (1981). The political atmosphere had changed to such an extent that when the government of another homeland, KwaNdebele, considered independence in the mid-1980s popular pressure led to its rejection. The international community rejected the homelands and refused them diplomatic recognition. The *New York Times* (26 October 1976) expressed the American and international official response to apartheid:

The reason for shunning the Transkei is moral and political rather than legal and juridical. To recognize the Umtata regime would be to condone South Africa's 'separate development' blueprint, perhaps the most drastic racial segregation policy ever devised ... a denial of our common humanity and a challenge to the conscience of mankind.

As a result, international recognition eluded the homeland governments. International legitimacy could not be established as the Organisation of African Unity, the United Nations and other bodies resolutely opposed the homeland policy. Internal legitimacy was compromised by the lack of economic development, the extreme poverty of the population and widespread government corruption, while the external liberation movements continued to exert pressure for the introduction of universal franchise in a unitary state. Military coups d'etat by the homeland armies and internal conflict ensued until the homelands were reincorporated into South Africa in April 1994 with the first universal franchise elections and the installation of Nelson Mandela as President.

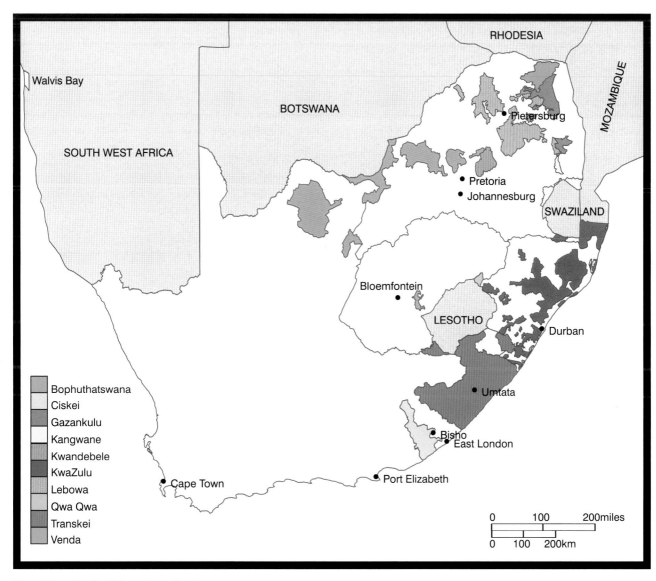

Map 9.7   South African homelands

9.8   SOUTH WEST AFRICA – NAMIBIA

Closely connected to the issue of apartheid in South Africa was that of its extension to South West Africa. Indeed, because of its international character, the debate over the future of the country was closely bound up with the Cold War and in time scale was coincident with it, lasting from 1946 to 1990. South West Africa, after the First World War, had become a South African mandated territory of the League of Nations. Unlike the other mandatory powers, South Africa did not convert its contractual obligations into a trusteeship agreement with the United Nations in 1946. The attempt to annex the territory was rejected by the world body and the terms of the mandate remained in force, with the United Nations assuming the prescribed supervisory role.

The continuing South African administration was challenged in the World Court of Justice in The Hague by Liberia and Ethiopia as the two other African members of the defunct League of Nations. The challenge failed, but in October 1966 the United Nations revoked the mandate and declared the South African administration to be illegal. In May 1967 a United Nations Council for South West Africa was established to oversee the transition to

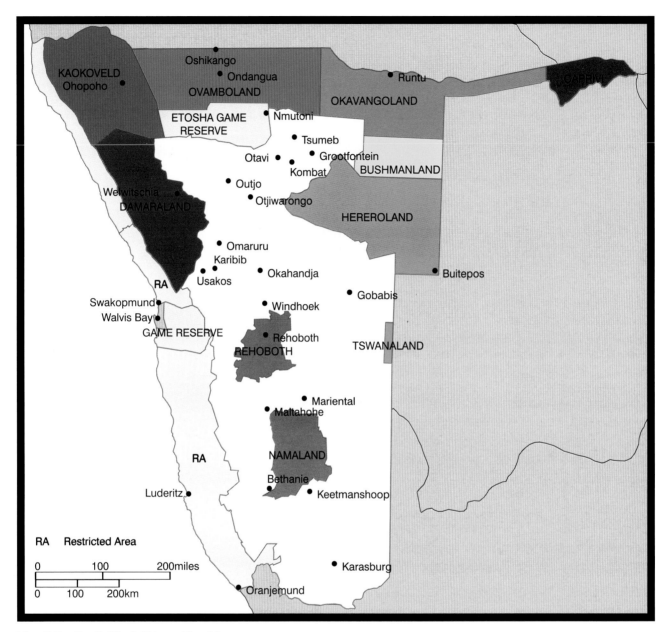

Map 9.8   South West Africa – Namibia

independence. In June 1968 the United Nations changed the name of the territory to Namibia as a symbolic indication of its new status. South Africa did not recognise the end of the mandate and continued to govern the country. The international impasse was thus complete.

The South African government proceeded to apply apartheid policies to the territory. Although the population then numbered under a million, the delimitation of homelands began. Ten tracts of African reserve were

designated as ethnic homelands. In all they covered nearly 40 percent of the territory. The numbers of people involved was often small. Thus the Tswanas who numbered only 10 000 were able to support only a few administrative functions, the remainder being supplied by the central government. The representatives of the San (Bushmen) consistently maintained that they wished to remain under the central government. However, the other ethnic homelands implemented the policy, resulting in the administrative fragmentation of the country. In the case of the Rehoboth Gebeid, self-government structures had been recognised by the German colonial administration and continued thereafter. This constituted the only area where significant support for autonomy, even independence, was to be found. None of the homeland governments sought separate independence and so the territorial integrity of South West Africa was maintained.

Opposition to South African administration strengthened as other African countries gained independence. In 1959 the South West African People's Organisation (SWAPO) was founded and seven years later began an armed insurrection. With the end of Portuguese rule in Angola the conflict merged with the civil war in that country, with South African forces operating in Angola against SWAPO and its allies. The Angolan war proved to be a major burden for the South African economy and by the mid 1980s international pressures to force a withdrawal from both Angola and South West Africa mounted. The widespread adoption of political and economic sanctions against apartheid in South Africa was made all the more worthwhile when it could be seen to benefit a settlement of the international dispute over South West Africa. The American Comprehensive Anti-Apartheid Act of October 1986 was the most significant move to isolate South Africa and promote change.

South Africa was forced by military and economic pressures to seek an accommodation with the international community. Negotiations over the future of South West Africa continued but with more urgency. Finally agreement was reached for a United Nations supervised transition, with the independence of Namibia proclaimed in March 1990. No international transitional administrative regime was introduced as originally conceived.

9.9 SECESSIONIST MOVEMENTS IN IN AFRICA

Given the organisational fragility of the majority of African states, the complex ethnic and linguistic make-up and the sudden assumption of independent status, the prospects for the new states were bleak. Indeed it was widely expected that fragmentation and reorganisation would take place to create a pattern more akin to the linguistic map (Hance, 1964). However, the states did not fragment. External assistance was frequently offered to stabilise the situation, while the international community adhered to the status quo, even if conflict between rivals for control of the state was fomented. Furthermore, the majority of states were too

weak to intervene actively in the affairs of their neighbours. Most armed conflict in Africa thus was of the character of civil war, rather than secessionism. As a result, the political maps of the mid 1960s and of the year 2000 resemble one another closely.

However, the potential for secession was enormous and the suppression of secessionist struggles has occupied disproportionate shares of the limited resources of a number of countries. The artificial character of the territorial constructs of the colonial period were immediately demonstrated at independence. The Belgian Congo at independence in June 1960 fragmented as the structures of the central government, most noticeably the army, disintegrated. The government of the major copper producing province of Katanga declared its independence in July 1960. In the colonial period the province had been administered by a special council and as the major producer of wealth for the country its interests were often at variance with the remainder which consumed wealth. In the chaos that ensued several other provinces attempted to secede, including diamond rich Kasai (August 1960 to February 1961). The counter secession of northern Katanga from Katanga further complicated the pattern. The United Nations intervened to support the government of the Congo Republic and preserve its territorial integrity. Essentially the ending of Katangan independence in January 1963 was the result of United Nations military intervention against the secessionists. The complex and disorganised state has remained nominally unified since then, although the writ of the central government has often been very weak in the peripheral regions.

It was the Congo struggle that induced the Organisation of African Unity to include the pledge to recognise the territorial integrity of member states in the Charter (Kamanu, 1974). The essential contradiction between the demands for self-determination and independence could not be resolved when the foundations of the nation-states were so weak. It should be noted that no government recognised Katanga or any of the other ephemeral states declared during the Congo civil war. The international community thus supported a highly coercive and corrupt government in the pursuit of 'nation building'.

Secessionism based on ethnic diversity has affected a number of other states, although this has often been no more than the demand for autonomy. The centralised one party and military dictatorships that in the first thirty years of independence characterised the continent resisted such demands as infringing their prerogatives. Some have been of particular significance. The unique nature of the Somali issue is examined later. The longest surviving secessionist

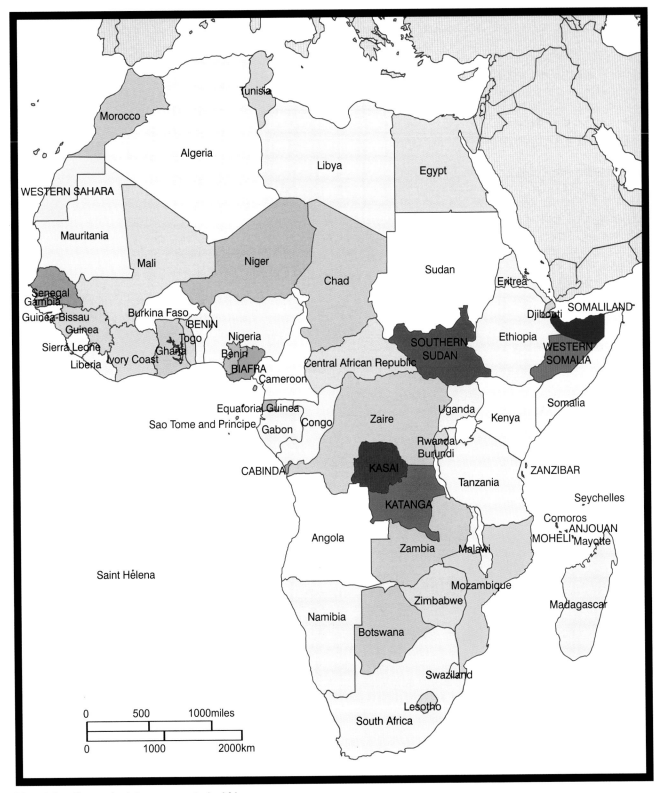

Map 9.9   Secessionist movements in Africa

movement has been based in the southern Sudan, where African Christian and Animist tribal groupings have fought against the Arab Moslem government in Khartoum. The southern Sudan was subject to a special British controlled condominium regime in the colonial period, ensuring its isolation from the influence of the other condominium partner and the Arab population of the North. At independence the special status ceased and integration was a difficult process as northerners took over most of the positions previously occupied by nationals of the condominium powers. The vague promise of a federal arrangement between North and South, which was given to satisfy the departing colonial power, was not honoured. The influence of Islam was particularly significant as the independent government identified closely with its Islamic roots and sought to spread the religion and later Sharia law over the whole country. The result was rebellion in 1955 and the demand for a separate Southern Sudanese state. The insurrection has persisted throughout most of the period since independence with little prospect of either the South Sudan People's Liberation Army or the Sudanese government achieving complete success. The first civil war ended in 1972 following a peace agreement granting autonomy to the South. However, this was repudiated in 1983 and the civil war began again.

Other secessionist movements were formed elsewhere on the continent, but few were in a position to establish any viable administration or conduct lengthy military operations aimed at securing independence. The particular problems of Eritrea, Somalia and Nigeria are dealt with in subsequent sections.

9.10 NIGERIA

Biafra is in a different category to other secessionist movements in that it gained formal recognition from some members of the African community of nations. The Nigerian civil war was rooted in the formation of the Nigerian Federation in 1914. The various British possessions in Nigeria with their multitude of ethnic, linguistic and religious groupings were joined together in 1914 as a matter of administrative convenience, although with a substantial measure of indirect rule, thereby retaining many pre-colonial indigenous political structures. Three major ethnic groups, the Hausa-Fulani, the Ibo and the Yoruba, dominated the Northern, Eastern and Western regions respectively. However, the country contained over 200 linguistic groups, with marked fracture zones between the three dominant peoples.

After independence in October 1960 the dominant political parties of the Northern and Eastern regions formed a parliamentary alliance. As a result, in August 1963 the Western Region was divided through the secession of the Mid-West Region for the Edo people, after a 99 percent vote in favour of the move. Politically the Northern Region was left as a remarkably powerful unit able to dominate the Federation in terms of voter numbers. It was suggested that to reduce this domination the regions should be subdivided further on linguistic lines to satisfy the demands of the minority groups. President Nnamdi Azikiwe (1965: 447) suggested that:

In order to evolve a near perfect union, the whole of Nigeria should be divided and so demarcated geographically and demo-graphically that no one region would be in a position to dominate the rest ... Irrespective of the number of regions suggested and in the light of dividing Nigeria into many regions this is basically sound because the aim is to consolidate national unity. There is wisdom in further splitting this country according to the main nationalities or linguistic groups not ethnic groups which form the bulk of the population.

The complex politics of the federation with alternating brief civilian governments and military coups d'etat resulted in heightened communal confrontation. As a result, the various groups, notably the Ibo, tended to withdraw to their ethnic homelands for security. In May 1967 the federal government redrew the map of Nigeria, dividing the Eastern Region into three units as part of a twelve state federation. The military government in the Eastern capital, Enugu, assumed that a genocidal attack upon the Ibo people was imminent and declared the region independent as the Republic of Biafra in July 1967. The war was lengthy and, because of the federal blockade of the ports, resulted in a famine in the besieged state. In the course of the war, the Biafran army briefly occupied the Mid-Western Region. In September 1967, as federal forces recaptured the region, it was declared independent as the Autonomous Republic of Benin. Biafra was defeated in January 1970 and reintegrated into Nigeria. Significantly four African states recognised the independence of the Biafran government. It was the only secessionist movement on the continent to achieve this diplomatic distinction (Stremlau, 1977).

At the end of the war the federal military government embarked upon a policy of reconciliation in order to bring the Ibo people back into the mainstream of Nigerian political life. The federation was restructured with further states established to protect local interest groups and weaken the ethnic blocks. The number of states was increased to 19 in 1976, 30 in 1991, and 36 in

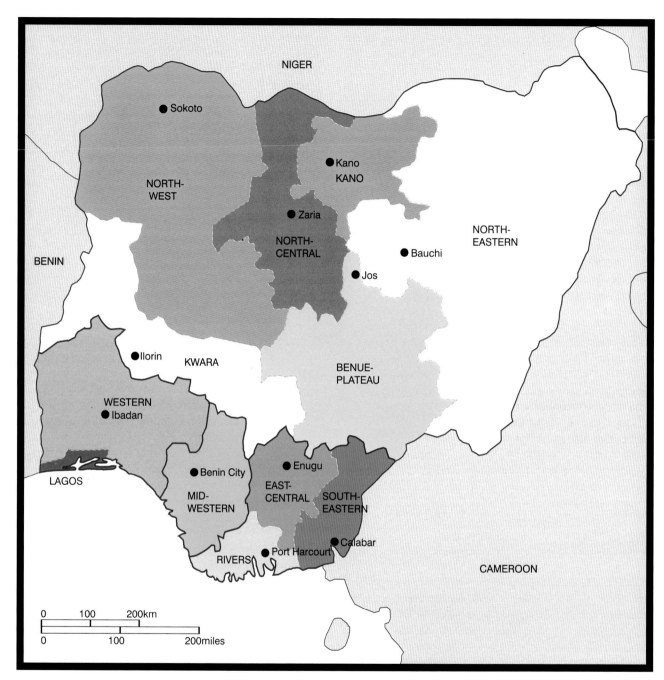

Map 9.10   Nigeria

1996. A separate capital territory of Abuja was established in 1976 in an attempt to move the federal government to a neutral location in the centre of the country. The states were created for administrative purposes, often to accommodate particular interest groups (Ikporukpo, 1986). It should be noted that the country spent most of the post-independence era under military rule, thereby negating the usual association of federalism with democratic institutions. However, the pressures for secessionism appear to have abated, but this may be no more than a reflection of the imposition of military rule.

9.11   SOMALIA

The definition of a Somali state has presented one of the major problems in African and international statecraft (Touval, 1963). Since 1991 there has been no recognised government in the area demarcated on the political map as 'Somalia'. It became the classic example of a 'collapsed state' (Zartman, 1995). During the colonial period, the Somali occupied region of the Horn of Africa was divided between five states or colonies. The coastal belt was occupied by Italy, Britain and France, each of which established a Somali colony. The interior was occupied by Ethiopia and to a lesser extent attached to British East Africa (Kenya). Briefly, during and after the Second World War, virtually the whole area fell under British control. However, the previous political boundaries were reasserted in the following period as Ethiopia regained independence and its pre-1936 territorial limits.

At the end of the colonial era, the British Somaliland Protectorate received independence in June 1960 followed by the Italian trusteeship territory of Somalia in July 1960. The two states proceeded to merge, and adopted a flag with a five pointed star to symbolise the five units of 'Greater Somalia', in which the new government sought to unite all the Somali people in one state. Ethiopia was challenged by these demands in two ways. First, the incorporation of French Somaliland (the French Somali Coast), renamed the French Territory of the Afars and Issas in July 1967 to remove the Somali connotation, would have placed control of the railway line from Addis Ababa to the sea in Somali hands, enabling economic pressure to be exerted. Secondly, the Haud and Ogaden region, which was the major part of the Somali claim, had been incorporated into Ethiopia in the late nineteenth century and more recently regained from Great Britain after the Second World War only in January 1955. This was not about to be relinquished. Insurrection and finally invasion by Somalia followed. In July 1977 the provisional government of Western Somalia was established only to be defeated in March the following year and the Ethiopians regained control of the region, displacing many of the inhabitants. It was only in September 1977 that the French nominally withdrew from their possession, which took independence as the Republic of Djibouti, without joining Greater Somalia. The demands for unity were in large measure deflected as the Somali state had ceased to have the attractive power it exercised in the 1960s. Somali secessionism in northern Kenya has been confined to a sporadic low level insurgency.

In January 1991 President Siad Barre of Somalia was overthrown and the country disintegrated without any recognisable government. The various clans and factions took control of 'their' sections of the country. Even the capital, Mogadishu, was divided into sectors between the warlords who assumed effective control. The collapse of the political infrastructure resulted in a famine. This in turn led to a United Nations humanitarian exercise to save lives and attempt to reconstruct the state administration in 1992–1995, which ended in failure.

Significantly in the former British Somaliland the breakdown of administration did not take place and the local Somali National Movement decided to 'revise the Act of Union' of 1960 and in May 1991 declared Somaliland independent (Prunier, 1994). The new state received no diplomatic recognition, although it was but claiming to re-establish a state which was merged after the independence of two separate colonies. Effective independence did mean that it was able to avoid the chaos afflicting the remainder of Somalia. It is notable that the Somali nationality state in Ethiopia, as established in 1994, did not exercise its right to secede and join Somalia, although the option remains open, at least on paper.

9.12   DECOLONISATION IN ARABIA

Great Britain at the end of the Second World War was still responsible for a series of nominally dependent states and a colony on the eastern and southern margins of Arabia extending from Kuwait to Aden. Between 1961 and 1971 the British withdrew entirely from the region, leaving behind five independent Arab states.

The first, Kuwait, was the most problematic. Its international status had been the matter of international negotiation in the twentieth century between the British and initially the Ottoman Empire and subsequently the Saudi kingdom and Iraq. In November 1914, following the entry of the Ottoman Empire into the First World War, Kuwait joined Great Britain, which recognised it as an independent sheikhdom under British protection. Kuwait was therefore able to conduct limited foreign relations but enjoyed protection from external threat. In line with the new power relations in the Middle East, the protection agreement was ended in June 1961 and the country's independence was recognised. However, Iraq immediately claimed the state as being part of its inheritance from the Ottoman Empire. This was duly rejected by the United Nations and the Arab League. It was only in October 1963 that Iraq formally recognised Kuwaiti independence. Repudiation of this

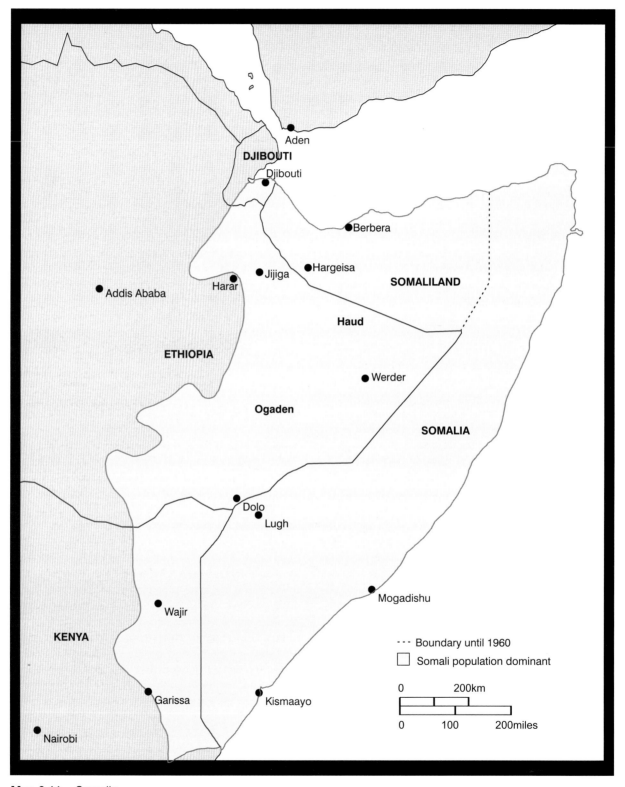

Map 9.11 Somalia

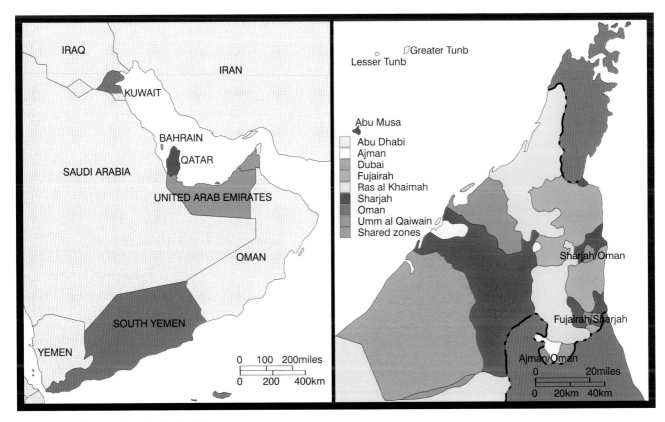

Map 9.12   Decolonisation in Arabia

agreement in August 1990 led to one of the major military confrontations of the post-Cold War era. Following the Iraqi invasion a 'Provisional Free Kuwaiti Government' was established, which declared a republic, and then requested incorporation into Iraq. Independence was only restored in January 1991 as a result of the victory of an American led expeditionary force against the invaders.

The British withdrawal from Aden and the adjacent protectorate states in 1967 was also problematical. A number of the sultanates of the western Aden Protectorate were grouped together in February 1959 to form the Federation of Arab Emirates of the South, subsequently renamed the Federation of South Arabia. In January 1963 the British colony of Aden joined the Federation, as did all but the three most easterly sultanates. Yemeni and Pan-Arab backed forces claimed the area as a part of the Yemen, leading to an armed insurrection. The British garrison gradually lost control of the interior as the National Liberation Army overthrew the sultanates between August and October 1967. Finally in November 1967 Aden was abandoned and the Republic of South Yemen, subsequently the People's Democratic Republic of Yemen, was duly

inaugurated (Gavin, 1975). It was only in May 1990 following the end of the Cold War and the elimination of ideological differences between them that the two Yemeni states united. However, in May 1994 the Democratic Republic of Yemen, based in Aden, declared its independence, as the union was not working as its leaders had expected. The secessionist state remained unrecognised and was defeated in a brief civil war in July 1994.

The British withdrawal from the remaining parts of Arabia in 1971 was more orderly, following the decision in February 1967 to withdraw from all bases east of Suez. The seven Trucial States had signed a peace treaty with the British authorities in India in 1820, which was codified in the agreement of 1853 as the Perpetual Maritime Truce. Only in 1892 did the states transfer control of foreign affairs into British hands, effectively assuming protected status. Bahrain's dealings with Great Britain were similar. Qatar remained under Ottoman suzerainty until 1916 when British protected status was accepted. Initially all nine states began negotiations for a joint organisation. However, after the United Nations 'test of opinion' in Bahrain in May 1970, Iran withdrew its claim to the islands and the Sheikh decided to opt for separate statehood. The Sheikhdoms of Bahrain and Qatar were recognised as independent states with the ending of the protection agreements in August and September 1971 respectively.

The remaining seven Trucial States presented a problem for the departing colonial power, as although the two larger states, Abu Dhabi and Dubai, could have functioned as independent states, the smaller entities were considered to be too fragmented territorially and too poor economically to do so. Much of the complexity was due to the often ambiguous tribal allegiances of the local populations. Thus in December 1971 six of the seven states ended the protection agreements and agreed upon a federal union to form the United Arab Emirates. Ras al Khaimah only joined in February 1972 after seeking better terms (Heard-Bey, 1996).

The Gulf states have undergone significant economic development since independence, with the boom in the petroleum industry. As a result, only a fifth of the population of the United Arab Emirates were citizens by the mid-1990s, with the implicit threat that such a situation poses for state stability. Dependence upon the ruling dynasties to embody the state-idea is also precarious in an era of republicanism and nationalism.

9.13   PLANS FOR ARAB UNITY

One of the largest territorial groupings united by a common language is the Arab world. The widespread use of the Arabic language, the language of the Koran and formal Moslem prayers, is a powerful unifying factor in acculturation, which has frequently been used for political purposes. After the First World War the emergent Arab nationalist forces in the Middle East hoped to establish an Arab state or grouping of independent states out of the Arab sections of the former Ottoman Empire. In large measure this programme was not achieved.

The League of Arab States was established in March 1945 to coordinate the policies of the independent Arab states on matters of mutual concern. Inevitably the creation and continued existence of the State of Israel dominated the political agenda. Severe disagreements over the signing of the Israeli–Egyptian peace treaty in 1979 reduced the League's effectiveness. The League did not produce tangible Arab unity, but it provided a significant support base for the Palestinian cause, although Palestine was only admitted to full membership in September 1976. However, a host of cooperative and technical organisations were linked to the League. Most ambitious was the Arab

Common Market, established in January 1964. It failed to achieve its objectives and was revived as the more limited Arab Market for Free Trade in January 1998, aimed at harmonising tariffs and liberalising trade regulations between Arab states.

Membership of the League grew as the recognisable Arab states gained independence. Subsequently the League took the first steps towards expanding its sphere of influence with the admission of Mauritania in October 1973. Somalia was admitted in February 1974 despite the national decision to transliterate the Somali language into Latin, not Arabic, script. Djibouti was admitted in September 1977 on the understanding that Arabic would be adopted as the official language as soon as possible. At the same time a decision on the application for admission by the Comoros was deferred as Arabic was not the official language and French was predominant. However, in September 1993 the Comoros were admitted in recognition of their Islamic heritage. The application by Eritrea in May 1993 was deferred pending the solution of outstanding problems with neighbouring Arab states, notably Yemen, over control of the Hanish Islands in the Red Sea.

In the aftermath of the Suez crisis of 1956 more restricted plans for Arab unity were pursued with more limited objectives. In February 1958 Egypt and Syria formed a political union, entitled the United Arab Republic, with the prime purpose of securing a coordinated policy directed towards the destruction of Israel. However, friction between the two administrations over the control of the centralised functions was such that in October 1961 Syria resumed its status as an independent state. It was only in September 1971 that the remaining section of the United Arab Republic changed its name to the Arab Republic of Egypt. Parallel with this venture, a symbolic agreement was reached between the United Arab Republic and Yemen for the establishment of a federal union in March 1958. It was dissolved in December 1961 as the governments were unable to agree upon an effective role for the union.

As a counter measure the Hashemite kingdoms of Iraq and Jordan formed the Arab Federation (subsequently Union) in February 1958. However, the subsequent revolution in Baghdad, with the assassination of King Faisal II and the overthrow of the monarchy, ended this route to unification, which was dissolved in August 1958.

Other states put forward schemes for the unity of sections of the Arab world. Libya in particular offered treaties of unification to many of its neighbours. These included the Federation of Arab Republics, with Egypt and Syria (September 1971), union with Egypt (September 1973), Tunisia (January 1974) and Syria (September 1980).

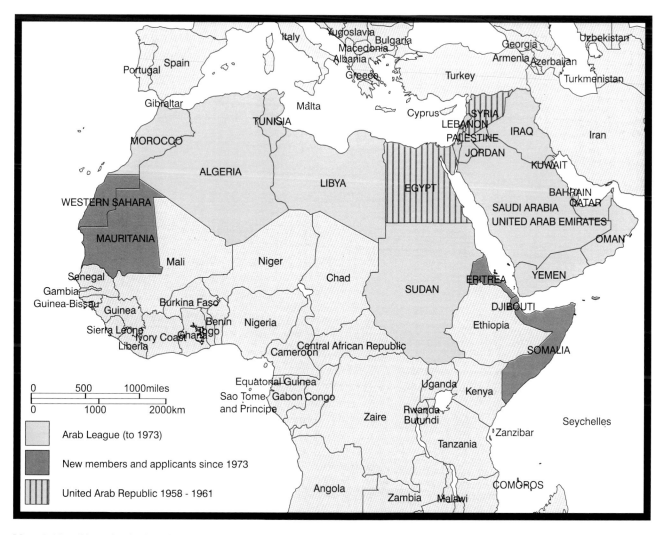

Map 9.13   Plans for Arab unity

None survived to establish viable governmental structures. Similarly plans for the unification of the Maghreb involving Morocco, Algeria and Tunisia have foundered as a result of mutual suspicions.

9.14   CYPRUS

The granting of independence to Cyprus was one of the more problematic decisions taken by a departing colonial power. In the 1950s the British administration had been confronted by a militant movement among the Greek-speaking majority aimed at achieving 'Enosis', union with Greece. The Turkish-speaking section of the population, constituting approximately a fifth of the total, would have preferred union with Turkey if the colonial regime was to end. As both Greece and Turkey were allies in the North Atlantic Treaty Organisation, the conflict between them over the issue was diffused through a compromise which satisfied no one. Independence was granted in August 1960 and guaranteed by the interested parties. Thus union with Greece or Turkey was ruled out, as was partition. Furthermore, control over two small portions of the island was retained by Great Britain as 'Sovereign Base Areas'.

The practical workings of the complex communally based constitution failed to accommodate the fears of the political leaders of the Turkish speakers and conflict resulted. Segregation levels between the two communities were high, reflecting the patterns of historic settlement since the conquest of the island by the Ottoman Empire in

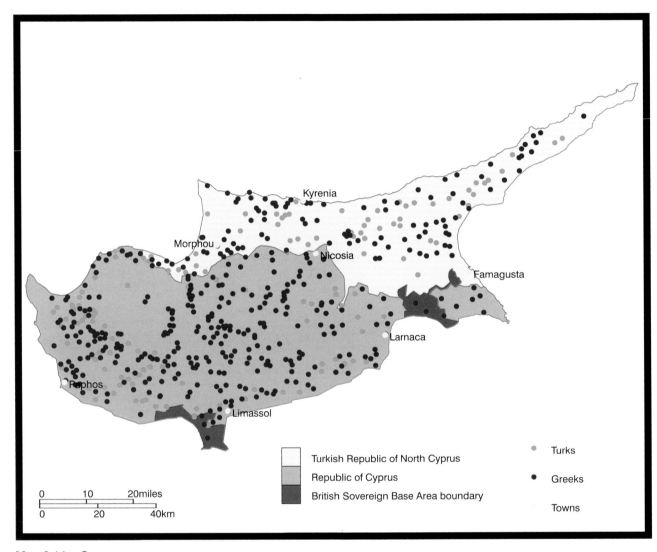

Map 9.14   Cyprus

the late sixteenth century. Thus villages and suburbs tended to be predominantly either Greek or Turkish. However, there was no overall spatial division of the island between them. Thus constitutional federal plans, based on community rather than territory, proved to be remarkably difficult to implement. Conflict between the two groups in December 1963 resulted in the Turkish community's abandonment of some outlying villages and concentration in a number of consolidated but isolated ethnic enclaves, together with the division of Nicosia, the capital.

An attempted Greek nationalist coup d'etat in Nicosia prompted military intervention by Turkey in July 1974, which proceeded to occupy approximately 40 percent of the island. The result was effective partition of the state, including the capital by the 'Atilla' line, which was policed by United Nations forces. A massive enforced population exchange took place, with virtually all the Greeks moving to the South and Turks to the North. The northern portion declared itself a separate Turkish Federated State of Cyprus in February 1975. Sporadic negotiations continued thereafter aimed at some reconciliation between the leaders of the two communities. No solution was devised and the split widened, leading to the declaration of independence by the Turkish Republic of North Cyprus in November 1983. The new state pursued a process of 'Turkification' in an effort to erase the previous Greek imprint within its territory (Kliot and Mansfield, 1997). However, international recognition has eluded the breakaway state.

9.15 DECOLONISATION IN THE CARIBBEAN

The Caribbean region was late to be decolonised, largely because the colonial powers considered the individual islands and territories to be too small to support themselves as independent states. Indeed the majority of colonial governments considered that the Caribbean region would continue under some form of political linkage to the metropolitan powers indefinitely. In March 1946 the French government decided to incorporate administratively their Caribbean colonies, Guadeloupe, Martinique and

Guiana (including the Territory of Inini), into the French Republic as overseas departments. Thereafter they were governed as integral parts of France.

The British pursued a different course through the promotion of self-government and independence. Initially this was viewed as the creation of a West Indies Federation, linking the colonies into an overall structure which could achieve independence. It was therefore in the grand tradition of British colonial federalism pursued in the establishment of other dominions, notably Canada, Australia and South Africa. Contemporary developments in Rhodesia and Nyasaland also indicated that the opportunities for the creation of federations had narrowed

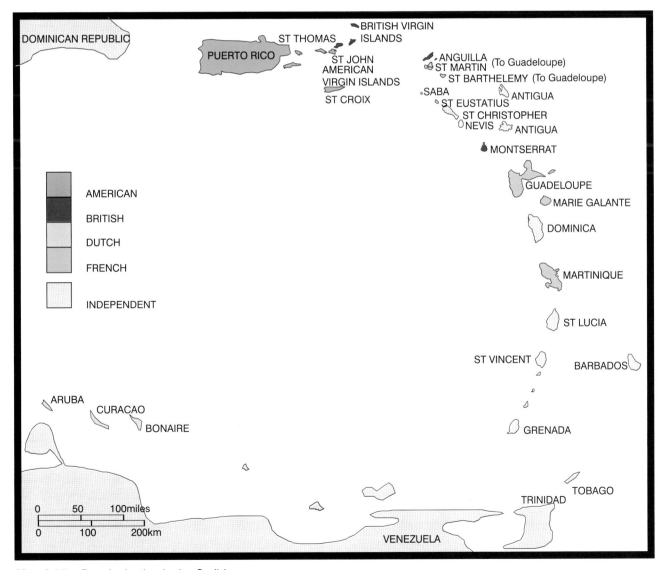

Map 9.15   Decolonisation in the Caribbean

substantially. In January 1958 the Federation was established and linked most, but not all, the British islands in the Caribbean. Significantly the two mainland colonies did not join, neither did the Bahamas or Bermuda. Even existing shared structures were broken. The Jamaican dependencies of the Cayman Islands and the Turks and Caicos Islands chose not to be linked and so became separate colonies. In the Leeward Islands, the Presidency of the British Virgin Islands chose to secede and become a separate colony. However, some ten colonies joined the Federation. Inter-island tensions, even over the site of the federal capital, rendered the structure ineffective and the two largest islands decided to secede (Dale, 1962). The Federation was wound up in May 1962 and both Jamaica and Trinidad and Tobago became independent states in August 1962.

Negotiations over the establishment of a smaller Eastern Caribbean Federation were conducted over the next two years, without finality. British Guiana, renamed Guyana, assumed independence in May 1966 and Barbados in November the same year. The remaining British small island colonies sought a continuing link with Great Britain. Constitutional lawyers devised the formal position of 'Associated State', whereby the colony became self-governing and the British government was only responsible for foreign affairs and defence. The status could be terminated at any time. The six Leeward and Windward islands which took this status opted for independent dominion status between February 1974 (Grenada) and September 1983 (St Christopher and Nevis).

The tendency for the islands to pursue their own interests in isolation was amply illustrated by the history of Anguilla, and its population of approximately 5000, after the breakdown of the Federation (Clarke, 1971). In February 1967 St Christopher–Nevis–Anguilla assumed the status of Associated Statehood. However, the inhabitants of Anguilla rejected the new government in May 1967, followed by a declaration of independence the following month. Negotiations between the various parties continued until February 1969 when the island declared itself a republic. In March 1969 Anguilla was occupied by British police forces and placed under the control of a British administrator. In July 1969 the government of Associated State St Christopher–Nevis–Anguilla agreed to the continuation of the British administration of the island. However, it was only in December 1980 that Anguilla officially left the Associated State and became a separate British dependency. The subsequent movement for the independence of Nevis failed to gain the necessary support of two-thirds of the electorate in the referendum in August 1998.

The British Caribbean colonies were thus reduced in number to the two former Jamaican dependencies, together with the British Virgin Islands, Montserrat and Bermuda. All were small states with under 35 000 inhabitants. Furthermore, the political stability and security implied by the continuation of British rule enabled their economies to be developed around financial and tourist services for the North American market. The Bahamas became independent in July 1973, while Bermuda opted in a referendum in August 1995 to remain a British colony. British Honduras (Belize) remained under nominal colonial rule until September 1981, when Guatemala finally dropped its claim to the territory, allowing the colony to become independent.

In December 1954, under the Statute of the Kingdom, the Dutch constitution was amended to incorporate the Netherlands Antilles and Suriname as full partners in the Kingdom. Subsequently Suriname became independent in November 1975. The island of Aruba seceded from the Netherlands Antilles in January 1986, with the object of gaining independence after ten years. This option was subsequently, in June 1990, rejected in favour of 'special status' under the Dutch Crown. Curaçao and the other four islands rejected special status in November 1993 and remained linked together.

The other colonial possessions were in American hands. In January 1952 Puerto Rico rejected independence and assumed Commonwealth status, as 'a country freely associated of its own will with the United States', with internal self-government. Decisions on further constitutional advance revolved around the, as yet unresolved, debate over the merits of independence or admission as a state to the Union. The American Virgin Islands remained a Territory with a large measure of self-government. Thus, although substantial decolonisation has taken place since the 1960s, the Caribbean remains as one of the main regions of colonial control.

9.16   DECOLONISATION IN THE PACIFIC

The last broad region of the world to experience decolonisation was the Pacific Ocean. The smallness of the islands, both in size and population, and the long distances between them, appeared to the colonial powers as late as the early 1970s, to render the Pacific islands their permanent wards (Overton, 1994). The renaming of the French Settlements in the Ocean as French Polynesia in August 1957 was the first official hint of Pacific island ethnic nationalism.

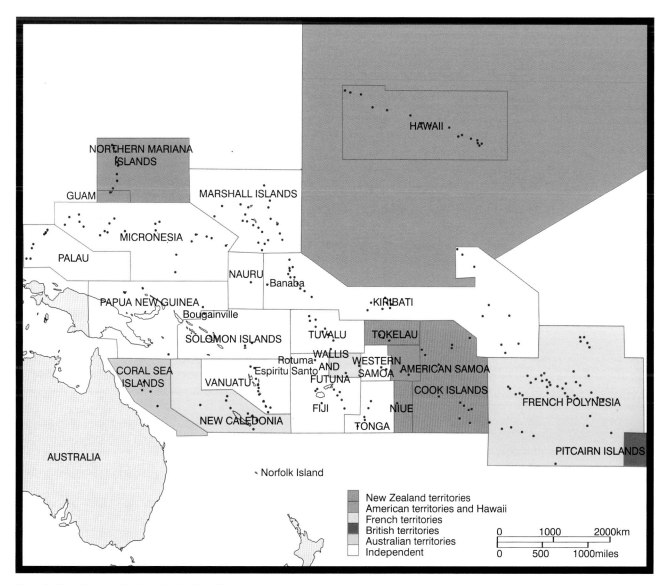

Map 9.16   Decolonisation in the Pacific

The first two independent states were created by the conclusion of the United Nations trusteeship regimes. Western Samoa achieved independence in January 1962 and Nauru in January 1968. The latter measured only 21 square kilometres with a population of approximately 6000 and was clearly a mini-state by any definition. Its financial resources have not extended to seeking membership of the United Nations and most diplomatic and consular affairs are dealt with by the former administrative power, Australia.

As was the case in the Caribbean, the French resisted decolonisation most strenuously, while the British government accepted its inevitability. The protected kingdom of Tonga gained independence in June 1970 and was followed by the largest island group, in terms of population, Fiji, in October the same year. Papua and New Guinea attained independence as a single country in September 1975. Other island groups followed, including the New Hebrides in July 1980. The condominium agreement between France and Great Britain was ended and the islands granted independence as the Republic of Vanuatu. This constituted the only French retreat from Empire in the region. The main French island groups of French Polynesia and New Caledonia had by this time independence movements, but the French settlers were effectively in political control to prevent such a move. The smaller Wallis and Futuna Islands, which had been raised to separate status in July 1961, avoided the conflicts of the larger French dependencies.

The American Pacific Trust Territory, acquired from Japan at the end of the Second World War, had been granted to the United States with the understanding that there would be significant political advancement. Creating a sense of nationhood was difficult for a territory of 75 inhabited islands spread over an area of 7.5 million square kilometres. In 1961 the United Nations prompted the American administration to speed up constitutional advance and in 1965 the Congress of Micronesia was established as an inter-island body. However, this disintegrated as the various island groups seceded. The Northern Mariana Islands opted for continuing the link with the United States through the attainment of Commonwealth status which entered into force in 1986. Palau (December 1994) and the Marshall Islands (October 1986), together with the rump Federated States of Micronesia (November 1986), considered that the advantages of self-governing Commonwealth status were outweighed by those of independent statehood. Instead of taking independence as a single entity the territory was thus divided into four separate states. The Northern Mariana Islands continued with Commonwealth status. Similarly no move to independence was made by the island of Guam, acquired in 1898 and administered as a United States territory since that date.

One of the significant features of the independence period and in more recent years has been the problem of island secessionist movements. At independence some colonies fragmented. Thus the Polynesians of the Ellice Islands sought separation from the majority Micronesians of the Gilbert Islands (including Ocean Island, the Phoenix and Line Islands). A referendum was held on the issue in August–September 1974 and separation took place in October 1975. Thus Tuvalu and Kiribati went to independence as separate states in October 1978 and July 1979 respectively. In the latter state the land area amounted to only 710 square kilometres situated across 5000

kilometres of ocean. Even within Kiribati, Ocean Island (Banaba) sought a special dispensation on the basis of its phosphate deposits on which the islands' economy was based and the population's own distinctive ethnic origins and history (van Trease, 1993). The population had been removed in the Second World War to Rabi Island in Fiji, where some subsequently elected to remain. With the exhaustion of the deposits in 1980 the economic incentive for secessionism disappeared, but not the ethnic tensions which remained.

The most significant fragmentation took place with the American Pacific Trust Territory alluded to above. The constitution of the Federated States of Micronesia hopefully affirmed that: 'To make one nation of many islands, we respect the diversity of our cultures. Our differences enrich us. The seas bring us together, they do not separate us. Our islands sustain us, our island nation enlarges us and makes us stronger' (Hinckley, 1981: 51). On the other hand, local particularism was to prove too great to sustain such rhetoric and the peripheral parts split off from the Federation.

Individual islands have sought independence from island groupings at various stages. The independence of Vanuatu (New Hebrides) was accompanied by the attempt of the inhabitants of the island of Espiritu Santo to secede in the same year, reflecting the Anglo-French split in the New Hebrides' administration in the colonial period. Similarly in Papua New Guinea, on the island of Bougainville, initially part of the Solomon Islands, the secessionist Bougainville Revolutionary Army sought to base a separate independence on control of the copper mine between 1988 and 1998. The position of Banaba in Kiribati has been mentioned. Special status for Rotuma in Fiji was accepted, based upon the recognition of a separate history and culture.

Even within the remaining dependencies fragmentation is noticeable. Thus the island of Niue seceded from the remainder of the Cook Islands. However, economic circumstances were such that the majority of the population had migrated to New Zealand, the colonial power. Indeed the possibility of each island opting for independence is a prospect that the colonial powers have resisted strongly.

CHAPTER 10

Post-Cold War Reordering 1990–2000

The end of the Cold War in the last decade of the twentieth century was accompanied by dramatic changes in the international system. The United States emerged as the undisputed global superpower. The end of Communism as an international revolutionary movement and the fragmentation of the Soviet Union were highly significant events leading to substantial changes on the world map (Crampton and Crampton, 1996). The two other Slavic federations, Yugoslavia and Czechoslovakia, similarly collapsed with the demise of their Communist ideology. Thus in the early 1990s some 22 states gained their independence, while two mergers took place. The year 1991 consequently ranks with 1918 and 1960 as one of the most significant years of the twentieth century for state formation.

The end of the Cold War also had major global repercussions with many of the international and internal tensions that had been held in suspense during the era of superpower confrontation now brought to the surface. Much discussion concerning the establishment of 'a New World Order' accompanied the American victory in the Cold War (e.g. Hendriksen, 1992; O'Tuathail and Luke, 1994; Polestsky, 1991; Smith and Borocz, 1995). However, there was little concerted effort by the dominant superpower to consolidate such a new order, beyond a few key international problem areas associated with the Cold War. Thus Germany, Palestine, South Africa and Northern Ireland were all revisited by American diplomacy, with, in general, considerable effect. However, the American debacle in Somalia in October 1993 ended the more interventionist phase of the post-Cold War era.

The almost universal success of liberal democracy and the defeat of the other major ideologies was hailed as 'the end of history' (Fukuyama, 1992). Indeed the 'end of geography' was also proclaimed as the world economy became increasingly integrated (O'Brien, 1992). Such an outcome had not been self-evident to the participants in the ideological conflicts of the previous eighty years. Indeed the experience of Europe between 1914 and 1991 was such as to prompt one observer to label it the 'Dark Continent' of the twentieth century, as communism and fascism appeared to prevail over liberal democracy in much of the continent for a long period of time (Mazower, 1998).

The optimistic expectations generated by the collapse of communism in eastern Europe and the Soviet Union were not fulfilled as the ghosts of the past returned and national conflicts over specific pieces of territory dominated the 1990s. By 1993 some 70 ethno-territorial area conflicts in central and eastern Europe and the former Soviet Union had been identified (Szajkowski, 1993). The Gulf War in January 1991 demonstrated the continuing international instability of the post-Cold War era. The challenge to the state system posed by the Iraqi seizure of Kuwait was defeated and the protective role of the United Nations world security system was enhanced, although the opportunity to place a more comprehensive collective security system in place was lost.

10.1   THE EX-SOVIET STATES

The collapse of the Soviet Union was sudden and in large measure unexpected by the international community. Indeed in the final stages of disintegration American efforts were directed to its reform and preservation, rather than disintegration (Kissinger, 1994). The last Soviet President, Mikhail Gorbachev, introduced programmes of glasnost (political liberalisation) and perestroika (restructuring) in an effort to transform the Soviet Union. However, the relaxation of the repressive system upon which the Soviet state was based released pressures for national liberation as well as democratisation. The result was the declaration by the Supreme Soviet in December 1991 that the Union of Soviet Socialist Republics no longer existed. The fifteen constituent republics were thus independent states.

The definition of the Union republics was therefore of considerable concern. The essential outlines had been drawn between 1917 and 1936 by Joseph Stalin in his roles as Commissar of Nationalities and then Secretary General of the Central Committee of the Communist Party. Indeed the 1936 constitution of the Soviet Union had specifically included a clause guaranteeing the right of each Union republic to secession and independence. It was this constitution that had finally settled the delimitation of states in the Caucasus and Central Asia. The Transcaucasian Soviet Federal Socialist Republic was disbanded and the three constituent republics resumed separate Union statehood. In Central Asia, Kazakhstan was separated from Kyrgyzstan and both promoted to separate Union republican status, bringing the number of Union republics in the region to five.

Subsequent changes were associated with Soviet territorial expansion in Europe in the Second World War. The Moldavian and Karelian Autonomous Soviet Socialist Republics had been raised to Union status in August and March 1940 respectively. In both cases the move was intended to incorporate lands seized from neighbouring states, namely Finland and Romania respectively. Indeed the Karelian Republic was renamed the Finno-Karelian Republic to emphasise the claims upon Finnish territory. In August 1940 the three Baltic republics of Latvia, Lithuania and Estonia were incorporated into the Soviet Union. The Soviet Union at this stage consisted of sixteen constituent republics.

In July 1956 the Finno-Karelian Republic was downgraded to the status of an autonomous republic within the Russian Soviet Federal Socialist Republic and the reference to the Finns removed. In the official request for the change of status, the Karelian President, Otto Kuusinen, claimed that the increasingly close economic and cultural ties with Russia and the small population (approximately 600 000) did not justify the continued existence of the Union republic. Furthermore, intensive Russification had severely reduced the Karelian component of the population (Harris, 1993b). The former strategic advantages of Union status, vis-à-vis Finland, were deemed to have diminished as the latter state had been neutralised under the post-war peace treaty. Thus the number of full Union republics was set at fifteen, a number which remained constant until the dissolution of the Soviet Union.

The relative decline of the Soviet Union with its rigid centralised command economy was not at first evident, but it was militarily and economically overextended as it expanded its confrontation with the United States beyond its traditional areas of concern in Europe and Asia. During this period of decline, the Communist parties in the various Union republics exercised ever greater independence of the centre (Smith, 1996). Thus the original concepts followed by Lenin and Stalin of a decentralised administration, to accommodate the nationalities, controlled by a centralised party, began to change. The introduction of perestroika (restructuring) and glasnost (political liberalisation) under President Mikhail Gorbachev in March 1985 weakened the structure of the Union yet further. Elections in May 1989 introduced an element of pluralism in the political system, which had been so noticeably lacking since 1918. The result was an intensification of demands for political reforms, which inevitably undermined the raison d'etre of the Union.

The Baltic and Transcaucasian republics began the move towards greater freedom from Russia. In the former case the governments of the three republics sought to have Stalin's annexation declared illegal and declarations of 'sovereignty' were followed by those of independence in the course of 1989 and 1990. Although at first opposed by the Soviet Union, the three republics were recognised in September 1991 as independent states. In the Caucasus the inter-ethnic conflicts had broken out in the late 1980s, notably between Armenia and Azerbaijan over the future of the autonomous republic of Nagorno-Karabakh. Other violent conflicts strained Russian resources to contain them.

The attempted military coup d'etat in August 1991 removed the central government from control of affairs, placing power in the hands of the Russian Federal president, Boris Yeltsin. In December 1991 the Ukraine, the second most populous constituent state, held a referendum which supported independence. In the same month the Soviet Union was formally dissolved and the remaining

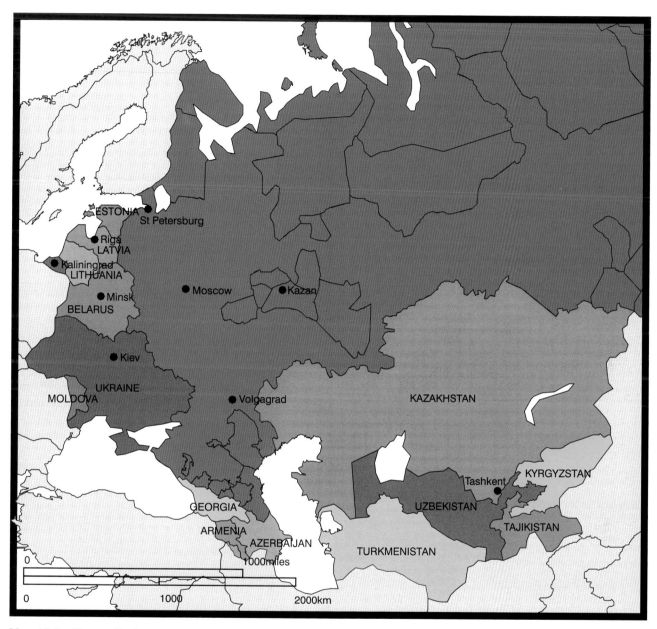

Map 10.1   The ex-Soviet states

constituent republics became independent states. The Commonwealth of Independent States was also established in the same month to promote economic and military, but no longer political, cooperation between most of the states.

The newly independent states were confronted by a number of severe problems. In most there were boundary disputes with neighbours and minority groups within (Harris, 1993a, 1993b). It was, after all, only the fifteen dominant nationalities which achieved self-determination and the independence of their nation-states. The other nationalities were still subject to alien rule. The particularly acute problems of Russia and the Caucasian regions are considered in later sections. In the other republics secessionist movements were also apparent. Thus previously autonomous republics attempted to gain greater autonomy, even independence. Hence the claims for autonomy raised by the administrations of Nakhichevan in Azerbaijan and Gorno-Badakhshan in Tajikistan were essentially overlooked in the interests of maintaining national unity. In others minority groups declared their own separate republics, as in the case of the Gaugauzs of Gaugauzia (August 1990) and the Russians of the Transnistria (September 1990), both in Moldova.

The complexities of the nationality question outside Russia and the Caucasus were most serious in the Crimea, where Russia mounted a challenge to the Ukrainian position. The dispute is both ethnic and historic. The Crimean Tatars had sought a separate state at the time of the Russian revolution. However, they had been deported in 1945 as a 'collaborator people' following the German occupation of the peninsula in the Second World War. Colonisation in the eighteenth century and again after 1945 had resulted in a substantial Russian majority of the population, thereby undermining the Tatar claims. Russian dominance was reinforced by the presence of the major Soviet naval base for the Black Sea fleet at Sebastopol.

However, in February 1954 the Crimea had been transferred from Russia to the Ukraine as a gift to commemorate the three hundredth anniversary of the union of the two states under the Romanov Czar Aleksei Mikhailovich. As the transfer document stated it was 'yet another affirmation of the great fraternal love and trust of the Russian people for Ukraine' (Magocsi, 1996: 653). It is maybe relevant to note that the Soviet leader at the time, Nikita Khrushchev, originated from the Ukraine. The conflict over the status of the Crimea was therefore intense, but eventually it was agreed by the members of the Commonwealth of Independent States that the boundaries inherited from the Soviet Union should not be altered. The parallel with the stance of the Organisation of African Unity on maintaining the status quo is notable. The Crimea, after a complex set of negotiations, obtained the status of 'an autonomous republic forming an integral part of Ukraine' in November 1995. The Crimean Tatars failed to obtain concessions on their special status (Allworth, 1998).

In the majority of cases conflicts were halted or mediated by Russian military intervention, whether in Moldova or Tajikistan. However, many states were not as homogeneous in population composition as the administrative map of the former Soviet Union might have suggested. Even the script in which languages were written became the subject of confusion and controversy. In the 1930s the various Central Asian languages had been transliterated into Cyrillic script, after a brief post-revolutionary phase of the adoption of Latin script, from the original Arabic script. Reversion to Latin script accompanied political independence from Russia. Even more confused was the situation in Moldova. As an element in the creation of a distinct Moldovan nation,

the Soviet authorities had decreed the use of the Cyrillic script to write Romanian. In September 1989 the Moldovan parliament reverted to the use of the Latin alphabet. Significantly, in September 1992, the Russian based breakaway Dnestr Republic authorised the use of Cyrillic script within its territory.

In contrast to the general movement towards fragmentation, the government of one state, Belarus, had doubts over the benefits of independence and sought a political accommodation with Russia. The indigenous Slavic population was in many ways closest in terms of language and culture to the Great Russians. In the immediate aftermath of the Russian revolution in 1917, the Byelorussians (White Russians) had not been able to establish an independent administration and the area was turned into a battleground. The Byelorussian Soviet republic established in January 1919 was from the start a creation of the Russian state. Furthermore, the Belarussian government after 1991 had pursued economic and political reforms more slowly than the other ex-Soviet states. Hence the country's economy declined dramatically. This prompted the Russian government to reject the moves towards complete political integration. However, an agreement on closer political and economic union with Russia was reached in April 1996 and reaffirmed the following year, although no surrender of national sovereignty was implied.

The position of Moldova was highly fragile at the time of independence. Union with Romania appeared a logical step as the reunification of territories lost to the Soviet Union in 1940. However, at the time of Moldovan independence integration into the Romanian economy and polity was not attractive to Moldovans emerging from dictatorship. Thus in January 1993 the Moldovan parliament rejected the call for a referendum on unification by an overwhelming majority.

10.2 THE RUSSIAN FEDERATION

The Russian Federal Republic as it emerged from the dissolution of the Soviet Union was still the most extensive country in the world, with an area of 17.1 million square kilometres. However, in terms of population, it housed only 148.7 million, of whom 81.5 percent were Russians. The independence of the other fourteen republics, which were mostly situated on areas conquered in the eighteenth and nineteenth centuries, had resulted in the re-emergence of a Russian nation-state, reduced to little more than the extent of Muscovy in the mid-seventeenth century.

Map 10.2   The Russian Federation

A	ADYGEY REPUBLIC	KP	KOMI-PERMYAK AUTONOMOUS OKRUG
AB	AGA-BURYAT AUTONOMOUS OKRUG	ME	MARI-EL REPUBLIC
C	CHUVASH (CHAVASH) REPUBLIC	M	MORDVIN REPUBLIC
CI	CHECHEN-INGUSH REPUBLIC	N	NORTH OSSETIAN REPUBLIC
J	JEWISH AUTONOMOUS OKRUG	T	TATARSTAN
KB	KABARDINO-BALKAR REPUBLIC	U	UDMURT REPUBLIC
KC	KARACHAI-CHERKESS REPUBLIC	UO	UST'-ORDA BURYAT AUTONOMOUS OKRUG

0 — 1500miles
0 — 2000km

AO   AUTONOMOUS OKRUG

As the name suggests the constitution retained the Soviet provisions for the minority nationalities, with nearly half the state area allocated to some 21 constituent national republics, ten autonomous areas and one autonomous region. The republics were small in terms of population. Only nine recorded a population in excess of one million in the mid 1990s and five of the autonomous areas recorded under 100 000 inhabitants. Only 21 000 people were recorded in the Evenki autonomous area, compared with 4.1 million in Bashkortostan and 3.8 million in Tatarstan. In terms of area, the republics and autonomous areas and region covered over half (53.3 percent) of the land areas of the Russian Federation, although they housed only 17.7 percent of the population. Some of the Federation's republics were extensive. The Sakha Republic with 3.1 million square kilometres was larger in extent than all but seven independent states. However, with only a little over one million inhabitants it was remarkably sparsely populated.

The constituent republics could be divided into two broad divisions, the sparsely populated areas of the northern regions and Asia on the one hand and the more compact regions of the middle Volga and the northern Caucasus on the other. The northern republics, because of their harsh physical environments, had been relatively uninhabited prior to the imposition of Russian rule. Subsequent settlement by Russians had resulted in the emergence of a Russian majority in virtually all of them as the numbers of the indigenous population remained small. Republican status had been granted in Soviet times as a means of preserving indigenous languages and culture in the anticipated transition phase towards complete absorption into the dominant nation. Thus Russians accounted for 79 percent of the population of Khakassia and 70 percent of Buryatia. Only Sakha (Yakutia) with 50 percent and Tuva with 32 percent, did not record a Russian majority. The latter, although a forced Stalinist acquisition, remained a part of the Russian Federation, despite rising national consciousness within the republic.

In the second group of republics, the Russians were generally in a minority, although as a result of economic developments numerically quite large and occupied key positions in the local economies. The largest, Tatarstan, was the titular homeland of a population of some 6.6 million in 1989. The Tatars, despite their numbers, had not gained full Union status in the former Soviet Union as their homeland was strategically placed on the middle Volga, centred upon the city of Kazan. The boundaries of all the Union republics had been drawn so that they were linked to a non-Soviet country. Thus in the event of secession the state would not have become an enclave, completely surrounded by Soviet territory, and thus be at the political and economic mercy of a single state. The Tatars were thus the largest nationality in the Soviet Union without its own Union republic. Even with the dissolution of the Union, the Tatars found themselves in the same position with regard to the Russian Federation. Despite moves towards independence the Tatar leaders had to settle in February 1994 for a treaty of union with Russia, which provided for their control of internal affairs, while still linked to the Federation for purposes of foreign affairs, defence and currency. The other middle Volga republics settled for varying degrees of autonomy, within the Federation.

The republics in the northern Caucasus region presented greater problems for the Russian Federal government. The Russian minorities were smaller, reflecting the relative isolation and lack of economic opportunities in the region. In Dagestan, Russians only constituted 9 percent of the population. With the exception of the Kalmyks, the population of the republics was Moslem, and could trace a long history of resistance to Russian encroachment in the Caucasus Mountains. Some of the nationalities, notably the Chechens, had been deported under Stalin and only allowed to return in the late 1950s (Szajkowski, 1995). Chechnya rejected continued association with Russia and declared its independence in November 1991. The attempts to suppress the independence movement by military means in December 1994 failed and negotiations on the final status of the country have been delayed until the year 2001, when the reconstruction programme should have been completed.

The Ingush authorities dissociated themselves from the Chechen move and seceded from the breakaway state to gain their own republic in June 1992. In contrast, the joint Karachai-Cherkessia Republic was retained after a referendum in March 1992, rather than re-establish a separate Karachai republic as had existed before the deportation of the titular nationality in November 1943.

The legacy of Empire has confronted the new Russian state with numerous problems. Two are immediately apparent in terms of territory and population. The country possesses a significant exclave at Kaliningrad on the Baltic coastline. This represents the major remaining territorial acquisition of the Second World War. It constitutes the northern section of the former province of East Prussia, which had itself been physically separated from the remainder of Germany by the Polish corridor at the end of the First World War. After 1945 the German population had been deported and Russian settlers introduced. A thoroughgoing Russification of the landscape erased most historical links with Germany. However, since September 1991 continued Russian access by land involves movement through independent Lithuania and either Belarus or Latvia. Exclaves have had a particularly poor rate of survival in the twentieth century, and the future of Kaliningrad in a changing Europe must inevitably be subject to speculation.

The other major issue facing the Russian government at the end of Empire is the future of the Russian population beyond the Federation's borders. Over 25 million Russians were enumerated in the 1989 Soviet census as living in the other Soviet republics. Numbers in the Caucasus and Central Asia had declined in the previous decade, but in Latvia and Kazakhstan members of the titular nationalities only just exceed Russian numbers. Subsequent indigenisation of the bureaucracy and industry has resulted in a return flow of Russians to their homeland. However, the presence of substantial minorities of the former colonial ruling nation is a matter of tension in the regions referred to in Moscow as 'the Near Abroad'.

10.3 GEORGIA AND THE CAUCASUS

The Transcaucasian region has been the most problematical of Soviet legacies. The three republics have been beset with crises and military confrontation since the late 1980s. As yet few issues have been satisfactorily resolved and continuing conflict appears to be likely in the ensuing years. The issues of overlapping national territorial claims and secessionism have dominated the politics of the region (Wright et al, 1996).

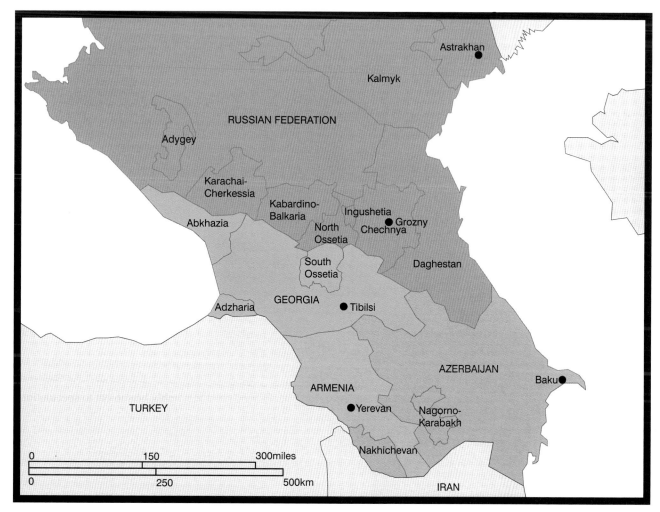

Map 10.3   Georgia and the Caucasus

In the 1980s the question of the status of the autonomous republic of Nagorno-Karabakh reached crisis point. When the boundaries of the Soviet republics were drawn in the early 1920s the area assigned to Armenia was severely circumscribed as Azerbaijan had been the major Russian ally in the region in the civil war. Thus Nagorno-Karabakh was included in Azerbaijan, despite the presence of an Armenian majority. In recognition of this situation, in July 1923 the enclave became an autonomous region and subsequently raised to autonomous republic level. In February 1988 the republic's government requested union with Armenia. The intervention of Soviet forces failed to achieve a solution and in September 1991 the enclave formally seceded from Azerbaijan. Following a civil war and the withdrawal of Russian troops in March 1992, Armenian forces invaded and by conquering a block of

Azerbaijani territory thereby consolidated Nagorno-Karabakh with its own territory. It is notable that the Armenian constitution adopted in August 1990 defined its national territory to include Nagorno-Karabakh. No agreement has been reached over the future of the republic.

Elsewhere in the region secessionism rather than interstate conflict has been most prominent. Georgia inherited a state with significant national minorities (Gachechiladze, 1997). Three, the Moslem Abkhazians, Ajarians and Ossetians, had established their own autonomous republics or areas in 1921–1922. Upon the dissolution of the Soviet Union all three attempted to gain greater autonomy or independence from Georgia. The Ajaria administration settled for greater autonomy, allowing it to establish closer links with neighbouring Turkey, of which it had been a part until 1878. In January

1992 South Ossetia voted in a referendum to join North Ossetia which was part of the Russian Federation, rather than remain within Georgia. Abkhazia first claimed full Soviet Union republic status, and then in July 1992 its independence from Georgia. Neither of these movements was recognised and inconclusive armed conflicts ensued. Once again ethnic conflict has dominated the politics of the country since the end of the 1990–1993 civil war.

10.4   YUGOSLAVIA, POPULATION DISTRIBUTION

After the Second World War the Federal People's Republic of Yugoslavia was established under Marshal Josep Broz Tito, the Communist partisan leader. The country's post-war constitution was modelled upon that of the Soviet Union. Six republics, Serbia, Croatia, Slovenia, Macedonia, Montenegro, and Bosnia and Herzegovina, were established, together with two autonomous regions, Kosovo and Vojvodina, located within the Serbian republic. Unlike the definition of the Soviet republics, historical units assumed greater significance in the drawing of Yugoslav republican boundaries. This was in large measure due to the greater complexity and inter-digitation of the different nationalities. Thus with only relatively minor modifications the resultant republics resembled state and provincial patterns of 1914. Even Montenegro reappeared on the map, although the Montenegrins were in most senses indistinguishable from the Serbs. The Macedonian republic was proclaimed as a separate entity in August 1944, legitimising the identification of a separate Slavic nationality as postulated in the Serbian propaganda of the pre-1913 era. In May–June 1945 the Macedonian language was formalised distinct from both Serbo-Croat and Bulgarian, completing the process of linguistic independence.

The Yugoslav state after 1945 continued to be dominated numerically and politically by the Serbs, as had been the pre-war kingdom. Although the constitution provided for national cultural and linguistic autonomy the economy and political system was run on highly centralised lines by the Communist Party.

Following the death of Marshal Tito in May 1980 the succeeding collective leadership and rotating presidency began to show national divergencies. The individual republican governments sought greater powers, while local politicians began to seek nationalist support. This had been regarded as inevitable by earlier politicians. Thus Milovan Djilas, one of Marshal Tito's close associates, who had become disillusioned with the system, wrote in 1967:

What brought and held different Yugoslav nationalities together was the common fear of foreign aggression or imperialism, the Turkish and Habsburg Empires in the first place, then Nazi Germany and Fascist Italy; later for a while Stalin's Russia. But now there are no such threats; nobody has designs on this country. It is only natural that the Slovenes, the Croats, the Macedonians and so on are seeking to affirm their own cultural identity and cultural independence. If Togo can be a state on its own, they ask, why not us?

(quoted in Owen, 1995: 36).

Nationalism and separatism had long historic roots which were revived for political purposes. Even the last King of Montenegro, Nicholas I, was reburied with due ceremonies in the former royal capital, Cetinje, in October 1989 as a demonstration of the republic's separate identity. In the same year the celebration of the 600th anniversary of the battle of Kosovo was turned into a demonstration of Serb nationalism and anti-Albanian rhetoric. As in the Soviet Union, the relaxation of the tight control exercised through the centralised Communist Party resulted in federal dissolution as nationalist forces re-emerged as dominant factors in politics.

Slovenia and Croatia declared their independence in June 1991. Slovenia, the most prosperous and ethnically uniform of the republics, also had the advantage of being peripheral to the main centres of the country. After a brief conflict the Yugoslav National Army withdrew and the country gained international recognition. Croatia was involved in a bitter war in Eastern Slavonia centred on the city of Vukovar and the Serb inhabited regions of the Krajina and Western Slavonia (Paulicevic, 1996). All three areas had been occupied by Serb settlers in the seventeenth and eighteenth centuries following the devastation caused by the Austro-Turkish wars. A truce between Yugoslavia (Serbia) and Croatia was signed in January 1992, and provided for United Nations supervision of the Serb held areas in the Krajina and Western and Eastern Slavonia. The former was occupied by Serb forces and declared a separate Serb republic, which survived until August 1995, when it was conquered by Croat forces and the Serb population expelled. The autonomous area of Western Slavonia was reoccupied by Croatian forces in May 1995, while Eastern Slavonia remained under Yugoslav (Serb) occupation until January 1998.

There followed the declaration of independence by Bosnia and Herzegovina and Macedonia in March 1992. The latter was the only republic to achieve independence without armed conflict. However, international recognition was delayed by the Greek government, which objected to the adoption of the name and the use of historic

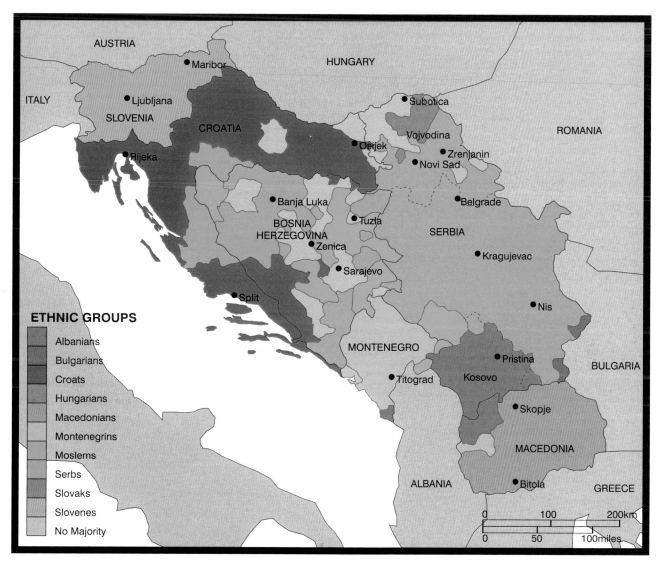

Map 10.4   Yugoslavia, population distribution

Macedonian symbols dating from the classical times of Philip of Macedon and his son Alexander the Great in the fourth century BC. This was alleged to undermine the Greek role in history and the historic Macedonian cultural links to Greece. Furthermore, the new country was accused of harbouring expansionist designs upon the Greek province of the same name which had been conquered in 1912, and of the promotion of a 'Greater Macedonia'. It was only in April 1993 that the country gained admission to the United Nations under the cumbersome title of 'The Former Yugoslav Republic of Macedonia'.

In March 1992 the electorate of Montenegro voted in a referendum to remain part of Yugoslavia. Thus the remaining two republics, Serbia and Montenegro, formed a new Federal Republic of Yugoslavia in April 1992. Relations between the two were at times uneasy, but differences were more related to economic questions than ethnicity. Significant internal problems were associated with the presence of ethnic minorities in the two autonomous regions. The autonomy of both was revoked as a result of political conflict. The most serious was in Kosovo, where ethnic Albanians had constituted 82 percent of the population in 1991 (Malcolm, 1998). The region was regarded as the historic core of the Serbian state, although subsequent Albanian immigration had reduced the Serb population to a small minority. Conflict between the two groups led to the abolition of regional autonomy, while a self-styled Republic of Kosovo was established (Milivojevic, 1992). The Serbian grip on the province was such as to stifle the secessionist movement until March 1999. In Vojvodina the presence of a substantial Hungarian minority was no longer considered to be sufficient to warrant the inconvenience of a separate administration and its autonomy was revoked.

Recurring features of the disintegration of Yugoslavia were ethnic cleansing, deportations and massacres. Large-scale changes throughout the country took place as people were moved or killed in order to fit the population to the new political patterns. It is worth noting that this has been a frequent feature of the present century as indicated by a report by Lev Bronstein (better known as Leon Trotsky), acting as a war correspondent from the Kosovo region during the Balkan War of 1913:

The Serbs in Old Serbia, in their natural endeavour to correct data in the ethnographical statistics that are not quite favourable to them, are engaged quite simply in systematic extermination of the Moslem population.

(quoted in Malcolm, 1998: 253).

10.5 BOSNIA AND HERZEGOVINA

The disintegration of Yugoslavia was a much more bloody process than that of the Soviet Union, reflecting the different processes in drawing the boundaries of the constituent republics. This was amply demonstrated by the fate of Bosnia and Herzegovina, which declared its independence in April 1992. In 1991 the population had been mainly divided between the Moslems (44 percent), Serbs (31 percent) and Croats (17 percent), representing a significant shift in the course of the century in favour of the Moslems (see page 29). All spoke the same Serbo-Croat language, although it was written differently, reflecting the religious divides. The imposition of over four decades of centralised dictatorial rule had in large measure overcome the legacy of bitterness from the Croat–Serb conflict in the Second World War. However, the nationalist parties, which gained control after the demise of Communism, were able to rekindle ethnic and religious animosities with remarkable ease (Malcolm, 1994).

The convoluted negotiations between the three main, ethnically defined political groupings degenerated into civil war at independence. The Serbs declared a separate Serb Republic, the Croats declared the Republic of Herzeg-Bosna, while the central government was dominated by the Moslems. Essentially three separate political entities vied

for control of the state territory, dividing it into complex and fragmented areas. A federation between the Croat government and the central Moslem dominated government in June 1994 resulted in the central government gaining majority support. The Serb Republic aimed at secession and linkage with the Serb dominated Yugoslav Federation, as did the neighbouring Serb republic of Krajina in Croatia. The Moslem enclave at Bihac in the north-west was completely surrounded by Serb held territory, including the Krajina. Its authorities throughout the war therefore pursued a highly autonomous course of action, but were able to prevent its capitulation. Against this background, the Croatian and Serbian leaders pursued unstated policies aimed at the eventual partition of the country between their two countries (Owen, 1995).

The civil war was conducted with great ferocity accompanied by large-scale 'ethnic cleansing', involving the wholesale forced removal and at times massacre of members of the various groups, as military front lines changed. Areas of integration were thus eliminated and the structures built-up between 1945 and 1990 largely destroyed, with a series of ethnically homogeneous regions being created. By 1993 some 70 percent of the area of Bosnia-Herzegovina had fallen into Serb hands, but the urban areas proved to be more difficult to capture. Thus the capital, Sarajevo, was besieged by the Serbs throughout the war, as were a number of urban Moslem enclaves in the east. The capital of Herzegovina, Mostar, was partitioned between the Croats and Moslems, demonstrating the fragility of the rapprochement between the two groups, and had to be placed under European Union authority in July 1994. The civil war was also noticeable for the involvement of the international community. The United Nations and later the North Atlantic Treaty Organisation were involved in providing humanitarian aid, military supervision and finally peacekeeping. Numerous peace plans were proposed in an attempt to end the war (Owen, 1995). However, no lines could be drawn which would satisfy all the contending sides and the international community was committed to the preservation of the territorial integrity of Bosnia-Herzegovina.

In November 1995 the war was ended by the military intervention of the North Atlantic Treaty Organisation and the United States against Serb forces and the negotiation of the Dayton Peace Accord, concluding four years of warfare in the former Yugoslavia. Bosnia-Herzegovina was divided into two sections, one controlled by the Moslem–Croat Federation and the other by the Serb Republic, but united under a joint central government (Crampton, 1996). The redefinition of the boundary between the two, notably in

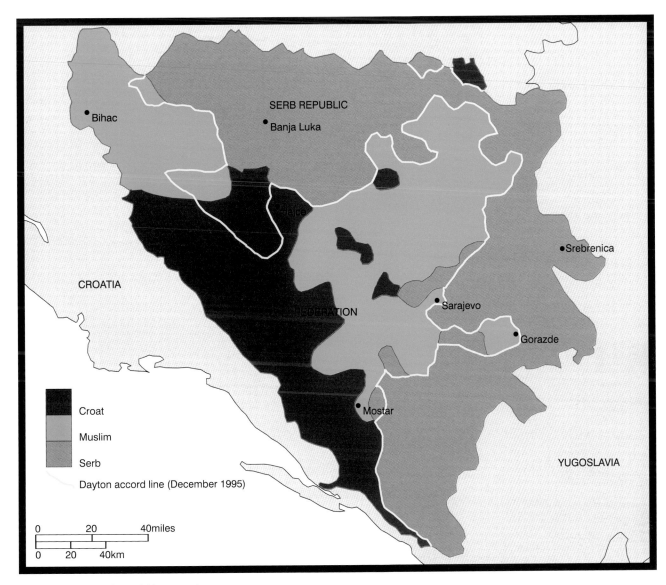

Map 10.5   Bosnia and Herzegovina

securing the whole of Sarajevo to the Federation, smoothed out many of the boundary irregularities, making the long-term survival of the partition line more feasible.

10.6   ETHIOPIA

Ethiopia was one of the more significant countries over which the Cold War was fought in the 1970s and 1980s. The country was the third most populous in Africa. Owing to its prestige as surviving the colonial era virtually unscathed and the personal renown of its then ruler, the Emperor Haile

Selassie, the Organisation of African Unity established its headquarters in Addis Ababa in 1963. The Emperor pursued a strongly pro-American policy in the post-war period. However, in September 1974 he was deposed and the following year a Socialist government was installed committed to a Marxist ideology of societal transformation. Soviet and Cuban aid was supplied to assist the government in its development programmes and the prosecution of the war against the various secessionist movements, notably the Somali and Eritrean (Abbink, 1995).

The war against the Somalis was successful, but that against the Eritreans failed to achieve permanent results

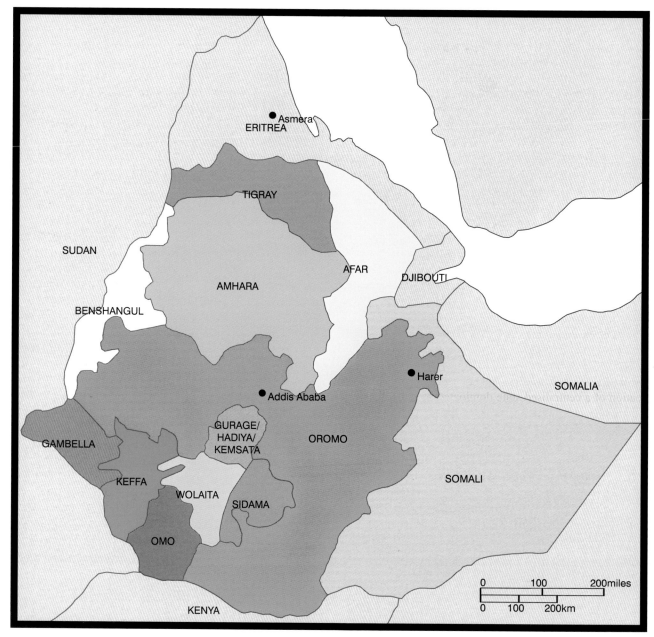

Map 10.6   Ethiopia

and the Eritrean People's Liberation Front continued to hold extensive parts of its homeland. In the course of 1988 the civil war widened with the Tigrean People's Liberation Front opening up a further insurrection against the central government in the province adjacent to Eritrea. These and other ethnic liberation movements, notably among the Oromo in the south of the country, combined in an effort to overthrow the government. In April 1991 the central

government was overthrown and a transitional administration installed.

The Eritreans were only concerned with the recognition of their right to secession and wished to have no further part in the government of Ethiopia. The transitional government agreed to allow Eritrea to secede after a supervised referendum, which was held in April 1993. With an electoral turnout of 98.2 percent, some 99.8 percent of the voters supported independence for the country, completing the country's constitutional secession and recognition of its separate statehood later in the month. This successful and internationally recognised secession effectively opened discussion on the merits of other secessionist movements in the region (Gurdon, 1994). The contradictions between the concepts of 'self-determination' and 'territorial integrity', the two major supports of the African state system, were underlined (Young, 1991).

The Tigrean People's Liberation Front had a major problem once it achieved power and militarily dominated the transitional government. The Eritreans, to whom they were closely linked, had gained secession on the basis of a separate colonial history and struggle for independence. The Tigreans had no such history and indeed had been closely linked to the Ethiopian state throughout much of recorded history, albeit one dominated by the Amharas. Although they constituted only 10 percent of the population their leaders sought to prevent the re-emergence of the type of centralised dictatorship which they had just overthrown. In this they were supported by the leaders of many of the other minority groups.

The Front therefore expanded the Stalinist concept of 'nationalities', not as a means of moving towards the creation of a centralised state dominated by a bureaucratic political party, but as a means of promoting effective autonomy. Accordingly it devised the system of an ethnic federation for Ethiopia. Over 60 nationalities were identified, although only nine states, for the major national groups or related groupings, were constituted. Significantly the constitution of December 1994 provided that each nationality had 'an unconditional right to self-determination, including the right to secession' (Clapham, 1996: 246). Indeed the constitution defined the boundaries of the Ethiopian state as the sum of the individual members of the federation. The constitution also provided that any self-identified group of people was given the right to constitute itself as a nation or nationality, with the same rights and privileges as the original nine states. The Tigreans therefore were instrumental in introducing one of the loosest people's federations anywhere in the world. The experiment may thus offer guidance for the governance of other multi-ethnic states.

10.7   SOUTH AFRICA

The race-based policy of apartheid in South Africa had elicited universal condemnation in the 1970s and 1980s. With the reduction of tensions towards the end of the Cold War, what little support was forthcoming from the Western powers ceased and international economic and political sanctions were tightened, notably the American Comprehensive Anti-Apartheid Act of 1986. In the deteriorating economic and security situation the South African government was forced to reconsider the prospect of African majority rule, while the liberation movements recognised that the military overthrow of the White-dominated, National Party government would take a great many more years and lives to achieve. Compromise was therefore urged upon all sides. The challenge was taken up by the incoming president, F.W. de Klerk, in February 1990.

Complex negotiations between all the interested parties, including the African homeland governments, occupied the ensuing years. Finally, in April 1994, the first universal franchise general elections were held to elect a Government of National Unity. The resultant government included representatives of the main liberation movement, the African National Congress, which gained 62.6 percent of the popular vote, the outgoing White dominated National Party and the main traditional Zulu ethnic party, the Inkatha Freedom Party. The leader of the African National Congress, Nelson Mandela, was installed as the first African president of South Africa in May 1994.

The interim constitution, and the subsequent final constitution incorporated a quasi-federal structure to accommodate significant regional and ethnic interests. The African homelands promoted by the previous South African government were erased from the map. Only the one name, 'KwaZulu', survived as a reminder of the apartheid era. In similar vein the Afrikaner settler name 'Transvaal' was erased from the map. The four homelands which had been granted independence between 1976 and 1981 were reincorporated into South Africa. The civilian governments of all four had been overthrown prior to the elections as a measure of their lack of legitimacy and support.

In view of the constitutional importance of new provinces, the drawing of their boundaries was subject to intense negotiations (Christopher, 1995). The planning regions devised in 1982 as part of the National Economic Development Plan were taken as the basis for the new dispensation. The resultant pattern increased the number of provinces from four to nine. The urban heartland, centred upon Johannesburg, the commercial capital, and Pretoria, the administrative capital, was created as a separate province, Gauteng. Generating some 40 percent of the national gross domestic product, it was placed in a remarkably strong economic position. In terms of population the provinces ranged in size from KwaZulu-Natal with 8.5 million inhabitants to the Northern Cape

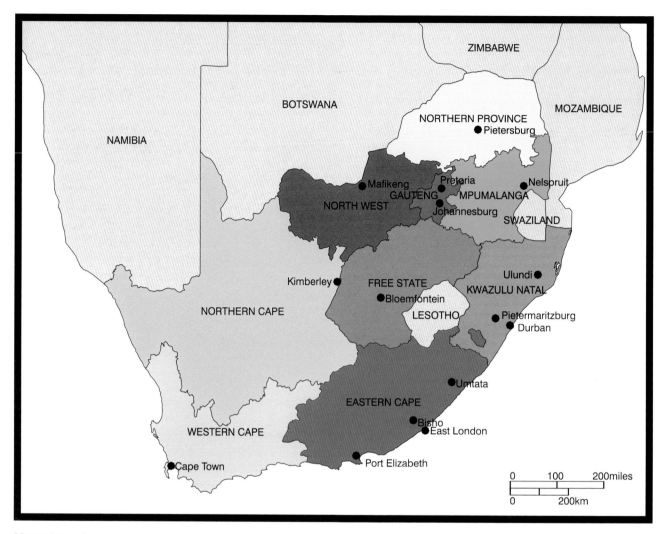

Map 10.7   South Africa

with only 760 000. The latter was created as a political compromise during the negotiations to boost National Party representation. The next smallest were the Free State and Mpumalanga with 2.8 million inhabitants apiece. In terms of area the Northern Cape was the largest, with 363 400 square kilometres, while Gauteng covered only 18 800 square kilometres.

Inevitably the new provinces bore some semblance to ethnic homelands, despite the African National Congress's disclaimers. Thus some 85 percent of the inhabitants of the Eastern Cape were Xhosa speaking, while 80 percent of the inhabitants of KwaZulu-Natal were Zulu speakers. The Free State, Northern Province and North West Province were similarly dominated by one linguistic group. Equally significant was the dominance of Afrikaans speakers in the Western and Northern Cape. However, these were not the Afrikaner homelands envisaged under the previous government as Whites constituted only small minorities in both provinces. Within Gauteng, Afrikaans speakers (20 percent) and Zulu speakers (18 percent) constituted the largest linguistic groups, in a thoroughly polyglot population.

In the April 1994 elections only two ethnic parties achieved any regional success: the Inkatha Freedom Party won control of KwaZulu-Natal and the National Party won control of the Western Cape. In the remainder of the country the celebratory and liberationary character of the election submerged ethnic differences. However, secessionism in KwaZulu-Natal remained a significant political force as the future status of the Zulu kingdom remained the subject of intense debate.

The White Afrikaner quest for racial exclusivity was not entirely forgotten under the new constitution. As a means of diffusing racial tensions in the pre-election period, an Afrikaner Volkstaat Council was convened to investigate the possibility of establishing such an Afrikaner homeland. Despite some ingenious territorial proposals its deliberations demonstrated the unattainability of such an ideal, and the Council became more concerned with the preservation of Afrikaner culture and language rights, within a united South Africa.

10.8   GERMANY

The symbolic end of the Cold War was the fall of the Berlin Wall in November 1989. The wall had been erected by the German Democratic Republic in August 1961 in an attempt to prevent the inhabitants of East Germany and East Berlin from emigrating to the West. The numbers involved in this migration had become a substantial flow as the rising prosperity and political freedom of the West contrasted with the relative stagnation and political authoritarianism of the East. Thereafter the wall became a symbol of the ideological divide between the two systems and of the apparently permanent partition of Germany. The breaking down of the Berlin Wall in November 1989 was therefore the most symbolic act of the end of the Cold War and the demise of the Soviet system.

The leaders of the German Democratic Republic celebrated its fortieth anniversary in October 1989. The guest speaker, Soviet President, Mikhail Gorbachev, had stated that 'We don't idealize the order that has settled on Europe. But the fact is that until now the recognition of the postwar reality has insured peace on the continent. Every time the West has tried to reshape the postwar map of Europe, it has meant a worsening of the international situation' (Kissinger, 1994: 795). The major changes which were about to take place were therefore totally unanticipated and not forcibly resisted, whether the unification of Germany or the demise of the Soviet Union.

The pace of German reunification proceeded rapidly, dynamically propelled by the German Federal Chancellor, Helmut Kohl. The most significant stage was the agreement of the four Allied powers of the Second World War to formally end the last remnants of the occupation, more particularly the four-power status of Berlin, as a preliminary to reunification (Harris, 1991). Soviet agreement to the withdrawal of its armed forces from the country in return for a German guarantee of the post-war

international boundaries was another major step towards redrawing the map of the continent.

Free elections in East Germany resulted in a remarkable change in support for the communist Socialist Unity Party and its allies. In May 1989, with no choice offered, the state parties' candidates had gained 99 percent of the vote in the communal elections. In the May 1990 local elections its level of support had slumped to 15 percent and the parties represented in the Federal parliament, notably the ruling Christian Democratic Union, received overwhelming support. The government of the German Democratic Republic therefore proceeded to negotiate itself out of office and merge the country with the German Federal Republic. The East German districts were reconstituted as the 1949–1952 provinces or länder and they joined the German Federal Republic in October 1990. East Berlin was absorbed by West Berlin as a separate länd, which was declared to be the national capital.

The reunified Germany is thus divided into sixteen länder which enjoy a high degree of autonomy. Despite the substantial reorganisations of provincial government, there remained substantial demographic and areal disparities between the länder. In terms of population, North Rhine-Westphalia with 17.4 million inhabitants dwarfed Bremen with only 700 000 inhabitants. In area, Bavaria was the most extensive with some 70, 554 square kilometres, while Bremen measured only 404 square kilometres. Apart from the national capital, Hamburg and Bremen were the only other city states to survive as a separate land.

The reunified Germany became the second most populous country in Europe, after Russia. As such the carefully negotiated balances which led to the formation of the European Union had assumed France, Great Britain, Italy and Germany were approximately equal in size. Unification demonstrated that German economic primacy was now accompanied by demographic dominance. The economic and social integration of western and eastern Germany proved to be more difficult to achieve than initially anticipated, paralleling the experience of other reunited nations, giving rise to some nostalgia for the defunct eastern state (Corson and Minghi, 1994).

10.9   PALESTINE

One of the recurring international issues throughout the post-1918 period has been the future of Palestine. After the signing of the peace treaty between Egypt and Israel in March 1979, the Israelis withdrew from the Sinai Desert, but they failed to pursue the wider sections of the

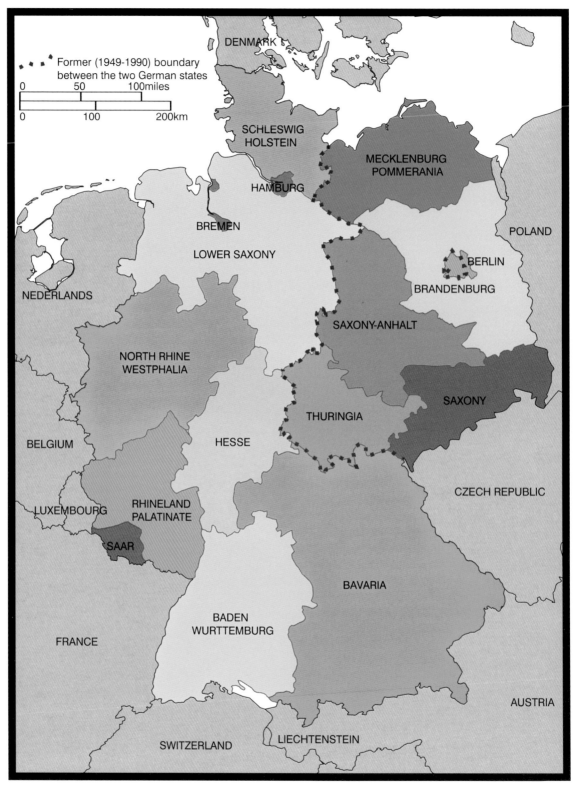

Map 10.8   Germany

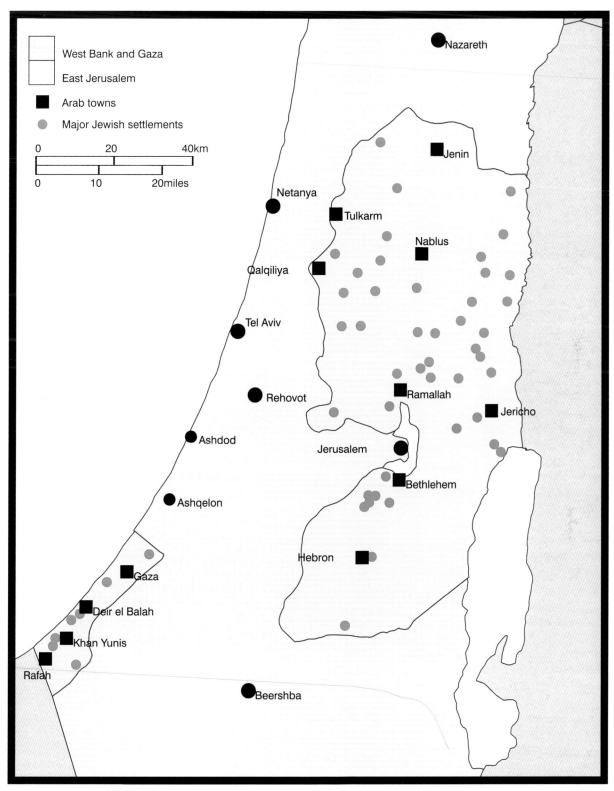

Map 10.9   Palestine

agreement, which provided for the granting of autonomy to the Palestinians. Indeed the Palestinian population of the West Bank and Gaza Strip became increasingly dissatisfied with their inferior status under military occupation. The result was the outbreak of the intifada or uprising in December 1987. Strikes, riots and bombings resulted in even stricter Israeli security measures with mutual distrust reinforced. The intifada prompted King Hussein of Jordan finally to dissolve the union between Palestine and Transjordan in August 1988, over twenty years after he had lost effective control over the West Bank to the Israelis. The Palestine Liberation Organisation thereupon made a declaration of an independent Palestinian state in November 1988 in an attempt to exert its moral authority over the Palestinians. However, effectively little changed, beyond the legal peculiarity of the West Bank joining Gaza as being outside the sovereignty of any internationally recognised state (McColl and Newman, 1992).

At the same time the West Bank and Gaza Strip were subject to colonisation by Jewish settlers who regarded the occupied territories of Samaria and Judea as part of the historic Land of Israel, 'Eretz Israel', which had been promised in the Bible to their forefather Abraham. By the confiscation of 'unused' and state land, the government was able to acquire areas for Jewish colonisation in amongst the Palestinian villages. Equally significant was the establishment of pockets of Jewish settlers in some of the towns. East Jerusalem had been formally annexed to Israel in June 1967 and active Jewish colonisation of the area had reduced the Palestinians to a small minority. Even in the Old City of Jerusalem, Jewish settlers had spread outside the rebuilt Jewish Quarter into the Moslem and Christian Quarters. The organisations and political parties which supported the settlers hoped that by establishing a physical presence in the areas concerned, later Israeli governments would find withdrawal impossible to effect. However, successive Israeli governments refused to annex the West Bank and Gaza as involving the incorporation of a large Arab population which would seriously jeopardise the Jewish character of the state.

The American government actively pursued the possibilities of a peace agreement between Israel and the Palestinians. The Oslo Accords signed in September 1993 provided for the Palestine Liberation Organisation's recognition of Israel's right to exist in return for Israeli withdrawal and the grant of autonomy for the West Bank and Gaza Strip – the 'land for peace' formula. The first withdrawal took place in May 1994 and a Palestinian National Authority was established for the administration of Jericho and Gaza (Newman, 1996). Subsequently other towns and villages of the West Bank were transferred to the Palestinian Authority, although the highly contested site of Hebron was only handed over in part in January 1997. The result was not an Israeli withdrawal from the whole of the West Bank and Gaza, but only a rather disconnected series of exclaves, with the Jewish settlements, the main roads and most of the Jordan valley remaining under Israeli military control (Newman and Falah, 1995). The threatened re-proclamation of Palestinian independence in May 1999 publicised the plight of the nation but could not lead to meaningful consolidation.

The negotiations for a final settlement of the boundaries of a Palestinian state have been postponed for the twenty-first century. The issues of the Jewish settlements, Israeli security, the return of Palestinian refugees, and ultimately the future status of Jerusalem appear intractable, but require a degree of compromise which has usually been lacking in the bitter series of confrontations between the two parties (Emmett, 1996). The separate issue of the return of the Golan Heights to Syria is dependent upon the wider Middle East peace settlement.

10.10   KURDISTAN

After the conclusion of the Gulf War in April 1991, international restrictions and sanctions were imposed upon Iraq. These included the declaration of a military exclusion zone in the north of the country, preventing any Iraqi military operations north of the 36th parallel. The main objective of this restriction was to provide a place of refuge for the Kurdish population in the region. The various Kurdish factions had waged a long war for autonomy or independence, in the course of which the civilian populations had been bombed and gassed by the Iraqi army. Autonomy agreements between the Kurdish movements and the Iraqi government, such as those of June 1966 and March 1970, had had no more permanence than any of those devised in the 1920s. However, the 'safe havens' created under the armistice came under the control of the Kurds in April 1991. Elections were held and an assembly formed to administer the area. Effective control fell into the hands of the different factions, which reflected the basic cleavages within Kurdish society. The result was sporadic internal conflicts, which were exploited by the Iraqi authorities (Keyenbroek and Sperl, 1992).

The administration and economy of the Kurdish region remained skeletal as aid had to be brought in overland from Turkey. No government was able to provide a level of military or diplomatic aid to secure the Kurdish position.

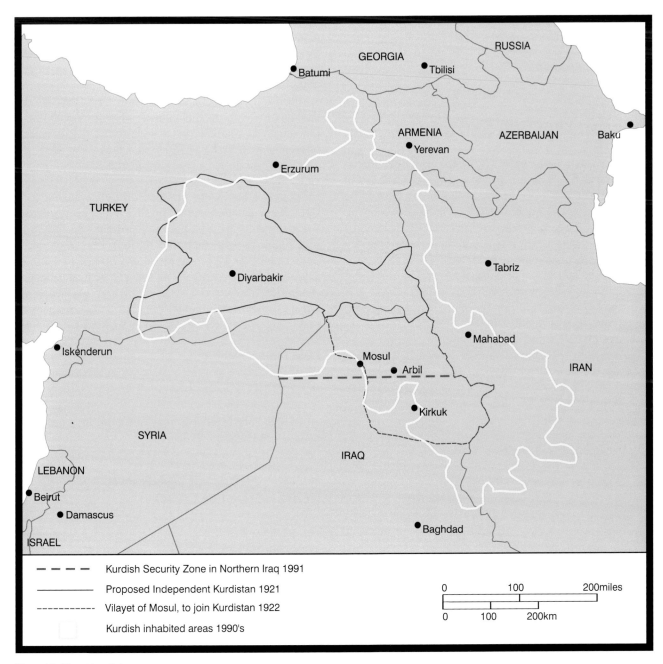

Map 10.10   Kurdistan

The Iraqi military incursion in August 1996 demonstrated the limits of the effective autonomy that the local administrations enjoyed. The long-term American commitment to preserving the enclave beyond the final settlement of outstanding differences with Iraq remained highly problematical. International diplomatic support for an independent Kurdish state was not forthcoming.

Concurrently Turkey was faced with an ongoing revolt initiated in August 1984 by the Kurdish Workers' Party in the south-east of the country, aimed at secession or at least the grant of autonomy. The ban on the use of the Kurdish language was lifted in January 1991, but the government did not accede to the wider political demands. Turkish support for the American defence of an autonomous Iraqi

Kurdistan was thus circumscribed, as the government still feared the emergence of a wider pan-Kurdish movement which would disrupt the Turkish state. Similarly Iran and Syria remained hostile to Kurdish aspirations throughout the region.

10.11   HONG KONG AND MACAO

The end of the colonial era was symbolically celebrated with the transfer of Hong Kong to Chinese sovereignty in July 1997. The territory had been the largest remaining British colony and after its transfer there remained no significantly large dependent territories. At the time of the transfer Hong Kong was a substantial state with 5.9 million inhabitants and a land area of 1045 square kilometres. This was approximately twice the area and population of Singapore, the economy of which was frequently compared with that of Hong Kong. However, the international status of the colony precluded the grant of sovereign independence.

Hong Kong had been acquired by Great Britain in three stages. In 1841 the island of Hong Kong had been seized and ceded to Great Britain as a base for its trade with China. In 1860 the Kowloon peninsula had been ceded as an additional area for development and to safeguard the anchorage in Victoria Harbour. However, in 1898 a further area, the New Territories, was acquired under a 99 year lease agreement from China. The area was extensive with the farmland and water resources required to provide a measure of self-sufficiency to the colony. It also pushed the military boundary away from the built-up area of the capital. The subsequent development of the colony took place as a single unit, without reference to the line separating British sovereign territory and the leasehold section. The influx of population into the colony, particularly upon the Communist takeover of mainland China in 1949, allowed for a dramatic expansion of the economy, which resulted in the emergence of a significant economic power in the region.

However, as the end of the 99 year lease approached, negotiations over the future of the colony commenced between Great Britain and China. China refused to consider a renewal of the lease agreement, which it regarded as one of the 'unequal treaties' forced upon it by the Western Imperialists in the nineteenth century. At the same time Great Britain realised that its sovereign area was not a separate viable entity and that it could not survive on its own. Under the Sino-British Joint Declaration of September 1984 the whole of the territory reverted to Chinese sovereignty in July 1997. As part of the agreement its existing social and economic systems were to remain unchanged for fifty years thereafter, within a Special Administrative Area.

The settlement of Macao was the last of the Portuguese colonies. Immediately after the revolution in Lisbon in April 1974 the new Portuguese government offered to return the territory to China. The offer was initially refused as it was considered to be of greater value to the Chinese People's Republic as an alternative entrepot to Hong Kong. However, the changing status of Hong Kong and the internal political situation resulted in a reappraisal of the situation. In April 1987 an agreement was signed for the return of the territory to China. In December 1999 Macao reverted to China with a similar status to Hong Kong. The millennium thus ended symbolically with the demise of the oldest of the European overseas colonial empires, which had played such a significant role in the history of Africa, Asia and South America in the previous five hundred years. However, the reunification of China took place at a time when the future government structures were liable to change. As in the case of the Soviet Union, there is the possibility of state fragmentation accompanying democratisation. Indeed the possibility of secession is open to speculation (Eronen, 1998).

10.12   GREAT BRITAIN AND NORTHERN IRELAND

The post-Cold War era also witnessed a review of the other major international issues that had defied solution in the Cold War era. The Northern Ireland issue was one such apparently insoluble problem (Boal and Douglas, 1982). The Irish Republican Army had begun another round of demonstrations, bombings and shootings in August 1969 in support of the creation of a united Ireland. In reaction the British army was sent to the province to restore order. Inter-communal confrontation culminated in the January 1972 'Bloody Sunday' shooting when 14 people were killed and the province entered a phase of low intensity civil war. Protestant loyalist organisations joined the general lawlessness with a counter campaign of demonstrations, bombings and shootings. Briefly (January–July 1972) sections of Belfast and Londonderry were converted into 'no-go' areas, controlled by the Irish Republican Army and administered as 'Free Belfast' and 'Free Derry'.

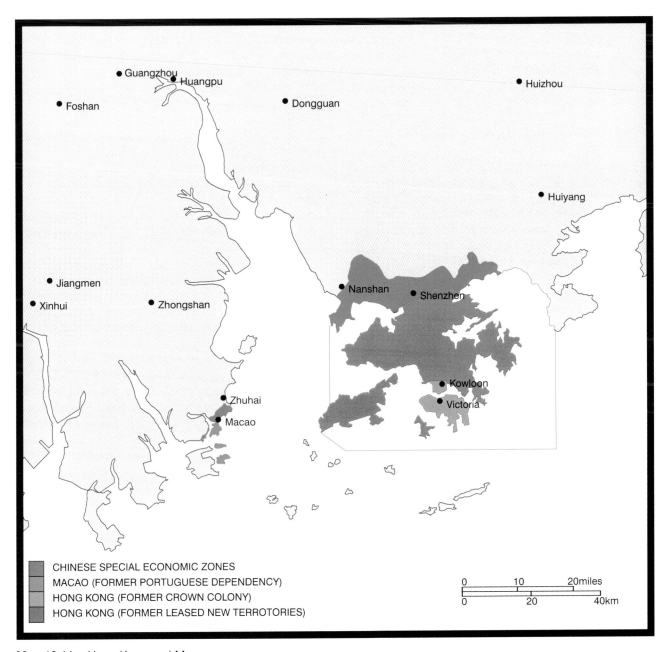

CHINESE SPECIAL ECONOMIC ZONES
MACAO (FORMER PORTUGUESE DEPENDENCY)
HONG KONG (FORMER CROWN COLONY)
HONG KONG (FORMER LEASED NEW TERROTORIES)

0   10   20miles
0   20   40km

Map 10.11   Hong Kong and Macao

In March 1972 the British government dismissed the Northern Ireland government and assumed direct control of the province. Subsequent negotiations, involving both the Irish and American governments, failed to secure any agreement for an elected body to replace the provincial government. All the elaborate constitutional schemes collapsed over the basic arithmetic of a Protestant majority in Northern Ireland, which wished to remain a part of the United Kingdom. However, for Sinn Fein, the political wing of the Irish Republican Army, 'a lasting and meaningful peace ... can only be achieved by the ending of partition arising from British rule in six of Ireland's 32 counties; British disengagement from Ireland and the restoration of the right to exercise self-sovereignty, independence and national self-determination' (Pringle, 1996: 382). Such a clear-cut statement ran up against the apparently unanswerable question 'whose self-determination?'

Only in April 1998 was a compromise solution to 26 years of politically motivated violence reached, involving a complex package of constitutional checks and balances. The Northern Ireland electorate of both communities endorsed the establishment of a new provincial government, together with the creation of joint North–South structures with 71.1 percent approval at a referendum in May 1998. At the same time the Republic of Ireland gave up its constitutional claim to Northern Ireland with 94.4 percent approval in a complementary referendum. The Irish government and electorate recognised that unification was only possible with popular support. New East–West links covering the whole of the British Isles were envisaged as a part of the settlement. The new dispensation was hailed by the *Irish Times* (25 May 1998) commenting that: 'people have been liberated to look afresh at relationships – not only with the North, but with the diverse peoples who live on the neighbouring island'. Whether this may mark the emergence of a separate identity, and potential state, for Northern Ireland, distinct from both the Republic of Ireland and the United Kingdom is uncertain (Graham, 1997; Graham and Shirlow, 1998).

The strains imposed upon the constitutional structures of 'the neighbouring island' in the twentieth century were nowhere near as extreme as those in evidence in Ireland. But, resurgent nationalisms increasingly came to the fore in British politics. In the 1960s and 1970s in particular the Scottish and Welsh nationalist parties gained considerable support. Indeed in 1969 the central government went so far as to appoint a Royal Commission on the Constitution 'in relation to the several countries, nations and regions of the United Kingdom' (Anderson, 1989: 45).

Ten years later, in March 1979, referenda were held on devolution of some functions to directly elected Scottish and Welsh assemblies. The concept of a Welsh assembly was rejected by 80 percent of the voters. Welsh nationalist demands had in large measure been driven by the Welsh language movement, which had a support base largely confined to the rural areas of west Wales, from which the nationalist movement traditionally gained its strength (Gruffudd, 1994). Thus the inhabitants of English-speaking areas, particularly the industrial heartland of South Wales, then had no desire to be separated from the central administration. In Scotland there was majority support for devolution (52 percent of voters), but the measure failed to satisfy the referendum criteria. In September 1997 further referenda resulted in 74.3 percent of voters supporting devolution in Scotland and 50.3 percent in Wales. The regionally based opposition to devolution in Scotland largely disappeared with broad-based support for an autonomous parliament, which was opened in July 1999 with the pomp and circumstance of a fully sovereign body by Queen Elizabeth II (but only I of Scotland). The Welsh result was not so clear-cut and the local assembly was given few powers. However, as a constitutional means of loosening, even ending, the union the emergence of separate national parliaments is significant.

Inevitably regional or national autonomy, home rule, or secession in the United Kingdom have always been viewed with regard to the relationship with the English core. In many respects this reflects the origin of the state and its institutions. However, through the avoidance of a political revolution or civil war since 1688 and through successful resistance to foreign occupation, England retained many institutions of a pre-modern nationalism. Only in January 1981, under the British Nationality Act, was the imperial terminology of 'subjects' finally deleted in favour of the more egalitarian term, 'citizens'. The point has also been made that even within England, there are degrees of political integration in a country viewed essentially in terms of distance from the royal court situated in the 'Home Counties', which were contrasted with the distant 'North Country' or 'West Country' (Taylor, 1991). The constitutional relationships between the various constituent parts of the United Kingdom became even more complex with European integration, which resulted in the loss of many of the functions of the central government, and rising republicanism, which sought to destroy the essentially pre-modern, monarchist, core to the British state-idea. Furthermore, the economic disparities between 'North' and 'South', which had prompted the concept of 'two nations' in the nineteenth century, remained in the late twentieth century (Martin, 1988).

The Crown dependencies of Jersey, Guernsey and the Isle of Man remained anomalies within the state system, possessing complete internal self-government, but ultimately dependent upon the British government for defence and the conduct of foreign affairs. No integration of these three or the other colonial dependent territories into the constitutional structures of the United Kingdom has yet been attempted.

It is a measure of the high degree of centralisation in the British state that the historic county boundaries could be redrawn in July 1974, with the abolition of some

Shetland

Orkney

SCOTLAND

NORTHERN
IRELAND

Isle
of
Man

IRELAND

WALES

ENGLAND

Monmouth

Gaeltacht

0   100   200miles

0   100   200km

Guernsey

Jersey

Map 10.12   Great Britain and Northern Ireland

counties with pedigrees of over a thousand years and the creation of other completely new entities. Popular disenchantment with the changes resulted in the resurrection of some of the historic units, notably Rutland in April 1997. One of the many changes which took place in 1974 was the transfer of Monmouthshire to Wales and its redesignation as 'Gwent'. The official redefinition of an internal 'national' boundary without public consultation was remarkable in the light of European political history in the twentieth century, particularly as Welsh speakers are virtually absent in the county (Aitchison and Carter, 1994).

CHAPTER 11

The World in the Year 2000

An examination of the map of the world at the dawn of the new millennium reveals that it is dominated by a host of nearly 200 independent sovereign states. Few are now inter-continental in scale, indeed many are extremely small. The map also reveals the great diversity of size, both in terms of area and population, between nominally equal sovereign entities. A few colonial possessions remain, but they are small and in the main retain their dependent status as they require continued financial support from the metropolitan power.

Behind the apparent stability of the state pattern, there remain a number of unresolved questions, weakening the position of the nation-state as the container of personal allegiances and the satisfaction of personal needs (Taylor, 1994, 1995). Internal divisions and external integration complicate the picture presented by the political map as governments have to adjust to changes in their raison d'etre. In the course of the twentieth century, inhabitants have changed from being subjects, to become citizens, and increasingly customers, in their relationship to the state. The present state system based on territorial nationalism is thus often unsuited to respond to these changes in function.

Secessionist movements are present in a large number of states. They seek to fragment the world political pattern yet further, so that the states may coincide more closely with the pattern of ethnic and other groups. In most cases national governments have sought to suppress or incorporate such movements and so maintain the territorial integrity of the state. Other potential sources of internal division and discord are posed by the presence of indigenous peoples in countries which have been recently colonised by outsiders. The grant of special land rights and resource dispensations together with cultural autonomy have been adopted frequently as a means to diffuse any separatist tendencies. The issues of secessionism and indigenous rights come together in the Canadian Confederation, which exhibits signs of severe constitutional strain.

In contrast to threats of fragmentation, the emergence of multi-national and supra-national organisations has eroded the sovereignty of the nation-state in terms of macro-economic and world political policies. The European Union offers a model for other multi-national organisations, which have sought to establish economic and subsequently political unions, without recourse to force. However, even within the European Union, the forces of ethnic nationalism have had to be confronted within the nation-states which form its constitutional base. Indeed the security offered by the larger continental Union has often been the catalyst for resurrection of internal divisions. Spain and Belgium represent two of the more radical departures from the centralised state model which has been such a significant feature of their past histories.

11.1 THE WORLD IN 2000

The world at the beginning of the third millennium is divided into 192 independent states and 42 small inhabited dependencies. The extensive intercontinental empires which had dominated the map of 1900 have virtually disappeared. However, a remarkable feature concerning the

Map 11.1   The world in 2000

Iceland

Norway
Sweden
Finland

Great
Britain
Denmark
Estonia
Latvia
Lithuania
Ireland
Netherlands
Belarus
Belgium
Germany
Poland
Ukraine
Switzerland
Czech R
Austria
H
Moldova
France
Italy
S
Romania
Georgia
Portugal
Spain
Albania
Macedonia
Bulgaria
Greece
Cyprus
Turkey
M
Lebanon
Syria
Iraq
Morocco
Tunisia
Algeria
Libya
Egypt
Kuwait
Iran
Pakistan
Afghanistan

Russia

Kazakhstan

Mongolia

Uzbekistan
Kyrgyzstan
T
TA
China
North Korea
South Korea
Japan

Western Sahara
CV
Mauritania
Mali
Niger
Chad
Sudan
Eritrea
United Arab Emirates
Saudi Arabia
Oman
Yemen
Nepal
Bhutan
Bangladesh
India
Burma

Gambia
Senegal
Guinea
Burkina Faso
Benin
Nigeria
Central
African
Republic
Ethiopia
Djibouti
Somalia
Sri Lanka
Thailand
Vietnam
Cambodia
Philippines
Palau

Sierra Leone
Ghana
Cameroon
TO
Maldives
Marshall Islands
Micronesia
Kiribati
Nauru

Liberia
Ivory Coast
E
Gabon
Congo
Uganda
Kenya
Seychelles
Malaysia
Brunei
Singapore
Indonesia
Tuvalu

Sao Tome and Principe
Congo-K
Bu
Tanzania
Papua New Guinea
Solomon Islands
Vanuatu
Fiji

Angola
Zambia
Malawi
Comoros
Mozambique
Mauritius

Namibia
Zimbabwe
Madagascar

Botswana
Swaziland
South Africa
Lesotho
Australia
New Zealand

Ar Armenia
A   Azerbaijan
B   Bahrain
BH Bosnia - Herzegovina
Bu Burundi
C   Croatia
CV Cape Verde Islands
E   Equatorial Guinea
GB Guinea - Bissau
H   Hungary
I   Israel
L   Laos
M   Malta
Q   Qatar
R   Rwanda
S   Slovakia
SI Slovenia
T   Turkmenistan
TA Tajikistan
TO Togo
Y   Yugoslavia

0   2000   4000km

0   1000   2000miles

map is the continued dominance of a few large states, despite the process of fragmentation that had been so prevalent in the twentieth century. Despite the disintegration of the Soviet Union, its primary successor, the Russian Federation, extending over 17 million square kilometres, remains the largest state in the world in areal terms. Six states (Russia, Canada, China, the United States, Brazil and Australia) covered some 46 percent of the earth's land surface, if Antarctica is excluded. In contrast, when attention is directed to the other end of the scale, half of the states of the world covered only 2.5 percent of the land surface of the earth. The decolonisation process had produced a substantial number of micro- and mini-states, to join the European mini-states. Indeed in the year 2000, there were some 26 states with land areas of under 1000 square kilometres apiece.

In terms of population there was an equally wide distribution, ranging from China with 1200 million people to the Vatican City with under 1000. The six most populous states (China, India, the United States, Indonesia, Brazil and Russia) accounted for just over half (51.6 percent) the total population of the world. In contrast, the smaller half of states housed only 3.3 percent of the world's population. Indeed some 44 states enumerated under one million inhabitants while 15 states counted under 100 000. Such disparities suggest that such concepts as national viability have little to do with size, whether measured in terms of area or population.

The global distribution of the sovereign states had become far more evenly spread in the course of the twentieth century. On a continental basis Africa with 53 states headed the list, followed by Europe (48), Asia (42), the Americas (35) and Oceania (14). The large number of African states is a reflection of inherited colonial administrative patterns, as well as the outcomes of the political ambitions of the local politicians to obstruct the wider imposed federal structures of the colonial era. The numerous island small states of the Caribbean and Oceania again illustrate the inability of local politicians to agree upon the erection of overarching political structures, although in economic terms cooperation is often close.

11.2   COLONIAL DEPENDENCIES

By the year 2000 there were only a few formal colonies remaining on the world map. Indeed such was the opprobrium in which colonialism was held that only two British possessions, Gibraltar and Bermuda, were still officially styled as colonies. The former was as much a

matter to emphasise the free choice of the population to remain a British Crown Colony, in the face of Spanish pressures for possession, as any constitutional peculiarity. The latter was the last of the North American colonies and traded upon its peculiar status for the tourist trade. The remainder of the extant colonies had been renamed 'dependent territories' (Great Britain), 'overseas territories' or 'territorial collectivities' (France), 'external territories' (Australia), or 'unincorporated territories' (United States). Their common political feature was a lack of sovereign independence and continuing dependency upon another state, in which they took no part in governing.

The majority of dependent territories were small in terms of physical extent and population. Colonial possessions covered some 1.8 percent of the earth's surface, but housed only 0.1 percent of the world's population in the year 2000. The inflated area calculation is due to the continued Danish sovereignty over Greenland, and that of Norway over Svalbard. Both were predominantly occupied by ice-fields. Puerto Rico with 3.3 million inhabitants accounted for half the inhabitants of dependent territories and is by far the most significant 'colony' after the return of Hong Kong to China in July 1997. This dubious distinction may help to induce a decision on the constitutional choice between admission to the United States as the fifty-first state of the Union and independence.

There were fifteen other dependencies with populations over 50 000, which could attain independence within the existing international framework. Even states as small as Montserrat, with 12 000 inhabitants, have considered the option, although the economic advantages of remaining within the British sovereign area appear to be considerable. The disastrous volcanic eruptions which destroyed two-thirds of the island in the two years after the initial explosion in July 1995 indicate the insecurity of many small island colonies confronted by natural calamity, economic forces and physical isolation. Indeed in the majority of cases continued association with the colonial power is considered advantageous by local leaders. A careful balance is therefore maintained as some territories opt for independence when local governments change and the pro-independence parties achieve power. Independence is a one-way process. Recolonisation after the following election is not a possibility. The attempt in August 1997 by the inhabitants of the islands of Anjouan and Moheli in the Comoros to secede and rejoin France was unsuccessful in the latter aim, although a significant commentary on the substantial differences in levels of economic development between their own and the French island of Mayotte.

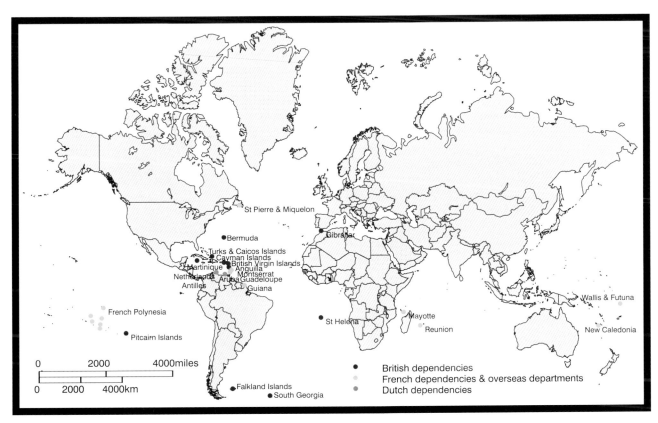

Map 11.2   Colonial dependencies

Incorporation of the remaining territories into the constitutional framework of the metropolitan power is a means of ending colonial status (Connell and Aldrich, 1991). This was the French approach for Reunion and its Caribbean colonies. However, the grant of special regional councils in control of local affairs, particularly in the 1990s, has helped to undermine the concept of complete integration into metropolitan France. In most cases the colonial power has been more concerned to prevent integration, taken to the extent of maintaining immigration controls against some of its overseas nationals in the case of Great Britain (Royle, 1995). Only in September 1998, after the return of Hong Kong to China, did the inhabitants of the remaining British colonies gain full British citizenship. However, the chasm between ruler and ruled in a colonial relationship may remain as wide at the end of the twentieth century as at the beginning. The remarks in August 1997, 'they will be wanting golden elephants next', by Clare Short, Secretary for International Development, concerning compensation requests by the Montserrat government, illustrate a lack of understanding of the colony's plight and that little had changed in a hundred years (*The Times*, 24 August 1997).

In a number of cases the remaining colonies are coveted by neighbouring states. In such circumstances of insecurity, independence as a separate state is not a viable proposition. Thus sovereignty over the Falkland Islands is also claimed by Argentina as the Ilas Malvinas, a claim projected and rejected by force in 1982. The same is true of Gibraltar, claimed by Spain, or Mayotte, claimed by the Comoros. In more peaceful vein, the British Indian Ocean Territory is the subject of a reversionary agreement, whereby Mauritius will obtain the islands when they are no longer required as a military base by Great Britain. Indeed the Territory no longer has a permanent population and the Commissioner is resident in London.

Some of the colonies are remarkably small and isolated. Thus the Pitcairn Islands with a population reduced by out-migration to approximately 50 living on an area of 47 square kilometres demonstrates the peculiar problems posed by the end of the colonial period. The islands are remarkably isolated, situated approximately 5000 kilometres from both South America and New Zealand. The isolation was historic as the island was uninhabited when the first settlers, the mutineers of the *Bounty*, arrived at the end of the eighteenth century seeking isolation and concealment from the Royal Navy. In similar circumstances governments have evacuated small poor communities from the islands, for example the Blasket Islands off the coast of Kerry in Ireland or St Kilda off the Hebrides in Scotland. In the case of the Pitcairn Islands a precedent was set by an evacuation of the population to Norfolk Island in 1856, but the islanders persuaded the authorities to return them five years later. A similar evacuation of Tristan da Cunha in October 1961, following a volcanic eruption, proved to be only temporary as the islanders were able to return two years later. Evacuation raises more problems than it solves, with regard to sovereignty, resource exploitation, and more especially the islanders' hostility to removal and place of relocation. The same problem of small isolated islands is repeated throughout the colonial world.

11.3   SECESSIONIST STATES AND UNRESOLVED STATUSES

Within the existing state structures there are a number of unresolved statuses which are often the cause of international conflict. Some, such as the status of Tibet, have been internationally regarded as internal matters for the Chinese government as Tibet before 1950 had been unable to establish its international credentials in the same manner as Mongolia. Despite numerous conventions and declarations, no effective international programme exists to protect the inhabitants of sub-national units, which might wish to establish separate statehood. The anti-colonial movement of the twentieth century has bequeathed no successor to promote self-determination for suppressed minorities. The doctrine of non-interference in the internal affairs of sovereign states has become another dominant theme in inter-state relations. However, there are territories where the international community has been involved in the resolution of the dispute, where the sovereign status is disputed, notably East Timor and Western Sahara. The latter even operates a functioning state-in-exile among the refugee camps in neighbouring Algeria. To this might be added disputed provinces such as Northern Ireland and Jammu and Kashmir, which are claimed by two states, and so rarely considered as potential separate independent states.

In some cases secessionist states have achieved a measure of governmental stability and effective control of a national territory. The prime example is the Turkish Republic of North Cyprus, which has enjoyed Turkish diplomatic recognition and a separate existence of over 25

years. All it lacks is the elusive endorsement of international recognition, which does not appear to be forthcoming. The Republic of Somaliland has operated as a separate state, within defined boundaries, with little outside interference for nearly a decade. Again international recognition of the dissolution of Somali unification has been withheld. The State of Palestine functions with many of the attributes of a secessionist state, yet despite the precision of its effective zone of control, its sovereign territory in ill-defined. Widespread international recognition has not been converted into effective political support vis-à-vis its occupying power. Even less secure are the Kurdish 'safe-havens' in Iraq, protected by an international armistice agreement and the enforcement of the American backed ban on Iraqi military activity. However, such an administration is unlikely to survive once that agreement can be safely abrogated by the Iraqi government.

De facto secession has occurred in Taiwan. It is a remarkable fact that the island was only under the control of the central Chinese government for four years (1945–1949) in the course of the twentieth century. The degree of political, social and cultural separation from the mainland and the presence of a numerically dominant indigenous population renders the formal secession from China a possibility, even if not contemplated immediately. At the time of the first democratic presidential elections in March 1996 the issue was largely ignored, although President Lee subsequently suggested that China might be regarded as a cultural rather than a political entity. The military and economic strength of the Taiwanese state is formidable, and it retains the international recognition of a number of smaller states.

Secessionist movements, without effective control of territorial bases, are active in a large number of states (Waterman, 1996). They range from tightly organised and violent groups such as the Basque ETA movement, to the Scottish National Party seeking mass electoral support. The majority of movements have followed ETA's path with varying degrees of violence, either where the minority group is suppressed by the majority and where resistance to autonomy or independence has produced state sponsored violence, such as in Tibet; or where the majority of the population is content with the existing political dispensation and a violent minority group seeks independence, such as the Sikh demand for a separate state of Khalistan.

One of the particularly intractable and violent conflicts has attended the Hindu Tamil secessionist movement in Sri Lanka (Ceylon). The Tamil minority, constituting

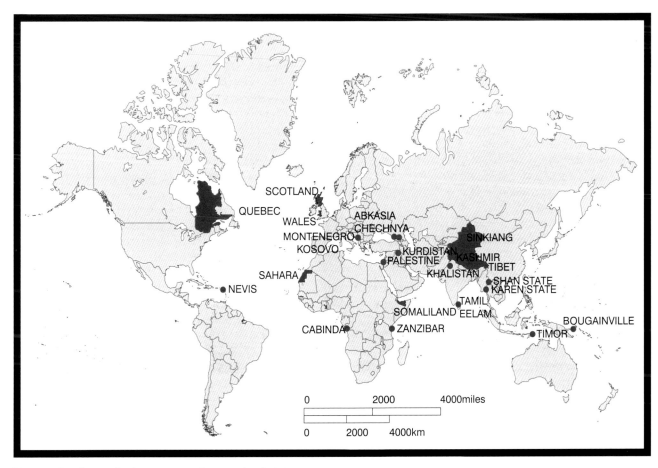

Map 11.3   Secessionist states and unresolved statuses

approximately 15 percent of the island's population, had the protection of their language and cultural heritage acknowledged in the constitution at independence in February 1948. However, in April 1956 the populist Sinhalese Buddhist party came to power and proceeded to impose Sinhalese as the sole official language and undermine the position of the minority through disenfranchising those considered to be the descendants of recent Indian immigrants. Inter-communal violence ensued in May 1958 and continued sporadically thereafter, as the communal elites refused to reach any accommodation (Stokke, 1998). A full-scale civil war broke out in July 1983, with the Liberation Tigers of Tamil Eelam seeking the establishment of the separate independent state of Tamil Eelam, in the Northern and Eastern Provinces of the island. Partition on ethnic grounds was rejected by the central government and a military solution was attempted. An Indian peace-keeping force was sent to the island between July 1987 and March 1990 to assist the central

government and provide security for the Tamil community. A symbolic formal declaration of independence by the North-Eastern Provincial Council in March 1990 was made immediately prior to the withdrawal of the Indian army. The civil war continued thereafter with no compromise in evidence. For a period the Tamil Tigers held and administered a portion of their proposed state, including the city of Jaffna, which they held for over five years from September 1990 to December 1995.

The status of East Timor remains highly contentious as only Australia recognised the Indonesian annexation of the former Portuguese colony (Jardine, 1996). The continuing conflict between the predominantly Christian population and its predominantly Moslem occupiers was highlighted in October 1996 when the Nobel Peace Prize was awarded to Carlos Belo, Bishop of Dili, and Jose Ramos-Horta, leader of the Fretilin Independence Movement. The international community thus demonstrated its continued support for self-determination by the people of East Timor.

11.4   INDIGENOUS PEOPLES

The secessionist movements mentioned above are in many cases the result of the re-emergence of historic territorial nationalisms suppressed by the state, whether colonial or independent. Government and particularly military leaders have regarded the preservation of the territorial integrity of the state as their most important task. The result has been conflict and the promotion of secessionism. Of a similar nature, but on a different scale, had been the resurgence of 'indigenous' claims. Symbolically the United Nations declared the year 1992 the 'Year of Indigenous Peoples', marking the five hundredth anniversary of Christopher Columbus's voyage between Europe and the Americas.

The indigenous peoples of the Americas and other parts of the globe colonised and permanently settled by European settlers were effectively dispossessed (Christopher, 1997). In many cases they were exterminated, reduced to a captive labour force, or forced to live in designated reservations, usually in environmentally problematical regions, notably the cold and arid desert lands. Frequently central governments assumed that the indigenous population would eventually be assimilated into the immigrant population and that any special status would therefore be temporary. However, just as the numerically more substantial ethnic groups of Europe, Asia and Africa sought political recognition, so too have the indigenous peoples of the Arctic, the Americas and Australasia.

In most cases political independence of the nature envisaged by European and Asian secessionist movements is not feasible owing to the small numbers of people involved, and their dependence upon the existing state structures. Indigenous peoples have often been reduced to very small proportions of the population and rarely constitute a majority outside highly restricted and fragmented areas. However, the areas set aside or claimed by indigenous peoples may be quite extensive. The autonomous republics of the Russian Federation present a significant solution to the recognition of indigenous rights and may be emulated in modified forms by other countries. In addition, a Congress of Small Peoples of the North met

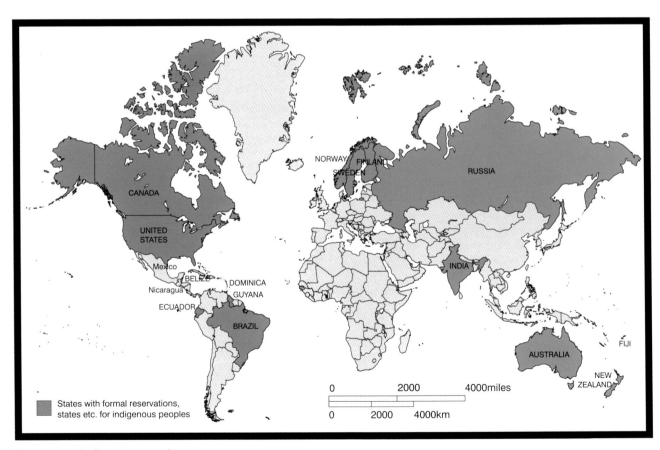

Map 11.4   Indigenous peoples

in Moscow in March 1990 to link indigenous peoples. In Scandinavia Finland established a Saami (Lapp) council in 1973 and this was followed by Norway in 1989 and Sweden in 1993 to protect the group from external encroachment. In the Russian Kola peninsula the Saami have also sought recognition and pan-Saami bodies appear likely to be established (Chaturvedi, 1996). Thus virtually all the lands surrounding the Arctic Ocean ended the twentieth century under some form of autonomous control by the indigenous peoples.

Accordingly in Australia the change in the governmental view of aboriginal land rights has substantially altered the internal arrangements of the state. Initially the 'terra nullius' principle assumed that there had been no established government or land rights prior to the British annexation. Reservations were set aside by the colonial governments to accommodate the aboriginal population, which by the 1930s had shrunk to under one percent of the total. Assimilation was the assumed final status for the aboriginal population. However, ethnic awareness and political action reversed the trend, with demands for the return of lands previously occupied.

The land restitution process began in the Northern Territory in 1970, with the establishment of legal mechanisms for aboriginal groups to claim their traditional lands. The process was slow, as the groups had to demonstrate their spiritual affinity to the land claimed through the continuity of performance of ceremonies (Berndt, 1982). However, because of the extreme aridity of the environment, the blocks awarded were extensive. In June 1992, in the settlement of the land claim brought in the Mabo case, the legality of the terra nullius assumption was overturned in the Supreme Court. Although the case only applied to a single island off the coast of Queensland, the ruling was assumed to apply to the whole of Australia. Substantial changes have since been made to the map of the country. However, the aboriginal political movement has done no more than produce the first separatist elements of a South African homeland plan.

It is notable that few colonised indigenous peoples in the Americas have sought independence. Even the Indian led Zapatista National Liberation Army, which seized control of much of Chiapas State in Mexico in January 1994, sought redress of their grievances by the central government, not secession or autonomy. In similar vein, the Moskito people of Nicaragua had by the 1980s only opposed the central government over land seizures and economic conditions, not as a bid to restore their independence (Gurr and Harff, 1994). Reservations for the indigenous Indian populations were established in countries

involved in the exploitation of the Amazon Basin, notably Brazil and Ecuador, but they have not been effective in withstanding continued encroachment.

11.5   EMERGING NATIONS AND STATES IN CANADA

The Canadian Confederation has undergone a number of constitutional crises in the course of the twentieth century and the country can be identified as one which may not survive in its present form in the twenty-first century. It is afflicted by both European style national secessionism and indigenous land claims. Although initially regarded as two issues, the secession of Quebec and the recognition of Indian and Inuit land rights overlap in northern Quebec.

The French-speaking population of Quebec remained a separate and in many ways an isolated community, as no large-scale immigration affected them after 1760. In the last quarter of the twentieth century it sought to redefine its position within the Canadian Confederation (Kaplan, 1994). In the late 1960s and 1970s the secessionist movement developed with a mixture of constitutional and violent measures. This was encouraged by General Charles de Gaulle's declaration 'Vive le Quebec libre' (Long Live Free Quebec), during his visit to the province in July 1967. Its success appeared complete when in November 1976 the Quebec Party won the provincial elections and declared French the sole official language. In May 1980 a referendum on independence was held but it was rejected by a margin of 59.5 to 40.5 percent, largely prompted by fears over the economic aspects of such a move. Subsequent negotiations failed to produce a constitutionally acceptable formula for the province and secession remains on the political agenda. In October 1995 a further referendum produced a narrower margin of under 1 percent. Supporters of independence confidently expect that the next referendum, early in the new millennium, will produce a result favourable to them.

Concentration upon the constitutional position of Quebec has tended to obscure events in other provinces and in the North West Territories. The isolation of Newfoundland from the remainder of English-speaking Canada has resulted in concern at the viability of the link in the event of Quebec independence. Newfoundland, however, receives a special federal subsidy covering approximately half of its budget expenditure (Watkins, 1993). No other sources of funds are available, making independence as unattractive as it was in 1934. The other Maritime Provinces of New Brunswick, Nova Scotia and

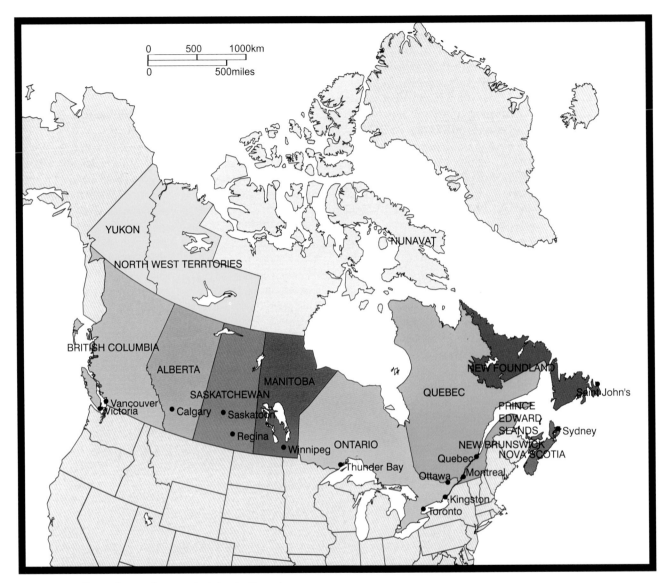

Map 11.5   Emerging nations and states in Canada

Prince Edward Island similarly could not support independent status, but have investigated joining the United States. However, in common with most Canadian provinces, their political party systems were generally not comparable with the American mould. The comparatively leftward orientation of Canadian politics and their volatility would not be attractive to the two mainstream American political parties, primarily concerned with the stability and internal dynamics of the United States (Doran, 1996).

The indigenous Indian and Inuit peoples constitute some 4 percent of the population of Canada. The approximately 800 000 people of Indian descent are scattered across Canada, with a large number of small Indian Reservations in each province, dating from the period of European settlement. In no cases are there large consolidated blocks of Indian land, as the general approach had been to assign subsistence areas to individual Indian bands, rather than larger confederacies. Land claims were raised, but these were adjudicated within the overall framework of the existing provincial structures.

The Inuit population in the North West and Yukon Territories amounted to under 50 000. The settlement of their claims against the Canadian federal government was ratified in November 1992. The area covered amounted to over 2.0 million square kilometres or more than 20 percent of the area of Canada, of which the communities retained some 350 000 square kilometres in private ownership. In April 1999 the main regions inhabited by the Inuit were removed from the jurisdiction of the North West Territories and received self-government as the territory of Nunavut. In this manner the Canadian Inuit joined the other Arctic indigenous peoples of Russia, Scandinavia, Alaska and Greenland, which had gained a large measure of self-government and control of the natural resources.

11.6   EMERGING ECONOMIC BLOCS

Against the background of increasing numbers of independent states there has been the opposite process of economic integration. In some cases economic integration is assumed to be the preliminary towards the establishment of a political union in the same manner as the German Zollverein in the period before 1871. The European Union is the prime example of this development, as well as being the most advanced towards economic integration (and is examined in the following section). Other regional groupings in South-east Asia, North America, Latin America and elsewhere have promoted economic integration, but with limited political agendas.

Economic integration in the Americas began in December 1960 with the establishment of the Central American Common Market, linking the six small Spanish-speaking states extending from Guatemala to Panama. This was followed in May 1969 by the formation of the Andean group, which linked states extending from Colombia to Chile, although subsequently Chile opted out and Venezuela joined. The Caribbean Community and Common Market was established in July 1973 to link the Commonwealth states extending from Belize to Guyana. It

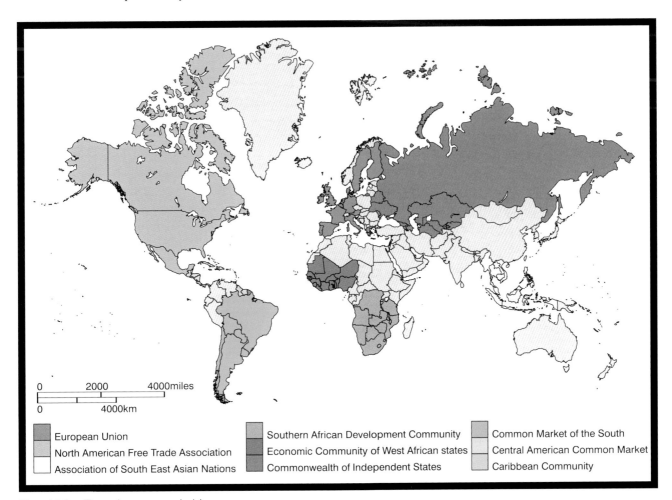

0   2000   4000miles
0   4000km

European Union
North American Free Trade Association
Association of South East Asian Nations

Southern African Development Community
Economic Community of West African states
Commonwealth of Independent States

Common Market of the South
Central American Common Market
Caribbean Community

Map 11.6   Emerging economic blocs

was subsequently enlarged with the accession of Suriname in July 1995. It was only in the 1990s that the two economically powerful extremities of the continent were organised. First in March 1991 the Common Market of the Southern Cone (Mercosur) linked Argentina, Brazil, Paraguay and Uruguay, with enlargement to include Chile and Bolivia as observer members. Finally in November 1993 the North American Free Trade Association, linking the United States, Canada and Mexico, was established, to promote trade between its three members. Unlike the European Union the American agreements specifically exclude any political unification.

Similarly in South-east Asia, the Association of South-east Asian Nations was formed in August 1967 to link a variety of states undergoing significant economic transformation, while avoiding direct political entanglements. Thus nominally neutralist Indonesia linked with pro-American Malaysia, Singapore, the Philippines and Thailand. Brunei joined in January 1984, upon gaining independence. However, in July 1995 the Association was expanded to include Communist Vietnam, indicating its essentially economic objectives in the post Cold War era. The Association was expanded in July 1997 to include Cambodia, Laos and the international pariah, Burma. Papua New Guinea assumed observer status. Political integration, even the harmonisation of political and social policies, was not on the agenda of the Association.

In Africa regional groupings such as the Economic Community of West African States, the Economic Community of Central African States, and the Southern African Development Community similarly linked states with widely differing political systems. The former, established in May 1975, linked the 15 West African states to overcome the divisions inherited from the colonial era. The Cape Verde Islands joined in November 1977. The latter Community, formed in April 1980 as the Southern African Co-ordination Conference, was designed as a means of countering South African dominance of the region (Gibb, 1987). It underwent dramatic transformation following South Africa's admission to the grouping upon the abandonment of apartheid in 1994. Its proposed enlargement in September 1997 to include the Democratic Republic of Congo (formerly Zaire) marked a significant new direction and possibly marked the abandonment of the Central African Community, which was only formed in 1983.

The Commonwealth of Independent States sought to retain some economic links between most of the former members of the Soviet Union. However, there are sections of the world where regional economic groupings have attained little success, largely due to political rivalries. North Africa, South-west, South, and East Asia were regions with poorly developed structures. The South Asian Association for Regional Cooperation established in 1985, and the Arab Maghreb Union dating from 1989, may provide the basis of future economic integration programmes.

Economic groupings appeared to have had greater success than the more nebulous political groupings. The Commonwealth had ceased to have any significant political purpose after the Second World War and was retained as a more broadly based cultural and aid organisation, with periodic meetings of national leaders. This was a rare survival of worldwide imperial connections. However, its expansion to include Mozambique and Cameroon, which lacked these links, has loosened whatever cohesion it once possessed. The French and Portuguese post-colonial equivalents similarly have little political content. Regional groupings were more widely developed. The Organisation of American States and the Organisation of African Unity constituted no more than continental links, which were aimed to increase continental solidarity and occasional political support against outsiders. None appeared to offer the basis for closer political integration. Cultural groupings including the Nordic Council and the Melanesian Spearhead group offered the same mutual support systems for smaller groups of countries.

11.7   THE EUROPEAN UNION

The nominal introduction of a single European currency in January 1999 symbolised the direction in which the European Union had progressed since the formation of the initial European Iron and Steel Community in July 1952. Other organisations followed, culminating in the Treaty of Rome in March 1957, which bound the signatories to widespread economic and political cooperation (Stirk, 1996). The European Economic Community followed in January 1958, with the intention of achieving a full economic union, making war between the members impossible. Both organisations linked a core of six states, France, Western Germany, Italy and the three members of the Benelux customs union, Belgium, the Netherlands and Luxembourg, which had come into force in January 1948 (Dedman, 1996).

In the 1950s and 1960s the longest and most substantial boom took place in the European economy, with the members of the European Economic Community recording high rates of growth. At the same time the structures of the community were organised around the Franco-German

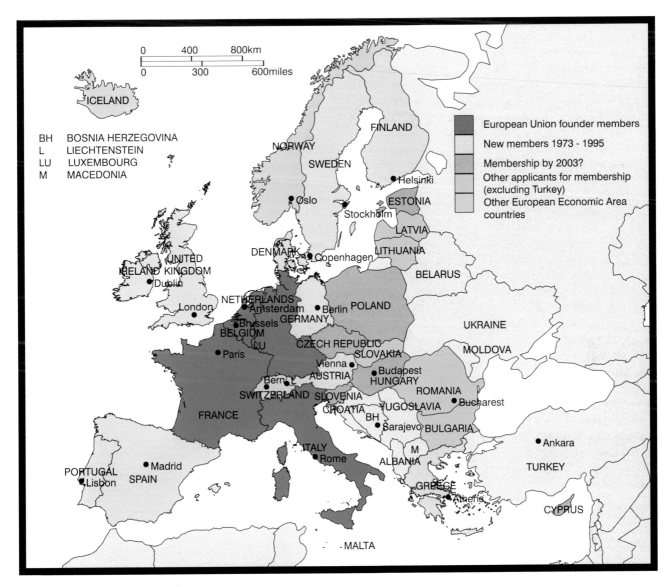

Map 11.7 The European Union

partnership. Thus the British application to join in 1963 was rejected as likely to compromise the ideals of the founders. Only in January 1973 were additional members admitted when the existing membership recognised that enlargement would not fundamentally alter the character of the organisation. In 1973 Great Britain, Ireland and Denmark joined. In 1981 Greece was admitted followed by Spain and Portugal in 1986. The reunification of Germany in 1990 led to further extension of the area of the Community. However, the grant of self-government to Greenland in May 1979 resulted in a reduction of the Community area, as the local government withdrew in 1985.

The leaders of the Community decided to advance the political aspects of the Community with the Treaty of Maastricht in December 1991, converting the organisation into the European Union. There followed a further expansion in January 1995 with the admission of Austria, Sweden and Finland. Equally significant was the rejection of membership by Norway (in November 1972 and November 1994), and Switzerland (in December 1994). Liechtenstein had little option but to follow Switzerland's lead, despite the earlier decision to accept the terms of accession. The main objections to membership were the political implications of joining what was increasingly taking on the appearance of a federation, without a mechanism for secession.

With the collapse of communism in eastern Europe, other countries applied for membership from April 1994 onwards. However, the social and economic problems encountered with the integration of East Germany were substantially greater than had been anticipated, and the inclusion of countries such as Poland, the Czech Republic, Hungary, Slovenia and Estonia may be postponed while their economies complete a number of structural adjustments to a post-Communist environment. Other applicants such as Romania, Bulgaria, Slovakia, Latvia and Lithuania may not gain admission for even longer, whereas Malta could gain admission more readily. The admission of Cyprus remains problematic in view of continued Greco-Turkish confrontation on the island. All told, some 12 countries have outstanding applications for membership.

Some countries, notably Norway and Iceland, have consistently chosen to stay outside the Union. They were offered the opportunity of an economic link through the creation of the European Economic Area in June 1996, as a preliminary to full membership. The position of Switzerland and Liechtenstein remains to be regularised. The question of Turkish membership remains the most contentious of all. Application for membership was made in April 1987, but a decision was deferred as various economic and political issues were raised, notably the forceful suppression of the Kurdish separatist movement. However, the basic issue of admitting a Moslem, if nominally secular, state, which therefore was not part of the overall ethos of a shared Christian heritage upon which the European Union was founded, has yet to be faced. So far only a customs agreement (January 1996) has been put in place.

It is a curious paradox that the economic and political integration has enabled smaller nations to revive. Western Europe thus acquired a 'nationalities question' as the grip of the centralised nation-state was loosened (Van Amersfoort and Knippenberg, 1991). Since the Second World War the strong nation-states of Europe have attempted to counter secessionist movements through autonomy agreements, such as that governing the German-speaking population of the Italian Tyrol (Markusse, 1997). Isolated island groups appear particularly susceptible to secession. The remaining constitutional links between the Faroes and Denmark are under strain, while the Aland Islands have secured greater autonomy from Finland (Hannikainen and Horn, 1997).

11.8   SPANISH DEVOLUTION

The Spanish monarchy under King Juan Carlos I was restored upon the death of General Francisco Franco in November 1975 (Preston, 1990). This set in motion a wide range of changes, including complete reintegration into the international community after a prolonged period of ostracism of the Fascist government following the Second World War. Fully democratic elections ensued and Spain later joined the North Atlantic Treaty Organisation and the European Union.

One of the significant results of the programme of democratisation was the accommodation of the demands for autonomy from the peripheral provinces and ethnic groups. During the period of the Spanish Republic (1931–1939) a high degree of regional autonomy had been granted to Catalonia and the Basque Country in September 1932 and October 1936 respectively. The two regional governments had been suppressed with the overthrow of the Republic in the course of the civil war between 1936 and 1939. The two regions remained centres of opposition to the Spanish government throughout the Franco era.

The restoration of autonomy to these two regions assumed a high priority for the new government. Enabling legislation was drawn up in September 1978 and referenda in October 1979 endorsed the autonomy statutes with 88.1 percent electoral support in Catalonia and 90.3 percent in the Basque Country. Significantly the Basque government, which had gone into exile in August 1937, formally dissolved itself in December 1979 in recognition of the grant of Basque autonomy under the post-Franco government. The establishment of new regional parliaments in March 1980 did not end the struggle by some members of the Euskadi Ta Askatsuna (Basque Nation and Liberty – ETA) movement to seek complete independence through violence. The relative strength of the national language was significant in both cases. Catalan was spoken by 64 percent of the population of Catalonia, and indeed by 70 percent in the Balearic Islands and 49 percent in Valencia. However, only 24.5 percent of the population of the Basque Country spoke the Basque language, limiting the potential support base demand for independence from Spain.

Catalonia and the Basque Country were followed by other regions in the course of the 1980s. Andalucia approved the negotiations for the grant of autonomy in a referendum in February 1980, but with only 54 percent support. Galicia, with its distinctive language akin to Portuguese, followed in September 1980. Self-government

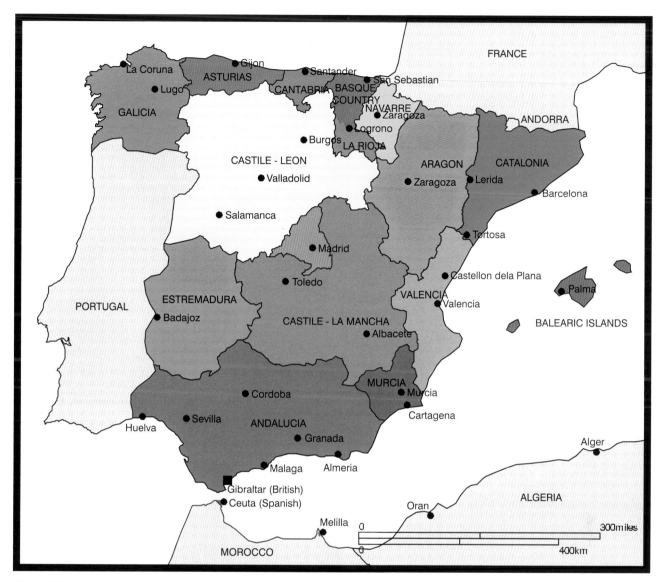

Map 11.8   Spanish devolution

for other historic provinces and grouping of provinces followed by May 1982. Significantly Navarre chose to establish its own government rather than join the Basque Country, reflecting the lower proportion of Basque-speakers (12 percent) in the historic kingdom. Most regions, termed autonomous communities, were based on regional particularisms of historical significance, such as Andalucia. Decentralisation was also extended to regions within the Spanish heartland, including (Old) Castile-Leon, (New) Castile-La Mancha and the national capital, Madrid. Finally some 17 autonomous communities were created through the linkage of the 50 inherited provinces.

11.9   BELGIUM

Decentralisation and ethnic self-government took place even in established democratic states at the same time as the centralisation of the European Union. There was therefore a marked tendency for the 'nation' states which appeared upon the world map not to reflect the reality of powers transferred from the sovereign state to both the supra-national continental communities and unions on the one hand and to sub-national regional and ethnic entities on the other. The nation-state in western Europe was thus

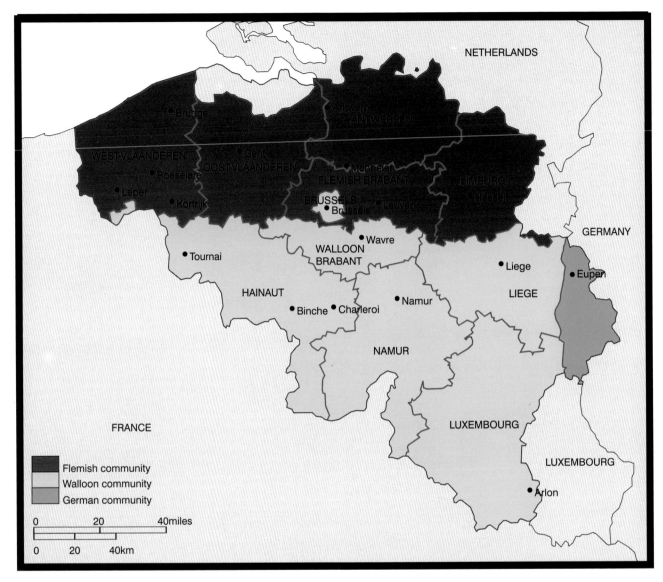

Map 11.9   Belgium

subject to continuing erosion both from 'above' and 'below' (Kolinsky, 1984). The emergence of regional superpowers, and the security which they engender, may unleash such centripetal forces elsewhere as the nation-state loses its central position in the state system.

Nowhere is this in greater evidence than in Belgium, the host to the central bureaucracy of the European Union. The bitter language conflict between the Flemish-speaking population of the north and the French-speaking Walloons of the south had bedevilled Belgian politics since the formation of the state in 1830. The recognition of Flemish as an official language in 1884 had done little to prevent

German exploitation of the language issue in both world wars. Political and economic crises were exacerbated by ethnic identification, particularly as the economies of the two regions exhibited markedly different structures. Furthermore, the expanding Brussels region, which was predominantly French-speaking, encroached steadily upon the Flemish-speaking rural areas of Brabant, providing a constant source of linguistic conflict. However, secession was not viewed as a practical proposition as the country's economic system was highly integrated.

In May 1993 the kingdom adopted a federal constitution with three communities (Flemish, Walloon and German)

and three regions (Flemish, Walloon and Brussels). A complex system of local and national government structures involved some redrawing of the nine historic provincial boundaries, including the partition of Brabant between the Flemish and Walloon communities. In addition, a permanent definition of the predominantly French-speaking Brussels metropolitan capital region was undertaken, to prevent future encroachment upon the surrounding Flemish region. Finally the German-speaking region of Eupen, which Belgium had annexed after the First World War, remained in the Walloon region, but constituted a separate community. The central government retained few powers beyond foreign affairs, defence and macro-economic policy, all of which were closely integrated within the European Union.

Even within this complexity, the presence of the European Union capital functions and the attractive power of the Belgian economy had resulted in nearly ten percent of the population being foreigners, adding a potential xenophobic element to the ethnic nationalism which has afflicted the Belgian kingdom for so long (Kesteloot and van der Haegen, 1987).

CHAPTER 12

Reflections

It is a truism to state that the world in the year 2000 is a very different place from that of one hundred years beforehand. Within the context of the system of sovereign independent states of the world, radical change is particularly noticeable. The increase in numbers from 56 to 192 independent entities represents an average growth of more than one state a year for the entire century. Yet the impact of the twentieth century upon the world map was most uneven, as a comparison of the stability of South America with the instability of Africa illustrates. At the same time the character of the state has undergone a number of significant changes, linked to the changes in the relationship between ruler and ruled and the relationship between individual states and the wider international community.

Certain themes require examination with a view to gaining a greater insight into the nature of states. Longevity is significant in that nearly a quarter of the states of the world were permanent features of the map throughout the century and they are predominantly European and American. In contrast the new states are predominantly African and Asian, having emerged from colonial rule, although the now fragmented multi-national empires and federations were not confined to those two continents. There remain the surviving colonies, whose anachronistic status still requires constitutional finality.

Intertwined with the birth of states has been death. In some cases countries have had a chequered history of birth, death and resurrection in the space of less than one hundred years. To add to the confusion the international community has in practice shifted its definition of sovereignty. International conferences of governments before the First World War and subsequently the League of Nations and the United Nations varied the rules on who was accepted and who was not. The sovereign state was thus not as readily identifiable as might at first appear. Non-governmental organisations were yet more problematical, extending recognition to entities which were frequently judged to be 'national', but not sovereign. At the other end of the scale, even sovereign states could be subjected to foreign military occupation and administration, which did not undermine the legitimacy of the state, only the government.

The recurring theme of the century relating nation to state and vice versa, demonstrates the complex relationship of both to the notion of ethnicity. The problem of reconciling ethnicity to the state and the state-created nation has been attempted in numerous ways, ranging from imposed unitarianism to federalism. Although the apparent ethnic uniformity of the nation-state has been assumed in most cases in the twentieth century, diversity is the general rule and states have had to be structured with this fact in mind. Two role models are offered, namely the two states which have accommodated the issue without either disintegration or excessive centralisation. The acceptance of often narrowly defined historic regionalisms, as in Switzerland, as part of personal identity creates a state of communities loosely bound in matters of mutual interest. In contrast, the idea that it is an individual's subscription to the state ideology which brings a common citizenship theoretically makes ethnicity irrelevant, as in the United States. Yet the concept of the 'clash of civilisations' has been placed on the international agenda for the post-Cold War era (Huntington, 1996).

Speculation on the establishment of new states and the demise of others is in the realm of prophecy or crystal ball gazing, but a few pointers to the future based on the experience of the past may be offered, if only to be confounded by the actual turn of events. Even less is there any intention of seeking to intervene in the political process. Here it is necessary to reiterate Manuel Castells' (1998: 358) recent warning to those that may wish for a direct involvement in shaping the future:

What is to be done? Each time an intellectual has tried to answer this question, and seriously implement the answer, catastrophe has ensued. This was particularly the case with a certain Ulianov (Lenin) in 1902. Thus, while certainly not pretending to qualify for this comparison, I shall abstain from suggesting any cure for the ills of our world.

12.1   STATES IN EXISTENCE 1900 AND 2000

Against the picture of turmoil, some 53 sovereign states were common to the maps of 1900 and 2000, allowing for changes in name and shape. However, six were removed from the map at some stage in the course of the century, but were subsequently able to regain their separate status. As might be expected the largest number (22) of survivors was situated in Europe. However, nineteen were situated in the Americas and only eight in Asia and four in Africa. The external stability of Latin America is particularly noticeable (Barton, 1997). The African figure was boosted by the resurrection of three after a period of colonial rule. Two European states and one Asian state experienced similar re-constitutions. Names have been changed reflecting political developments. Most symbolically, the Russian Empire became the Union of Soviet Socialist Republics and later reverted to the Russian Federation. Persia became Iran and Siam became Thailand, but such changes did not invalidate the continuity of the state.

The 46 states in continuous existence throughout the century were the success stories so far as survival is concerned. This does not mean that many of them did not suffer defeat in war, military occupation, civil war and loss of territory in the course of 100 years. Indeed the majority did suffer one, if not all, of these fates, but the state itself survived. The question thus arises: 'Is it possible to determine any common characteristics of these successful states?' At first sight there appears to be little to distinguish them from the current body of states. Survivors range in size from China and Russia on the one hand to Monaco and Liechtenstein on the other. Thus physical size and

population numbers have little to offer in seeking to explain longevity in a state. Furthermore, the second largest country in terms of population (India) and the second largest country in terms of area (Canada) were both part of the British Empire in 1900 and only gained independence in the 1930s and 1940s respectively. Other factors are clearly significant, although at the end of the century half the population of the world lived in the survivor states, indicating their larger than average nature.

The great powers, whether defined as those derived from the nineteenth century peace settlement of the Congress of Vienna, the post-First World War alliance, or the superpowers of the post-Second World War eras, were all survivors. Thus Great Britain, France, Prussia (Germany), Russia and Austria were regarded as the five great powers between 1815 and the outbreak of the First World War almost a century later. That war added the United States, Japan and nominally Italy to the list of great powers, while demoting Austria. After the Second World War only the United States and Russia, in the guise of the Soviet Union, remained as superpowers, although Great Britain, France and China also gained permanent seats on the Security Council of the United Nations. These nine states, with the temporary exception of Austria, were constant features of the world map, despite a marked fluidity in their boundaries. The great powers, even when defeated and occupied, were not annexed as they were assumed by the victors to be permanent components of the state system, which might somehow be jeopardised if they were erased.

To this list might be added other countries which although suffering military defeat or occupation were not incorporated by the victor. As the century unfolded annexations and wholesale incorporations became less frequent. Thus a rump Turkish republic survived the defeat of the Ottoman Empire in the First World War. The elaborate sets of plans which had been devised for the country's demise over a period of more than a hundred years were not put into effect when the final opportunity arose. In this respect Europe and Asia were regarded in a different light to Africa in the first half of the twentieth century. Apparently permanent African historic entities on the map, such as Morocco and Ethiopia, were incorporated into colonial empires, whereas others in Asia such as Iran and Thailand were not.

At the hub of the international state system in 1900 were the established nation-states and mini-states of western and central Europe which survived with only boundary modifications. Thus France, Spain, Portugal, Switzerland and others traced their pedigree back through the centuries and

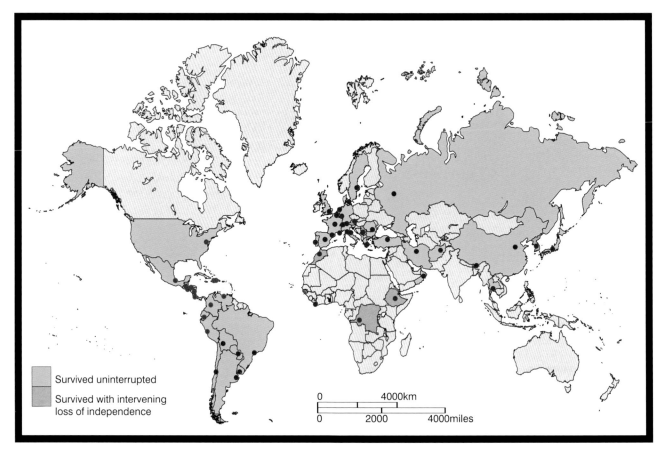

Map 12.1   States in existence 1900 and 2000

were undisturbed in their statehood by war, decolonisation and economic crisis. Even the newly unified nation-states of Germany and Italy were not permanently dismembered after defeat and occupation. In some cases the detachment of territories gained through imperial expansion took place even within Europe. Hence Great Britain, Russia and Sweden lost significant parts of their territories, while retaining the basic national core. This development was independent of the fate of the extra-European colonial empires. In view of the previous history of state aggrandisement, the survival of the four European mini-states deserves some comment. States regarded as insignificant to their neighbours' security could be successful in maintaining their independence through careful diplomacy.

It was in the Americas that the state system exhibited the greatest degree of stability. All nineteen states on the map of 1900 survived, with comparatively little territorial modification when compared with that of 2000. All were republics, usually modelled constitutionally upon the United States of America, even if reality sometimes fell far short of

national aspirations. Since 1823 the United States had operated the Monroe Doctrine, which sought to exclude European influence from the continent. With rare exceptions this was successful and the governments of the newly independent republics were able to consolidate themselves in comparative isolation from the events of the Old World. In economic terms, the term 'informal empire' was applied to the extent of British economic penetration of South America, but the extension of a formal empire was never considered. Indeed in most areas of potential territorial conflict such as the Mosquito Territory (Nicaragua) and Bay Islands (Honduras), the British withdrew. French intervention in Mexico and Spanish recolonisation of the Dominican Republic during the American civil war in the 1860s ended with the Federal victory. The American state system was essentially in place by 1900 and the immediate post-independence conflicts had been resolved. The system demonstrated its resilience through the following century. The Americas present therefore the model to which other continents in the post-colonial era might aspire.

Africa, in contrast, exhibited a remarkable lack of continuity, with the current state pattern largely the product of the international relations of the colonial powers and their subsequent administrative policies. Only one of the six states in existence in 1900 survived without incorporation into the European colonial empires. Liberia owes its unique status to its close American association. Ethiopia and Morocco survived brief colonial eras, with institutions virtually intact. In contrast, the Congo Free State had little institutional relationship to the subsequent independent republic of Congo (Zaire), beyond its external boundaries. The Orange Free State and South African Republic (Transvaal) were reduced to provinces within the new South African union.

12.2   NEW STATES 1900–2000

The emergence of 139 new states on the world map is the most dramatic change of the twentieth century. In terms of distribution the greatest increases took place in Africa, with 49 additional states, and Asia, with 34 new states. Limited numbers of new states were established in the Americas (16) and Europe (8). Some 14 independent states were created in Oceania, which had been entirely under colonial rule in 1900. In view of the comments in the previous section, the almost doubling of the number of states in the Americas is particularly surprising. If the special case of Canada is excluded, the new states were small and with one exception (Panama) represented the granting of independence to small colonial territories and islands.

The two forces of decolonisation and nationalism account for the development of the majority of the new entities. The terminology of self-determination was often cloaked in anti-colonialist and nationalist terms, although the objectives might be quite different. Self-determination involved the creation of new nation-states, which seceded from existing multi-national empires. In some cases this involved no more than the constitutional ending of the link between the empire and the new state, which possessed a prior recognisable status. Thus Norway gained independence from Sweden through peaceful means,

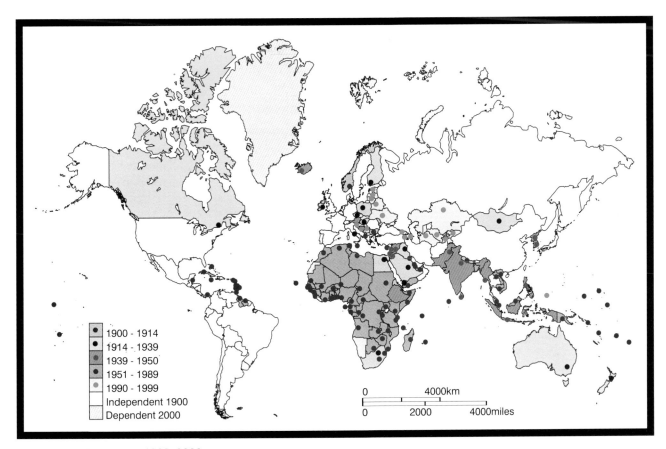

Map 12.2   New states 1900–2000

within historic boundaries. Others only seceded after conflict, as for example Finland, which during and after the First World War established its formal separation from Russia. In many cases there was no prior political entity before independence for the secessionists to use in pursuit of their objectives. Thus Poland was established with few clear guidelines other than the distribution of the Polish population and the political maps of Europe in the eighteenth century to aid the statesmen in the demarcation of its boundaries. Sometimes the new state was defined by the great powers, in the interests of maintaining the international balance of power, before national demands were closely focused, as in the case of Albania and Cyprus.

Imperial disintegration, as in the case of Austria-Hungary in 1918, presented the greatest problems in delimiting the new states and determining to what extent national self-determination should extend. This went to the very heart of the question of defining a nation, and at what size an ethnically defined nation became a viable entity. Similarly the disintegration of the Soviet Union in 1991 resulted in the independence of certain nations, but not of others. Again definition of the meaning of nation and its relation to the state was significant in this determination.

In general new states came into being as a result of the disintegration of empires, rather than the success of struggling national movements. The major European overseas colonial empires were granted independence on the basis of the individual colonies. These had often been defined for administrative convenience within an empire and as a result of diplomatic bargaining between empires. The results frequently had little relationship to pre-existing political and ethnic structures. The resulting states were in most cases multi-ethnic, and therefore afflicted with the subsequent problems associated with the integration of multi-ethnic states, at a time when western Europe appeared to have virtually completed the process of establishing mono-ethnic nation-states. The new governments and bureaucracies were therefore the inheritors of the colonial boundaries and colonial administrations. Attempts to create ethnic or linguistic nation-states out of these entities were resisted. The international community underwrote the system of quasi-states, offering aid and discouraging any challenge to their territorial integrity.

In all these cases it is noticeable that the governments of secessionist states, whether post-colonial or installed after achieving national self-determination, are remarkably unwilling to offer self-determination to smaller nations or nationalities falling within their newly defined territory. The result has frequently been that yesterday's freedom fighters have often become today's oppressors. The

outcome has been a tendency for independence boundaries to fossilise and achieve a degree of permanence, which may only be challenged when new movements seeking national self-determination achieve success.

One of the noticeable features of the process of decolonisation has been the emergence of a large number of mini- and micro-states. The strategic bases and isolated islands of the colonial era were granted independence after 1945, with little attempt to group them into larger political units. Thus by the year 2000 an additional 20 states measured less than 1000 square kilometres and 38 states counted populations of under one million people at the beginning of the new millennium. This development has had a profound effect upon the state system, which has had to come to terms with the particular problems of so many small, and generally poor, members.

12.3   THE DEFINITION OF COLONIES

The establishment of separate administrative colonies within the overseas colonial empires was clearly a highly significant factor so far as the evolution of the political map of the world is concerned. Just over half the states of the world in 2000 were dependencies of one of the intercontinental colonial empires in 1900. The definition of colonial boundaries was thus a particularly important factor. In the majority of cases the colony was defined by international treaty and internal subdivision was undertaken. Thus at independence entities such as Gambia and Sierra Leone were constituted within existing international boundaries. The most common such definition was the single island colony, or associated group of islands. In this manner Dominica, Grenada, St Lucia and St Vincent became independent as separate states, as they had been separate colonies beforehand, not a part of the wider Windward Islands or West Indies groupings. Similarly the Cape Verde Islands archipelago achieved independence as a group, as they had previously been administered as such. Sometimes two islands with markedly different histories were linked together to economise on administrative costs, thus Nevis was linked to Saint Christopher and Tobago to Trinidad.

In some cases the colonial definition was large and cumbersome. The territories acquired by Leopold II of Belgium to form the Congo Free State were very extensive and diverse. Whatever the internal administrative divisions, the government of the Free State and subsequent Belgian colony was essentially unified and hierarchical. Thus at independence the whole inadequate structure was bequeathed to the new Republic, whose government then

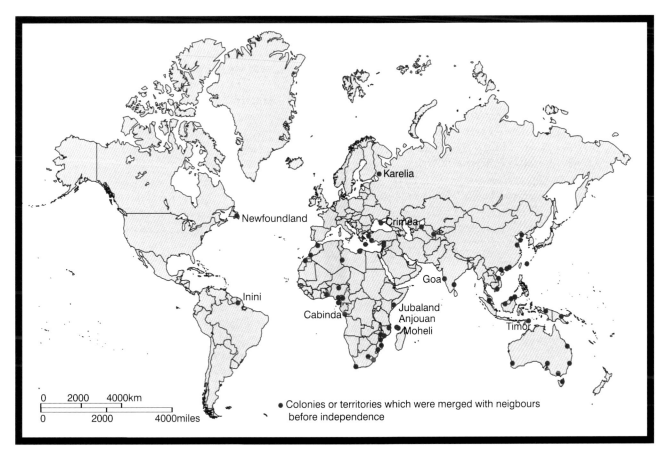

Karelia

Newfoundland

Crimea

Goa

Inini

Cabinda

Jubaland
Anjouan
Moheli

Timor

| 0 | 2000 | 4000km |

| 0 | 2000 | 4000miles |

● Colonies or territories which were merged with neigbours before independence

Map 12.3 The definition of colonies

proceeded to suppress a wide range of secessionist movements, based on the administrations of the outlying provinces. Even where administrative unity had not initially been considered possible the various units were subsequently grouped to fill out the extent defined by the international boundary, as in the case of Nigeria and Mozambique.

However, in a number of cases the internationally defined boundaries enclosed colonial territories which were too cumbersome or complex to administer as a single entity. French West Africa became an extensive territory covering some 3.6 million square kilometres. Although a Governor-General, based in Dakar, administered the common services for the whole federation, considerable powers were retained by the individual colonial governors. To ease the problems of administration, colonial boundaries were redrawn on a number of occasions after the French conquest of the interior French Sudan in the 1890s. The jurisdictions of individual coastal colonies were extended inland, while the interior colony was divided in 1919–1920

into three, including Upper Volta, as the homeland of the Mossi people. In 1932 as a result of the great depression, savings in the costs of colonial administration were effected, and Upper Volta was divided with the major portion merged with the Ivory Coast. In the course of the Second World War, the government of French West Africa declared for the Vichy government. However, the Mossi leaders supported the Free French. Thus in 1947 they were rewarded with the reconstitution of Upper Volta as a separate colony. In the drive for independence, political activity was centred upon the individual colonies. Hence French West Africa disintegrated into its constituent colonies, which happened to include Upper Volta at that particular time. In this respect it may be possible to speak of a fortuitous accident of history that the colony was in separate existence when independence took place.

Even more complex in design and results was the definition of South Africa. The British colonial empire in southern Africa was extensive, but administratively complex, reflecting the acquisition of colonies, protectorates, territories governed by the British South Africa Company, and in 1900 the annexation of the previously independent Afrikaner republics. Again an overarching administration was envisaged under a High Commissioner, but when constituted in 1910, only the four self-governing British possessions in southern Africa were included in the Union. Furthermore, the protectorate of Basutoland, despite its enclave position, resisted incorporation into the new Union and subsequent Republic, because of racial discrimination. Moves towards incorporation under the post-apartheid dispensation will be expected. The other British possessions were also not incorporated so that the boundary of South Africa in 2000 was virtually that of 1910. The definition of the surviving colonies and protectorates in British southern Africa thus becomes of some importance, as the 1910 pattern was effectively fossilised.

The same process of administrative division within colonial empires took place elsewhere. French Indo-China was divided into three states on historic grounds. The historic area of Burma was detached from India prior to the more publicised partition of 1947. In some cases regroupings were effected at the end of colonial rule to expedite withdrawal. The Spanish linked Rio Muni and Fernando Póo to form a single state, Great Britain incorporated North Borneo and Sarawak into Malaysia, despite their markedly separate statuses under colonial rule. The colonial powers created and demoted separate administrations with some ease. Independent states could not be created and disposed of with such alacrity, nor with hindsight have the former colonies necessarily disappeared as potential independent states, as the successful re-emergence of the Republic of Singapore indicates.

12.4   EPHEMERAL STATES

The emergence of new states was not all a one-way process of ever greater fragmentation and decolonisation. Some states, although obtaining independence, were unable to sustain that status, becoming only ephemeral entities on the world map. Others had remarkably chequered histories paralleling the experience of the French colony of Upper Volta, with subsequent resurrection. However, yet others disappeared permanently, with no revival. In this discussion secessionist movements which may have achieved a measure of effective but unrecognised independence for short periods must be excluded.

Sovereign states have lost their independent status throughout the century, beginning in 1900 with the annexation of the Orange Free State and the Transvaal by Great Britain, a fact subsequently recognised by their deposed governments two years later. Military force or the threat of force has been a frequent factor in the demise of states. The Emperor of Korea accepted protectorate status in 1905 and subsequent annexation because the country was under Japanese military occupation. A similar fate befell Latvia, Lithuania and Estonia in 1940 and Tuva in 1944 when under Soviet military occupation. The results of tightly controlled referenda were not reliable tests of public opinion on separate statehood.

Other states were occupied and annexed with no reference to the previous government. The kingdom of Hejez was conquered by the Saudi kingdom in 1925 and King Hussein was forced into exile, never to return. Similarly, Ethiopia was conquered by Italy in 1935 and annexed. This was not accepted by the Emperor Haile Selassie who went into exile and staged an unexpected return as a result of the Italian defeat in the Second World War. In the two World Wars similar occupations and annexations took place. In the Second World War Poland was effectively erased from the map of Europe and incorporated entirely into the two partitioning powers. In none of these cases was a test of national opinion undertaken, as the outcome would certainly have been to retain national independence as subsequent events were to prove, when such options were offered.

It has been rarer for countries to lose their raison d'etre and seek incorporation into a neighbouring state. The government of one of the few European ephemeral states, Montenegro, sought incorporation into the wider Yugoslav state in 1918, although King Nicholas was resistant. In others the overthrow of the existing government was a necessary preliminary for the process of integration to begin. Thus Sultan Seyyid Jamshid bin Abdulla of Zanzibar was overthrown in 1964, and the successor republican government sought its preservation through unification with its larger neighbour Tanganyika. The Zanzibari national raison d'etre, defined as an Arab Moslem sultanate, was redefined in Africanist revolutionary terms and found wanting.

It is significant that the loss of national identity has been rare. The classic example was that of Austria after the First World War. The republican government after the overthrow of the monarchy described itself as governing 'German-Austria'. Incorporation into Germany was requested but under the terms of the Treaty of Versailles could not be accepted. In 1938, in an act of international defiance, Germany occupied Austria. The subsequent referendum demonstrated overwhelming support for the merging of the

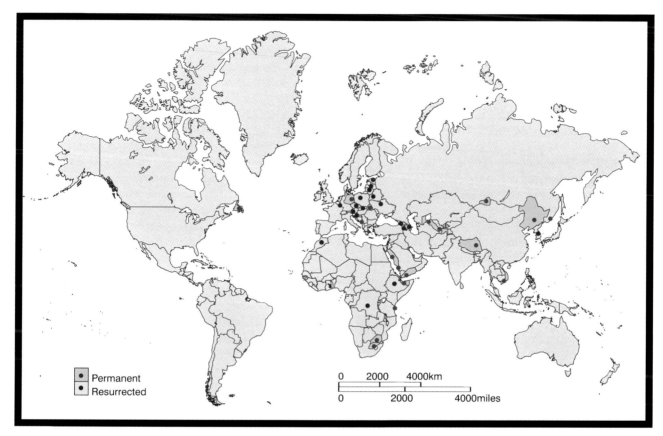

Map 12.4   Ephemeral states

country into Germany. However, the Austrian state was resurrected by the Allied powers in 1945 and granted independent statehood in 1955. The individual and collective trauma of the 1938–1945 period under National Socialism and military occupation afterwards effectively ended any coherent support for union with Germany and the recognition of a separate Austrian state identity.

National reunification has been the aim of a number of governments throughout the century. The reunification of Germany in 1990 was accomplished through democratic means as the German Democratic Republic had been maintained by Soviet forces and had never been able to achieve internal legitimacy. The withdrawal of Soviet support opened the way to reunification. Similarly countries such as Somaliland and Somalia in 1960, and the Republic of Yemen and the People's Republic of Yemen in 1990 merged to establish unified nation-states. In both cases the union was uneasy as Somaliland's reassertion of independence in 1992 and South Yemen in May 1994 attested (Kostiner, 1995). The reunification of Vietnam in 1976 was expedited by the northern state, which considered

the southern state to be showing signs of reconsidering the desirability of reunification after the overthrow of its ideologically hostile predecessor. The Korean nation is one of the few to remain politically divided. Such a division is only likely to survive for as long as the ideological division between the two states.

A number of states only survived as a result of powerful patronage by a neighbour. Their ultimate fate was thus bound up with that neighbour. Hence the ephemeral Slovak state of 1939–1945 was intimately related to that of its sponsor, Germany, in the course of the ensuing Second World War. The survival of an independent Croatia in the period 1941–1945 was similarly bound to an ultimate victory by Germany. Manchuria similarly was completely dependent upon Japanese support between 1933 and 1945. In this category might be placed internationally unrecognised states such as North Cyprus supported by Turkey since 1974 and the South African 'independent' homelands between 1976 and 1994, which were dependent entirely upon their single sponsors' willingness to back their proteges by force.

In some cases independent states were established purely as temporary buffers between powerful contenders, only to be reincorporated once the crisis had passed. The brief independence of the Far Eastern Republic situated between Russia and Japan between April 1920 and November 1922 was one such temporary solution for reducing the potential for international conflict. Similarly, the Soviet Republic of Gilan in northern Persia survived from June 1920 to October 1921 and was intended by its creators to be no more than a move in the international relations between the two countries, which when regularised led to the collapse of the state. Similar ephemeral states were established under Soviet patronage in northern Iran after the Second World War.

Some states survived for long periods of time before they were eliminated, others survived only a few days. Thus Carpetho-Ukraine, which declared its independence in March 1939 on the disintegration of Czechoslovakia, was occupied by Hungary after only one day. In contrast, Montenegro traced its history as an independent state back to the fourteenth century.

Numerous ephemeral states were declared during periods of civil war and international conflict. These generally did not receive widespread international recognition and thus usually only appear in the footnotes of history. However, some achieved long periods of independence. Tibet between 1912 and 1950 had effectively seceded from China and acted in most respects as an independent state. Biafra during the Nigerian civil war maintained its independence from 1967 to 1970 and achieved limited international recognition. Its protege, Benin, lasted one day (20 September 1967) and received no recognition.

Some of the ephemeral states emerged only once and disappeared completely thereafter, such as the German Democratic Republic. However, others reappeared as sub-national units of administration and so remain as incipient states. Tibet is probably the most distinctive such national entity. To this could be added such entities as Somaliland, Western Sahara, Xinjiang (Sinkiang), East Timor, Tuva and Zanzibar, which have the potential to achieve resurrection.

12.5 RECOGNISED STATES: THE HAGUE CONFERENCES

One of the significant attributes of a sovereign state has been its participation in international affairs, notably diplomatic gatherings designed to reach binding decisions and conventions for the conduct of international relations. In this respect the acknowl-

edgement of sovereign status by other countries became increasingly important in the course of the twentieth century. The various gatherings of state representatives prior to the twentieth century had usually been restricted to the European powers. Thus the Congress of Vienna and the subsequent Congress system was completely Eurocentric, as was the system which it represented. In terms of military power the European states remained supreme throughout the nineteenth century and it was they that were involved in the majority of international confrontations. However, the emergence of the United States and Japan from self-imposed isolation in the 1890s, and their pursuit of more aggressive foreign policies, altered the global situation.

The concept of a permanent international court or authority charged with the settlement of inter-state disputes has a long history. However, the unprecedented scale of the arms race which developed in the 1890s led to a greater appreciation among diplomats and politicians of the need to establish a mechanism to prevent minor incidents from developing into a major war (De Bustamante, 1925). Thus in 1899 a conference was organised to promote world peace, convened by Czar Nicholas II of Russia in the Dutch capital, The Hague. The first conference was attended by the representatives of only 26 countries, of which 20 were European, 4 Asian and 2 American. It might be noted that Bulgaria was represented, although nominally an Ottoman dependency. The final treaty established the Permanent Court of Arbitration for the settlement of international disputes. The Peace Palace in The Hague, built from funds contributed by Andrew Carnegie, the American steel magnate and philanthropist, remains as a permanent monument to this endeavour.

Between 1899 and 1907 there were several gatherings of the representatives of the powers to deal with global issues, notably those relating to the conduct of war (Malloy, 1910). The Hague Convention signed in December 1904 included a Korean representative, while the Geneva Convention of July 1906 was signed by the Japanese delegate on behalf of the Emperor of Korea. Similarly the 1906 Geneva Convention was signed by the Belgian delegate on behalf of the Sovereign of the Congo Free State, Leopold II of Belgium. The International Sanitary Convention of December 1903 and the agreements establishing the Institute of Agriculture in June 1905 and the International Office of Public Health in December 1908 included an Egyptian signatory, in the first instance with powers delegated by the Ottoman imperial government. The interpretation of a sovereign state therefore still possessed a degree of flexibility.

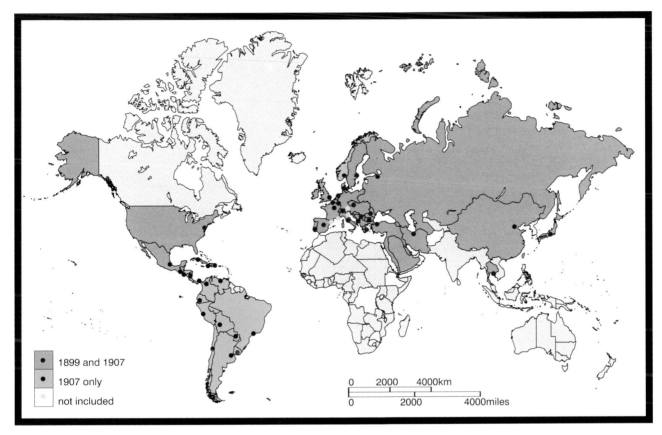

Map 12.5   Recognised states: The Hague conferences

The second Hague conference, which was concluded in October 1907, was far more universal in its conception, and attempted to embrace all the states of the world. The number of states represented increased to 44, including 21 states from Europe, 19 from the Americas, and 4 from Asia. The increased representation of the Americas, which brought a different and often the deciding point-of-view to the conference, is notable. Again Bulgaria participated as a full member. Korea was barred from the proceedings as no longer being a sovereign power. Among the European states, the mini-states (Andorra, Liechtenstein, Monaco, and San Marino) were again ignored, while Luxembourg and Montenegro were accorded the status of full states. The four independent African states were again conspicuous by their absence.

The later foundation and development of the Permanent Court of International Justice, at The Hague, was bound up with the Versailles treaty and the League of Nations, although membership was always wider than the membership of the latter body. After 1945 the Court was linked to the United Nations.

12.6   RECOGNISED STATES: LEAGUE OF NATIONS

The organisation of the world political system took a significant step forward after the First World War with the establishment of the League of Nations (Walters, 1952). The body was established under the terms of the Treaty of Versailles and its Council met for the first time in January 1920. The name is somewhat of a misnomer, as with its successor after the Second World War, the organisation linked governments not peoples. The objective was to provide a forum where threats to peace could be discussed and resolved without recourse to war. Most significantly the members of the League undertook to defend the independence and territorial integrity of its members. This binding commitment to the maintenance of the status quo offered little to those countries which sought to change the existing system. It was organised through an Assembly of all the members, and a Council of four or five permanent members and initially four others chosen from the

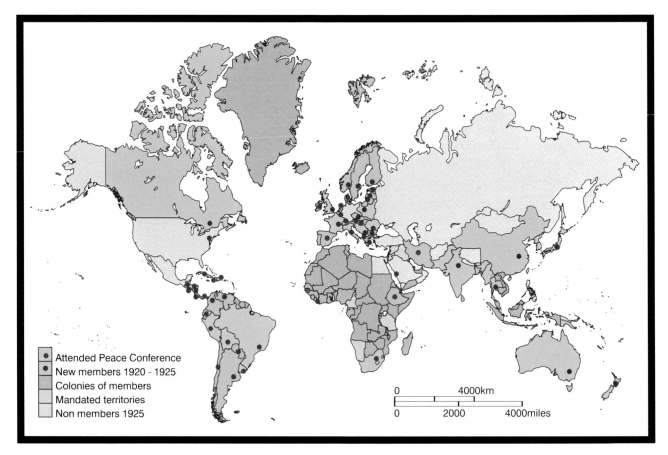

Map 12.6   Recognised states: League of Nations

remaining membership. Various technical bodies such as the International Labour Office and the Bank of International Settlements were also established to facilitate cooperation.

The League possessed administrative functions through the supervision of the colonial mandate system, the Free City of Danzig and the Saar Territory. In the former case the mandates for Iraq, Palestine and Syria were regarded as significant in recognising a group of communities 'which were so highly developed that their independence could be provisionally recognised, subject to a limited period of "administrative advice and assistance" until they were able to stand on their own feet' (Northedge, 1986: 64). The other mandated territories had no time limit placed on their period of supervision, but the administrative powers were subject to the oversight of the League's Mandates Commission in an effort to maintain good governance.

The four permanent Council members were Great Britain, France, Japan and Italy. The absence of the other great powers was to cripple many of the initiatives

contemplated by the organisation. The United States refused to join in March 1920, as membership would impose international obligations which an isolationist Senate was not willing to endorse. Russia and its successor the Soviet Union only joined in September 1934 but was to be expelled in December 1939 following its invasion of Finland. Germany was admitted in September 1926 and obtained a permanent seat on the Council, but withdrew in October 1933 as the new National Socialist government regarded the League as one of the primary instruments for the enforcement of the Treaty of Versailles. Japan withdrew in March 1933 after the League's criticism of its invasion of Manchuria. Italy similarly withdrew in December 1937 after the condemnation of its invasion of Ethiopia.

The remainder of the membership fluctuated. Brazil withdrew in June 1926 as it rejected its reduction to second-class status after the expiry of its term as a member of the Council. Costa Rica withdrew in January 1925 as the financial burdens of membership were regarded as too high and the League's interpretation of the Monroe Doctrine was considered to infringe the country's sovereign rights. The losses, notably in the 1930s, reflected the rise of Fascist governments in Latin America, which withdrew in support of their mentors. To counter this exodus others joined, notably Mexico in September 1931, Turkey in July 1932 and both Ecuador and Afghanistan in September 1934.

At one stage or another most of the states of the world, with the exception of the United States, were admitted to membership. The acceptance or rejection of applications for membership were significant and reflected differing definitions of a state. In 1920 the League was confronted with a substantial number of applications and potential applications. Some states such as Azerbaijan and the Ukraine were rejected as having lost their independence and being no more than extensions of Soviet Russia. States such as Khiva and Bokhara would have been rejected in similar terms. Although Armenia and Georgia took part in the Paris deliberations, they too had been occupied by Soviet and Turkish forces before they could be admitted to membership. Montenegro similarly was rejected as having been incorporated into Yugoslavia. Liechtenstein applied for membership in July 1920, but was also rejected as 'it could not discharge all the international obligations which would be imposed upon her by the Covenant' (Duursma, 1996: 171). More particularly the lack of an army was deemed to reduce its status, as did its dependency in matters of posts, customs, diplomatic relations and the judiciary.

In another respect membership was wider than the pool of recognised sovereign states. Four of the British dominions and the Indian Empire were admitted to membership in 1920, although the British government initially signed international treaties on their behalf. The Irish Free State joined in 1922. The constitutional reality of the position, for all but India, was attained in 1931 with the Statute of Westminster. None of the other empires were able to include their nominal dependencies in the membership; thus Iceland did not gain membership but remained diplomatically attached to Denmark.

Subsequent additions to the membership encountered the same problems of definition. Hejez, although a signatory of the peace settlement in 1919, did not pursue its membership and neither did its successor, Saudi Arabia, as no tangible advantages were to be gained. Ethiopia was only admitted once it had given specific undertakings to suppress slavery, indicating an inferior status. Egypt only gained admission in May 1937 after the conclusion of the Anglo-Egyptian Treaty, which granted the country control over the conduct of its foreign affairs. The admission of Mongolia and Tibet encountered Chinese opposition, which

claimed them as integral parts of its own territory. Independent states such as Oman, Nepal and Bhutan did not apply as their foreign relations were effectively controlled by Great Britain. The international definition of a state as adopted by the League of Nations was therefore both rather more restrictive and expansive than the nominal reality of accepted sovereignty.

12.7 RECOGNISED STATES: UNITED NATIONS

The founders of the United Nations in October 1945 intended the organisation to be far more inclusive and unified in purpose than the previous League of Nations. All the Allied powers were included and indeed membership was offered as a reward to countries which joined the Allied powers late in the war. Thereafter approval of admission to membership was often used as a political weapon in the early years of the Cold War. Thus the two German states were only admitted in September 1973 following an easing in Soviet–American relations. The admission of the two Korean states in September 1991 symbolically marked the end of one of the last legacies of the Cold War exclusion policies. On the other hand, the admission of the two Chinese states has been defeated as their constitutional positions are mutually exclusive and consequently only one has been a member at a given time (Nationalist 1945–1971 and Communist since 1971). The General Assembly was composed of all the members, while the Security Council was composed of the five great powers (United States, Soviet Union, China, Great Britain and France) as permanent members and a varying number of others filled by regional elections.

Membership initially was similar to that of the League of Nations. India, although still nominally a British dependency, obtained admission, while the Ukraine and Byelorussia secured independent seats, although then constituent republics of the Soviet Union. The European mini-states were not invited to join for the same reasons as in 1920. Although a few new members such as Pakistan (September 1947), Burma (April 1948) and Israel (May 1949) were subsequently allowed to join, deadlock between the two global power blocks ensued. It was only in December 1955 that a group of Communist countries were admitted in return for the admission of a group of non-Communist states. A similar reciprocal agreement in October 1961 resulted in the admission of Mongolia and Mauritania. The independence of Mongolia had been disputed by China and that of Mauritania by Morocco.

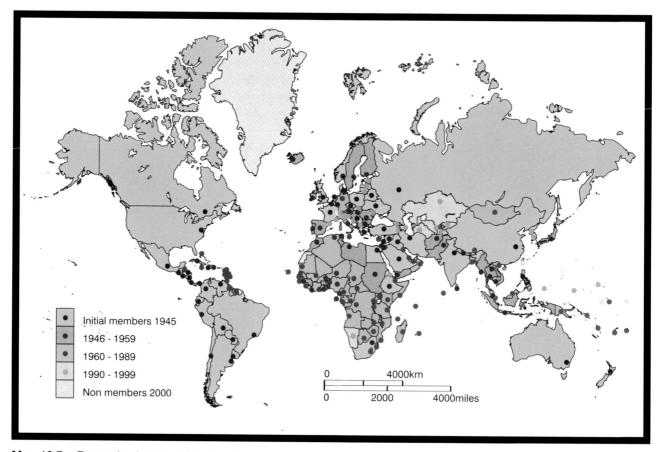

Map 12.7   Recognised states: United Nations

However, with the passing of time, most noticeably with the independence of some 69 predominantly African and Caribbean countries in the 1960s and 1970s, the question of universal inclusivity was raised once more. Thus Liechtenstein was admitted in September 1990 and Monaco in 1993. With the exception of Switzerland and the Vatican City, both concerned with possibly compromising their neutrality, those states still outside the United Nations were the very small micro-states, which were unable to afford even the nominal dues of membership (Kiribati, Nauru, Tonga and Tuvalu). This did not preclude some of the very small states from obtaining membership, notably Palau with a population of only 17 000 inhabitants at the time of admission in December 1994.

The United Nations, as the League of Nations before it, operated as a major support structure for the state system. Once substantial numbers of quasi-states, with limited resources to claim statehood, were admitted, then the United Nations became an essential component of the structure underpinning their survival. International aid and technical support organisations, ranging from the Food and Agriculture Organisation to the World Health Organisation, assisted the new states to overcome their numerous developmental problems, while the political sector guaranteed their independence, and most noticeably, their territorial integrity. In this respect the organisation was highly conservative in attempting to prevent further change in the state system, by fossilising the post-independence status quo. The United Nations' support for self-determination was thus limited to peoples struggling to achieve independence from colonial control, not from subsequent domination.

At times the international community withheld recognition of states to demonstrate its condemnation of their policies, creating a set of isolated or pariah states (Geldenhuys, 1990). Israel, South Africa and Taiwan were subject to this ultimate sanction of non-recognition and indeed the recognition of movements planning the overthrow of the existing governments.

12.8 RECOGNISED STATES: NON-GOVERNMENTAL ORGANISATIONS (NATIONAL OLYMPIC COMMITTEES)

Nations or groups of people often operate at levels other than governmental. International non-governmental organisations can have memberships which reflect other quasi-national groupings, rather than the formally recognised states. This is particularly true of that most independent, yet emotional, sector of civil society, namely sport. Thus the International Federation of Football Associations (FIFA), formed in May 1904, admitted to membership the four separate English, Welsh, Scottish and Irish associations, rather than a single British association. Within the International Cricket Council (originally the Imperial Cricket Conference), the West Indies was admitted in May 1926 as a single 'national' entity, linking all the English-speaking states and dependent territories in the Caribbean region into a single team. For the administration of baseball, Canadian teams operate within the American framework and play for the World Cup. In this manner sports teams may indicate public emotional acceptance of broader groupings or indeed of more restrictive separate nationhoods independent of the state pattern.

Possibly the most influential and universal of the sporting bodies is the Olympic movement. Baron Pierre de Coubertin revived the Olympic movement with the formation of the International Olympic Committee in Paris in 1894. The Committee sought to link the countries of the world together through the promotion of a 'peace through sport' programme, with regular quadrennial games, beginning with the First Olympiad in Athens in 1896. The scale of the games has changed dramatically in the course of the twentieth century. The Second Olympiad in Paris in 1900 attracted 1078 competitors from 19 countries, while the Eleventh Olympiad in Berlin in 1936 was attended by 3936 athletes from 49 countries. In 1996 the Twenty-sixth Olympiad in Atlanta in the United States attracted 10 332 competitors from 197 countries.

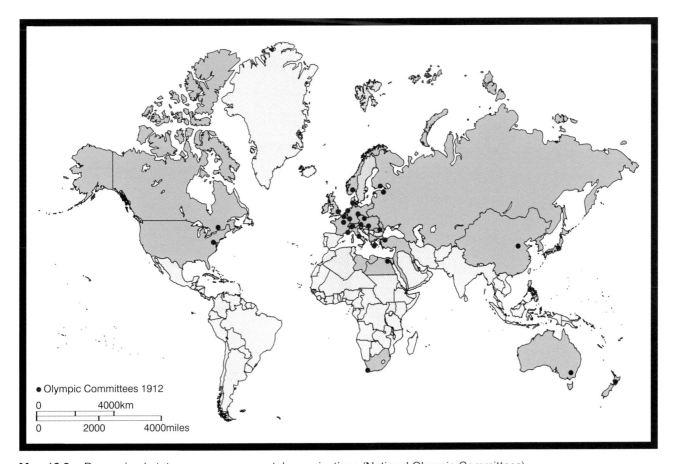

Map 12.8   Recognised states: non-governmental organisations (National Olympic Committees)

Since the inception of the games, the organisers have been confronted with the problem of drawing up the invitation list. National Olympic committees have been formed for political entities which did not enjoy internationally recognised sovereignty. Representatives from Hungary and Bohemia were present at the foundation of the International Olympic Committee. In subsequent games before the First World War competitors from non-sovereign counties such as Finland and Iceland won gold medals. As a means of overcoming political sensitivities, the International Olympic Committee recognised that the Czar of All the Russias was also the Grand Duke of Finland, in the same manner that the Emperor of Austria was also King of Bohemia and King of Hungary (Henry, 1976). The British Empire was similarly fragmented from the first, with South Africa represented before the formation of the Union in 1910. Yet the United Kingdom fielded a single British team, although at the Fourth Olympiad in London in 1908 an English team played an Irish team in the finals of the field hockey. Individual colonies and territories formed their own Olympic committees and participated independently in the games. Thus of the 28 national Olympic committees represented at the Fifth Olympiad in Stockholm in 1912, ten represented nations which were not fully independent.

After the First World War the political element in international competition became ever stronger, despite the strenuous attempts of the International Olympic Committee to keep political interference out of the conduct of sport. Thus the Russians withdrew altogether after the revolution and established a rival 'Red Sport International' in 1921, but this organisation achieved little in the international field. Only in 1952 did the Soviet Union begin to participate in the Olympic Games. The problems created by the divided states of China, Germany and Korea exercised the attention of the organisers from 1945 onwards, as both unified and separate team solutions were adopted (Espy, 1979). The concept of geographical areas rather than nations was introduced to satisfy over-sensitive politicians. The recognition of two Chinese entities for the Sixteenth Olympiad in 1956 in Melbourne was a significant breakthrough in negotiations, emulated by the representation of two Germanies at the Nineteenth Olympiad in 1968 in Mexico City.

International conflict became particularly significant in the 1960s as the pariah states of Israel, Rhodesia and South Africa were boycotted by the Afro-Asian countries in all fields of endeavour, including sport. The Games of the New Emerging Forces (GANEFO) was held in November 1963 as a challenge to the International Olympic Committee, but

again it had no long-term effect. Recognition of the Rhodesian national Olympic committee was withdrawn after the country's unilateral declaration of independence in 1965. Similarly, South Africa was barred from the games due to its apartheid policies. Mass, politically motivated, boycotts of the 1976 games in Montreal and the 1980 games in Moscow further complicated the subject. However, by 1984 at the Twenty-third Olympiad in Los Angeles the games returned to the universal meeting intended by its founders. In 1992 at Barcelona 12 of the ex-members of the Soviet Union participated as the 'Unified Team' but at Atlanta in 1996 they appeared as separate national teams.

Once again the structure of the international state system has been modified by international non-governmental organisations, which sought to operate within a more realistic division of the world's population. In some respects the formation of separate national Olympic committees has been a precursor, or pointer, to the future, as sport has reflected national aspirations. Accordingly the recognition of the Palestinian committee is an indicator of that nation's status.

12.9   MILITARY OCCUPATION STATUS

One of the most severe restrictions that can be placed upon sovereign statehood is military occupation by the forces of another state upon defeat in war or intervention to overthrow a government. However, in the majority of cases, troops of one country are stationed in another as a result of the invitation of the host in terms of a treaty of alliance. The American bases which have existed in Great Britain since January 1942 are one such long-term example. One of the essential aspects of such a mutually beneficial arrangement is that the forces stationed in the host country do not interfere in its internal affairs. Usually such forces are withdrawn on the request of the host. Thus American forces withdrew from France in March 1966 when that country withdrew from the integrated North Atlantic Treaty Organisation command structures and requested American withdrawal. Soviet forces similarly withdrew from Romania in 1964 at the government's request.

Powerful countries have occupied portions of territory deemed to have some military significance, usually in a strategic location. Before the First World War such areas were generally annexed and incorporated into the colonial empires. It is notable that the Panama Canal Zone established early in the century had been subject to formal administration by the American government as a separate

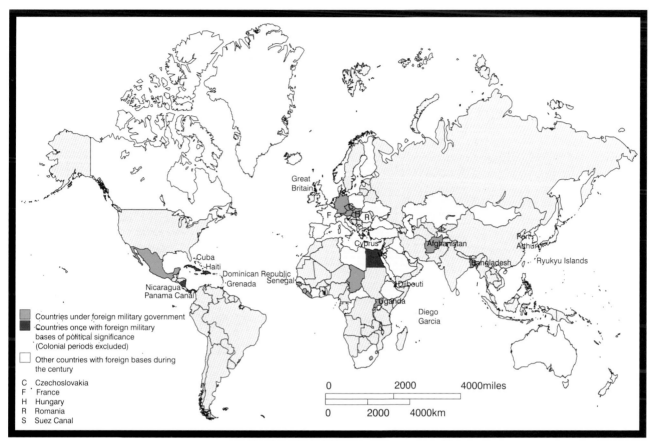

Map 12.9 Military occupation status

colonial entity. To this could be added such strategic territories as Port Arthur, possession of which was viewed by both Russia and Japan as essential to the maintenance of their influence in north-eastern China. However, in the post-First World War era such a course of action was no longer regarded as morally acceptable and less formal military occupation regimes took their place. Thus the Suez Canal Zone, where British forces were based after Egyptian independence in 1922 until 1954, is one of the most notable post-colonial examples. After the Second World War such action was even more limited. However, the Ryukuyu Islands, with the strategic Okinawa base, were detached from Japan in 1945 and remained under American military administration until May 1972. The British Indian Ocean Territory was detached from Mauritius in 1965 in order to secure the military installations on the island of Diego Garcia. A reversionary clause provided for its return when the facilities were no longer necessary for British security. The British 'sovereign bases' on Cyprus, retained at independence in 1960, were of a similar nature.

Military occupation has frequently been used to establish control of entire states, which the occupying power had no desire to annex. The United States in the period up to 1934 extended its control over several Central American states, or intervened directly in their politics by military means, yet did not seek to incorporate additional territory. Nicaragua was occupied by American marines in August 1912 and they stayed until January 1933. During that time the Americans controlled the customs administration, railways, national bank and established a National Guard under American officers. The country became a protectorate in all but name. In the First World War the Marines occupied Haiti between July 1915 and 1934 and the Dominican Republic between November 1916 and September 1924 in order to secure the approaches to the Panama Canal. American military intervention in the Mexican civil war between March 1916 and February 1917 ensured the success of a pro-American president in the face of German diplomacy. Short-term American interventions in the region have continued throughout the century, culminating in Grenada and Haiti.

Military intervention in the twentieth century has been used as an instrument of foreign policy following the end of formal empire. French military forces intervened frequently after 1960 in its former colonies in Africa, in order to secure friendly governments and maintain the status quo. The scale and frequency of such interventions had by the time of the Rwandan genocide of mid-1994 caused the policy to be questioned domestically and subsequent troop withdrawals reduced the French military presence to a small number of key countries, notably Djibouti and Senegal. In contrast, Great Britain and Portugal generally withdrew their forces at independence and resisted any temptation to intervene thereafter.

Military intervention was frequently designed to install client governments in the Cold War, as the example of the Russian intervention in Hungary in 1956 and Czechoslovakia in 1968 demonstrate. In these cases the overthrow of one government and its replacement by another was the desired result of the occupying power. This led to the establishment of a satellite state, which operated many internal and external policies as an effective dependency of the occupier. On rare occasions the installation of a satellite government has been no more than a technical means of legitimising the subsequent incorporation of the country into that of the aggressor. The German occupation of Austria in 1938 and Iraqi occupation of Kuwait in 1990 were two of the more infamous uses of such an approach.

The most extreme form of occupation has been the imposition of a military administration, where the country is run by and for the benefit of the occupying army. This was usually associated with the First and Second World Wars, where countries were conquered, and local governments were not reconstituted pending the conclusion of hostilities. Thus most of Belgium and northern France were administered by the German army for the duration of the First World War, and exploited for the propagation of the war effort. The same was true of the extensive areas conquered by Germany in eastern Europe in both world wars. Military administrations were introduced to the Italian colonies during the Second World War. The complete collapse of the civil government in Germany and Austria at the end of the Second World War resulted in the imposition of Allied military government. Civilian administration was subsequently resumed, but it was only in the 1950s that recognisably independent governments were established. In Germany the occupation forces

remained behind as part of military alliances, while in Austria all foreign forces withdrew.

On occasion military occupation was designed to guarantee rights or interests in only portions of a country. Thus Soviet troops occupied key positions in Sinkiang, Chinese Turkestan, before 1949 to guarantee its interests in that part of the country, but not the remainder of China. Secessionism was thus encouraged, but ultimately abandoned when a pro-Soviet regime was established throughout China (Hasiotis, 1987). The state of Israel has occupied portions of all its neighbours in the course of its history in order to secure its borders, leaving a remarkably complex heritage of conflict.

12.10   ETHNIC DIVERSITY: SWITZERLAND

One of the major problems faced by governments in the twentieth century was the accommodation of ethnic diversity within a single state structure. All states included people who were not completely assimilated into the mainstream of national identity, whether expressed in terms of language, culture, religion or some other significant attribute. The official response to the challenge of incorporating diversity has been highly problematic. Attempted solutions aimed at the maintenance of the nation-state have ranged from government sponsored genocide and the expulsion of the minorities, to state partition and fragmentation. In order to counter such trends, the processes of economic assimilation and constitutional autonomy have frequently ensured at least the acquiescence and frequently the active support of virtually the entire population for the state's continued survival.

Switzerland is often held up as the prime example of accommodating linguistic and religious diversity within one state through the constitutional mechanism of promoting local autonomy. The struggle for independence in medieval times was essentially waged at local cantonal level and each canton preserved most of the attributes of an independent state upon gaining admission to the Confederation. The title 'Swiss Confederation' is now a misnomer, as the right to secede was repudiated in 1846 as an outcome of the civil war. However, the new 1848 constitution confirmed the federal character of the state and established German, French and Italian as the official languages. Romansch was added as a fourth in 1938. The cantons enjoy a high degree of autonomy, with only limited functions assigned to the central government. The frequent employment of referenda to settle most important and sometimes minor issues provides for a significant measure

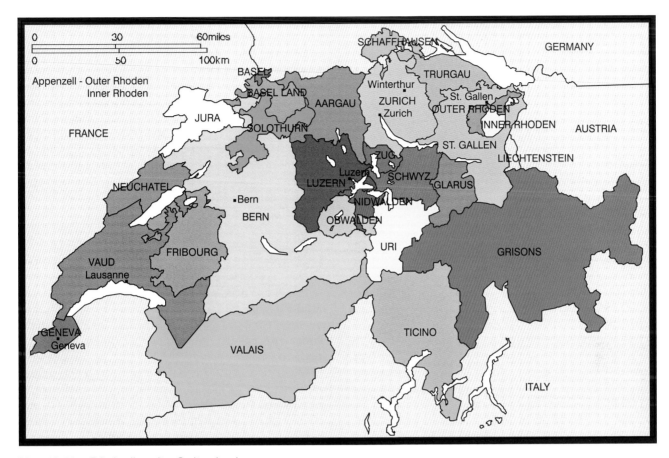

Map 12.10 Ethnic diversity: Switzerland

of direct participation in decision making by the citizenry at both local and national level. The national government's role is therefore highly circumscribed and the conduct of politics has traditionally been viewed in local terms.

The country is divided into twenty cantons and six half cantons. They vary substantially in size and population. Even in 1992, nine cantons recorded populations of under 100 000 and only two (Zurich and Bern) over one million. In terms of linguistic composition, at mid-century, 72.1 percent of the population was German-speaking, 20.3 percent French-speaking, 5.9 percent Italian-speaking and 1.1 percent spoke Romansch. The population was also split on confessional lines between 56 percent espousing Protestant churches and 42 percent Roman Catholic. Subsequent immigration and differential growth rates has tended to change the proportions in favour of Italians and Roman Catholics, while a significant number recorded other languages and no religion. The linguistic and confessional divides do not correspond, thereby preventing the consolidation of compact mutually antagonistic blocks.

However, it is notable that the cantons specify their official languages and that in 1970 some 96 percent of German speakers lived in the German cantons, 92 percent of French speakers in French cantons and 79 percent of Italian speakers in the Italian region. Permanent migration outside the linguistic heartlands was thus rare and difficult (Laitin, 1992).

Despite its antiquity, the cantonal structure proved to be remarkably flexible in the twentieth century. In the 1970s secessionist agitation by the French-speaking population in the northern section of the predominantly German-speaking canton of Bern reached significant levels. As a result of lengthy negotiations and comprehensive tests of public opinion, the new canton of Jura was approved in September 1978. It was the first new canton to gain admission to the Confederation since its reconstitution in 1815. It is noteworthy that at no stage did the campaign for a separate Jura canton become an irredentist movement to join France, as the Swiss ethos of the movement was paramount (Jenkins, 1986). It was this element of the recognition of an over-riding Swiss citizenship, based upon a common historic experience within a stable local homeland, that bound people of diverse backgrounds together and provided one of the complex solutions to the survival of the multi-ethnic state.

12.11   THE MELTING POT: THE UNITED STATES

An alternative approach to the unification of a multi-ethnic state was adopted by the United States. Local particularism is present in the historic experience and the struggle for independence, paralleling that of Switzerland. Yet the basic ethos of the Founding Fathers of the republic was essentially White Anglo-Saxon Protestant (WASP), as befitted their ethnic origins and that of the dominant group of European settlers. Indeed under the Naturalization Act of 1790 only White immigrants could be granted American citizenship, a restriction which remained in force for 162 years.

Subsequent immigrants have had to adjust to the modified heritage of this dominant ethos, which until recently included the powerful influence of compulsory schooling through the medium of the English language. Acculturation, however, was a two-way enterprise. The successive waves of immigrants in the nineteenth century from first northern Europe, then southern and eastern Europe produced an American culture which was no longer a copy of that of the British Isles. The Wasps remained a highly influential group within American society, but others increasingly shared power and economic prosperity. In the twentieth century immigrant groups from Latin America and Asia have further diversified the ethnic origins of the population (Glazer and Moynihan, 1963).

The theory of 'the melting pot' was applied to the development of the American nation from the disparate immigrant peoples who have flocked to the country (Ward, 1989). The poem by Emma Lazarus, 'The New Colossus', inscribed at the base of the Statue of Liberty presents the aspiration of this bold exercise in nation formation:

Give me your tired, your poor,
Your huddled masses yearning to breathe free,
The wretched refuse of your teeming shore.
Send these, the homeless, the tempest-toss'd to me.
I left my lamp beside the golden door.

(Johnson, 1997: 480)

The ideals so movingly expressed appeared to be capable of fulfilment in the creation of a new American society, which defined the nation. The regional distribution of the various immigrant groups provided no pattern for the identification of historic homelands (Allen and Turner, 1988). Indeed the proverbial mobility of the American population precluded regionalism being converted into the potential for political secessionism. Segregationism was transferred to the individual cities which experienced high degrees of segregation but the pattern was reproduced throughout the country (Frey and Farley, 1996). Later modifications of the melting pot theory suggesting the survival of several mutually exclusive components did not materially alter the basic outcome (Takaki, 1993).

The three outstanding exceptions to the general idea of assimilation into a single culture were the descendants of the African slaves, the Spanish-speaking population of the South-west, and the indigenous Indian population (see Section 2.20). In the case of the African-Americans, political separatism offered no solution to the problems of discrimination and poverty. As a group, by the middle of the twentieth century they had become too thinly spread across the country to achieve anything but highly localised majority areas, which could be used to gain representation in Congress (Webster, 1993). Integration into American society as promoted by the Civil Rights movement offered the way to economic and social advancement, within the wider American context. However, the integration of the African-American population did not come and multi-culturalism was adopted as a means of reconciling this failure. As Nathan Glazer (1997: 120) expressed the dilemmas: 'whatever the causes, the apartness of blacks is real. And it is this that feeds multiculturalism. For this one group, assimilation by some key measures has certainly failed.'

The more geographically concentrated Spanish-speaking population possessed an historic territorial base in the lands which had belonged to Spain and Mexico until the 1830s. However, as in the case of the Spanish-speaking population of New Mexico, later immigrants effectively fragmented the homeland (Nostrand, 1992). More recent immigration from Mexico, however, offers the prospect of Spanish-speaking majorities in some of the south-western states in the twenty-first century, when the state raison d'etre may be severely tested.

African-American ethnic pride was revived through the television screening of Roots, written by Alex Haley (1976), which provided an identifiable group history. Others were to follow. The French-speaking population of Louisiana has been subject to a re-invention even 'forging' of a regional identity as part of the rise in ethnic awareness (Trepanier, 1991). Regionalism, even powerfully promoted distinctive

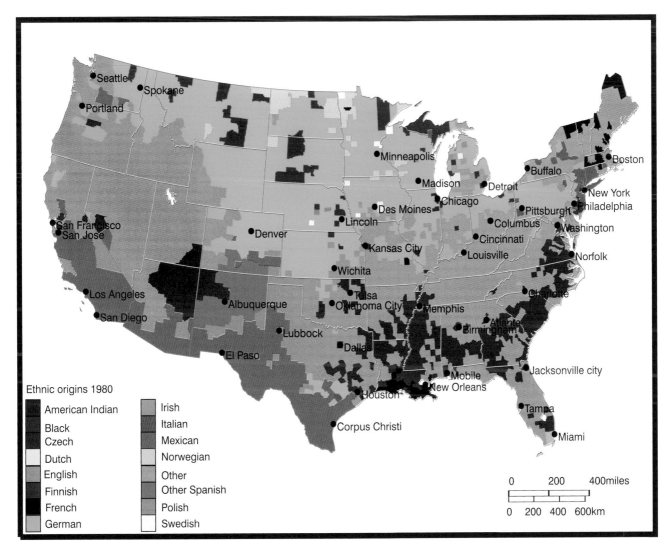

Map 12.11   The melting pot: United States

state identities such as that of Texas, presents no threat to the continuation of the Union (Meinig, 1976).

The American experience had a profound effect upon American official attitudes to the nationhood of others, which because of the diplomatic and military importance of the United States has impacted dramatically upon world politics. There is a significant truism that the American state essentially created the nation from diverse origins. If this could be done in the New World, why should it not be done in the Old World? To confirm the favourable American view of the universality of the legally defined nation, the experience of most of the Latin American countries appeared to parallel that of the United States. The attachment of societies living in historic homelands to those

homelands, and often hostility to outsiders, appeared remarkably antiquated and even abhorrent to American politicians, who worked and lived with other Americans of diverse ethnic backgrounds. Thus by the 1960s there was a general consensus that state structures should be preserved even where historic groups were intent upon slaughtering one another. The American intervention in Bosnia-Herzegovina in 1995 demonstrated the government's desire to preserve the territorial integrity of the state and with it the legally defined nation, against the spectre of the ethnically defined nations, intent upon separation. Thus the American approach to statehood and nationhood was offered as the universal panacea to the solution of the problems of the multi-ethnic state.

12.12 'CIVILISATIONS'

The case has been persuasively argued by Samuel Huntington (1996) that just as the rise of nationalism dominated the politics of the pre-1914 era, and the conflict of ideologies between 1917 and 1991, so the immediate post-Cold War era has been dominated by 'the clash of civilisations'. Such a conclusion was derived from an examination of the intermediate scale of organisational unit, between the bipolar world of the Cold War and its highly fragmented multi-national successor. The existence of a set of historic 'civilisations', which have survived the rise and fall of individual states and empires, appeared to offer such a scale (Braudel, 1994; Wallerstein, 1991). It has further been suggested that the political and economic dominance of 'the West', in the 'New World Order', which was anticipated after the fall of the Berlin Wall, has not been sustainable. Even the outward trappings of American hegemony may similarly be fleeting (Taylor, 1996). The alternative has been the identification of regional blocks united on the basis of common cultures, although internally divided into sovereign states. Such an approach also represents an equally significant break with the frequently projected Western–Oriental dichotomy inherited from the colonial period (Said, 1994).

The number of civilisations is open to dispute, but allowing for the anticipated success of the projected 'African Renaissance', there are nine recognisable civilisations, of sufficient size to warrant inclusion, which are in existence at the beginning of the new millennium. They are Western Christian, with its distinctive offshoot Latin America, Eastern Orthodox Christian, Islamic, Hindu, Buddhist, Confucian, Japanese, and African. Each of these possesses a set of distinctive traits derived from its historic experience, and particularly from its religious ethic and organisational character. It has been observed that cooperation between states within such groupings is easier than between states in different civilisations, because of shared ideas and methods of working; they therefore offer the basis for broad multi-state unification programmes, such as the European Union.

It was these civilisations which formed the basis of most of the loosely connected separate world systems of the pre-1500 era (Abu-Lughod, 1989). In the main they were dominated by a core state, which usually claimed 'universal' status. Thus China represented the core of a Confucian realm, which extended over several of its tributary states. After the fall of the Byzantine Empire, Russia formed the core of the Orthodox Christian realm,

rendering assistance to co-religionists both before 1917 and since 1991. However, following the collapse of the Ottoman Empire, there was no core state in the Islamic realm, although there are several contenders for the position. Most significantly the Western Christian realm did not have a core state after the Reformation in the sixteenth century and the contention for supremacy contributed to the constant technological and economic change of the era (Landes, 1998). Again, several states laid claim to hegemony and after 1945 the United States was effectively the core state in political and economic terms.

It is further postulated that conflict is more likely between states or sub-sections of states belonging to differing civilisations, where the opportunities for misunderstanding are consequently greater (Black, 1998). The cultural and religious cleavages between civilisations tend to exacerbate national conflicts, making multi-civilisational states particularly difficult to sustain. The tripartite, three civilisational, conflict of 1992–1995 in Bosnia-Herzegovina is a particularly stark example, with echoes of earlier ages of inter-civilisational conflict in the Mediterranean region (Braudel, 1976). Furthermore, greater media attention is given to such conflicts than those within a single civilisation (Myers, Klak and Koehl, 1996). In the study of conflict it is possible to overlook the achievements of those multi-civilisational states, such as Thailand, which have retained internal stability through the accommodation of significant minorities (Forbes, 1982).

With the relative decline of the West and the revival of other civilisations, which were subject to severe repression by the West in its period of global ascendancy, realignment and conflict are inevitable. The reassertion of submerged national and civilisational identities, whether Chechen, reinforced by Islam, Southern Sudanese identified as African, or Tamils in Sri Lanka claiming their Hindu heritage, has become a central factor in the post-Cold War redrawing of the world map, as it was beforehand. In the 1980s and 1990s it was Islam which had provided the most powerful civilisational support to the national revival of those peoples conquered by the West over the previous 500 years. The Islamic realm therefore exhibits the most noticeable ring of conflict around its periphery. However, in view of the territorially expansive nature of the West until the twentieth century, it is possibly the continuing deflation of this realm that may offer an equally unstable set of disputed borderlands.

Differential population growth rates between the different civilisations in the post-Cold War era have tended to emphasise the decline of the West, and indeed of the Eastern Orthodox region. Rapid population increases in

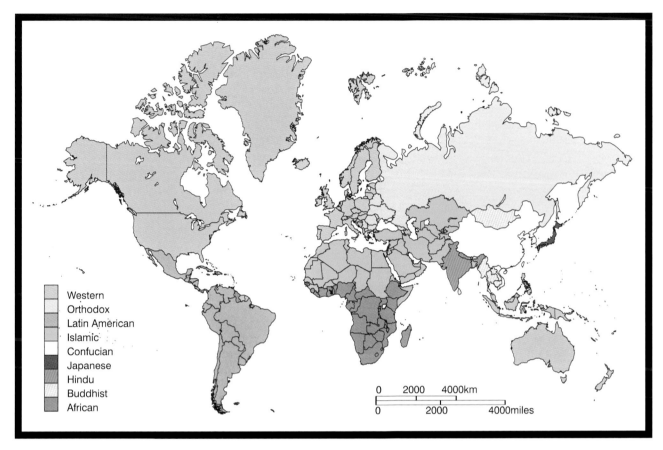

Map 12.12   'Civilisations'

Latin America and the Islamic world have changed the balance in significant areas of the world. Thus population projections indicating Mexican majorities in some of the south-western states of the United States by the year 2025, and the reversal in the numerical balance between Jews and Moslems in Israel–Palestine are but two of the demographic equations which have the potential to destabilise the map of the world. However, this is not to say that all multi-civilisational states have no chance of survival. Tolerance is possible as governments, such as those in India, seek to preserve the state's secular identities, but the opportunities to mobilise the cultural strength of the Hindu civilisation in support of the state are considerable.

The revival of the recognition of the significance of the broad civilisations in the forging of group identities offers a warning to the universal acceptance of the Western legalistic definition of the nation and the state. It also offers a reminder that many nations owe their origins to cultural and emotional factors, rather than the coercion of the state, and that the state is therefore the reflection of the nation,

rather than the other way around. Although questions of ideology dominated much of the political debate in the twentieth century, nations and civilisations formed the basis of an alternative, and once more, dominant discourse.

12.13   POTENTIAL STATES

At the beginning of the new millennium there is understandable speculation over what the future has to offer. This survey of the development of the pattern of states in the twentieth century offers some pointers in that direction. Futurology, in contrast to speculation over alternative outcomes of events, is remarkably dangerous (Ferguson, 1998). Predictions about the future political order have been significantly inaccurate. Siegfried Passarge, for example, accurately predicted two world wars in the twentieth century, but inaccurately that they were both won by Germany. The resultant world which was expected to emerge thus looked very different from the reality of 1945 (Sandner, 1989). Adolf Hitler's predictions of the Thousand Year Reich in Nazi Germany were obviously far too long-term as well as over-optimistic for a state which lasted little more than 12 years.

Even in the realms of well researched space fiction, the political element has been remarkably inaccurate. Thus in *2010: Space Odyssey Two* written in 1983, the author, Arthur Clarke, assumed that the Soviet Union would last well into the new millennium, although the picture he painted of space travel was far closer to reality. Similarly works such as *Amerika* by Brauna Pouns (1987) even postulated a Soviet victory in the Cold War and the territorial fragmentation of the United States. Jacques Neiryck (1996), in *The Siege of Brussels*, presented a picture of Flemish nationalism violently tearing apart the fabric of the Belgian and European Union in the early twenty-first century, and offered an alternative view to that of national cooperation and European political integration presented by the European Commission.

It would be most foolish to predict the fate of individual states. The major changes to the map of the world in the twentieth century were the outcomes of the two world wars and the Cold War. Conflict on this global scale does not appear to be imminent in the same way that leaders feared the arms race of the early twentieth century. Whether this results in world-wide peace and minimal political change is possible, although probably unlikely. The processes of regional and global integration will continue, while ethnic separatism will pull in the opposite direction. The possibilities of state fragmentation and supra-national coordination appear to parallel one another. Thus a strengthened European Union accompanied by an independent Scotland and independent Catalonia would not appear incompatible outcomes. Even Padania (Northern Italy) has been suggested as an independent state (Eva, 1997). Defining 'the state' would thus become the more difficult.

The supra-national federation or confederation is a paradoxical outcome for an era which witnessed the disintegration of many attempts to integrate wider political structures, whether the continental scale Soviet Union, or the inter-continental British Empire. The European Union is furthest in the quest for unification. Whether this will be the loose federal construct as a union of sovereign states, as envisaged by General Charles de Gaulle, or the closer political union subsequently envisaged by Chancellor Helmut Kohl, remains open to question. The political leaders of no other regional grouping appear ready to undertake such a significant surrender of state sovereignty to a supra-national body. Elsewhere economic policy making may be

surrendered but political identity remains, whether in the North American Trade Agreement, or the Association of South East Asian Nations. Fear of domination by the most powerful regional countries, Nigeria and South Africa, preclude the political integration of the Economic Community of West African States and the Southern African Development Community respectively. Political unity of the Arab world equally appears unlikely in view of the diversity of state interests within the Arab League.

The propensity towards fragmentation would therefore appear to be the main area of attention for changes in the pattern of states. The final stages of decolonisation will result in the emergence of several quasi-states, linked to the former imperial power for support. Thus some of the remaining West Indian and Pacific island colonies are likely to achieve independence at an opportune time. Certain of the self-governing dependencies such as Puerto Rico, Bermuda, Aruba, Curaçao, New Caledonia, Polynesia and possibly Guadeloupe, Martinique, and Cayenne (French Guiana) can be expected to opt for independence. In February 1991 the Danish government indicated that Greenland could gain independence if the electorate so wished. The peculiar constitutional problems of Gibraltar, the Faroe Islands, Jersey and Guernsey may also be overcome and accommodated within the structures of the European Union. Other colonies, such as Montserrat, Pitcairn Islands and St Helena, will in all probability remain too small for separate statehood and constitutional arrangements to accommodate them within the democratic framework of the imperial power will become all the more necessary.

However, the greatest propensities towards fragmentation lie within existing 'nation-states'. Federal state structures designed to accommodate ethnic diversity may be insufficient to hold the state together. The future shape of the Russian Federation is highly dependent upon the quality of the political leadership of the country. The recognition of the independence of Chechnya in 2001 would open up the possibilities for the independence of other republics. The resurrection of Tuva is thus not impossible. In most cases the permanent presence of a dominant Russian population is likely to prevent widespread secessionism. On a smaller scale the federal kingdom of Belgium with some 10 million inhabitants is politically fragile and open to partition. On an even smaller scale, the Comoro Islands state appears liable to complete disintegration with separate statehood for the four individual islands.

Self-determination in the form of secession, however, opens up the question of the viability and persistence of the nation-state. Indeed it is one of the

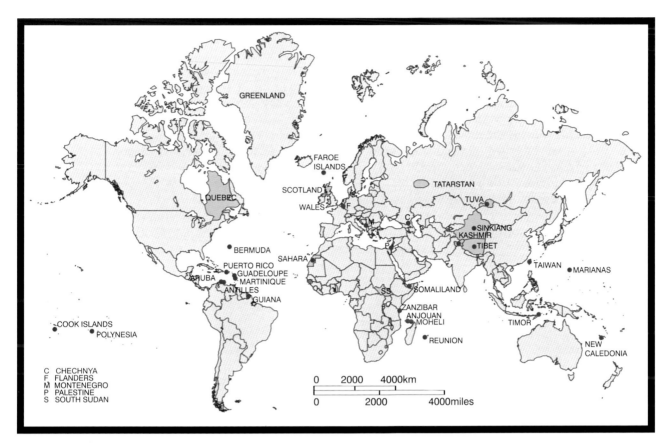

Map 12.13   Potential states

few areas where questions of state morality are raised, reflecting the American historical experience of the nineteenth century civil war (Buchanan, 1992). In contrast, self-determination as decolonisation was viewed in Western, American, terms as highly desirable (Louis, 1978). However, minority groups were expected to seek accommodation within the existing states and not venture over the fine line between demands for autonomy as opposed to independence in the new millennium (Mikesell and Murphy, 1991). In view of the wide range of groups seeking autonomy, the line may require careful consideration and a change from coercion to participation in the response to autonomist demands (Orridge and Williams, 1982). The independence movements in Tibet and Sinkiang (Xinjiang) can expect to achieve little beyond the implementation of programmes of cultural autonomy by the Chinese government. In contrast, an elected separatist Scottish nationalist government would encounter little resistance to its demands for independence from the British government.

As in the twentieth century, existing states may not survive. The governments of Belarus and Moldova have experienced problems in establishing viable state-ideas in the post-Soviet era. The reunification of Korea and China is the expressed aim of the two sets of parties. Only the ideological form of the reunification government is disputed. Some realignments among the Arab Gulf states are virtually certain if the ruling dynasties were to be overthrown. There are other states which may be inclined to join their larger, more powerful and prosperous neighbours.

The twentieth century witnessed a remarkable degree of integration both politically and economically. Concepts such as 'one world' and 'the common heritage of mankind' dominated the political rhetoric, while the emergence of the 'global market' paralleled the warnings of 'the end of history' and 'the end of geography'. In an effort to suppress the perceived evils of nationalism, multi-culturalism has been promoted and the role of the state and nation downplayed as no longer of major significance. As a result, international institutions, which have multiplied dramatically in the past one hundred years, have tended to be remarkably conservative, in guaranteeing the territorial status quo and attempting to suppress change. Ultimately, in a completely free enterprise economy, the state is relatively unimportant in the conduct of affairs by multi-national corporations (Yergin and Stanisław, 1998). However, regulation and national distinctiveness suggest that such a uniformity is unlikely, if not as unattainable as it was one hundred years ago. The state is not about to fade away.

The innate instability in the state map of the world is a continuing factor in international politics. Although pointers to the future may be discerned, it is remarkable that the details, even the broad outlines, and the timing of change have usually eluded the prophets of the past. The greatest upheavals in the twentieth century have occurred as a result of wars, notably the two world wars and the Cold War. At other times changes have been slower as pressures for change build up when societies evolve and perceptions of the state are modified. It is sincerely to be hoped that the catastrophic global conflicts of the twentieth century are not repeated in the twenty-first century. However, that does not mean that change in the pattern of states is not inevitable and even desirable. The world map of the year 2000 is not sustainable forever after and rigid conservatism is as dangerous as revolutionary initiatives in the management of change. In the new millennium a more humanitarian approach is necessary to accommodate and facilitate the essential changes in the state system – changes which may be equally as far-reaching as those experienced in the recent past.

APPENDIX

List of States of the Twentieth Century

Symbols

#, independent in 1900 (date of independence or state formation indicated)

*, date of independence

+, date of loss of independence

Afghanistan: #1747

Albania: *1913 (previously Turkish); +1914 (occupied by Austria, Greece and Italy); *1920 +1939 (occupied by Italy); *1943

Algeria: *1962 (previously French)

Andorra: #1278

Angola: *1975 (previously Portuguese)

Antigua and Barbuda: *1981 (previously British)

Argentina: #1810

Armenia: *1918 (previously Russian); +1922 (joined USSR); *1991 (upon dissolution of USSR)

Australia: *1931 (previously British, dominion status 1901)

Austria: *1918 (upon dissolution of Austria-Hungary); +1938 (incorporated into Germany); *1945 (upon defeat of Germany)

Austria-Hungary: #1867; +1918 (union dissolved)

Azerbaijan: *1918 (previously Russian); +1922 (joined USSR); *1991 (upon dissolution of USSR)

Bahamas: *1973 (previously British)

Bahrain: *1971 (previously British)

Bangladesh: *1974 (previously part of Pakistan)

Barbados: *1966 (previously British)

Belarus: *1919 (previously Russian); +1922 (joined USSR); *1991 (upon dissolution of USSR; known as Byelorussia before 1991)

Belgium: #1830

Belize: *1981 (previously British, named British Honduras)

Benin: *1960 (previously French, named Dahomey until 1975)

Bhutan: #1656

Bolivia: #1825

Bosnia and Herzegovina: *1992 (previously part of Austria-Hungary (until 1918), part of Yugoslavia (1918–1941 and 1945–1992) and Croatia (1941–1945))

Botswana: *1966 (previously British, named Bechuanaland Protectorate)

Brazil: #1822

Brunei: *1984 (previously British)

Bulgaria: *1908 (previously under Turkish suzerainty)

Burkina Faso: *1960 (previously French, named Upper Volta until 1984)

Burma: *1948 (previously British, part of British Indian Empire (until 1937)). Independent under Japanese 1943–1945. Renamed Myanmar in 1989

Burundi: *1962 (previously German (until 1915) and Belgian (1915–1962), jointly administered with Rwanda as Ruanda-Urundi in Belgian period)

Cambodia: *1949 (previously French)

Cameroon: *1960 (previously German (until 1915) and French and British (1915–1960))

Canada: *1931 (previously British, dominion status 1867)

Cape Verde Islands: *1975 (previously Portuguese)

Central African Republic: *1960 (previously French, named Oubangi-Chari)

Chad: *1960 (previously French)

Chile: #1810

China: #Ancient empire

Colombia: #1810

Comoros: *1975 (previously French)

Congo: *1960 (previously French, named French Congo (until 1904) and Middle Congo (1904–1960)). Sometimes given name Congo-Brazzaville to distinguish it from its neighbour.

Congo: #1884; +1908 (annexed by Belgium); *1960 (renamed Zaire 1971–1997). Sometimes given name Congo-Kinshasa to distinguish it from its neighbour.

Costa Rica: #1839

Croatia: *1941 (previously part of Austria-Hungary (until 1918) and Yugoslavia (1918–1941)); +1945 (reincorporated into Yugoslavia); *1991

Cuba: *1902 (previously under United States administration)

Cyprus: *1960 (previously British)

Czech Republic: *1993 (previously part of Czechoslovakia)

Czechoslovakia: *1918 (previously part of Austria-Hungary); +1939 (occupied by Germany); *1945 (upon defeat of Germany); +1992 (federation dissolved)

Denmark: #960

Djibouti: *1977 (previously French, named French Somali Coast (until 1967), French Territory of the Affars and Issas (1967–1977))

Dominica: *1978 (previously British)

Dominican Republic: #1865

Ecuador: #1830

Egypt: *1922 (previously Turkish (until 1914) and British (1914–1922)). Joined United Arab Republic (1958–1961), and retained the name until 1971

El Salvador: #1839

Equatorial Guinea: *1968 (previously Spanish Guinea, comprising Fernando Póo and Rio Muni)

Eritrea: *1993 (previously Italian (until 1941), British (1941–1952) and Ethiopian (1952–1993))

Estonia: *1918 (previously Russian); +1940 (incorporated into the USSR); *1991 (upon dissolution of USSR)

Ethiopia: #Ancient Empire; +1935 (occupied by Italy); *1941

Fiji: *1970 (previously British)

Finland: *1917 (previously Russian)

France: #Ancient kingdom and republic

Gabon: *1960 (previously French)

Gambia: *1965 (previously British)

Georgia: *1918 (previously Russian); +1922 (joined USSR); *1991 (upon dissolution of USSR)

Germany: #1871. Partitioned 1949–1990 between German Federal Republic (West) and German Democratic Republic (East); reunited 1990

Ghana: *1957 (previously British, named Gold Coast)

Greece: #1830

Grenada: *1974 (previously British)

Guatemala: #1839

Guinea: *1958 (previously French Guinea)

Guinea-Bissau: *1974 (previously Portuguese Guinea)

Guyana: *1966 (previously named British Guiana)

Haiti: #1804

Hejez: *1916 (previously Turkish); +1925 (occupied by Nejd)

Honduras: #1838

Hungary: *1918 (personal union with Austria dissolved)

Iceland: *1944 (previously linked to Denmark, personal union after 1918)

India: *1947 (previously British Indian Empire)

Indonesia: *1945 (previously Netherlands Indies)

Iran: #Ancient empire (named Persia until 1935)

Iraq: *1932 (previously Turkish (until 1917) and British (1917–1932))

Ireland: *1931 (previously part of United Kingdom: dominion status 1922)

Israel: *1948 (previously Turkish (until 1917) and British (1917–1948))

Italy: #1861

Ivory Coast: *1960 (previously French)

Jamaica: *1962 (previously British)

Japan: #Ancient empire

Jordan: *1950 (Union of Transjordan and Palestine). Name retained following dissolution of union in 1982

Kazakhstan: *1991 (upon dissolution of USSR)

Kenya: *1963 (previously British, called British East Africa (until 1920))

Kiribati: *1979 (previously British, called Gilbert Islands)

Korea: #1895; +1905 (Japanese protectorate, annexed 1910, occupied by Russian and American forces 1945)

Korea (North): *1948 (previously Russian northern zone)

Korea (South): *1948 (previously American southern zone)

Kuwait: *1961 (previously British). Annexed to Iraq (1990–1991)

Kyrgyzstan: *1991 (upon dissolution of the USSR)

Laos: *1949 (previously French)

Latvia: *1918 (previously Russian); +1940 (incorporated into USSR); *1991 (upon dissolution of USSR)

Lebanon: *1943 (previously Turkish (until 1918) and French (1918–1943))

Lesotho: *1966 (previously British, named Basutoland)

Liberia: #1847

Libya: *1951 (previously Turkish (until 1912), Italian (1912–1943) and British (Tripolitania and Cyrenaica) and French (Fezzan) (1943–1951))

Liechtenstein: #1719

Lithuania: *1917 (previously Russian); +1940 (incorporated into the USSR); *1991 (upon dissolution of USSR)

Luxembourg: #1890; +1941 (incorporated into Germany); *1944 (upon defeat of Germany)

Macedonia: *1992 (previously Turkish (until 1913), Serbian (1913–1918) and Yugoslav (1918–1992). Occupied by Bulgaria in both world wars (1915–1918) and (1941–1944))

Madagascar: *1960 (previously French)

Malawi: *1964 (previously British, named British Central Africa (until 1908), then Nyasaland (1908–1964))

Malaysia: *1957 (previously British Malaya, including Straits Settlements, renamed in 1963 upon incorporation of Singapore, and Sabah (formerly British North Borneo) and Sarawak in northern Borneo)

Maldives: *1965 (previously British)

Mali: *1960 (previously French, named Senegambia and Niger (until 1904), Upper Senegal and Niger (1904–1920) and French Sudan (1920–1960). Joined Federation of Mali (1959–1960); dissolved 1960)

Malta: *1964 (previously British)

Manchuria: *1932 (previously Chinese); +1945 (reincorporated into China)

Marshall Islands: *1986 (previously German (until 1914), Japanese (1914–1945) and American (1945–1986))

Mauritania: *1960 (previously French)

Mauritius: *1968 (previously British)

Mexico: #1810

Micronesia: *1986 (previously German (until 1914), Japanese (1914–1945), and American (1945–1986))

Moldova: *1991 (upon dissolution of the USSR)

Monaco: #1297

Mongolia: *1921 (previously Chinese)

Montenegro: #1878; +1918 (incorporated into Yugoslavia); *1941 (occupied by Axis powers); +1944 (rejoined Yugoslavia)

Morocco: #Ancient empire; +1912 (partitioned between France and Spain); *1956

Mozambique: *1975 (previously Portuguese)

Namibia: *1990 (previously German (until 1915) and South African (1915–1990), named (German) South West Africa)

Nauru: *1968 (previously German (until 1914) and Australian (1914–1968))

Nejd: *1918 (previously Turkish); +1932 (united with Hejez to form Saudi Arabia)

Nepal: *1912 (previously Chinese)

Netherlands: #1813

New Zealand: *1931 (previously British, dominion status 1907)

Newfoundland: *1931 (previously British, dominion status 1917); +1934 (reverted to colonial status, joined Canada 1949)

Nicaragua: #1839

Niger: *1960 (previously French)

Nigeria: *1960 (previously British, incorporating Northern Nigeria and Southern Nigeria (until 1914) and Lagos (until 1906))

Norway: *1905 (previously united with Sweden)

Oman: #1650

Orange Free State: #1854; +1900 (annexed by Great Britain, subsequently (1910) joined South Africa)

Pakistan: *1947 (previously part of British Indian Empire)

Palau: *1994 (previously German (until 1914), Japanese (1914–1945) and American (1945–1994))

Palestine: *1948 (previously Turkish (until 1917) and British (1917–1948)); +1950 (united with Transjordan to form Jordan). In 1982 the union was dissolved

Panama: *1903 (previously part of Colombia)

Papua New Guinea: *1975 (South previously British New Guinea (until 1906) and subsequently Papua under Australian administration (1906–1975). North previously German New Guinea (until 1914) and then Australian (1914–1975))

Paraguay: #1811

Peru: #1821

Philippines: *1946 (previously American). Declared independent by the Japanese (1943–1945)

Poland: *1916 (previously Russian); +1939 (partitioned between Germany and USSR); *1944 (upon defeat of Germany)

Portugal: #1640

Qatar: *1971 (previously Turkish (until 1916) and British (1916–1971))

Romania: #1878

Russia: #1480; +1922 (joined USSR); *1991 (upon dissolution of USSR)

Rwanda: *1962 (previously German (until 1915) and Belgian (1915–1962), jointly administered with Burundi as Ruanda-Urundi in Belgian period)

Sahara: Status undetermined (previously Spanish (until 1976) and Moroccan (since 1976))

Saint Christopher and Nevis: *1983 (previously British)

Saint Lucia: *1979 (previously British)

Saint Vincent: *1979 (previously British)

San Marino: #301

Sao Tome and Principe: *1975 (previously Portuguese)

Saudi Arabia: *1932 (union of Hejez and Nejd)

Senegal: *1960 (previously French) Part of Mali Federation 1959–1960

Serbia: #1878; +1918 (formed Yugoslavia, merging with Montenegro and formerly Austrian and Hungarian territories). Briefly revived 1941–1945 following dissolution of Yugoslavia

Seychelles: *1976 (previously British)

Sierra Leone: *1961 (previously British)

Singapore: *1965 (previously British (until 1963) and Malaysian (1963–1965)). Part of Straits Settlements until 1946

Slovakia: *1939 (upon dissolution of Czechoslovakia); +1945 (reformation of Czechoslovakia); *1993 (dissolution of Czechoslovakia)

Slovenia: *1991 (previously part of Austria-Hungary (until 1918), Yugoslavia (1918–1941 and 1945–1991), Italy (1941–1943), Germany (1943–1945))

Solomon Islands: *1978 (previously British)

Somalia: *1960 (previously Italian (until 1941 and 1950–1960), and British (1941–1950)).United with Somaliland 1960.

Somaliland: *1960 (previously British); +1960 (united with Somalia)

South Africa: *1931 (previously British, dominion status 1910. Incorporated previously independent Orange Free State and Transvaal)

Spain: #1479

Sri Lanka: *1948 (previously British, named Ceylon until 1972)

Sudan: *1956 (previously Anglo-Egyptian condominium, administered by Great Britain)

Suriname: *1975 (previously Dutch)

Swaziland: *1968 (previously British)

Sweden: #1523

Switzerland: #1291 (1648)

Syria: *1944 (previously Turkish (until 1918) and French (1918–1943)). Independent state briefly established 1920

Tajikistan: *1991 (upon dissolution of the USSR)

Tanganyika: *1961 (previously German, named German East Africa (until 1915/18) and British (1915/18–1961)); +1964 (United with Zanzibar to form Tanzania)

Tanna Tuva: *1921 (previously Chinese); +1944 (incorporated into the USSR)

Tanzania: *1964 (union of Tanganyika and Zanzibar)

Thailand: #Ancient kingdom (named Siam until 1939)

Togo: *1960 (previously German (until 1914) and French (1914–1960))

Tonga: *1970 (previously British)

Transjordan: *1946 (previously Turkish (until 1918) and British (1918–1946)); +1950 (united with Palestine to form Jordan)

Transvaal: #1881; +1900 (annexed by Great Britain and incorporated into South Africa (1910))

Trinidad and Tobago: *1962 (previously British)

Tunisia: *1956 (previously French)

Turkey: #1288 (named Ottoman Empire until 1923)

Turkmenistan: *1991 (upon dissolution of the USSR)

Tuvalu: *1978 (previously British, named Ellice Islands)

Uganda: *1962 (previously British)

Ukraine: *1917 (previously Russian); +1922 (joined the USSR); *1991

Union of Soviet Socialist Republics (USSR).: *1922 (union including previously independent states of Russia, Armenia, Azerbaijan, Belarus, Georgia and Ukraine); +1991 (dissolved)

United Arab Emirates: *1971 (previously British, named Trucial States)

United Kingdom of Great Britain and Northern Ireland: #1707 (name changed in 1922 in recognition of secession of Irish Free State)

United States of America: #1776

Uruguay: #1828

Uzbekistan: *1991 (upon dissolution of the USSR)

Vanuatu: *1980 (previously Anglo-French condominium of New Hebrides)

Vatican City: *1929 (established by treaty with Italy)

Venezuela: #1830

Vietnam: *1949 (previously French). Two states operated until unification in 1976

Western Samoa: *1962 (previously German (until 1914) and New Zealand (1914–1961))

Yemen: *1918 (previously Turkish). Incorporated Yemen (South) in 1990

Yemen (South): *1967 (previously British, part of British Indian Empire (until 1937), then named Aden (1937–1962), and South Arabia (1963–1967)); +1990 (united with Yemen)

Yugoslavia: *1918 (union of Serbia, Montenegro and various Austrian and Hungary territories, including Croatia and Bosnia-Herzegovina); +1941 (dissolved into component parts); *1944 (reconstituted as a federation of six republics) In 1991–1992 all but Serbia and Montenegro left the federation.

Zambia: *1964 (previously British, named Northern Rhodesia)

Zanzibar: *1963 (previously British); + 1964 (united with Tanganyika to form Tanzania)

Zimbabwe: *1980 (previously British, named Southern Rhodesia). Between 1965 and 1979 an independent state of Rhodesia was in control

BIBLIOGRAPHY

Background reference works

Eastern Province Herald. (Port Elizabeth, 1900–).

Irish Times. (Dublin, 1900–).

Keesing's (Contemporary) Archives. (London, 1931–).

New York Times. (New York, 1900–).

Statesman's Year Book. (London: Macmillan, 1900–).

The Times. (London, 1900–).

Time. (New York, 1923–).

Times Atlas. (London, 1900–).

Books and articles

Abbink, J. (1995) Breaking and making the state: The dynamics of ethnic democracy in Ethiopia. *Journal of Contemporary African Studies* 13, 149–163.

Abu-Lughod, J.L. (1989) *Before European Hegemony: The World System AD 1250–1350*. Oxford: Oxford University Press.

Ageron, C.R. (1979) *Histoire de l'Algerie contemporaine*. Paris: Presses Universitaires de France.

Ahmad, K.M. (1994) *Kurdistan during the First World War*. London: Saqi Books.

Ahmed, I. (1996) *Nation and Ethnicity in Contemporary South Asia*. London: Pinter.

Ahonsi, B.A. (1988) Deliberate falsification and census data in Nigeria. *African Affairs* 87, 553–562.

Aisin-Gioro, P.Y. (1987) *From Emperor to Citizen: The autobiography of Aisin-Gioro Pu Yi*. Oxford: Oxford University Press.

Aitchison, J. and Carter, H. (1994) *A Geography of the Welsh Language 1961–1991*. Cardiff: University of Wales Press.

Ajayi, J.F.A. and Crowder, M. (1985) *Historical Atlas of Africa*. London: Longman.

Akbar, M.J. (1985) *India: The Siege Within, Challenges to a Nation's Unity*. Harmondsworth: Penguin.

Akenson, D.H. (1992) *God's Peoples: Covenant and Land in South Africa, Israel and Ulster*. Ithaca: Cornell University Press.

Alexander, L.M. (1957) *World Political Patterns*. Chicago: Rand McNally.

Allen, J.P. and Turner, E.J. (1988) *We the People: An Atlas of America's Ethnic Diversity*. New York: Macmillan.

Allworth, E. (1998) *The Tartars of the Crimea: Return to the Homeland*. Durham, N.C.: Duke University Press.

Al-Rasheed, M. (1991) *Politics of an Arabian Oasis: The Rashidi Tribal Dynasty*. London: I.B. Tauris.

Anderson, B.R.O'G. (1983) *Imagined Communities: Reflections on the Origin and Spread of Nationalism*. London: Verso.

Anderson, J. (1989) Nationalisms in a disunited kingdom. In Mohan, J. (ed.) *The Political Geography of Contemporary Britain*. Basingstoke: Macmillan, pp. 35–50.

Anderson, M.S. (1966) *The Eastern Question 1774–1923: A Study in International Relations*. London: Macmillan.

Andrews, J.H. (1960) The 'Morning Post' Line. *Irish Geography* 4, 99–106.

Ashton, S.R. (1982) *British policy towards the Indian States 1905–1939*. London: Curzon Press.

Azikiwe, N. (1965) Essentials for Nigerian survival. *Foreign Affairs* 43, 447–461.

Bairoch, P. (1982) International industrialization levels from 1750 to 1980. *Journal of European Economic History* 11, 269–334.

Balfour, M. (1964) *The Kaiser and His Times*. London: Cresset Press.

Barnett, A.D. (1993) *China's Far West: Four Decades of Change*. Boulder: Westview.

Barrier, N.G. (1981) *The Census in British India: New Perspectives*. New Delhi: Manohar.

Barros, J. (1968) *The Aland Islands Question: Its Settlement by the League of Nations*. New Haven: Yale University Press.

Barton, J.R. (1997) *A Political Geography of Latin America*. London: Routledge.

Bayart, J.-F. (1993) *The State in Africa: The Politics of the Belly*. London: Longman.

Beeley, B.W. (1978) The Greek-Turkish boundary: conflict at the interface. *Transactions of the Institute of British Geographers* 3, 351–366.

Bennett, N.R. (1978) *A History of the Arab State of Zanzibar*. London: Methuen.

Beresford, M. (1989) *National Unification and Economic Development in Vietnam*. London: Macmillan.

Berndt, R.M. (1982) *Aboriginal Sites: Rights and Resource Development*. Perth: University of Western Australia Press.

Biger, G. (1994) *An Empire in the Holy Land: Historical Geography of the British Administration in Palestine 1917–1929*. Jerusalem: Magnes Press.

Black, J. (1998) *War and the World: Military power and the fate of continents 1450–2000*. New Haven: Yale University Press.

Bled, J.P. (1994) *Franz Joseph*. Oxford: Blackwell.

Blouet, B.W. (1996) The Political Geography of Europe 1900–2000 AD. *Journal of Geography* 95, 5–14.

Boal, F.W. and Douglas, J.N.H. (1982) *Integration and Division: Geographical Perspectives on the Northern Ireland Problem*. London: Academic Press.

Bowman, I. (1928) *The New World: Problems in Political Geography*. New York: World Book Company. (First published 1921.)

Braudel, F. (1976) *The Mediterranean and the Mediterranean World in the Age of Philip II* (2 vols). New York: Harper.

Braudel, F. (1994) *A History of Civilisations*. London: Penguin.

Breton, R.J.-L. (1997) *Atlas of the Language and Ethnic Communities of South Asia*. New Delhi: Sage.

Brook-Shepherd, G. (1996) *The Austrians*. London: Harper-Collins.

Brownlie, I. (1978) *African Boundaries*. London: Hurst.

Buchanan, A. (1992) *The Morality of Political Divorce from Fort Sunter to Lithuania and Quebec*. Boulder: Westview Press.

Bull, P. (1996) *Land, Politics and Nationalism: A Study of the Irish Land Question*. Dublin: Gill and Macmillan.

Cameron, I. (1980) *To the Farthest Ends of the Earth: The History of the Royal Geographical Society 1830–1980*. London: Macdonald.

Capps, E. (1963) *Greece, Albania and Northern Epirus*. Chicago: Argonaut.

Carrere d'Encausse, H. (1981) *Stalin: Order Through Terror*. London: Longman.

Castells, M. (1998) *End of Millennium: The Information Age: Economy, Society and Culture*, Volume III. Oxford: Blackwell.

Catudal, H.M. (1975) The plight of the Lilliputians: an analysis of five European microstates. *Geoforum* 6, 187–204.

Catudal, H.M. (1979) *The exclave problem of Western Europe*. Montgomery: University of Alabama Press.

Cervenka, Z. (1977) *The Unfinished Quest for Unity: Africa and the OAU*. New York: Africana Publishing.

Chaliand, G. and Rageau, J.P. (1995) *The Penguin Atlas of Diasporas*. New York: Viking Penguin.

Chaturvedi, S. (1996) *The Polar Regions: A Political Geography*. Chichester: John Wiley.

Christopher, A.J. (1976) *Southern Africa: Studies in Historical Geography*. Folkestone: Dawson.

Christopher, A.J. (1984) *Colonial Africa*. London: Croom Helm.

Christopher, A.J. (1988) *The British Empire at its Zenith*. London: Croom Helm.

Christopher, A.J. (1994a) *The Atlas of Apartheid*. London: Routledge.

Christopher, A.J. (1994b) South Africa: the case of a failed partition. *Political Geography* 13, 123–136.

Christopher, A.J. (1995) Regionalisation and ethnicity in South Africa 1990–1994. *Area* 28, 1–11.

Christopher, A.J. (1997) *Spatial aspects of indigenous lands and land claims in the Anglophone world*. Cambridge: University of Cambridge, Department of Land Economy.

Chua, B.H. (1995) *Communitarian Ideology and Democracy in Singapore*. London: Routledge.

Clapham, C. (1996) Boundary and Territory in the Horn of Africa. In Nugent, P. and Asiwaju, A.I. (eds.) *African Boundaries: Barriers, Conduits and Opportunities*. London: Pinter, pp. 237–250.

Clark, G.L. and Dear, M. (1984) *State Apparatus: Structures and Language of Legitimacy*. Boston: Allen & Unwin.

Clarke, A.C. (1983) *2010: Space Odyssey Two*. London: Granada.

Clarke, C.G. (1971) Political fragmentation in the Caribbean: The case of Anguilla. *Canadian Geographer* 15, 13–29.

Clayton, A. (1981) *The Zanzibar Revolution and its Aftermath*. London: Hurst.

Clericy, A. (1910) *Plan de la Principaute de Monaco, 1:12,500*. Grasse-Nice: Lambert & Cie.

Clymer, K.J. (1995) *Quest for Freedom: The United States and India's Independence*. New York: Columbia University Press.

Collins, R.O. (1971) *Land Beyond the Rivers: The Southern Sudan 1898–1918*. New Haven: Yale University Press.

Connell, J. and Aldrich, R. (1991) The last colonies: failures of decolonisation? In Dixon, C. and Heffernan, M. (eds.) *Colonialism and Development in the Contemporary World*. London: Mansell, pp. 183–203.

Conrad, J. (1993) *The Heart of Darkness*. London: Everyman's Library.

Corson, M.W. and Minghi, J.M. (1994) Reunification of partitioned states: theory versus reality in Vietnam and Germany. *Journal of Geography* 93, 125–131.

Crampton, J. (1996) Bordering Bosnia. *GeoJournal* 39, 353–361.

Crampton, R. and Crampton, B. (1996) *Atlas of Eastern Europe in the Twentieth Century*. London: Routledge.

Crossley, P.K. (1997) *The Manchus*. Oxford: Blackwell.

Cyprus (1976) *Distribution of Population by Ethnic Group 1960 and Positions of the Invading Turkish Forces*. Nicosia: Department of Lands and Surveys.

Dahm, B. (1969) *Sukarno and the Struggle for Indonesian Independence*. Ithaca: Cornell University Press.

Dale, E.H. (1962) The state-idea: Missing prop of the West Indies Federation. *Scottish Geographical Magazine* 78, 166–176.

Darby, H.C. and Fullard, H. (1970) *The New Cambridge Modern History Atlas*. Cambridge: Cambridge University Press.

Darkoh, M.B.K. (1996) Sub-Saharan Africa in crisis and the need for a new domestic order. In Yeung, Y.-M. (ed.) *Global Change and the Commonwealth*. Hong Kong: Chinese University of Hong Kong, pp. 45–56.

Davidson, B. (1992) *The Black Man's Burden: Africa and the Curse of the Nation State*. London: James Currey.

Davies, W.D. (1982) *The Territorial Dimension of Judaism*. Berkeley: University of California Press.

De Bustamante, A.S. (1925) *The World Court*. New York: Macmillan.

Dear, I.C.B. and Foot, M.R.D. (1995) *The Oxford Companion to the Second World War*. Oxford: Oxford University Press.

Dedman, M.J. (1996) *The Origins and Development of the European Union 1945–95: A History of European Integration*. London: Routledge.

Derry, T.K. (1973) *A History of Modern Norway 1814–1972*. Oxford: Clarendon Press.

Dickason, O.P. (1992) *Canada's First Nations*. Norman: University of Oklahoma Press.

Dikshit, R.D. (1976) *The Political Geography of Federalism: an Inquiry into Origins and Stability*. London: Macmillan.

Dikshit, R.D. (1997) *Developments in Political Geography: A Century of Progress*. New Delhi: Sage.

Doran, C.F. (1996) Will Canada unravel? *Foreign Affairs* 75, 97–109.

Duursma, J. (1996) *Fragmentation and the International Relations of Micro-States*. Cambridge: Cambridge University Press.

Dziewanowski, M.K. (1969) *Joseph Pilsudski: A European Federalist 1918–1922*. Stanford: Hoover Institution Press.

Dziewanowski, M.K. (1977) *Poland in the Twentieth Century*. New York: Columbia University Press.

East, W.G. and Moodie, A.E. (1956) *The Changing World: Studies in Political Geography*. London: George G. Harrap.

Ehrenreich, B. (1997) *Blood Rites: Origins and History of the Passions of War*. New York: Henry Holt.

Ehret, C. and Posnansky, M. (1982) *The Archaeological and Linguistic Reconstruction of African History*. Berkeley: University of California Press.

Ellis, G. (1976) Alsace and the French nation 1789–1871: A view from the Archives. In Benyon, J.A. (ed.) *Studies in Local History*. Cape Town: Oxford University Press, pp. 15-27.

Ellis, P.B. (1985) *The Celtic Revolution: A Study in Anti-Imperialism*. Talybont, Wales: Y Lolfa.

Emmett, C.F. (1996) The capital cities of Jerusalem. *Geographical Review* 86, 233–258.

Engel, J. (1962) *Grosser Historischer Weltatlas* (3 vols). Munich: Bayerischer Schulbuch Verlag.

Eronen, J. (1998) A geopolitical approach to China's future as an empire. *Tijdschrift voor Economische en Sociale Geografie* 89, 4–14.

Espy, R. (1979) *The Politics of the Olympic Games*. Berkeley: University of California Press.

Eva, F. (1997) The unlikely independence of Northern Italy. *GeoJournal* 43, 61–75.

Fagge, A. (1914) *The National Anthems of the Allies: Belgium, Russia, France and Great Britain*. London: Boosey and Co.

Ferguson, N. (1998) *Virtual History: Alternatives and Counterfactuals*. London: Macmillan.

Fischer, F. (1967) *Germany's Aims in the First World War*. New York: W.W. Norton.

Fonseca, I. (1996) *Bury Me Standing: The Gypsies and Their Journey*. New York: Alfred A. Knopf.

Forbes, A.D.W. (1982) Thailand's Muslim minorities, assimilation, secession or coexistence. *Asian Survey* 21, 1056–1073.

Forbes, A.D.W. (1986) *Warlords and Muslims in Chinese Central Asia: A political history of republican Sinkiang 1911–1949*. Cambridge: Cambridge University Press.

Forrest, R.A.D. (1973) *The Chinese Language*. London: Faber.

Forsyth, J. (1992) *A History of the Peoples of Siberia: Russia's North Asian Colony*. Cambridge: Cambridge University Press.

Freeman, M. (1987) *Atlas of Nazi Germany*. London: Croom Helm.

Frey, W.H. and Farley, R. (1996) Latino, Asian and Black segregation in US metropolitan areas: Are multiethnic metros different? *Demography* 33, 35–50.

Friters, G.M. (1951) *Outer Mongolia and its International Position*. London: George Allen and Unwin.

Fukuyama, F. (1992) *The End of History and the Last Man*. New York: Free Press.

Gachechiladze, R. (1997) National idea, state-building and boundaries in the post-Soviet space (the case of Georgia). *GeoJournal* 43, 51–60.

Gavin, R.J. (1975) *Aden under British rule 1839–1967*. London: C. Hurst.

Geldenhuys, D. (1990) *Isolated States: A Comparative Analysis*. Johannesburg: Jonathan Ball.

Gerteiny, A.G. (1967) *Mauritania*. New York: Praeger.

Gibb, R.A. (1987) The effect on the countries of SADCC of economic sanctions against the Republic of South Africa. *Transactions of the Institute of British Geographers* 12, 398–412.

Gilmour, D. (1994) *Curzon*. London: Macmillan.

Glassner, M.I. (1996) *Political Geography*. New York: Wiley.

Glazer, N. (1997) *We are All Multiculturalists Now*. Cambridge: Harvard University Press.

Glazer, N. and Moynihan, D.P. (1963) *Beyond the Melting Pot: The Negroes, Puerto Ricans, Jews, Italians and Irish of New York City*. Cambridge, Massachusetts: MIT Press.

Graham, B. (1997) *In Search of Ireland: A Cultural Geography*. London: Routledge.

Graham, B. and Shirlow, P. (1998) An elusive agenda: the development of a middle ground in Northern Ireland. *Area* 30, 245–254.

Great Britain (1903) *Tientsin, 4 inches to 1 mile*. London: Intelligence Branch, North China Command.

Great Britain (1960) *Report of the Advisory Commission on the Review of the Constitution of Rhodesia and Nyasaland*. [Cmnd 1148] London: HMSO.

Griffiths, I.L. (1995) *The African Inheritance*. London: Routledge.

Griffiths, P. (1974) *A Licence to Trade: The History of English Chartered Companies*. London: Macmillan.

Gruffudd, P. (1994) Back to the land: historiography, rurality and the nation in interwar Wales. *Transactions of the Institute of British Geographers* 19, 61–77.

Grunfeld, A.T. (1987) *The Making of Modern Tibet*. London: Zed Books.

Gurdon, C. (1994) *The Horn of Africa*. London: University College London Press.

Gurr, T.R. and Harff, B. (1994) *Ethnic Conflict in World Politics*. Boulder: Westview Press.

Haley, A. (1976) *Roots: The Saga of an American Family*. New York: Dell.

Hamdan, G. (1963) The political map of the New Africa. *Geographical Review* 53, 418–439.

Hance, W.A. (1964) *The Geography of Africa*. New York: Columbia University Press.

Hannikainen, L. and Horn, F. (1997) *Autonomy and Demilitarisation in International Law: The Aland Islands in a Changing Europe*. The Hague: Kluwer Law International.

Harris, C.D. (1991) Unification of Germany in 1990. *Geographical Review* 81, 170–182.

Harris, C.D. (1993a) New European countries and their minorities. *Geographical Review* 83, 301–320.

Harris, C.D. (1993b) A geographical analysis of Non-Russian minorities in Russia and its ethnic homelands. *Post-Soviet Geography* 34, 543–597.

Harris, R.C. (1977) The simplification of Europe overseas. *Annals of the Association of American Geographers* 67, 469–483.

Hartshorne, R. (1950) The functional approach in political geography. *Annals of the Association of American Geographers* 40, 95–130.

Hasiotis, A.C. (1987) *Soviet Economic and Military Involvement in Sinkiang from 1928 to 1949*. New York: Garland Publishing.

Headmasters' Conference (1949) *The Public School Hymn Book*. London: Novello.

Headrick, D.R. (1981) *The Tools of Empire: Technology and European Imperialism in the Nineteenth Century*. New York: Oxford University Press.

Heard-Bey, F. (1996) *From Trucial States to United Arab Emirates: A Society in Transition*. London: Longman.

Hendriksen, T.H. (1992) *The New World Order: War, Peace and Military Preparedness*. Stanford: Stanford University, Hoover Institution.

Henley, D.E.F. (1995) Regional nationalism in a colonial state: a case study from the Dutch East Indies. *Political Geography* 14, 31–58.

Henry, B. (1976) *An approved history of the Olympic Games*. New York: Putnam's Sons.

Herb, G.H. (1997) *Under the Map of Germany: Nationalism and Propaganda 1918–1945*. London: Routledge.

Hinckley, T.C. (1981) The United States and the Pacific Trust Territory. *Journal of the West* 20(1), 41–51.

Hitchman, J.H. (1971) *Leonard Wood and Cuban Independence 1898–1902*. The Hague: Martinus Nijhoff.

Hobsbawm, E.J. (1995) *Age of Extremes: The Short Twentieth Century 1914–1991*. London: Abacus.

Hobsbawm, E.J. and Ranger, T. (1983) *The Invention of Tradition*. Cambridge: Cambridge University Press.

Hodson, H.V. (1969) *The Great Divide: Britain–India–Pakistan*. London: Hutchinson.

Hopkirk, P. (1990) *The Great Game: On Secret Service in High Asia*. London: Murray.

Horne, A. (1977) *A Savage War of Peace: Algeria 1954–1962*. London: Macmillan.

Horowitz, D.L. (1985) *Ethnic Groups in Conflict*. Berkeley: University of California Press.

Hsu, I.C.Y. (1983) *The Rise of Modern China* (3rd Edn). New York: Oxford University Press.

Huntington, S.P. (1996) *The Clash of Civilizations and the Remaking of the World Order*. New York: Simon and Schuster.

Husain, A. (1970) *British India's Relations with the Kingdom of Nepal 1857–1947: A Diplomatic History of Nepal*. London: George Allen and Unwin.

Hyam, R. (1972) *The Failure of South African Expansion 1908–1948*. London: Macmillan.

Hyam, R. (1976) *Britain's Imperial Century 1815–1914: A Study of Empire and Expansion*. London: Batsford.

Ikporukpo, C.O. (1986) Politics and regional policies: The issue of state creation in Nigeria. *Political Geography Quarterly* 5, 127–139.

India (1913) *Census of India 1911, Vol VI City of Calcutta, Part I*. Calcutta: Bengal Secretariat Book Depot.

India (1914) *Topographic Map of India 1:250,000*. Dehra Dun: Survey of India.

India (1955) *Report of the States Reorganisation Commission*. New Delhi: Manager of Publications.

Jackson, R.H. (1990) *Quasi-states: Sovereignty, International Relations and the Third World*. Cambridge: Cambridge University Press.

Jardine, M. (1996) Pacification, resistance, and territoriality: prospects for a space of peace in East Timor. *GeoJournal* 39, 397–404.

Jaszi, O. (1929) *The Dissolution of the Habsburg Monarchy*. Chicago: University of Chicago Press.

Jelavich, B. (1987) *Modern Austria: Empire and Republic 1815–1986*. Cambridge: Cambridge University Press.

Jelavich, C. and Jelavich, B. (1977) *The Establishment of the Balkan National States 1804–1920*. Seattle: University of Washington Press.

Jenkins, J.R.G. (1986) *Jura Separatism in Switzerland*. Oxford: Clarendon Press.

Joerg, W.L.G. (1932) *Pioneer Settlement*. New York: American Geographical Society.

Joesten, J. (1943) German rule in Ostland. *Foreign Affairs* 22, 143–147.

Johnson, N.C. (1993) Building a nation: an examination of the Irish Gaeltacht Commission Report of 1926. *Journal of Historical Geography* 19, 157–168.

Johnson, P. (1997) *A History of the American People*. London: Weidenfeld and Nicolson.

Johnston, R.J. (1982) *Geography and the State: An Essay in Political Geography*. London: Macmillan.

Jordan, D.P. (1979) *The King's Trial: The French Revolution vs. Louis XVI*. Berkeley: University of California Press.

Josephy, A.M. (1994) *500 Nations: An Illustrated History of North American Indians*. New York: Knopf.

Kamanu, O.S. (1974) Succession and the right of self-determination: An OAU dilemma. *Journal of Modern African Studies* 12, 355–376.

Kaplan, D.H. (1994) Two nations in search of a state: Canada's ambivalent spatial identities. *Annals of the Association of American Geographers* 84, 585–606.

Kennedy, P. (1988) *The Rise and Fall of the Great Powers: Economic Change and Military Conflict from 1500 to 2000*. London: Unwin Hyman.

Keogh, D. (1996) The role of the Catholic Church in the Republic of Ireland 1922–1995. In *Forum for Peace and Reconciliation, Building Trust in Ireland*. Belfast: Blackstaff Press, pp. 85–213.

Kesteloot, C. and van der Haegen, H. (1997) Foreigners in Brussels 1981–1991. *Tijdschrift voor Economische en Sociale Geografie* 88, 105–127.

Keyenbroek, P.G. and Sperl, S. (1992) *The Kurds: A Contemporary Overview*. London: Routledge.

Khoury, P.S. (1987) *Syria and the French Mandate: The Politics of Arab Nationalism 1920–1945*. Princeton: Princeton University Press.

Kidron, M. and Segal, R. (1995) *The State of the World Atlas*. London: Penguin.

Kim, C.I.E. and Kim, H.K. (1967) *Korea and the Politics of Imperialism 1876–1910*. Berkeley: University of California Press.

Kimmich, C.M. (1968) *The Free City: Danzig and German Foreign Policy 1919–1934*. New Haven: Yale University Press.

Kissinger, H. (1994) *Diplomacy*. New York: Simon and Schuster.

Kliot, N. and Mansfield, Y. (1997) The political landscape of partition: The case of Cyprus. *Political Geography* 16, 495–521.

Kliot, N. and Waterman, S. (1991) *The Political Geography of Conflict and Peace*. London: Belhaven.

Knippenberg, H. (1997) Dutch nation-building: a struggle against the water? *GeoJournal* 43, 27–40.

Kohn, H. (1960) *Pan-Slavism: Its History and Ideology*. New York: Vintage Books.

Kolinsky, M. (1984) The nation-state in Western Europe: erosion from 'above' and 'below'? In Massey, D. and Allen, J. (eds.) *Geography Matters!* Cambridge: Cambridge University Press, pp. 166–180.

Kosinski, L.A. (1969) Changes in the ethnic structure of East-Central Europe 1930–1960. *Geographical Review* 59, 388–402.

Kostiner, J. (1993) *The Making of Saudi Arabia 1916–1936: From Chieftaincy to Monarchical State*. New York: Oxford University Press.

Kostiner, J. (1995) *Yemen: The Tortuous Quest for Unity 1990–94*. London: Royal Institute of International Affairs.

Krishan, G. (1988) The world pattern of administrative area reform. *Geographical Journal* 154, 93–99.

Laclavere, G. (1978) *Atlas de la Republique du Zaire*. Paris: Editions Jeune Afrique.

Lagerberg, K. (1979) *West Irian and Jakarta Imperialism*. London: C. Hurst.

Laitin, D.D. (1992) *Language Repertoires and State Construction in Africa*. Cambridge: Cambridge University Press.

Laitin, D.D. and Samatar, S.S. (1987) *Somalia: Nation in Search of a State*. Boulder: Westview Press.

Landes, D. (1998) *The Wealth and Poverty of Nations: Why some are so rich and some so poor*. New York: W.W. Norton.

Large, S.S. (1992) *Emperor Hirohito and Showa Japan: A Political Biography*. London: Routledge.

Laroche, L. (1903) Pays bizarres: armées minuscules. *Revue Française* 28, 388–395.

Lehn, W. (1988) *The Jewish National Fund*. London: Kegan Paul International.

Levine, H.S. (1973) *Hitler's Free City: A History of the Nazi Party in Danzig 1925–39*. Chicago: University of Chicago Press.

Li, L. (1975) *The Japanese army in North China 1937–1941: Problems of political and economic control*. Tokyo: Oxford University Press.

Louis, W.R. (1978) *The United States and the Decolonization of the British Empire 1941–1945*. New York: Oxford University Press.

Lower, A.R.M. (1959) *Colony to Nation: A History of Canada*. Toronto: Longmans Green.

McAlister, J.T. (1970) *Viet Nam: The Origins of Revolution*. New York: Alfred A. Knopf.

McColl, R.W. and Newman, D. (1992) States in formation: The ghetto state as typified in the West Bank and Gaza Strip. *GeoJournal* 28, 333–345.

McIntyre, W.D. (1977) *The Commonwealth of Nations: Origins and Impact 1869–1971*. Minneapolis: University of Minnesota Press.

Mackinder, H.J. (1904) The Geographical Pivot of History. *Geographical Journal* 23, 421–444.

Mackinder, H.J. (1919) *Democratic Ideals and Reality; A Study in the Politics of Reconstruction*. New York: H. Holt.

McLeod, K. (1983) *The Last Summer: May to September 1914*. London: Collins.

Macmillan, H. (1972) *Pointing the Way 1959–1961*. London: Macmillan.

Magocsi, P.R. (1993a) *The Persistence of Regional Cultures: Rusyns and Ukrainians in their Carpathian Homeland and Abroad*. New York: Columbia University Press.

Magocsi, P.R. (1993b) *Historical Atlas of East Central Europe*. Seattle: University of Washington Press.

Magocsi, P.R. (1996) *A History of Ukraine*. Toronto: University of Toronto Press.

Mahajan, V.D. (1983) *History of Modern India (1919–1982). Volume I (1919–1974)*. New Delhi: S. Chand.

Maimela, S.S. (1996) Culture and ethnic diversity as sources of curse and blessing in the promotion of democratic change. In Hulley, L., Kretzschmor, L. and Pato, L.L. (eds.) *Archbishop Tutu: Prophetic Witness in South Africa*. Cape Town: Human and Rousseau, pp. 80–92.

Malcolm, N. (1994) *Bosnia: A Short History*. London: Macmillan.

Malcolm, N. (1998) *Kosovo: A Short History*. London: Macmillan.

Malloy, W.M. (1910) *Treaties, Conventions, International Acts, Protocols and Agreements between the United States of America and other powers 1776–1909*. Washington: Government Printing Office.

Mamdani, M. (1996) *Citizen and Subject: Contemporary Africa and the Legacy of Late Colonialism*. Princeton: Princeton University Press.

Mansfield, P. (1971) *The British in Egypt*. New York: Holt, Rinehart and Winston.

Marcus, H.G. (1983) *Great Britain and the United States 1941–1974: The Politics of Empire*. Berkeley: University of California Press.

Markusse, J. (1997) Power-sharing and 'consociational democracy' in South Tyrol. *GeoJournal* 43, 77–89.

Marriott, J.A.R. (1917) *The Eastern Question: An Historical Study in European Diplomacy*. Oxford: Clarendon Press.

Martin, R. (1988) The political economy of Britain's north–south divide. *Transactions of the Institute of British Geographers* 13, 389–418.

Mazower, M. (1998) *Dark Continent: Europe's Twentieth Century*. London: Allen Lane.

Medved, F. (1997) Nation and patria in the emerging world order. *GeoJournal* 43, 5–15.

Mehra, P. (1974) *The McMahan Line and Thereafter*. London: Macmillan.

Meinig, D.W. (1976) *Imperial Texas: An Interpretive Essay in Cultural Geography*. Austin: University of Texas Press.

Meinig, D.W. (1986) *The Shaping of America: A geographical Perspective on 500 Years of History. Volume 1: Atlantic America, 1492–1800*. New Haven: Yale University Press.

Mendelson, M. and Hulton, S. (1994) Iraq's claim to sovereignty over Kuwait. In Schofield, R. (ed.) *Territorial Foundations of the Gulf States*. London: University College London Press, pp. 117–152.

Mikesell, M.W. and Murphy, A.B. (1991) A framework for comparative study of minority group aspirations. *Annals of the Association of American Geographers* 81, 581–604.

Milivojevik, M. (1992) *Wounded Eagle: Albania's Fight for Survival*. London: Institute for European Defence and Strategic Studies.

Monmonier, M. (1991) *How to Lie with Maps*. Chicago: University of Chicago Press.

Moorehead, C. (1998) *Dunant's Dream: War, Switzerland and the History of the Red Cross*. London: HarperCollins.

Morris, B. (1990) *1948 and After: Israel and the Palestinians*. Oxford: Clarendon Press.

Moseley, C. and Asher, R.E. (1994) *Atlas of the World's Languages*. London: Routledge.

Motyl, A.J. (1992) *Thinking Theoretically about Soviet Nationalities*. New York: Columbia University Press.

Muir, R. (1975) *Modern Political Geography*. London: Macmillan.

Myers, G., Klak, T. and Koehl, T. (1996) The inscription of difference: News coverage of the conflicts in Rwanda and Bosnia. *Political Geography* 15, 21–46.

Newcomer, J. (1984) *The Grand Duchy of Luxembourg: The Evolution of Nationhood, 963 AD to 1983*. London: University Press of America.

Newman, D. (1996) Shared spaces – separate spaces: the Israel–Palestine peace process. *GeoJournal* 39, 363–375.

Newman, D. and Falah, G. (1995) Small state behaviour: on the formation of a Palestinian state in the West Bank and Gaza Strip. *Canadian Geographer* 39, 219–234.

Newton, G. (1996) *Luxembourg and Leetzebuergesch: Language and Communication at the Crossroads of Europe*. Oxford: Clarendon Press.

Neirynck, J. (1996) *Le Siege de Bruxelles*. Paris: Desclee De Brouwer.

Nolan, W. (1988) New farms and fields: migration policies of the state land agencies 1891–1980. In Smyth, W.J. and Whelan, K. (eds.) *Common Ground: Essays on the Historical Geography of Ireland*. Cork: Cork University Press, pp. 296–319.

Norman, J. (1988) *Chinese*. Cambridge: Cambridge University Press.

Northedge, F.S. (1986) *The League of Nations: Its Life and Times 1920–1946*. Leicester: Leicester University Press.

Nostrand, R.L. (1992) *The Hispano Homeland*. Norman: University of Oklahoma Press.

O'Ballance, E. (1993) *Afghan Wars 1839–1992: What Britain Gave Up and the Soviet Union lost*. London: Brassey's.

O'Brien, R. (1992) *Global Financial Integration: The End of Geography*. London: Pinter.

Orridge, A. and Williams, C.H. (1982) Autonomous nationalism. *Political Geography Quarterly* 1, 19–40.

O'Tuathail, G. and Luke, T.W. (1994) Present at the (Dis)integration: deterritorialization and reterritorialization in the New Wor(l)d order. *Annals of the Association of American Geographers* 84, 381–398.

Overton, J. (1994) Small states, big issues? Human Geography in the Pacific Islands. *Singapore Journal of Tropical Geography* 14, 265–276.

Owen, D. (1995) *Balkan Odyssey*. London: Victor Gollancz.

Paasi, A. (1996) *Territories, Boundaries and Consciousness: The Changing Geographies of the Finnish–Russian Border*. Chichester: John Wiley.

Paddison, R. (1983) *The Fragmented State: The Political Geography of Power*. Oxford: Basil Blackwell.

Parker, G. (1985) *Western Geopolitical Thought in the Twentieth Century*. New York: St Martins.

Parker, W.H. (1968) *An Historical Geography of Russia*. London: University of London Press.

Parsons, J.J. (1967) *Antioquia's Corridor to the Sea: An Historical Geography of the Settlement of Uraba*. Berkeley: University of California Press.

Paterson, J.H. (1987) German Geopolitics reassessed. *Political Geography Quarterly* 6, 107–114.

Paulicevic, D. (1996) A review of the historical development of the Republic of Croatia. *GeoJournal* 38, 381–391.

Peires, J.B. (1995) Ethnicity and Pseudo-ethnicity in the Ciskei. In Beinart W. and Dubow, S. (eds.) *Segregation and Apartheid in Twentieth Century South Africa*. London: Routledge, pp. 256–284.

Pepper, D. and Jenkins, A. (1985) *The Geography of Peace and War*. Oxford: Basil Blackwell.

Peterson, J.E. (1982) *Yemen: The Search for a Modern State*. Baltimore: Johns Hopkins University Press.

Pipes, R. (1964) *The Formation of the Soviet Union: Communism and Nationalism 1917–1923*. Cambridge: Harvard University Press.

Platt, D.C.M. (1986) *Britain's Investment Overseas on the Eve of the First World War: The Use and Abuse of Numbers*. Basingstoke: Macmillan.

Platzky, L. and Walker, C. (1985) *The Surplus People: Forced Removals in South Africa*. Johannesburg: Ravan.

Pocock, T. (1998) *The Battle for Empire: The very first World War 1756–63*. London: Michael O'Mara Books.

Polestsky, M. (1991) *The New World Order: Opposing Viewpoints*. San Diego: Greenhaven Press.

Pounds, N.J.G. (1963) *Political Geography*. New York: McGraw-Hill.

Pouns, B. (1987) *Amerika*. New York: Pocket Books.

Prescott, J.R.V. (1987) *Political Frontiers and Boundaries*. London: Allen and Unwin.

Preston, P. (1990) *The Triumph of Democracy in Spain*. London: Routledge.

Pringle, D.G. (1985) *One Island, Two Nations? A Political Geographical Analysis of the National Conflict in Ireland*. New York: John Wiley.

Pringle, D.G. (1996) The peace process in Ireland: new challenges for the geographical imagination. *GeoJournal* 39, 377–385.

Prunier, G. (1994) Somaliland: birth of a new country? in Gurdon, G. (ed.) *The Horn of Africa*. London: University College London Press, 61–75.

Prunier, G. (1997) *The Rwanda crisis 1959–1994: History of a Genocide*. London: Hurst.

Putzger, F.W. (1997) *Putzger Historischer Weltatlas*. Berlin: Cornelsen.

Ratzel, F. (1897) *Politische Geographie*. Munich: Verlag von R. Oldenbourg.

Roberts, B.R. (1995) *The Making of Citizens: Cities of Peasants Revisited*. London: Arnold.

Robinson, K.W. (1975) The geographical context of political individualism. In Powell, J.M. and Williams, M. (eds.) *Australian Space Australian Time: Geographical Perspectives*. Melbourne: Oxford University Press, pp. 226–249.

Rodney, W. (1974) *How Europe Underdeveloped Africa*. Washington: Howard University Press.

Royle, S.A. (1995) Economic and political prospects for the British Atlantic Dependent Territories. *Geographical Journal* 161, 307–321.

Rudolph, R.L. and Good, D.F. (1992) *Nationalism and Empire: The Habsburg Empire and the Soviet Union*. New York: St Martins Press.

Rupen, R.A. (1971) The absorption of Tuva. *Studies on the Soviet Union* 11(4), 145–162.

Said, E.W. (1994) *Culture and Imperialism*. London: Vintage.

Sandner, G. (1989) The Germania triumphans syndrome and Passage's Erdkindlicke Weltanschauug: the roots and effects of German political geography beyond Geopolitik. *Political Geography Quarterly* 8, 341–351.

Schofield, R. (1994) *Territorial foundations of the Gulf States*. London: University College London Press.

Schofield, V. (1996) *Kashmir in the Crossfire*. London: I.B. Tauris.

Segal, R. (1995) *The Black Diaspora*. London: Faber and Faber.

Selth, A. (1986) Race and Resistance in Burma 1942–1945. *Modern Asian Studies* 10, 483–507.

Seton-Watson, H. (1977) *Nations and States: An Enquiry into the Origins of Nations and the Politics of Nationalism*. London: Methuen.

Seward, D. (1995) *The Monks of War: The Military Religious Orders*. Harmondsworth: Penguin.

Sharp, A. (1991) *The Versailles Settlement: Peacemaking in Paris 1919*. Basingstoke: Macmillan.

Shaw, M. and Coleman, H. (1963) *National Anthems of the World*. London: Blandford Press.

Shirer, W.L. (1964) *The Rise and Fall of the Third Reich*. London: Pan.

Short, J.R. (1993) *An Introduction to Political Geography*. London: Routledge.

Siddle, R.M. (1996) *Race, Resistance and the Ainu of Japan*. London: Routledge.

Sire, H.J.A. (1994) *The Knights of Malta*. New Haven: Yale University Press.

Slezkine, Y. (1994) *Arctic Mirrors: Russia and the Small Peoples of the North*. Ithaca: Cornell University Press.

Smalley, W.A. (1994) *Linguistic Diversity and National Unity: Language and Ecology in Thailand*. Chicago: University of Chicago Press.

Smith, A.D. (1986) *The Ethnic Origins of Nations*. Oxford: Blackwell.

Smith, A.D. (1991) *National Identity*. London: Penguin.

Smith, D.A. and Borocz, J. (1995) *A New World Order? Global Transformations in the Late Twentieth Century*. Westport, Conn.: Greenwood Press.

Smith, G. (1996) *The Nationalities Question in the Post-Soviet States*. London: Longman.

Smith, J. (1998) *The Cold War 1945–1991*. Oxford: Blackwell.

Smith, M. (1991) *Burma: Insurgency and the Politics of Ethnicity*. London: Zed Books.

Smith, P.A. (1984) *Palestine and the Palestinians 1876–1983*. London: Croom Helm.

Sneath, D. (1994) The impact of the Cultural Revolution in China on the Mongolians of Inner Mongolia. *Modern Asian Studies* 28, 409–430.

Spate, O.H.K. (1947) The Partition of the Punjab and of Bengal. *Geographical Journal* 110, 201–222.

Stein, K.W. (1984) *The Land Question in Palestine 1917–1939*. Chapel Hill: University of North Carolina Press.

Stirk, P.M.R. (1996) *A History of European Integration since 1914*. London: Pinter.

Stockwell, A.J. (1992) Southeast Asia in War and Peace: The End of European Colonial Empires. In Tarling, N. (ed.) *The Cambridge History of Southeast Asia, Vol 2 The Nineteenth and Twentieth Centuries*. Cambridge: Cambridge University Press, pp. 329–385.

Stokke, K. (1998) Sinhalese and Tamil nationalism as post-colonial political projects from 'above', 1948–1983. *Political Geography* 17, 83–113.

Stone, G. (1972) *The Smallest Slavonic Nation: The Sorbs of Lusatia*. London: Athlone Press.

Stremlau, J.J. (1977) *The International Politics of the Nigerian Civil War 1967–1970*. Princeton: Princeton University Press.

Stuart-Fox, M. (1995) The French in Laos 1887–1945. *Modern Asian Studies* 29, 111–139.

Sukhwal, B.L. (1971) *India: A Political Geography*. Bombay: Allied Publishers.

Sutton, I. (1976) Sovereign states and the changing definitions of the Indian Reservation. *Geographical Review* 66, 281–295.

Swietochowski, T. (1995) *Russia and Azerbaijan: A Borderland in Transition*. New York: Columbia University Press.

Szajkowski, B. (1993) *Encyclopaedia of Conflicts, Disputes and Flashpoints in Eastern Europe, Russia and the Successor States*. London: Longman.

Szajkowski, B. (1995) Chechnia: The Empire strikes back. *GeoJournal* 37, 229–236.

Takaki, R. (1993) *A Different Mirror: A History of Multi-cultural America*. Boston: Little, Brown and Company.

Taylor, A.J.P. (1954) *The Struggle for Mastery in Europe 1848–1918*. Oxford: Clarendon Press.

Taylor, P.J. (1990) *Britain and the Cold War: 1945 as Geopolitical Transition*. London: Pinter.

Taylor, P.J. (1991) The English and their Englishness: a curiously mysterious, elusive and little understood people. *Scottish Geographical Magazine* 107, 146–162.

Taylor, P.J. (1993a) *Political Geography: World-Economy, Nation-state and Locality*. Longman, London.

Taylor, P.J. (1993b) *Political Geography of the Twentieth Century: A Global Analysis*. London: Belhaven Press.

Taylor, P.J. (1994) The state as container: Territoriality in the modern world-system. *Progress in Human Geography* 18, 151–162.

Taylor, P.J. (1995) Beyond containers: internationality, interstateness and interterritoriality. *Progress in Human Geography* 19, 1–15.

Taylor, P.J. (1996) *The Way the Modern World Works: World Hegemony to World Impasse*. Chichester: Wiley.

Thomson, C.N. (1995) Political stability and minority groups in Burma. *Geographical Review* 85, 269–285.

Thomson, D. (1957) *Europe since Napoleon*. London: Longmans.

Thrower, N.J.W. (1972) *Maps and Men: An examination of Cartography in relation to Culture and Civilization*. Englewood Cliffs: Prentice-Hall.

Toschi, U. (1931) The Vatican City State from the standpoint of Political Geography. *Geographical Review* 21, 529–538.

Touval, S. (1963) *Somali nationalism in International Politics and the Drive for Unity in the Horn of Africa*. Cambridge Mass: Harvard University Press.

Trepanier, C. (1991) The Cajunization of French Louisiana: forging a regional identity. *Geographical Journal* 157, 161–171.

Tuchman, B.W. (1967) *The Proud Tower: A portrait of the World before the War: 1890–1914*. New York: Bantam.

Turnock, D. (1989) *Eastern Europe: An Historical Geography 1815–1945*. London: Routledge.

United States (1992) *Yugoslav Republics March 10, 1992*. Washington DC: Department of State, Office of the Geographer.

Vail, L. (1976) Mocambique's Chartered Companies: The Rule of the Feeble. *Journal of African History* 17, 389–416.

Van Amersfoort, H. and Knippenberg, H. (1991) *States and Nations: The rebirth of the 'nationalities question' in Europe*. Amsterdam: Royal Dutch Geographical Society.

Van Trease, H. (1993) *Atoll Politics: The Republic of Kiribati*. Christchurch: University of Canterbury, Macmillan Brown Centre for Pacific Studies.

Velychenko, S. (1993) *Shaping identity in Eastern Europe and Russia: Soviet Russian and Polish Accounts of Ukrainian History 1914–1991*. New York: St Martins Press.

Wagner, D. and Tomkowitz, G. (1971) *Ein Volk, Ein Reich, Ein Fuhrer: The Nazi Annexation of Austria 1938*. London: Longman.

Wakeman, F. (1995) *Policing Shanghai 1927–1937*. Berkeley: University of California Press.

Walker, B.M. (1978) *Parliamentary election results in Ireland 1801–1922*. Dublin: Royal Irish Academy.

Wallerstein, I. (1974) *The Modern World-System I: Capitalist Agriculture and the Origins of the European World-Economy in the Sixteenth Century*. New York: Academic Press.

Wallerstein, I. (1989) *The Modern World-System III: The second era of great expansion of the capitalist world-economy, 1730s–1840s*. New York: Academic Press.

Wallerstein, I. (1991) *Geopolitics and Geocultures: Essays on the Changing World-System*. Cambridge: Cambridge University Press.

Walters, F.P. (1952) *A History of the League of Nations*. London: Oxford University Press.

Ward, D. (1989) *Poverty, Ethnicity, and the American City, 1840–1925: Changing Conceptions of the Slum and the Ghetto*. Cambridge: Cambridge University Press.

Waterman, S. (1987) Partitioned states. *Political Geography Quarterly* 6, 161–170.

Waterman, S. (1996) Partition, secession and peace in our time. *GeoJournal* 39, 345–352.

Watkins, M. (1993) *Canada*. New York: Facts on File.

Webb, W.P. (1951) *The Great Frontier*. Austin: University of Texas Press.

Weber, E. (1976) *Peasants into Frenchmen: The Modernization of Rural France 1870–1914*. Stanford: Stanford University Press.

Webster, G.R. (1993) Congressional redistricting and African-American representation in the 1990s: An example from Alabama. *Political Geography* 12, 549–564.

Welensky, R. (1964) *Welensky's 4000 Days: The Life and Death of the Federation of Rhodesia and Nyasaland*. London: Collins.

Wilkes, J.J. (1992) *The Illyrians*. Oxford: Blackwell.

Wilkinson, H.R. (1951) *Maps and Politics: A Review of the Ethnographic Cartography of Macedonia*. Liverpool: University Press of Liverpool.

Wilkinson, J.C. (1983) Traditional concepts of territory in South East Arabia. *Geographical Journal* 149, 301–315.

Williams, C.H. (1994) *Called Unto Liberty! On Language and Nationalism*. Clevedon: Multilingual Matters.

Winslow, C. (1996) *Lebanon: War and Politics in a Fragmented Society*. London: Routledge.

Woolf, S. (1979) *A History of Italy 1700–1860: The Social Constraints of Political Change*. London: Methuen.

Wright, D. (1987) Curzon and Persia. *Geographical Journal* 153, 343–350.

Wright, J.F.R., Goldenberg, S. and Schofield, R. (1996) *Transcaucasian Boundaries*. London: UCL Press.

Wyndham, G. (1904) *The Development of the State*. London: Archibald Constable.

Yergin, D. and Stanisław, J. (1998) *The Commanding Heights: The battle between government and the market place that is remaking the modern world*. New York: Simon and Schuster.

Young, C. (1991) Self-determination, territorial integrity, and the African state system. In Deng, F.M. and Zartman, I.W. (eds.) *Conflict Resolution in Africa*. Washington: Brookings Institution, pp. 320–346.

Younger, C. (1970) *Ireland's Civil War*. London: Fontana.

Zamir, M. (1985) *The Formation of Modern Lebanon*. London: Croom Helm.

Zartman, I.W. (1995) *Collapsed States: The Disintegration and Restoration of Legitimate Authority*. Boulder: Lynne Rienner Publishers.

Zevelev, A. (1972) *The Nationalities Question: How it was solved in the USSR*. Moscow: Novosti Press Agency Publishing House.

Index of States and Placenames

Index compiled by Annette Musker

Subject Index

Index compiled by Annette Musker